Theofatalism™
Personal Reformation for Troubled Souls

Lewis Tagliaferre

iUniverse, Inc.
Bloomington

Theofatalism™
Personal Reformation for Troubled Souls

iUniverse books may be ordered through booksellers or by contacting:

iUniverse
1663 Liberty Drive
Bloomington, IN 47403
www.iuniverse.com
1-800-Authors (1-800-288-4677)

ISBN: 978-1-4620-2247-2 (pbk)
ISBN: 978-1-4620-2248-9 (cloth)
ISBN: 978-1-4620-2249-6 (ebk)

Printed in the United States of America

iUniverse rev. date: 06/14/2011

PREFACE

Where do you go when your life is shaken and you realize it is God who is doing the shaking? When it comes to the real problems in life, especially things you desperately want to be different or wish had never happened, formal religion may seem to be impotent and irrelevant to many thinking people. Many churches in America have become little more than social clubs with Sunday entertainment that pay no taxes. This is what I discovered when my traditional church "family" provided no help after the untimely and traumatic death of my wife at age 52. They even treated me like I had a contagious disease, and I did. It is called grief. So I had to find some other way to survive that immense loss and go on working until I could retire. One therapist led to another and another and one book led to another and another until I discovered Sedona, AZ while on a business trip to the southwest.

In subsequent trips I was "introduced" to its matron, Mrs. Sedona M. Schnebly, wife of the founding post master. Although she died in 1950, I believe she led me to this understanding through "meeting" five imaginary teachers on metaphorical trips of discovery. They provided me with a new belief system that could enable people like me to survive and maybe even grow through the great tragedies of life. Such principles can never be created, only discovered. Albert Einstein said that imagination is more important than knowledge. Wherever it came from, this product of my imagination may stir some responses in your own thinking about the issues of reality in human life on this planet.

The formation of these principles I call Theofatalism™ is narrated in the basic book, Voices of Sedona. From that foundation, and through many hours of silent contemplation I have been given a series of essays to expand on the principles and relate them to modern living, and I feel compelled to share them with those who are ready to receive them. Perhaps they will be helpful to someone, somewhere, sometime. The full volume of essays is presented in <u>Lessons From Sedona</u>. A special selection of essays from that book is presented for the aging generation in <u>Baby Boomer Lamentations</u>, i.e., those who face retirement in America with no place to turn for security and spiritual comfort. They are available from www.IUniverse.com, www. amazon.com, and Barnes & Noble book stores.

This specialized work is for all those who find their traditional beliefs provide no comfort for the spiritual needs of real life. Perhaps it will be of some help to church leaders who don't really believe what they preach on Sundays and may change their homilies to something more helpful . . . and realistic. Perhaps it also will be some help to the members sitting in congregations who take home nothing of any relevance to their daily lives once they leave the sanctuary. One may question if the politically correct separation of church and state held so aloof in American culture has not created a chasm or mote so wide separating them that little if any relation exists any longer between the two, except possibly for the Amish and Mennonites. Perhaps Islam is growing so rapidly precisely because it has no such separation, but rather integrates the secular and non-secular as one solid mass of society such as the laws of Moses originally demanded. [Actually, "law enforcement" is an oxymoron because police may not arrest someone for illegal intentions or thoughts, only for breaking the law after the fact. Celebrated trial lawyer, Clarence Darrow (1857-1938) proclaimed, "The law does not punish everything that is dishonest as that would interfere too much with business." Darrow always contended that psychological, physical, and environmental influences - not a conscious choice between right and wrong - control human behavior. Being an agnostic, he never invoked God's will. Moreover, what is legal and illegal varies with time and culture, so there is no absolute book of laws for everyone. Think about it.]

Except for the quotes from secondary sources, the word "sheeple" replaces the word "people" throughout because the relationship of the shepherd to his flock of sheep flows from Genesis to Revelation in the Bible and provides the basic voice for this work, that of a shepherd/Jesus tending and feeding his sheep. "The third time he said to him, Simon son of John, do you love me? Peter was hurt because Jesus asked him the third time, Do you love me? He said, Lord, you know all things; you know that I love you. Jesus said, Feed my sheep." (John 21:17) This work concludes that people naturally fall into two groups:

1) those who are living God's will 24/7 and know it and;
2) those who are living God's will 24/7 but do not know it.

Many sources unknowingly contributed to this work, often posthumously. For all of them I am very grateful. The miracle is how they were gifted to me by powers beyond my understanding. I could never have discovered them by searching on my own. All sources and quotations are included for educational purposes with legal advice under the "fair use" doctrine of the U.S. laws on copyright in accordance with Title 17 U.S. Code, Section 107. Bible scriptures are from the New International Version, used by permission. Some of the quotes, data and statistics were obtained from internet sources and are not directly referenced because they may be temporary. No claim is made about their accuracy or validity. Published sources of quotations are integrated with text wherever possible. The Chicago Manual of Style does not apply as this is not presented as a scholarly work. It also is published without formal professional editing, so there are no doubt errors of commission and omission that could be improved. [However, author editorial remarks are bracketed.]

IUniverse Publishing deserves much credit for enabling unknown authors to make their contributions to this publishing genre, because they may have something valuable to say worth reading. If you find this book somehow and think it worthwhile, please recommend it to others. If this work is to be discovered and used by others, it will be up to you.

Taken together, all this work may add up to a new virtual School of Theofatalism™. [Visit www.schooloftheofatalism.org] And, like any school, it will do you no good unless you attend, take notes, and do the homework. But it takes special eyes or the shock would be too great. It is represented on the cover design by the ancient labyrinth from the Cathedral of Our Lady of Chartres, France. The labyrinth, where there is only one way to go, is opposite to a maze that is a puzzle full of dead ends. The first half of life is like the walk to the center marked by various accumulations; family, friends, careers, assets, etc. The second half is the return process of discarding the accumulations until we return to our origins as naked as we arrived. As in the walk of life, you just put one foot in front of the other. There are only two rules, begin and continue.

Caution: If the essays about reality in this work make you feel scared and confused, that could be normal because all growth comes with suffering. But, if they make you feel panic and uncontrollable anxiety, please seek professional care immediately from a qualified counselor. Nothing in this work is intended to be a substitute for competent medical or mental health treatment.

TABLE OF CONTENTS

INTRODUCTION

Hang out a banner in America offering health, wealth, and happiness and sheeple will line up to enter. But offer a course in reality and the line gets a lot shorter. Offer a book guaranteeing fame and fortune and it climbs to the best seller list. Get real and there are few buyers. So I don't expect this work to be a best seller. The Buddha, along with Pope Benedict XVI [aka Joseph Cardinal Ratzinger] in his <u>Eschatology, Death and Eternal Life</u> (1988) discovered, "History is real, it really continues, and its reality is suffering." American-born English Nobel poet, T.S. Eliot (1888-1965) said, "Humankind cannot bear very much reality." Like the Jack Nicholson character proclaimed in the movie, "A Few Good Men," (1992) "You can't handle the truth." President Harry Truman said, "I don't give people hell. I just tell the truth and they think it's hell." This seems to be the essential question: how much truth can you handle? Shakespeare wrote in "As You Like It", that "all the world's a stage and men and women merely are the players" . . . so perhaps this is a tour behind the curtain to show you how things really work. Think you can handle that?

Like the Buddha, many sheeple were shielded from reality since their childhood so they have no coping skills to see them through this disaster called life. If supported at their level, children can handle tragedy, sorrow and tears much better than they can handle lies, deceit, and evasions. Such parenting can help youngsters gain the inner resources needed for adult challenges they will surely face. Someone said life can only be understood backwards, but it must be lived forwards. This means making choices with consequences that are unpredictable, and that creates anxiety and fear from indefinite uncertainty if you stop to think about it. There may be no mistakes, only choices and consequences. Children who never learn this truth must suffer for its lack later in life. You have to reach a certain degree of spiritual maturity after you finish playing "let's pretend" to be interested in reality.

Reality is like drinking straight whiskey; you can only take a small sip at a time. That is why this work is presented in small doses of essays and organized the way they are. They move forward and backward as one does walking through a labyrinth, often encountering a spot visited earlier but with new insight, to reach the core at the center. It may seem at first that one is meandering about in a path to nowhere but although it may appear to be meaningless it may lead one to the center of being where there lies the peace that passes understanding. Some of the essays are longer than others, but that must be necessary or they would be different. Beloved opera diva, Beverly Sills (1929-2007) opined, "there are no short cuts to anywhere worth going." [You can buy a Chartres Labyrinth in table top placemat size at www.labyrinthcompany.com wherein you can let your fingers do the walking.]

In this modern age of 140-character "tweets," a book as long and serious as this may attract very few readers. One may process a tweet in a few seconds but it could take a lifetime to absorb all this wisdom. So please do not treat this book as a quick read to be discarded and forgotten. Treat it as you would some valuable insight into human nature that becomes more valuable as it is read over and over . . . sort of like the Bible. Most sheeple in spiritual distress would rather pretend things are different than to look into reality and see what is really there. That is why so many sheeple seek diversions from their normal lives by stalking celebrities in sports and entertainment and filling the arenas of celebrity preachers who sell "prosperity religion." Fantasy sells, reality sucks. Perhaps there is no growth without distress. Get used to it, or go outside and play. Arthur Schopenhauer (1788-1860) stipulated that new truth goes through three stages. First it is ridiculed, then it is opposed, and finally it is accepted as self-evident. Perhaps this work will have to survive the first two in order to achieve the latter, if it ever does. It can be unwise to assault the assumptions of common sense that authorities hold in high esteem, but that is a risk that must be taken in order to achieve any growth at all. Sometimes the process takes centuries. So, take your time . . . even if it takes the rest of your life . . . or more.

French philosopher Voltaire [aka Francois-Marie Arouet (1694-1778)] wrote, "It is dangerous to be right in matters on which the established authorities are wrong." Most sheeple prefer to be wrong with the support of a group than to be correct all by themselves. You may find yourself out on a very long limb all alone if you accept the principles of Theofatalism™. Those who are called to further knowledge often must be able to live without social approval. The trouble with making new discoveries is that they destroy our confidence in the establishment. But you will be in some very good company. [Galileo was forced to recant his discovery that proved Copernicus was right in concluding the Earth was not the center of the Universe. It took the Church 400 years to apologize for its arrogance and his unjust censure.]

Every major change in human beliefs originally began as a heresy, and the originator usually was condemned for his efforts. Sometimes a common sense belief becomes so strong that suggesting it might be wrong is nearly impossible. Apostle Paul wrote, "Do not deceive yourselves. If any one of you thinks he is wise by the standards of this age, he should become a fool so that he may become wise. For the wisdom of this world is foolishness in God's sight." (1 Corinthians 3:18-19) The collapse of banking and the failure of mortgage financing in 2008 shows how true this warning can be. The consequent recession has eliminated eight million jobs. Read on.

The history of science is full of discoveries that went unnoticed because the establishment did not recognize the author until some time later when another one got the attention with the same message. For example, a French astronomer named Ole Roemer predicted in 1676 that light traveled at a finite speed when everyone thought it was instantaneous, but it took 50 years for anyone to agree with him. Vesto Melvin Slipher actually discovered that the Universe is expanding at increasing velocity, using the Clark telescope at the Lowell observatory in Flagstaff, AZ. But it was Edwin P. Hubble who became famous for it after repeating the same discovery from the Mount Wilson observatory in Pasadena, CA. Many discoveries have been made several times before they actually were perceived, and often legacy beliefs linger long after they are obsolete. In surveys reported by Newsweek of March 2007, 48 percent of U.S. respondents claimed they believe that God created man as is about 6,000 years ago. How long will it take for belief in this God to die off? Must we wait for eons of evolution to finally surpass the remnants of Paleolithic man that still occupies our brains?

Whether you read this work like a novel from front to back or skip around from essay to essay, you will arrive at the same place. And wherever that is for you it is the only place you can be. However, I recommend that you read the first three essays in order first. Then you may find more benefits in reading the others as the spirit moves you. The principles of Theofatalism™ explained in the second essay set the stage for all the essays that come after it. Such principles can never be created, only discovered. And, as Thomas Paine stated, one should look beyond the content to the author, in this case not the writer who is only a scribe, but the source of all creation. It does not matter if you believe in God or not. If he/it exists and is omnipotent then what you believe is what you are given. God makes atheists too. And if there is no God, then Homo sapiens must do the best they can with what is. However, if there is a spirit that gives life then you may be about to begin the adventure of a lifetime.

Trappist monk, Thomas Merton, (1915-1968) [aka Fr. M. Louis] wrote in <u>No Man Is an Island</u>, (1955) "Without a life of the spirit, our whole existence becomes unsubstantial and illusory. The life of the spirit, by integrating us in the real order established by God, puts us in the fullest possible contact with reality—not as we imagine it but as it really is." So read on and you may find the benefits are worth the burdens . . . or not.

1. The Need for Personal Reformation

Ever since Martin Luther posted his little memo on that church door in 1517 there seems to be a continuing interest in reforming the church initiated by Jesus Christ. Modern communications makes it possible for a few reformers to organize hosts of like minded rebels in continuing attempts to change the world. Someone said the more things change, the more they seem to stay the same. Nevertheless, a crisis now is brewing among religions of the world. Things are changing rapidly in modern societies, and human consciousness is moving into a new expansion. But religion commonly is stuck in legacy beliefs that have not kept up with the times. The sources of faith sheeple have relied upon for centuries now are obsolete, but very few sheeple realize it yet. They are irrelevant and impotent in helping sheeple live with reality in science, politics, economics, philosophy, medicine, psychology and the basic issues of life and death. It is time for a quantum leap in religious thinking . . . a big change.

The Chinese ideogram for "change" also contains elements of both "threat" and "opportunity." Whichever way this present spiritual crisis evolves, it certainly includes both/and rather than either/or. There was a time when church and state were integrated with religion throughout Europe providing guideposts for society, as it still is in Islam. When this situation became enslavement to state dogma from the Pope or the King many sheeple left Europe to organize a new form of pluralistic society, separating government from religion in America. Now, their ways of defining God are being challenged in western culture, but the replacement has not yet been clearly defined. Perhaps a clue pointing to the source of this challenge comes from some ancient Hindu concept of God translated from Sanskrit that means Generator, Operator, Destroyer. (G.O.D.) And he never asks our permission first. So, the next time you enter a house of worship, perhaps you can see it

1

as the symbol of that God. This could be the model of a new Trinity . . . or not.

The old ways always must make way for the new, but this time the reformation will be devastating to those who cannot or will not move with the times, like using the Internet for information transfer. Martin Luther could change the world with only one page tacked onto a church door in 1517, but today one must use the latest information technology to spread the word. Luther lamented, "I never would have thought that such a storm would rise from Rome over one simple scrap of paper." Imagine what God can do with the Internet. Because there are no new continents to explore we must live among each other for better or worse, in sickness and health, for richer or poorer, in peace and war, until death do us part each with our own version of information display in the palms of our hands.

The schism between Islam and Christianity, for example, that now threatens to explode into open warfare between the intolerant extremes in both camps is but a symptom of the inner struggle among mankind to choose who they will serve, God or Baal, self or technology. Space travel and the modern physics make it no longer possible for many to accept the old laws of Moses compiled in the Torah and re-formalized in the shari'ah law of Islam. Neither does the teaching of passivity by Jesus from Nazareth stand up to the challenge of modern minds under the reality of science in new warfare. We cannot look at the Earth from the orbiting space station or look into the Universe through the orbiting Hubble telescope and continue believing in the Gods of our ancestors or even our fathers, church leaders, and Sunday-school teachers. The emergence of this new reformation will require real suffering and challenge to the faith of our ancestors before it is fully birthed. It is an old struggle continuing to balance faith and reason among mankind, and the end is not yet in sight.

Retired Episcopal Bishop, John Shelby Spong (1931 . . .) is the spox [new term for spokesperson] of a more progressive form of religion. [The San Francisco Chronicle says of Bishop Spong, "He provides enlightenment for those who no longer believe in the God of Sunday school and are looking for something else to give their lives meaning."] He puts it this way; "People can talk about their understanding of God until the cows come home, but we have not yet come to grips with the fact that there is no supernatural, parental deity above the sky, keeping the divine record books on human behavior up to date and ready at any moment to intervene in human history to answer prayers. Moreover, our concept of God must change as we discover more about the Universe, our home planet, and human life. When we do embrace this fact then prayer [and worship] becomes an increasingly impossible idea and inevitably a declining practice. To get people to embrace this point clearly,

I have suggested that the popular prayers of most people are little more than adult letters written to a Santa Claus God. There are then two choices. One says that the God in whom I always believed is no more, so I will become an atheist. The other says that the way I have always thought of God has become inoperative, so there must be something wrong with my definition . . . This stance serves to plunge us deeply into a new way of thinking about God. Can God, for example, be conceived of not as a supernatural person, but as a force present in me and flowing through me as life itself? The spiritual life is then transformed from the activity of a child seeking the approval of a supernatural parent to being a spontaneous journey into self-discovery and into the mystery of existence. It also feeds my sense of growing into oneness with the source of all life [in its many forms and manifestations.]"

Spong goes on; "We once defined human life as a special creation made in the image of God, endowed with an immortal soul and just a little lower than the angels. Then came Charles Darwin who defined us instead as just a little higher than the apes. We began to see ourselves not as fallen angels, but as highly developed animals linked by DNA to everything from the plankton of the sea, to the cabbages, to the chimpanzees. Suddenly we wondered if there was any meaning to life other than the biological processes of being born, maturing, mating, reproducing and dying." [Now there is space travel with views of the Universe that reduce the Earth to another dot among infinite dots and mankind to nothing but a zit in the scale of space/time it is now possible to envision.]

"So it is that faith wavers in the modern world and the external supernatural being we once thought of as God might just turn out to be little more than a stage in human development. Certainly the God who rewards and punishes is little more than the behavior controlling parental deity that immature children seek [not unlike belief in Santa Claus.] I urge you to turn your attention inward not outward, to go so deeply into your own humanity that you escape its limits and begin to experience that which is transcendent or the divine presence. That is the only doorway that in my experience enables me to contemplate life after death."

The Asian ancients attempted to make that journey through the practices of yoga, the Buddhists by the practice of meditation, and lately the Church of Scientology provides its techniques of psychoanalysis to break out of the bounds of mind/body mortality and emerge into the spiritual condition of "Clear." Jesus declared, "The kingdom of God is within you," but only after he described it in a dozen parables as outside oneself. C.G. Jung observed, "Those who look outward dream, but those who look inward awake." The least likely place to experience this transcendence is in a modern church service on Sunday morning.

There always is an opposing opinion, as stated by The Very Rev. Canon Robert S. Munday, "People who allow unbelief and prayerlessness to rob them of intimacy with God do not know what they are missing. The precious truth of the Gospel is that God loves us, that he created us for fellowship with him, and when we had fallen into sin, God sent Jesus Christ to redeem us, not only so that we can enjoy heaven later, but so that we can experience the joy of daily, constant fellowship with God now. The unbelief of the skeptics will never destroy what the saints know to be true: You can petition the Lord with prayer!" Catholics have designated some 10,000 or more saints posthumously as personal advocates with such standing in heaven that they can indeed change the mind of God. But, what kind of God would change his plans whenever his creation asks him to? Answer: The kind that Jesus described . . . "Therefore, I tell you whatever you ask for in prayer, believe that you have received it and it will be yours." (Matthew 17:20, 21: 21-23, Mark 9:23, 11:24) And what kind of God would create a Universe with such suffering and injustice while giving the supreme creatures the power to disobey his every command? Such beliefs are badly in need of reformation.

Most Christians, Jews, and Muslims have been taught to believe that God is a good and loving God, and he wants sheeple to do good things to get good rewards in this as well as some afterlife, but their reality often belies this claim. The weekly worship service and ongoing weekday committee meetings, with a short dose of Sunday school for children, hardly provides more than a social gathering for sheeple who are programmed to avoid the guilt of secular weekend activities. When sheeple enter church, many of them check their brains at the door. The dogma of authentic Christian doctrine—universal brotherhood, suppression of national distinctions, abolition of private property, and the strange injunction of non-resistance to evil by force—demand what is seemingly impossible to human nature. Indeed, that is so, because the authentic Christian life is manifested by a change in human nature and so it is very rare. Many sheeple haven't really read the Bible, as Muslim students must read the Koran, or just read certain passages in church designated by the leader. This is understandable, as the holy books are hard to read due to archaic language and obscure translations. Why would anyone in their right mind believe any of them unless God makes them do it? Also many rabbis, priests, and preachers, and imams don't like to disclose many passages because they present a message that does not conform with socialized orthodoxy and would threaten church survival. Professional religious who have a career vested in church social practices cannot risk losing their incomes by speaking the truth when it challenges established dogma.

For example, it is amazing how many times God ordered the killing of innocent sheeple in the Old Testament even after the Ten Commandments said *"Thou shall not kill."* God killed 70,000 innocent sheeple to punish David for his disobedience. (1 Chronicles 21:14). God also ordered the destruction of 60 cities so that the Israelites can live there. He ordered the killing of all the men, women, and children of each conquered city, and the looting of all personal property. (Deuteronomy 3: 3-7). He ordered another attack and the killing of "all the living creatures of the city: men and women, young, and old, as well as oxen sheep, and asses." (Joshua 6: 20-21) He empowered the Jews to kill all the innocent inhabitants of a city, including hanging its king in public for all to see. (Joshua 8: 24-29) In Judges 21, he ordered the murder of all the sheeple of Jabesh-gilead, except for the virgin girls who were taken to be forcibly raped and married. When they wanted more virgins, God told them to hide alongside the road and when they saw a girl they liked, "kidnap her and forcibly rape her and make her your wife!" (Judges 21:20-23) In 2 Kings 10:18-27, God ordered the murder of all the worshipers of a different God in their very own church! The God of the Bible also allowed slavery, including selling your own daughter as a sex slave (Exodus 21:1-11), child abuse (Judges 11:29-40, Isaiah 13:16), and bashing babies against rocks. (Hosea 13:16 & Psalms 137:9) Moreover, God [voiced by Apostle Paul] ordered, "Slaves, obey your earthly masters in everything; and do it, not only when their eye is on you and to win their favor, but with sincerity of heart and reverence for the Lord. Whatever you do, work at it with all your heart, as working for the Lord, not for men." (Colossians 3:22-23, Ephesians 6:5) Shall we not forget the birth of Jesus, "king of the Jews," prompted Israel's King Herod to order the slaughter of all male children under the age of two in Bethlehem, fulfilling Old Testament prophecy. (Matthew 2:16-18) [It is curious that only the writer of Matthew reports this atrocity.]

In addition, what shall we do with the account of incest between Lot and his two daughters that founded the tribes of Moabites and Ammonites? (Genesis 19:30-36) After that, the foundation of Jews as the chosen people is based upon the deception of Jacob and his mother that deprived Esau, as the rightful heir, of his birthright from their father, Isaac. (Genesis 27) It is written that God hated Esau but he loved Jacob for no apparent reason. (Malachi 1:2-4) Thus Jacob became Israel and father of the twelve tribes of chosen sheeple by fraud. Moreover, God chose David as the first King of Israel. But David stole the wife of Uriah through adultery and had him murdered in battle, and then he was punished by the death of their first child . . . who was an innocent victim. But the second son was Solomon who began the reign of kings in Israel and thence the ancestor of Jesus Christ who was born from adultery and murder. There is no record of David and Bathsheba ever getting married. (2 Samuel 11-12) Now, why would the

Creator of the Universe, the God of love, do such a thing? And, why would so many sheeple believe that he did? All this goes to show that God does whatever he wants, with whoever he wants, whenever he wants. And that includes telling you what to think too.

Surveys by the Princeton Religion Research Center disclosed that 60 percent of Americans over age 60 believe the Bible is the inspired Word of God and contains no errors. If true, then God apparently needs a better editor. Actually, any scholar with moral integrity must admit that the Bible is full of contradictions, inconsistencies, and imaginations about what a few Jewish writers thought God really was like more than 2,000 years ago. No scientist would rely upon a text book that is 2,000 years old, but those who find comfort in their legacy faith must overlook its primitive origins. Any serious reader of the New Testament must contend with its obvious insult to logical reasoning. One scholar has described thirty unsolved problems with the New Testament. Here is one of them concerning judgment: "Moreover, the Father judges no one, but has entrusted all judgment to the Son." (John 5:22) By myself I can do nothing; I judge only as I hear, and my judgment is just, for I seek not to please myself but him who sent me. (John 5:30) You judge by human standards; I pass judgment on no one. But if I do judge, my decisions are right, because I am not alone. I stand with the Father, who sent me." (John 8:15-16) "As for the person who hears my words but does not keep them, I do not judge him. For I did not come to judge the world, but to save it." (John 12:47) "There is a judge for the one who rejects me and does not accept my words; that very word which I spoke will condemn him at the last day." (John 12:48)

If the inspired writer of the Gospel of John is this confused, how can we hope to find the truth? Jesus was given that name instead of Immanuel (which means God with us) because he "would save his people from their sins." (Matthew 1:21) But, only if they freely believe in him. (John 3:16) And that only if they are called/enabled by God the Father. (John 6:63-65) This obviously did not work out that way because his sheeple, the Jews, rejected him and within one generation they revolted against Rome and were massacred and dispersed to wander as a nationless race until 1947 when Israel was reconstituted by the United Nations under prodding by President Harry Truman. Perhaps if he were named Immanuel, "God with us," as instructed in the Old Testament it would have been different. (Isaiah 7:24, Matthew 1:23) So you might conclude that Jesus failed in selection of the twelve apostles . . . they all cut and ran at his crucifixion. And on the cross he felt abandoned by God, exclaiming, "My God, why have you forsaken me?" (Matthew 27:46, Mark 15:34) If the Bible is the Word of God, why does it leave so many holes for thinking sheeple to fall into?

The Old Testament is a flawed history of the Jews and the New Testament is a flawed history of Jesus of Nazareth, separated by several hundred years of silence from God. The later the account of the beginnings of Christianity, the more miraculous the details seem to become. For example, in the writings of Paul (50-64 CE) which precede the Gospels according to scholars, there are no miracles, no virgin birth and the resurrection is assumed from hearsay. He was not an eyewitness to the crucifixion so his authority was based upon his schizophrenic encounter on the road to Damascus. (Acts 9:3-8) Without belief in the resurrection of Jesus, the Jews had no Messiah. [Although it is believed to represent the time of Jesus Christ's resurrection, the festival of Easter existed in pre-Christian times. As cited by D.M. Murdock (aka Acharya S), according to the Christian saint Venerable Bede (672-735 CE), Easter was named for the Teutonic or German Goddess Eôstre, who was the "Goddess of dawn" or returning Sun and who symbolized the annual fertility among plants and animals occurring abundantly during the springtime of each year. Hence the Easter bunny and those decorated eggs.] It was Apostles Paul and John who argued most for belief in the resurrection; "I am the resurrection and the life. Those who believe in me will live even though they die. (John 11:25)] If there is no resurrection of the dead then not even Christ has been raised . . . and our preaching is useless and so is your faith." (1Corinthians 15: 12-14) However, with such faith, the Apostle Paul declared, "Death, where is your sting . . . . Death where is your victory?" (1 Corinthians 15:55) The desire for immortality has sponsored many different beliefs about the afterlife among various tribes of Homo sapiens. They cannot all be true, and maybe none of them are. Whether these beliefs are created by imagination or discovered like laws of physics is known only to God, the Generator, Operator, and Destroyer. Think you can handle that?

The miracles of Jesus were first introduced by Mark when the gospel was written after the letters of Paul somewhere around 70-72 CE. The virgin birth was introduced by Matthew, the second gospel to be written, about 82-85 CE. The resurrection of Jesus understood as physical resuscitation was introduced or at least strongly emphasized by only Luke written about 88-93CE and by John in 95-100 CE. The account of first century Christians in the book of Acts, presumably written by Luke, is composed of many direct quotations with no sourcing to affirm their accuracy or validity although he claims it as accurate history. The Catholic Encyclopedia declares, "The book of Acts does not contain the acts of all the apostles, nor does it contain all the acts of any apostle." None of these events are verified by Roman historians of those times, although Jesus is introduced as hearsay briefly by the Jewish writer, Josephus. Then the story goes silent for two hundred years until picked up in the fourth century of Roman history. These facts are elementary in reputable Christian seminaries, but for a variety of reasons this knowledge has not filtered down to those who sit in the pews of our churches Sunday after Sunday.

If God really wanted to disclose himself to his creation, why hide among sources that seem undependable to skeptics? Moreover, after 2,000 years the faith of Christians has not become contagious among most of the Homo sapiens on planet Earth. Instead, mankind is more troubled by wars, disease, poverty, and disasters than ever before as well as the competing claims of various different religions. Are they all from the same God, or what? Sheeple generally all grow up believing and practicing the religions of their tribes and families. Only among a few thinking sheeple are they ever critically examined to sort out the facts from fiction, if that is even possible.

Consider the God of Genesis who created a perfect world that includes knowledge of good and evil and then induced mankind to act out their given will to disobedience that condemns all mankind to eternal punishment a-priori according to the last written letter from Apostle Paul. (Romans 5:18-19) Consider then how the Church attempts to assign blame for the evils of creation to willful mankind rather than to the actual Creator of it all. If everyone is born a sinner, where is the free will? Nowhere does the book of Genesis say the sin of Adam is imputed to all of his heirs. It does not even punish Cain for killing his brother, Abel, because God refused his sacrifice of garden produce and preferred the blood sacrifice by Abel instead. Without that inheritable foundation, the Church has no claim for the universal need of a savior. Compare, for example, John 6:64-66 and John 6:44 which claim that no one can accept Jesus unless the Father wills it with John 14:6 which says just the opposite. Jesus says, ". . . to sit at my right or left is not for me to grant. These places belong to those for whom they have been prepared by my Father." (Matthew 20:18) But, he also says, "All authority in heaven and on Earth has been given to me." (Matthew 28:18) They would seem to be mutually exclusive claims; if one is right the other must be wrong. Go figure.

The Gospel of John is the most metaphysical of the four and the most controversial. Actually, it contains much of the Gnostic teachings that somehow were not filtered out by the Roman Catholic editors of the Latin Bible, the Vulgate. Much of its teaching appears to be symbolic rather than literal and posed a great deal of discomfort for the disciples. Surely no one should take literally the claim of cannibalism described in John. "Whoever eats my flesh and drinks my blood has eternal life . . ." (John 6: 53-56) If this is not to be taken literally how much more is symbolic also? The Gospel of John contains no claim for a virgin birth of Jesus, it excludes the lineage of his ancestors back to King David, it has no temptation by Satan in the wilderness, and it omits the ascension into heaven at the end. The miracle of turning water into wine at a wedding in the gospel of John is in no other gospel.

The Gospel of John includes no parables of Jesus about the Kingdom of God and also has no "sermon on the mount" or "plain" included in the other gospels. It substitutes a symbolic feet washing by Jesus for the cannibalistic blood sacrifice of the other gospels at the last supper. (John 13:1-12) It includes an expanded account of his arrest and crucifixion, including some confusion about the first interrogation by the high priest. (John 18:12-19) It puts words into the mouth of Jesus in the first person during his private moments with the disciples and prayers to the Father that no scribe writing decades later could possibly have known first hand. And it provides the foundation of Christianity with its famous verse in John 3:16 that promises everlasting life to believers—only to believers who may not come to Jesus unless the Father causes/enables them. (John 6:63-65) [The Gospel of John is thought by scholars to have been written around 90 CE, a full generation after the death of Jesus when none of the eyewitnesses were still living.] Any account of history written from hearsay decades after the events can hardly be relied upon as accurate, unless of course God wills it so to be.

The writer of John opens by declaring, "In the beginning was the Word, and the Word was with God, and the Word was God. He was with God in the beginning. Through him all things were made; without him nothing was made that has been made." This apparent or assumed attribution to Jesus was the first major controversy among church bishops that was settled at the Council of Nicaea in 325 CE in favor of this version. The rest of John, Chapter 1 makes it clear that "the Word" refers to Jesus Christ. Although Jesus referred to and prayed to the Father in the second person, he also proclaimed, "I and the Father are One . . . whoever has seen me has seen the Father." (John 10:30, 12:44) Thus John introduces a seemingly impossible contradiction, that Jesus both "was with God" and "was God" at the same time, and that was true from the beginning of creation. So, if you don't like something about your life, blame it on Jesus. Throughout the book of John, Jesus speaks of God in the second person as his father so he obviously did not think he was God. This split personality is more Gnostic than Christian. Gnostics believed that there is a true God who is the essential source of every living and non-living creation and a false God or Creator God, who created the flawed world. According to the Gnostics, humans mirrored the duality found in the created world; they are flawed from the creation of the false Creator and yet also contain the light of the true God.

None of the other gospels present Jesus in this dual light, but always separate Jesus from the Father as in two persons, as does John throughout most of the book. Read the Jesus conversation with God for more Gnostics

9

thought. (John 17) Fundamental Christians use this scripture to prove that Jesus was God and man simultaneously, even though Jesus obviously was talking to another person. There is no logical way to accommodate this mutually exclusive duality except to say both/and. Actually, no one knows how many other versions of the gospels that may have raised even more controversy were circulating at the time the Roman Catholic Church limited scripture to these four in the Latin Vulgate Bible in the late fourth century. The Dead Sea Scrolls found in Qumran in 1947-1956 provided manuscripts of Old Testament theology in Hebrew from the first century, but were withheld from scholars for several decades by Israel Antiquities Authority. They mention one called the Teacher of Righteousness, but do not mention Jesus and his life as in the gospels. So, there is no source outside of the New Testament to confirm the life and teachings of Jesus.

Also, one must stretch the scriptures beyond reality to contrive the doctrine of the Trinity as nowhere does it say that God exists as one in three parts. Jesus always prayed to the Father in the second person. (John 17: 1 . . .) The trinity, three parts in one, is a concept made up by the Roman Catholic Church in the Vulgate, its Latin Bible, during the fourth century. The unified Trinity does not appear in any Greek Bible manuscript until the sixteenth century. In this criticism of Christianity, the Muslims may be right in saying God is One and has no Son and needs no concubine. The Old Testament says, "You are my witnesses, declares the LORD, and my servant whom I have chosen, so that you may know and believe me and understand that I am he. Before me no God was formed, nor will there be one after me. I am the LORD, and apart from me there is no savior. I have revealed and saved and proclaimed—I, and not some foreign God among you. You are my witnesses, declares the LORD, that I am God." (Isaiah 43:10-12) "I am the Lord your God who brought you out of Egypt. You shall acknowledge no God but me, no savior except me. (Hosea 13:4) But, skipping forward 400 years one discovers a new idea. "Today in the town of David a savior is born to you; he is Christ the Lord."(Luke 2:11) "We have seen and testify that the Father has sent his Son to be the savior of the world." (John 4:14) "From this man through David's descendents God has brought to Israel the savior Jesus, as he promised." (Acts 13:23) It seems like God must have changed his mind. Muslims are willing to fight and die for what they believe . . . how many Christians are?

Perhaps the Christian concept of triune God was influenced by the Trinity of Gods in Hinduism, as some scholars reason. The Hindu trinity is composed of Gods Brahma, Vishnu and Shiva. They are respectively the creator, preserver and destroyer of the Universe. They are also aligned as the transcendent Godhead, Shiva, the cosmic lord, Vishnu and the cosmic mind,

Brahma. In this regard they are called Sat-Tat-Aum, the Being, the "Thatness" or immanence and the Word or Holy Spirit. This is much like the Christian trinity of God as the Father, Son and Holy Ghost. The trinity represents the Divine in its threefold nature and function, i.e., creation, operation, and destruction. Each aspect of the trinity of Hinduism contains and includes the others. Each God in the trinity has his consort. To Brahma it is Saraswati, the Goddess of knowledge. For Vishnu it is Lakshmi, the Goddess of love, beauty and delight. For Shiva it is Kali (Parvati), the Goddess of power, destruction and transformation. The three Goddesses often are worshipped by Hindus along with their spouses. This trinity of Gods occupies the second highest tier among the pyramid of Gods in Hinduism, with the highest God Brahman occupying the supreme seat at the top. But along came Muhammad in the seventh century who taught God/Allah is only One and needs no son or holy spirit to make up the whole. So, who you gonna believe? Little wonder there is constant strife among Jews, Christians, Muslims, Hindus and the rest. Why is that? Perhaps it is the will of God the Almighty One, as there can be no other. Let's continue.

Jesus portrays the Father sending the Counselor/Holy Spirit—that is the Father and the Holy Spirit are two distinctly different entities, and he portrays both the Father and the Holy Spirit/Comforter/Counselor/Teacher as distinct from Jesus himself. ". . . the Counselor, the Holy Spirit, whom the Father will send in my name, will teach you all things and will remind you of everything I have said to you." (John 14:26) That does not sound like three-in-one. Thus even apart from whether Jesus was God, Jesus declares that the Father and the Holy Spirit are not one and the same. Again, Jesus claims that he came to bring life, and that more abundantly. (John 10:10) But he also claims that he came not to bring peace, but a sword that would cleave families asunder. (Matthew 10:34) Apostle Paul claims that, "Just as man is destined to die once, and after that to face judgment, so Christ was sacrificed once to take away the sins of many people . . ." (Hebrews 9:27-28), but the Roman Catholic Church teaches that souls not bad enough for hell go to Purgatory for penance to purify them for heaven. So, is it either/or or both/and? Actually, it could be all of the above . . . think you can handle that? If there is only one God and nothing happens outside its will, how can anyone in the creation ever hope to conquer the Creator?

Trappist monk, Thomas Merton (1915-1968) [aka Fr. M. Louis] recognized this problem of Bible contradictions with a discussion of "salvation" in his book, No Man Is An Island (1955). "This matter is a very simple thing, but when we analyze it, it turns into a tangle of paradoxes. We become ourselves by dying to ourselves. We gain only what we give up, and if we give up everything we gain everything. We must love our neighbors as ourselves, but to be a disciple we must not only hate mother and father but our own life also. The only answer to the problem [of mutually exclusive contradictions] must therefore reach out to embrace both extremes of a contradiction at the same time. Love must reach over the both sides and draw them together. [Both/and instead of either/or.] Hence the answer must be supernatural. All the answers that are not supernatural are imperfect for they only embrace one of the contradictory terms and they can always be denied by the other." In short, humankind has a long way to go to achieve such spiritual maturity.

To claim that the Bible is a perfect documentary about God is folly. So also is reading the Book of Mormon or the Holy Koran as the word of God. Yet, Apostle Paul says, "God is not the author of disorder/confusion, but of peace." (1 Corinthians 14:33) As for peace, Jesus declared, "Do not suppose that I have come to bring peace to the Earth. I did not come to bring peace, but a sword. "(Matthew 10:34, Matthew 24:7-11) He does not sound like the God of peace described by Apostle Paul. Since the Bible obviously contains confusion and various interpretations cleave the ministry of Jesus, it must not be authored by God or the Apostle was confused. For example, compare the commandment to honor father and mother with this declaration of Jesus, "If anyone comes to me and does not hate his own father and mother and wife and children and brothers and sisters and even his own life he cannot be my disciple." (Luke 14:26) He also commanded disciples to love one another. (John 13: 34-35, 15: 12, 17) It seems like his left hand did not know what his right hand was saying or the writer of John did not read the book of Luke and vice versa.

So if it was authored by God, he intentionally inserted so much confusion in the Bible that various interpretations are possible, keeping the scholars in continuous turmoil for some reason he is not telling us. It is more likely an imperfect record of the Jewish imagination about God. How close that account comes to reality no one can tell. But, the opposite syllogism says that since God does not create confusion and God wrote the Bible, it cannot contain confusion and if you think so, you just don't understand it. The many contradictions merely are dismissed by conservative Church leaders as some of the "mysteries" of the gospels. To continue using Bible scripture as the basis for an international religion is close to insanity and reflects the primitive mentality that still exists among Homo sapiens, in spite of their social and scientific evolution. Which you believe is all in the will of God the Almighty One, of course, as there can no other.

Most pastors and priests and rabbis in the mainstream American churches and synagogues are systematically preaching from their pulpits teachings which they themselves know to be blatant lies, or at most traditional myths. Why the systematic lying? The basic problem in western churches is a divergence during the last several centuries between "academic" religion taught in the seminaries and "popular" Christianity as practiced in churches to raise money from childish sheeple sitting in the pews. As early as the Renaissance, scholars such as Erasmus (1466-1536) began applying the intellectual tools that were being developed in science, history, and medicine to better understand, purify, and solidify their Christian faith. But, they were lost on the common man who had no education. By the eighteenth-century Enlightenment, an increasing number of scholars and intellectuals were coming to realize that biblical Christianity could not actually be historically true in all respects.

In the nineteenth century, the floodgates opened. From David Strauss's <u>Life of Jesus</u> (1902) to Albert Schweitzer's <u>The Quest of the Historical Jesus</u>, (2005) scholarly research proved that the Bible was a crazy mish-mash of garbled history, Jewish mythology, and fantasies based on pagan stories of virgin births, resurrected savior Gods, etc. In fact, the idea of a dying and resurrecting God/man had its beginning in pagan mythology hundreds of years before the time of Christ. In Egypt he was known as Osiris, in Greece as Dionysus, in Syria as Adonis, in Asia Minor as Attis, in Mesopotamia as Marduk, and in Persia as Mithras. The conclusion behind the myth of Christian sheeple is they must think they need a savior because God the Creator planted that idea in their minds as there is no other source. The mystery is where that need comes from. It seems to be in the genes, or maybe in some kind of unconscious conscience we are born with that includes innate guilt and the need for making amends.

By the early twentieth century, F. C. Burkitt, (1864-1935) in an introduction to Schweitzer's famous book, could confidently assert as an established fact among educated sheeple, "Every one nowadays is aware that traditional Christian doctrine about Jesus Christ is encompassed with many difficulties, and that many of the statements in the Gospels appear incredible in the light of modern views of history and nature." The popular view of Jesus as an adult equivalent of the child's invisible friend, always there to smooth over the difficulties of life, and to bring health, wealth, and happiness to the flock, is untrue to the Gospels. Jesus healed only to show the power of God, he condemned wealth, and he scarcely spoke about happiness at all while he blessed those who mourn. His ministry of pacifism brought persecution and suffering to his followers beyond their wildest dreams, and the Jews were all but destroyed by Rome in their uprising of 69-74 CE. This was a crazy act of gross hubris, so the Jewish leaders who drove them to battle the Roman legions must have been some of the best leaders in history, although history has forgotten them. How could such a stupid thing happen, almost mass suicide like the final group did at Masada, unless God willed it so? The God/Father of Jesus was a different concept from that of the Jews and many modern churches today. Sometimes this truth comes through in disguised forms in secular literature.

No less than Russian novelist and philosopher Leo Tolstoy (1828-1910) attempted to right perceived wrongs of modern churches in his essay titled, "The Kingdom of Heaven is Within You." (1893) Not many Christians were or are ready for it, then or now. "It is terrible to think what the churches do to men. But if one imagines oneself in the position of the men who constitute the Church, we see they could not act differently. The churches are placed in a dilemma: the Sermon on the Mount or the Nicene Creed—the one excludes the other. If a man sincerely believes in the Sermon on the Mount, the Nicene Creed must inevitably lose all meaning and significance for him, and the Church and its representatives together with it. If a man believes in the Nicene Creed, that is, in the Church, that is, in those who call themselves its representatives, the Sermon on the Mount becomes superfluous for him. And therefore the churches cannot but make every possible effort to obscure the meaning of the Sermon on the Mount, and to attract men to themselves. It is only due to the intense zeal of the churches in this direction that the influence of the churches has lasted hitherto. Let the Church stop its work of hypnotizing the masses, and deceiving children even for the briefest interval of time, and men would begin to understand Christ's teaching. But this understanding will be the end of the churches and all their influence. And therefore the churches will not for an instant relax their zeal in the business of hypnotizing grown-up sheeple and deceiving children. This, then, is the work of the churches: to instill a false interpretation of Christ's teaching into men, and to prevent a true interpretation of it for the majority of so-called believers." All in God's will of course . . . AIGWOC. Think you can handle that?

Tolstoy quoted one Adin Ballou, an American Christian patriot of Massachusetts who justified nationalism and war in 1838; "Jesus Christ forbids me to resist evil doers but my government demands from me quite the opposite, and bases a system of self-defense on gallows, musket, and sword, to be used against its foreign and domestic foes. For this we have a succession of Christian priests to pray for us and beseech the blessing of Heaven on the holy work of slaughter. The U.S. Constitution says the government has the right to declare war, and I assent to this and support it, and swear that I will support it. And I do not for that cease to be a Christian. Is it not a Christian duty to kill hundreds of thousands of one's fellow-men, to outrage women, to raze and burn towns, and to practice every possible cruelty? It is time to dismiss all these false sentimentalities. One man cannot plunder and pillage, but a whole nation can. But precisely how many are needed to make it permissible? Why is it that one man, ten, a hundred, may not break the law of God, but a great nation may?" Would you believe that? Jesus said, "For if you forgive men when they sin against you, your heavenly Father will also forgive you. But if you do not forgive men their sins, your Father will not forgive your sins." (Matthew 6: 14-16) That seems to put eternal destiny in the power of individuals to choose forgiveness or war. How can this simultaneous dichotomy still exist a century later and more unless it is the will of God the Almighty One, for it could not be sustained within human logic without his power.

How can it be that most religious Americans are ignorant of this gap between first century myths about Christian living and its modern reality? Much of the explanation is simply economic self-interest. Clergy fear the loss of their jobs. After all, religion is a gigantic tax-exempt business in the U.S. that would be threatened with extinction if its true basis in mythology actually were disclosed. Denominational officials and professional theologians perpetuate the present state of affairs because they have come to enjoy too much their role as sole owners and manipulators of the sacred symbols. Consciously or unconsciously, they leave their church members in a state of darkness because otherwise they would have to share prestige and authority with Christ. Many pastors honestly believe that the adults in their congregations simply lack the maturity to handle the truth and that telling the truth would therefore result in the destruction of Christianity. They could be right. Like the resurrection of Santa Claus each December, it seems that many sheeple need to believe that they are born as lost sinners who must be saved by the sacrificial death and resurrection of Jesus Christ. This may be the greatest scandal of our age. How could it be unless God willed it so? For rational, educated people who know the truth the appeal of Christianity is simply nostalgia. If everyone comes to know the truth about indefinite uncertainty and there are no more true believers, the Church will fade away. The new variety of "pseudo progressive" Christianity is simply a temporary rest stop on the road from orthodox Christianity to the emerging evolution of a new cosmic religion called for by Albert Einstein that integrates science and faith, the known and the unknown.

For all of its 2,000 years of trying to obey the command of Jesus to go and preach the gospel and teach all nations, Christianity has barely recruited one third of the Homo sapiens on planet Earth. The other two thirds either have not yet gotten the message or fail to realize its benefits. Maybe the problem is its hypocrisy, which Jesus condemned then as now. (Matthew 16:11-12) In several different scriptures, Jesus described the Kingdom of God as purified and released from the leaven of the self-righteous Pharisees, as leavened bread was prohibited to the Jews. (Exodus 12: 19-21) He condemned their hypocritic behaviors, calling them "snakes and vipers." (Matthew 23:33)

In spite of their professions of faith, most Christians and their religious leaders do not actually follow the teachings of Jesus as taken literally. If they really believe he was the divine son of God and the New Testament contains his word, then why do they not obey it? "If you love me keep my commandments." (John 14:15) From the very beginning work of the apostles it appears that distortions leaped into the dialogue that threatened to destroy the Gospel. Jesus taught, "Not everyone who says to me, Lord, Lord, will enter the kingdom of heaven, but only he who does the will of my Father who is in heaven." (Matthew 7:20-22) And James says, ". . . you see how that by works a man is justified, and not by faith only" (James 2:24) while Paul says, "A man is justified by faith without the deeds of the law." (Romans 3:28) and "no man is justified by the law in the sight of God." (Galatians 3:21) Both of them seem to ignore the instruction of Jesus to practice charity if you want to receive his support in judgment. (Matthew 25: 40-45)

This argument still rages in some churches; are we saved by faith unilaterally through grace, or by works? Or does it require both? Other conflicts among the first century preachers: James tells sheeple not to become teachers [in James 3:1, the word "masters" should be translated "teachers"] whereas Paul encourages sheeple to become teachers. (I Corinthians. 12:31) Apostle Paul warned about deception from anyone who disagreed with him, "I marvel that you are so soon removed from Him that called you into the grace of Christ unto another gospel: which is not another; but there be some that trouble you, and would pervert the gospel of Christ. But though they/we, or an angel from heaven, preach any other gospel unto you than that which we have preached unto you, let him be accursed." (Galatians 1:6-8) He would not tolerate any rivals either, "If anybody thinks he is a prophet or spiritually gifted, let him acknowledge that what I am writing to you is the Lord's command. If he ignores this, he himself will be ignored." (1 Corinthians 14:37-38) This type of declaration of divine infallibility seems to be a prerequisite for all succeeding religious leaders, whether it is true or not.

Another example of hypocracy: Apostle Paul had some very specific instructions for women in the early church that are hardly practiced today. "In like manner also, that women adorn themselves in modest apparel, with shamefacedness and sobriety; not with braided hair, or gold, or pearls, or costly array; But, which becomes women professing Godliness, with good works. Let the woman learn in silence with all subjection. But I permit not a woman to teach, nor to usurp authority over the man, but to be in silence. For Adam was first formed, then Eve. And Adam was not deceived, but the woman being deceived was in the transgression." (1 Tim. 2:9-14) "Let your women keep silence in the churches: for it is not permitted unto them to speak; but they are commanded to be under obedience, as also says the law. And if they wish to learn anything, let them ask their husbands at home: for it is a shame for women to speak in the church." (1 Corinthians. 14:34) Perhaps Muslims are closer to this teaching in their treatment of women than are modern Christian churches. For sheeple who believe the entire Bible is the Word of God without exception, there is only one explanation for selective disobedience of such dialogue. It is the will of God the Almighty One. So, if the words of Apostle Paul and Jesus are taken as commands from God, then the modern church is in a heap of trouble. [God the Almighty One is used throughout this text to distinguish the ultimate Source from the God created by mankind in all of their religions.]

Seldom do you hear Christian leaders actually preaching the words of Christ, as for example Luke 6: 20-49. Go ahead, check it out. How can Christians read this passage and continue making war? Answer: because Jesus said they would. (Matthew 24:6, Mark 13:7) The dogma of Christian doctrine: universal brotherhood, suppression of national distinctions, abolition of private property, and the strange injunction of non-resistance to evil by force all demand what is seemingly impossible to human nature and free market capitalism. Indeed, that is so, because the authentic Christian life is manifested by a change in human nature and so it is very rare. For Apostle Paul, the controlling human ego is replaced with possession by Christ spirit. "I have been crucified with Christ and I no longer live, but Christ lives in me." (Galatians 2:20) Jesus condemned the self-righteous scribes and Pharisees. For them he said he brought a sword that would separate families and require his disciples to hate mother and father and siblings to follow him. "I have not come to call the righteous, but sinners to repentance." (Luke 5:32)

Jesus also taught The Golden Rule, as did most other religious philosophers, "So in everything, do to others what you would have them do to you, for this sums up the Law and the Prophets." (Matthew 7:12) And he expanded that notion with this; "Give, and it will be given to you. A good measure, pressed down, shaken together and running over, will be poured into your lap. For with the measure you use, it will be measured to you." (Luke 6:38) Not many Christians practice this instruction, do they? However, Jesus said, "If you love me keep my commands..." (John 14:15, 14:21, 15:10) This same idea is found in Buddhism from 600 BCE and among the Greek philosophers too. It was rediscovered by Ralph Waldo Emerson, (1803-1882) "It is one of those beautiful compensations of this life that no one can sincerely try to help another without helping himself." A much more practical and useful axiom may be that offered by German philosopher Johann Goethe (1749-1832); "Treat people as if they were what they ought to be, and you help them become what they are capable of being." This statement is the fundamental idea in the growth of humanist psychology. But, the law of reciprocity works in human nature too; tit for tat; insult for insult, tooth for tooth, and eye for eye in the realms of justice.

Churches are not exceptions to human nature. For many modern churches in a secular capitalist society their golden rule is, "Do unto others as they would have you do unto them." They may not realize this is a fundamental idea in Buddhism, and it works to shift attention and desire from self to other better than that other one . . . "do unto others as you want them to do unto you." That is why smart preachers will only present scriptures that keep sheeple coming to church and contributing their money, the current supreme example being Joel Osteen, who packs arenas without any seminary education. However, countless gullible sheeple have been defrauded of their savings by illegal schemes based in religion to get their money with only broken dreams in return. The sociopath gets it mixed up and returns ill for good, while the saint may return good for ill. And the religious bully would demand unilateral servitude and obedience to his version of scriptures. Such are the likes of Benny Hinn and Mike Murdock who seemed to have duped a large following of those poor in spirit who wish they were rich in fact. All in the will of God the Almighty One, of course.

If sheeple could act like Jesus taught in non-secular society to the extreme, then everyone would be acting in the best interest of every other to the point that there would be no separation and all would be ONE. But, this notion is opposite to the secular western idea of self reliance and individual pursuit of health, wealth, and happiness in competition with everyone else. Compare the vast tax exempt real estate holdings and cathedrals of the churches with this teaching of Jesus, "Do not store up for yourselves treasures on Earth, where moth and rust destroy, and where thieves break in and steal. But store up for yourselves treasures in heaven, where moth and rust do not destroy, and where thieves do not break in and steal." (Matthew 6:19-20)

Nevertheless, telling sheeple only what they want to hear works. It sells cars, fills movie theaters, and brings sheeple to church on Sunday. It also sells books and packs sheeple into stadiums to worship the orators of "prosperity preaching" such as the best-selling sermons of Joel Osteen and others stemming from the school of positive thinking led by the late Norman Vincent Peale and his predecessors. [All these preachers make the same fundamental and common error in classical logic, i.e., some people are rich so you can be also. They elevate a true specific scripture to a false universal generality, and the sheeple poor in spirit accept it as real. They could not exist unless their congregations believed them.] They ignore the real logic of the bell curve of income distribution which always has a bottom side, but sheeple keep hoping they will be the next winner so they keep on buying those lottery tickets. But no matter how you scale it, there is only one winner and many losers in the lotteries of life. Nevertheless, all the losers think they can be winners . . . sometimes. Such is human nature . . . all in God's will of course. AIGWOC.]

But, that is not what Jesus taught . . . sometimes. Calvinist theologian, John Piper wrote an opposing view: "Luring people to Christ to get rich is both deceitful and deadly. It's deceitful because when Jesus himself called us he said things like: Any one of you who does not renounce all that he has cannot be my disciple." (Luke 14:33). "And it's deadly because the desire to be rich plunges people into ruin and destruction." (1 Timothy 6:9). "The most dangerous thing in the world is the sin of self-reliance and the stupor of worldliness." When a rich man asked Jesus how to obtain eternal life, he replied by instructing him to obey the law and the commandments. Then he added, ". . . One thing you lack, he said. Go, sell everything you have and give it to the poor, and you will have treasure in heaven. Then come, follow me. At this saying the man's face fell. He went away sad, because he had great wealth. Jesus looked around and said to his disciples, How hard it is for the rich to enter the Kingdom of God! It is easier for a camel to go through the eye of needle than for a rich man to enter the Kingdom of God." (Mark 10:21-25)

Jesus expanded this notion with the parable in Luke 12:42-48, "From everyone who has been given much, much will be demanded, and from one who has been entrusted with much, much more will be asked." So, perhaps the poor are necessary in order for the rich to earn their place in the Kingdom of God by charitable giving as unto the Lord. (Matthew 25: 39-46) Therefore, be careful what you ask for. But, Jesus caused massive confusion by promising that anything is possible if you ask in prayer and believe that you have it . . . even to casting mountains into the sea. (Matthew 21:21-23, Mark 11:23-24) Go ahead, look it up. Can you believe that? The mystery is why, if it is the Word of God, the Bible contains such apparent contradictions. Are these necessary opposites, or what?

Jesus also added considerable confusion and negation of all his other descriptions of it in his parables by warning sheeple against trying to find the Kingdom of God here or there or now or later by saying, "The kingdom of God does not come with your careful observation, nor will people say, Here it is, or There it is, because the kingdom of God is within you." (Luke 17:20-21) [Although some scholars prefer "among," the Greek word translated "within" is used in only one other scripture, Matthew 23:26. So, it must mean what it says.] But Jesus said, "My kingdom is not of this world." (John 18:36) Nor would his disciples any more be of this world. (John 17:14) Notice usage of the present tense, is. This dual other-worldly theme runs throughout the Gnostic book of John, unlike the other synoptic gospels. Clearly, either Jesus was both man and God or the Gospel writers got it wrong, or the opposites must co-exist. Heaven is both out there and in here. Hmmm.

The first Christians reportedly were ordered to sell all they had and live under rules of community property laid out by Apostle Peter under penalty of death. (Acts 5:1-10) Isn't that what they call Marxist-Socialism or maybe even a religious cult? How many organized modern churches would pass this test posed by Jesus, which places communal charity above all else? "When the Son of Man comes in his glory, and all the angels with him, he will sit on his throne in heavenly glory. All the nations will be gathered before him, and he will separate the sheeple one from another as a shepherd separates the sheep from the goats. He will put the sheep on his right and the goats on his left. Then the King (Jesus) will say to those on his right, Come, you who are blessed by my Father; take your inheritance, the kingdom prepared for you since the creation of the world. For I was hungry and you gave me something to eat, I was thirsty and you gave me something to drink, I was a stranger and you invited me in, I needed clothes and you clothed me, I was sick and you looked after me, I was in prison and you came to visit me . . . I tell you the truth, whatever you did for one of the least of these brothers of mine, you did for me. Then he will say to those on his left, Depart from me, you who are cursed, into the eternal fire prepared for the devil and his angels. For I was hungry and you gave me nothing to eat, I was thirsty and you gave me nothing to drink, I was a stranger and you did not invite me in, I needed clothes and you did not clothe me, I was sick and in prison and you did not look after me . . . I tell you the truth, whatever you did not do for one of the least of these, you did not do for me. Then they will go away to eternal punishment, but the righteous to eternal life." (Matthew 25:31-46) [The Amish must take this commandment literally as some of them are volunteering to help rebuild housing for the residents left homeless by hurricane Katrina in the Louisiana bayou. How many other mainline denominations are acting likewise? And who will help rebuild the homes lost to the earthquake and tsunami that destroyed thousands of lives in Japan?]

Jesus taught, "No one can serve two masters. Either he will hate the one and love the other, or he will be devoted to the one and despise the other. You cannot serve both God and Money." (Matthew 6:24) He might as well have said you cannot serve both God and Rome or Washington, D.C. How disappointed he must have felt when the Jews rejected him. "O Jerusalem, Jerusalem, you who kill the prophets and stone those sent to you, how often I have longed to gather your children together, as a hen gathers her chicks under her wings, but you were not willing." (Matthew 23:37) But another scripture says this was their destiny. (1 Peter 2:7-8) Jesus, himself, could not change the destiny of the Jews, who would be routed, killed, and dispersed in their revolt against Rome just 40 years after his departure. "Not my will, but thine." (Luke 22:42) Also, Jesus hung out with the social rejects and said they would achieve the kingdom of heaven ahead of the rich and leaders of the religious establishment. "The first shall be last and the last shall be first" and, "It is easier for a camel to get through the eye of a needle than for a rich man to enter the kingdom of God." (Mark 10:24) Time and again he shouted to the self-righteous, "Woe to you scribes and Pharisees . . . there shall be wailing and gnashing of teeth." (Luke 13: 28-30) And so the Jews were demolished and their temple destroyed in the uprising against Rome of 67-74 CE. All in God's will of course . . . AIGWOC.

During the first three centuries CE many different interpretations and translations of the gospel message apparently strived among the Gentiles, although Jesus promised; "the counselor, the holy spirit whom the father will send in my name will teach you all things." (John 14: 16, 26, 15: 26) During the fourth century, the winners gradually organized their position with the help of several Caesars who finally adopted Christianity as the state religion of Rome in 382 CE. With the power of the state behind them, Roman Catholic Church leaders controlled the subsequent propagation of the gospels and the Pope became the new Caesar in all but name only. The power of the sword was replaced with the power of Word. [Actually the first few popes of the first century are lost to history and only tradition exists to connect them with the ordination of St. Peter.]

Writing the story of Jesus must have been a slow laborious task from oral history for those disciples of the first century who thought it should be done up to six decades after his death . . . after Apostle Paul spurred them into action. There must have been many versions of it circulating by the fourth century, maybe some in Hebrew, some in Greek, and some in Latin, each one embellished by the inspiration of its scribe, combining other versions with oral traditions passed down for generations. Which one/s of them were the most accurate, no one can tell. At least four organized groups, the Zealots, Gnostics, Nazarenes, and the Essenes have all but disappeared, rejected by the priests of the Roman Catholic persuasion. How the original canon was chosen for the New Testament is lost in history. But, one development suggests an intriguingly plausible explanation. The first official adoption of Christian doctrine occurred at the Council of Nicaea convened by Constantine I (presently Iznik in Turkey) May 20-June 19 in 325 CE and turned on the argument between bishops from Alexandia, Arius and Athanasius . . . bottom line is that Athanasius won the debate and we got the Roman Catholic Church. If Arius had won his argument the world would be much different but Arianism has not been forgotten totally. It resurfaced again in the seventh century with Muhammad in Mecca and became Islam. Maybe he was right, and the world should all be Muslims with only one God with no Trinity, and Jesus being one of his many sons.

In 331 CE the Roman Emperor Constantine sent a letter, the text of which has survived, to Bishop Eusebius in Caesarea asking him to arrange for the production of fifty bibles using the approved canon. The scribes that he employed are lost to history. These books were to be skillfully executed copies of "the divine scriptures" on fine parchment for use in the churches of the new capital of the empire, Constantinople, now called Istanbul, in Turkey. Constantine not only promised to pay all of the expenses incurred in this project, he also provided two carriages to assure the swift shipment of the completed copies for his personal inspection. Eusebius was an advisor to and confidant of the Emperor. He is widely regarded as the principal architect of the political philosophy of Constantine's reconstituted empire. He was a trusted ally of the Emperor in advocating and implementing the policies of the newly Christianized state. Eusebius knew that Constantine was concerned about the unity of the church and the unity of the state as one and the same. Eusebius also knew that these new bibles prepared for the capital city would play an important role in the unity of the church. In other words, the New Testament canon was settled for all practical purposes when Constantine gave the order to create those fifty bibles. Their publication was palpable evidence of the unity of the church and hence the unity of the empire. The Roman Catholic Church did not issue another official statement about the contents of the Bible until 1546, when the Council of Trent in northern Italy, by a vote of twenty-four to fifteen, with sixteen abstentions, declared the writings in Jerome's Latin Vulgate version to be the church's official canon.

After Rome hijacked the church of Christ with the Edict of Milan on February 13, 313 CE and made it the defacto state religion in 382 CE under the first official Roman Pope, Damascus, things changed mightily for the worse. Christianity, by allying with political power in the days of Emperor Constantine, and by continuing to develop in such conditions, became completely distorted. Much as the Church would like to claim itself as the creation of Christ, it really is the creation of Roman politics in the fourth century CE. The debate over Jesus' degree of divinity escalated from heated argument to violence and bloodshed. It was led by two charismatic bishops in Alexandria, Arius who preached that Jesus, though uniquely holy, is less than God, and Athanasius who argued that Jesus is God himself in human form. Jesus was declared God in order to assist Roman emperors to consolidate their fading power base and restore their throne to its previous world domination. This was true for Constantine, who called the council of bishops to Nicaea in 325 CE, through Theodosius, a Spanish general who became the new Augustus of the East in January, 379 CE. Under Theodosius, Arianism was outlawed and bishops were allowed to incite Christian zealots to attack and kill non-believers in Christ's divinity. From this bloody beginning, the Catholic priests took advantage of general ignorance to appoint themselves the arbiters of the faith and the door to atonement for illiterate sinners. A long wave of religious violence followed, consolidating the power of those who declared Jesus as God in their own names. Within a century the Roman Empire was gone, but the Roman Catholic Church replaced control by the sword with control by the Word and a new world empire was organized during the following two hundred years, led by politically appointed Popes.

From its outset, the Church of Rome declared itself infallible by the Holy Spirit and impossible of error. Subsequent historical developments and scientific discoveries refute this claim, but it still persists. It even told the sheeple what to believe and what to ignore, and it kept them illiterate in the dark for 1500 years while it amassed wealth beyond measure until Martin Luther and the printing press liberated them. Pope Benedict XVI, [aka Joseph Cardinal Ratzinger] wrote in his Eschatology, (1988) "If the communal life of the Church, which vouches for the permanence and thus the future of the Word, is no longer recognized then all interpretations simply are predictions without any validating authority." Indeed. The Pope seems to have overlooked one little detail at least as Jesus said, "Do not call anyone on Earth father, for you have one Father, and he is in heaven." (Matthew 23:9) This command does not appear in any other gospel, so perhaps it was meant to be excluded but was overlooked by the Catholic editorial redactor. All in God's will of course . . . AIGWOC.

That Jesus taught much that was not included in the Bible is claimed by the writer of John, "Jesus did many other things as well. If every one of them were written down, I suppose that even the whole world would not have room for the books that would be written." (John 21:25) It is too bad they were not written down because we only have some scraps of his teaching and nothing much at all of what he said after the alleged resurrection. Scholars have concluded the Gospels account for only 29 days out of the three years Jesus possibly served his disciples. Since he wrote nothing, his followers disputed for decades after his death what he actually taught. Based on the dating difficulties and other problems, the belief in the authorship of the gospels by Matthew, Mark, Luke and John is a matter of faith, as such a conclusion is not merited in light of detailed textual and historical analysis by Biblical scholars. The gospel authors are in fact anonymous. The book of Acts claims that all we know about Christian origins came from the Holy Spirit after its declaration on the day of Pentecost. The dogmatic Latin version of the Roman Catholic Vulgate Bible was compiled by Jerome under commission by Pope Damasus I in 382-385 CE from Hebrew and Greek resources several hundred years after the fact, so no one knows what material was discarded during its compilation. Because it was copied by hand from one scribe to another, literally hundreds of different versions have existed from time to time.

One can only imagine what secret manuscripts are kept in the Vatican library to this day that would dispute official church dogma. Perhaps among them are original books of The Nag Hammadi Library, a collection of ancient codices containing more than fifty texts, which was discovered in Egypt in 1945. These documents include mythical Gnostic writings that cast a different image upon the youth of Jesus, the family of Joseph as a widower with children prior to his betrothal to the virgin Mary, the role of Mary Magdelene as a feminine apostle, and even the interpretation of Genesis that accounts for a first wife named Lillith for Adam before the creation of Eve. The translation and printing of the Nag Hammadi library, published in the 1970's, have provided impetus to a major re-evaluation of early Christian history and the nature of Gnosticism, which was a prevailing belief system among first century Christians.

The Gnostics preceded Jesus in searching for a personal realization of God. While Christianity emphasizes faith and spiritual possession by Christ for salvation, Gnosticism focuses on attaining a state of divine consciousness and spiritual knowledge so that Godliness can be personally realized, not unlike Hinduism. They believed that only by getting rid of the material body and leaving it behind in death can we manifest our true spiritual nature. This immensely important discovery in the Dead Sea scrolls includes scraps from a large number of primary Gnostic scriptures—texts once thought to have been entirely destroyed during the early Christian struggle to define Catholic orthodoxy. Through the second century, its writers apparently attempted to integrate the teachings of Jesus. These include scriptures excluded from the Bible including the Gospel of Thomas, the Gospel of Philip, the Gospel of Truth, the Gospel of Mary, and the Gospel of Judas. It apparently was the political power of Irenaeus, the Bishop of Lyons in 180 CE which helped to get them classified as heresy and therefore excluded from the Bible.

The Gnostics believed that there actually are two Gods that mankind deals with. One is the God of this Earth who rules this planet and lords over its chaos. Gnostics concluded that God created by man was faulty, perverse, and needed to be superseded by a higher being that provided balance for the male and female aspects of nature. Then, there is a God who has no day to day dealings with mankind, but is the true, great and beautiful Spirit. This God, according to the Gnostic Gospel of Judas is God and Parent, Father and

Mother of All, the invisible one that is over all that is incorruptible, that is pure light. Further, Gnostics believed in a perfect parallel spiritual world that contrasts with the physical one full of struggle and suffering, the ultimate duality. They encouraged all individuals to seek to know God through their own experience and to achieve personal enlightenment through rigorous spiritual discipline and self-discovery, much like Hindus. "Liberation in life comes through self-realization. When the spirit is liberated from the bondage of the world, then the stage of liberation of the soul is reached." Jeremiah reported that women worshipped the "Queen of Heaven" and so it appears did the Gnostics. (Jeremiah 44: 17-25)

A Gnostic "Gospel of Mary" dated to the second century seems to support a leadership role for women in the early church. Some scholars claim that one scrap of its manuscript says that Jesus loved Mary Magdalene and kissed her "on the . . ." (the word is missing.) The Roman Catholic Church leaders opposed this notion, and they required unquestioning allegiance to the paternalistic Church as an obvious extension of the Holy Roman Empire which was in decline. They had Jesus live a celibate life and claim there was no marrying in the resurrection and declare, "My kingdom is not of this world." (Matthew 22:30, Mark 12:25) Princeton scholar, Elaine Pagels suggests that Gnosticism was too spiritual for Roman Caesars to understand, so it was all but eliminated by the fifth century. Had it survived, perhaps the Christian religion would look much different today. Nevertheless, the veneration of Mary as Holy Mother shows that first-fourth century Catholic leaders must have read the Gnostics and integrated what they liked while they discarded what was not politically correct for the times. How could all this be unless God the Almighty One willed it so to happen? Something is wrong with this picture. Maybe it is time for a different view of God. Can we ever hope to know the God that Jesus knew as the Father or is he forever lost, buried under the growth of dross that hides the pearl of great wisdom?

The Upanishads of ancient Hinduism states, "Who sees all beings in his own self and his own self in all beings loses all fear. When a sage sees this great Unity and his self has become all beings, what delusion and what sorrow can be near him?" Jesus seems to have expressed this state when he said, "I and the father are one . . . who has seen me has seen the father." (John 10:30, 14:9) A Course in Miracles (1975) [claimed to be a new revelation from Jesus] also would have us eliminate all suffering and conflict by replacing the projections of fear and guilt within separated selves by extending only love and forgiveness to all, and in that all we become One. It would have us believe that spirit and God are one inseparable and the only separation is an illusion that we have created to support insistence upon attack.

[Christians believe God has begotten only one Son. But that idea conflicts with the inclusion principle of Hinduism, that all of the souls that God created are his Sons, and if you also believe that the Sonship is One, then every soul must be a Son of God, or an integrated inseparable part of the Sonship that Jesus prayed for. (John 17: 20-23) If you do not find the concept that the whole is greater than the sum of its parts difficult to understand, you should therefore not have too great difficulty with this. The Sonship in its Oneness does transcend the sum of its parts. However, it loses this special state as long as any of its parts are missing. This is why the unity cannot ultimately be resolved until all of the individual parts of the Sonship have returned. Only then, in the true sense, can the meaning of wholeness be understood and manifested. The correction of this error is the At-One-Ment. Islam attempts to correct this error by proclaiming there is no God but Allah. Of course there must always be an opposite thought, and it was provided by Prof. Stephen Prothero, chair of the religion department at Boston University, in his book God is Not One (2010) By describing beliefs and practices of eight world religions he hopes to gain more tolerance for the vast diversity among religions. But some critics argue that he failed to prove his objective.]

Jesus thought the family of Christ was united in some form of oneness among his followers but everyone else seems to be excluded. (John 17:9-11) Apostle Paul apparently had the same idea but he went much further. "There is one body and one Spirit. In the same way you were called to share one hope." (Ephesians 4:4) "There are different kinds of spiritual gifts, but the same Spirit is the source of them all. God works in different ways, but it is the same God who does the work in all of us." (I Corinthians 12:4) Perhaps he got that notion from Jesus, "I have given them the glory you gave me, so they may be one as we are one." (John 17:22)

Rarely, an evolved soul is born with this insight. One such was juvenile philosopher and poet, Mattie Stepanek (1991-2004). If all the tribes of mankind originated in a single family somewhere in Africa as DNA evidence seems to indicate, perhaps this young man had access to deep pre-birth memories most of us cannot access, what Hindus and theosophists call the Akashic records and C.G. Jung called the collective unconscious. At age six, Mattie wrote this poem:

"We are many colors of skin and languages
We are many sizes and many countries
But we are one Earth and we have one heart and one life
We are growing up together
So we must live as one family."

If this be true, then to harm another is to harm one's self and to help another is to help one's self. But, unfortunately, many Christians assume this applies only to fellow Christians in the church. It certainly excludes Muslims, and vice versa. So do other religions practice exclusion and oppression of those who disagree with them . . . such as the eternal war between Jews and Palestinians in Israel . . . pity.

Jesus seems to have prayed to God for the coming of such unity among sheeple in John 17: 20-23, but alas, instead we got wars and rumors of wars. Religious wars seem to unite sheeple/soldiers into one family better than any other human enterprise, except for competitive sports. Consider the alignment of western Christian nations against the Arabic nations that follow Muhammad and rule by shari'ah law connected back to the laws of Moses. Add in the Zionist attitude among supporters of Israel that claims it has a divine right ordained by God to the land occupied by Palestine in the West Bank and the Gaza territory, and one gets perpetual conflict and threats of war. However, an emerging countermovement is underway that may have an opposing impact using the latest in Internet technology of video podcasts and personal blogs attempting to raise the human consciousness to the Oneness that Jesus attempted to demonstrate. He admonished, "I tell you the truth, anyone who has faith in me will do what I have been doing. He will do even greater things than these . . ." (John 14:12) If you are ready for this much unity, you can find a good site at http://weareoneinspirit.blogspot.com/ All in the will of God the Almighty One, of course.

If God wanted his humans to live in peace as one family, doubtless they would but this obviously is not the case. Unfortunately, it seems that humans require exclusionary groups in their social cultures. The uniform of a sports team or military unit sets them apart from their "enemies" and assures some kind of unity among the group to sustain the herd mentality among humankind. Researchers at Stanford University discovered that coordinated group activities give sheeple a feeling of belonging that may derive from primitive needs to support the tribal culture for mutual survival. Wars and competitive sports ultimately are the result. They discovered that "synchrony rituals," dances, games, festivals and such, are powerful—so much so that they may have endowed certain groups with a competitive advantage over the eons, perhaps even causing some cultures to flourish while others perished. Sheeple seem to have a need to belong to some kind of social group, even by virtual membership in a sports team, and its absence can impair their immune system and hasten death. Perhaps that is why there are so many different religious groups.

It is no wonder that such potent impulses for "belonging but separate" remain entrenched in today's sports teams, marching bands, churches, armies, and families, neighborhoods, country clubs and corporations, and it could even explain the attraction of synchronized swimming. [My high school colors were red and white, so I am naturally partial to any team that wears the colors of my youth.] One of the most effective experiences of this kind is close order drill in the military. Anyone who has completed basic military training knows the feeling that emerges after a few weeks resisting the emotion of the collective movement in drilling . . . a sense of pervasive well being emerges, becoming larger than self when "I" passes into "we" and individual fate loses its central importance in that communal state where self becomes submerged into the unit. Once that integration into the military unit is achieved, the self never again fully returns to "me." If you have not had that experience you cannot understand or appreciate its importance in human society, both collectively and individually. Only the veterans of war can know what this means.

Sages know that happiness comes from having something to do, someone to love, and something to look forward to, i.e., losing self in other, what psychology calls "flow." Military psychologists know this principle very well so they make sure that soldiers are always busy training. Lebanese poet Kahlil Gibran (1883-1931) described such an ideal in work; "It is to weave the cloth with threads drawn from your heart even as if your beloved were to wear that cloth, to build a house as if your beloved were to dwell in it, to sow seeds even as if your beloved were to eat the fruit." In other words, whatever you are called to do, do it with love. In this state, work becomes devotion to humanity, even if it is cleaning the floors or washing the windows. When that is all rolled into one, there is bliss. Perhaps one day we can change the focus from self to other and be liberated from ego in the process; maybe without resorting to wars for these benefits.

But, here is the rub because there always is a rub. Call it an opposing view. Homo sapiens in present form are newcomers to life on planet Earth, extending back less than 150,000 years, while many other species have had millions of years of evolution bringing them to the present state. We have a long way to go; in many ways we still are a primitive species. Our genetic natural selection has fitted us to unite into teams and also to divide us from other teams, while blinding us to this truth. Moreover, the illusion of separation keeps us not only separated from each other in perpetual defensive mode, but it also keeps us separated from the original unit of God in a world of fear that drives out love. You can see this throughout history that is driven by synchronized groups fighting each other for their self interest. Immature egos want to support a tribe where rank can be obtained, i.e., winners and losers, masters and slaves, employers and employees, government and governed, et al. The winner of Donald Trump's "Apprentice," television show gets a job while all the losers just get a learning experience, but there is no shortage of applicants each season. Competition seems to be in human nature as legendary football coach, Vince Lombardi (1913-1970) declared, "If winning isn't important, why do they keep score . . . winning isn't everything, it's the only thing." [Sports fans may know that bicycle racer Lance Armstrong won the Tour de France seven times, but no one knows who came in second.]

Would competitive sports be as interesting without the scoreboard and the playoffs? In fact, some would suggest that the will to compete and to win is a basic part of human nature that is thwarted by government entitlements which prevents winners and losers. Carried into war, this notion could include the body counts in mass graves at the end of battles. This is not a gender issue as competitive sports for women now will prove. In fact, women in military combat roles now are no longer the exception including snipers, fighter pilots, and submarine crews. But there is one gender component to natural competition . . . that is the way male sperm cells must race to get to the female egg in uterus first . . . there is no prize for second place in that bell curve. It is either do or die, and so it is for the poorest among us. Those who proclaim that anyone can achieve whatever they want just are not being realistic. For some to win others must lose in the contests of life. For each seller there must be a buyer and one will lose and one will gain. It is the law of necessary opposites. Get it? By the way, how living sperm cells are manufactured from scratch in the human testes and fertile female eggs are produced in their ovaries is a medical mystery. But it does seem that after conception their destiny is set. All in God's will of course . . . AIGWOC.

The problem in society is that sheeple must balance individual freedom to compete in global markets with the need for security and cooperation provided by a group. Security and personal freedom seem to be mutually exclusive. Homo sapiens have continually tried many different forms of government, but none of them have eliminated poverty and an increasing range between the poorest and the richest. Indeed, Jesus said the poor would never be eliminated so he had no solution either, and the disparity considers to widen with the rich getting richer. Oddly, security is obtained by letting organizations absorb personal freedoms. The worst cases are soldiers who must give up their freedom to preserve the freedom of others. Perhaps great national leaders, including Napoleon Bonaparte and Adolf Hitler and Franklin D. Roosevelt, were instinctively able to use this trait of Homo sapiens in organizing and leading their immense military campaigns. President Roosevelt successfully organized millions of unemployed youth in his Civilian Conservation Corps during the Great Depression to offset their angst by regimenting their lives in return for secure shelter, food, and clothing. So did President George W. Bush use fear of security to justify his doctrine of pre-emptive war against anyone suspected of planning terrorism against Americans.

It is of more than passing interest that the largest selling book of all time next to the Bible is <u>Mein Kampf</u>, (1926) the autobiographical dogma of Adolf Hitler which described regimentation of an entire nation. It seemed to work very well so long as God willed. The experience of this family of unity, one nation under God, is profound and can be hinted at only vaguely by the words of scripture. In contrast, the go-it-alone style of traditional American lifestyles deprives individuals and the culture of the advantage of being synchronized with a larger group. So they make up for it through vicarious participation in sports teams beginning with the community youth clubs on up to the professional sports business. There is no other explanation for what prompts sheeple to pay out large sums of money to watch their favorite teams compete. Winners are worshipped and losers are abandoned. But they all are inseparable parts of the whole.

The Buddhist master, Longchenpa Rinpoche taught, "Even the duality of truth and falsehood is one reality. Attachment to pleasure brings misery. Do not latch onto happiness, do not eliminate misery. Thereby everything is accomplished." This message is that where there is thought of duality, as in spirit and flesh, there also must be thought of non-duality, as in spirit only and the illusion of flesh or vice versa as they seem to be mutually exclusive. Opposites cannot exist one without the other, even in thoughts. C. G. Jung saw it as the integration of consciousness with the universal unconscious, or preconscious. If there is such a library of human experience, how it can be transmitted from generation to generation through merger of sperm and egg and where it may reside in each individual is not understood. Perhaps there is some energetic medium of transmission not yet discovered. It encompasses both union with God, or absolute reality, and union with all existence, the dissolution of subject and object, as knower and known become one. It is as though the id [just do it] and superego [just say no] both can exist as a merged singularity and the mediating function of ego vanishes, for it is no longer needed.

Either/or becomes both/and synthesis where the dualities in nature are merged. We are both "one out of many," as illustrated by your family tree, and "many out of one," if you believe the story of creation in the Bible or in the evolution of species from a single ancestor. The true self emerges above the suffering of life and merges with the Spirit of the Whole for those few who are so gifted. The struggle for control and safety is ended, and inner peace is achieved when selfish egotism is defeated. Until this state of being is attained by all Homo sapiens, there always will be wars. Until e Pluribus Unum becomes e Orbis Unum, sheeple will continue killing each other to prove who is "right." When it comes, this new religion will be a virtual church, with no clergy, no buildings, and no treasury. Its treasury will be in the hearts of Homo sapiens for Jesus taught that, ". . . where your heart is there will your treasure be also." (Matthew 6:21) Some modern churches have that reversed, and that must change for peaceful unity to be achieved.

Possibly the greatest crusader for updating outdated ideas about God in America is retired Episcopal Bishop, John Spong. He has written in his online blog, "Since human beings are creatures of both time and space, and since we know from the work of Albert Einstein that time and space are relative categories that expand and contract in relation to each other, then we must conclude that any statement made by anyone, who is bound by time and space, will never be absolute. There are no propositional statements, secular or religious, that are exempt from this principle. The old evangelical language commonly used is badly dated and I believe quite distorting to my understanding of what Christianity is all about. Religion is a journey into the mystery of God. It is not a system of beliefs and creeds and when it becomes that, it always becomes idolatrous and begins to die. Human concepts of God have been mortally wounded by the successive blows of Copernicus, Galileo, Isaac Newton, Charles Darwin and Albert Einstein, just to name a few. I do not believe, however, that this means that God has been mortally wounded even if the anthropomorphic definition of God has been. Suppose God is not defined as a being in the image of man, but is simply experienced as a power, a presence. Then the question is; Are we delusional or is this experience real? I think the experience of God is real, [as Generator, Operator, Destroyer] but I believe we are in the process of defining our God experience in a new way that will replace the dying theistic definition of the past."

Spong continues. "If you can no longer imagine God as a benevolent father answering all your prayers or like Santa bringing you presents at Christmas, you may be ready for a new relationship with the real God . . . God lives in me, loves through me and empowers me to escape that drive to survive that is in every living thing in order to give my life away. So I am drawn by God beyond my boundaries and I perceive that God becomes real when I enter into the task of living and loving and being. This makes me rather a deeply infused, God-intoxicated human being who no longer has the words to describe the God in whom I live and move and have my being." This conversion experience was expressed by Apostle Paul; "So from now on we regard no one from a worldly point of view. Though we once regarded Christ in this way, we do so no longer. Therefore, if anyone is in Christ, he is a new creation; the old has gone, the new has come!" (2 Corinthians 5: 16-17) This rebirth can only be experienced, never explained.

Frank Schaeffer, a former conservative Calvinist evangelist, reported in his book, <u>Crazy for God</u> (2008) that preachers are taught in seminary historical facts about the Bible they don't dare discuss from the pulpit for fear of destroying the childish faith of sheeple who finance their careers. If we cannot rely upon the words of New Testament scripture and the literature of its patriarchs as historical foundations of the Church, what can we rely upon for spiritual guidance into a new personal reformation? How can we navigate through the cruelty, suffering, and struggles of life unless there is some hope that it is all leading to some better life form ahead? Must we all just close the church doors and go about business as usual without that hourly respite on Sunday from anguish and existential anxiety? As for where we go after we die, no one knows, not even the Pope.

A wise Hindu sage commented, "Man wastes his time in futile thoughts. He expends all this energy in attachment and desire. For want of a proper aim in life he wanders in darkness and blames his karma or God." Possibly the greatest scientist who ever lived, Albert Einstein (1879-1955) wrote, "The religion of the future will be a cosmic religion. It should transcend a personal God and avoid dogmas and theology. Covering both the natural and the spiritual, it should be based on a religious sense arising from the experience of all things, natural and spiritual as a meaningful unity." If you can look up at the stars at night and not be overwhelmed at the true greatness of the creation, you just have not looked. The creator of it all is so majestic that humankind cannot imagine its grandeur. And although we are created "just a little lower than the angels," there is no measure for the chasm between the Creator and the created. (Psalm 8:5, Hebrews 2:7)

The ultimate unitive state is described in <u>World Scripture: A Comparative Analogy of Sacred Texts</u> (1991) by Andrew Wilson as . . . "the final goal of Spiritual evolution expressed in both Hinduism and Buddhism. If you know you are the Self, the Lord of Life, the supreme source of light; the supreme source of love, you will be free from suffering. You will transcend duality and live in a state of Oneness . . . Only the one-pointed mind attains the state of unity. There was and there will be only One. You are already fulfilled. How can you be bound or free? Whoever sees separation but not the one indivisible Self must wander on and on from death to death. A person in union with the Self is not concerned with what is without and what is within, for in that unitive state all desires find their perfect fulfillment. There is no other desire that needs to be fulfilled, and one goes beyond sorrow to inner peace." At this exhalted stage of evolution, the functions of ego, id, and superego no longer will be needed and wars between the self and the ego, spirit and flesh, called "Jihad" in Islam, will cease. But, too many Muslims have this interpretation of jihad attributed to prophet, Muhammad, "I am commanded to fight until everyone believes there is no God but Allah and Muhammad is his messenger."

Bishop Spong has observed that we should not be too critical of religion, although it flows at a glacier pace into the new and different. He wrote, "The Church, like most human social institutions, is in an inner struggle continuously between the values of yesterday and the rising consciousness of a changing world. Because the church [leaders are so] autocratic and allow so little dissent, it is very difficult for them ever to change their thinking until new truth is so established in the world at large that their position becomes embarrassing. In the evolution of human thought, time is of the essence. No one can fully escape the culture and ideas that form a particular age. The rise in human consciousness toward such things as war, the role of women and homosexuality is never implemented at once by all. It grows, beginning with a single protest, until it becomes a heresy, then a movement and finally a reformation. It then becomes a new orthodoxy equally resistant to change and the cycle goes on." Thus, the last reformation may be just the continuation of religious evolution from the old to the new. Each individual is both an insignificant and an indispensable part of the whole. All in the will of God the Almighty One, of course. Feel good inside no matter what happens outside.

2. The virtual Church of Theofatalism™

Perhaps you are beginning to wonder if the traditional things you were taught in church, synagogue, mosque, or temple really are true. Maybe you are even beginning to doubt whether religion actually is based in reality. Perhaps it merely is some form of universal mental illness or delusion based in fiction and imagination. So many theologians are culpable in loss of respect and authority by organized religion the very word "church" is repulsive to many seekers of inner peace. Many sheeple live in a gap between an old religion that no longer works and a new religion that has not yet been developed. Perhaps most sheeple live in that gap but are afraid to admit it for fear of the unknown consequences. Perhaps there is a need for some new kind of church that would support sheeple through this evolution towards a new spirituality that describes the world as it really is. What would it look like and what would it teach? Let it begin here.

Welcome to the church like no other but which includes all the others. The virtual Church of Theofatalism™ is like no other because it is "the universal spiritual pathway to serenity and contentment for all people." Instead of a corporate form of organized church, this is the most unorganized, random existence of spiritual souls embodied in human form that is possible. French poet and author extraordinaire of "Les Miserables" and "The Hunchback of Notre Dame," Victor Hugo (1773-1828) observed, "There is nothing more powerful than an idea whose time has come." If it is time, this could be it.

Like gravity, Theofatalism™ exists whether you believe in it or not and it certainly does not need your permission. Whether your organized social religion is Hindu, Buddhism, Jewish, Muslim or Christian, or some other including Atheism, this virtual church embraces them all. Everyone is a member and no one can ever live outside of it. It has no treasury, no buildings, and no clergy. It is pure soul. The Universe and all it contains is its

34

sanctuary, and its central theme is "God always wins." Everyone is a member, and no one can leave or be expelled. Theofatalism™ says that we all are on the pathway of life . . . exactly where we need to be here and now . . . like walking the Chartres labyrinth used for its universal symbol. All the ageless arguments about the existence—or not—of Gods in philosophy and religions considered, in this view God the Almighty One is "that which makes all things happen."

This definition arises from the law of physics that says a body at rest tends to remain at rest unless some external force is applied to it. It also arises from the various laws of thermodynamics that avoid a specific definition of energy because it only exists as a mathematical abstraction. Still, it is assumed that nothing happens of itself without some force or cause behind it. The definition of "all things" refers to everything from the smallest subatomic particle to the largest interstellar galaxy, in all the Universes however many there may be, with the lives of Homo sapiens barely discernable among them when seen from the satellites orbiting in space, each one insignificant but also indispensable. Considering all the happenings in the Universe, it is the ultimate hubris for Homo sapiens to think they are anything special, and yet each individual is both insignificant and indispensable. Of course, hubris also must have a cause, that which is called God the Almighty One. However, its essence is the universal energy or Theos, not the God of mythology but the one that created the mythology.

The symbol of Theofatalism™ is the Chartres Labyrinth tiled into the Cathedral of Our Lady of Chartres in France. With its roots in ancient mythology the design reappears throughout history in different forms. Unlike its opposite maze, which is a primitive symbol of chaos intended to confuse and frustrate, the labyrinth provides a clear and undistorted pathway to the center, which contains its distinctive central feature of the Lotus blossom. The Lotus blossom symbolizes the inseparability of cause and effect, the provision and reality, and the source and manifestation of enlightenment. Many churches and spiritual centers are using the Chartres Labyrinth to provide a walk of comfort and serenity for seekers of inner peace as the symbolic walk of life. The practice of labyrinth walking integrates the body with the mind and the mind with the spirit. It can be perceived as a sacred pilgrimage to the center Source after meandering about in reversing directions. There are three stages to walking a labyrinth: 1) releasing control by the ego on the way in by surrendering to the pathway ahead, 2) receiving sublime energy, comfort, and peace in the center, and 3) returning to serve as you follow the path back out of the labyrinth. At its most basic level the labyrinth is a metaphor for the journey to the center of your deepest self and back out into the world with a greater acceptance of who you really are.

The evolution of Theofatalism™ arises from awareness of reality as it really is. So you may call it a metaphysical form of reality gospel. Such awareness was experienced by the writer during his search for inner peace and contentment during several spiritual encounters on trips to Sedona, AZ which were chronicled in a book describing his discoveries. The present set of essays in this book is a study guide that explores principles of Theofatalism™ you will find detailed in the reference book titled, <u>Voices of Sedona</u>. Each essay presents a challenging discussion of contemporary issues, but taken together they compile a belief system to feel good inside no matter what happens outside.

Churches usually are based upon some creed or standards of belief. The virtual Church of Theofatalism™ has its own belief system as described in five principles of Theofatalism™ that are fully developed in <u>Voices of Sedona</u>, by imaginary teachers brought together to advance the spiritual evolution of Homo sapiens. The affirmation of this virtual Church is, "Feel good inside no matter what happens outside." Sheeple who no longer find comfort or useful coping resources in their traditional faith may find this pathway a more effective way to deal with reality. If you went searching for inner peace and contentment, this is what you found.

The Principles of Theofatalism™

Principles can never be invented, only discovered. The principles of Theofatalism™ are summarized here to stimulate readers to complete their full development by reading <u>Voices of Sedona</u>, to learn them and to make them a part of living twenty-four hours each and every day. There are only two rules to follow in their application to life: begin and continue.

1. Absolute Predeterminism: Everything is happening as it must or it would be different. The divine will of God the Almighty One cannot be disobeyed. It is the utmost arrogance and ignorance to assume that the creature can disobey the Creator or the clay can control the potter . . . or the puppet can pull its own strings. Disobeying God's will is imagined only by the insane because it is impossible. God's will be done, and that includes the arrogance and ignorance to assume otherwise. Everything that is or is not must be as it is or is not and everything must go as it goes, or it would be different. That includes both belief and disbelief in this principle. God creates atheists too. Everything is happening exactly as it was meant to be throughout the Universe, from the smallest subatomic particle to the largest and remotest galaxies. Each form of life on planet Earth is a small but

necessary element of the whole. Individual choices are driven by unseen forces incomprehensible to our conscious minds. The "I Am" that we are merely watches the mind/body as it manifests the will of God the Almighty One as there can be no other. [We cannot know what it is that we are outside of a body because that would be like spinning around fast enough to see your own back. Psychology calls it the "self" but words cannot describe what cannot be seen. Some things really are impossible.]

This principle presumes existence of a superior source called God the Almighty One that controls the will of Homo sapiens no less than all other forms of matter in the Universe. We must make decisions, and we are affected by their consequences through cause and effect, but the choices all were predetermined at the time of creation, which occurs outside of time/space. The greatest challenge sheeple face in life may be letting go of the wishful dream that things should be different. If they could be, they would be. You are right where you are supposed to be here and now. And so is everyone else . . . believe it or not. That would include the rich and famous as well as the homeless and criminals. Of course, this principle exposes belief in free will as a necessary illusion and concludes that God makes atheists too. But, that belief in illusion too must be necessary or it would be different as nothing can happen outside the will of God the Almighty One. So, this work either will be discovered and become widely distributed or it will not. All in God's will of course . . . AIGWOC. Get it? Think you can handle that?

2. Necessary Opposites: We readily accept the existence of opposites in the polarities of electromagnetism, in the ones and zeros of Boolean digital logic, and in the use of words with opposite meanings that we call "antonyms." For every action there is an equal and opposite reaction; but as in physics so in human thoughts and actions. Human beings either think they are a little lower than angels or a little higher than apes. Saints are one and imbeciles are the other, except that apes do some things better than humans and imbeciles are all too plentiful. The creation myth of the Bible and the Darwinian theory of evolution seem to be incompatible, either/or ideas. Charles Darwin observed that everything is continually changing and life forms must either adapt or die out. He noted that supplies of food never keep up with demand of geometric growth in consuming populations, making it necessary for individuals to compete for scarce resources, thus his law of "survival of the fittest" which causes suffering and

death. One such mystery in evolution is whether domesticated dogs evolved from wild wolves or sprang up on their own more than 12,000 years ago.

Indeed, death is a way of making way for change and improvement through genetics in all species. If God the Almighty One is the what, evolution is the how. What still is missing is a "theory of why." Unfortunately, among human societies it seems that reproduction is not always based upon fitness to compete, so many sheeple suffer from lack of resources to support health, wealth, and happiness. There is no law against being stupid and no restraint against the sexuality of stupid sheeple. But, creationists say all it takes is the voice of God to change things, so he must want things the way they are, opposites and all. Some sheeple find it curious that Lincoln and Darwin share the same birthday. Both were called to interpret death so that life could prevail, one with the pen and one with the bayonet and bullet. But, maybe these are both/and ideas that must be accommodated.

Indeed, Charles Darwin set off a civil war in western religion that forced Christians to choose whether they believed the Bible was the inerrant and infallible Word of God or merely the best attempts by its writers to describe their understanding of God that must be interpreted for modern times with aid of the Holy Spirit. The former became fundamentalists and the latter became the reformed modernists and progressives. This split reached its zenith in the trial of John Scopes in Tennessee in 1925 for his attempt to teach evolution in the public schools that was defended by the American Civil Liberties Union. This court debate reached across the whole country and set up the battleground engaged to this day. Scopes lost his case but his lawyer, Clarence Darrow launched the modernist movement. Its opponents included the evangelical likes of Dwight L. Moody, Amy S. McPherson, Billy Sunday, and Billy Graham, and Jerry Falwell, all great orators. It was like the religious energy aligned with opposing north and south poles of a magnet. It is interesting that during the same time period, politics was separating into the Democrats and Republicans, the former being the modernists and the latter aligning with the fundamentalists; and the former appealing more to educators and creative artisans while the latter appealing more to the workers and their masters.

Perhaps, all energy of the Universe is distributed about a neutral center like the air in a balloon, with equal power invested in opposing forces manifested in life events as well as laws of physics.

A magnet must have both north and south poles to be complete, with like poles demonstrating the law of repulsion and opposite poles demonstrating the law of attraction . . . both/and rather than either/or. Physics now assumes that both matter and anti-matter are necessary to sustain the Universe. The opposite ideas, God the Almighty One is and God the Almighty One is not, must both exist in order to have the center between faith in God and faith in no God. For every action, there is an equal and opposite reaction in nature, and so in thought. The idea that everything sensible is changing, and everything is impermanent must be balanced with an idea that permanence in some form also exists, so sheeple invented the ideas of immortality, heaven, hell, and eternity. Even the concept of Christ is balanced with the necessary anti-Christ. Jesus said that he was come to bring life, and that more abundantly. But he also said he came to bring a sword that would put family members against each other. You could look it up.

[The logical necessity of opposites to make up the whole was expressed by Greek philosopher, Heraclitus (535-475 BCE) who took as a first principle the notion that, "Opposites all are the same." The corollary would be all units are composed of opposites, i.e., all atoms are balanced between equal positive and negative charges of energy with matter having one set of polarities and anti-matter having the opposite. Moreover, the self-contradictory statements which can be found in the scriptures of every major world religion are taken by many sheeple to have a very profound meaning. If apparently contradictory expressions can in fact carry some meaning, then they must do so by depending on some other type of logic called the "logic of paradox," i.e., two seemingly mutually exclusive things that coexist but not in the same realm . . . sort of like Homo sapiens in New York City and mountain gorillas in Rwanda or whales in the ocean and mankind on shore. However, it was George Wilhelm Friedrich Hegel (1770-1831) who developed a system of higher logical thought he called dialectical reasoning, thesis-antithesis-synthesis, that could accommodate the necessary opposites. Examples would include; "the ten thousand things are one" and "right is not right" (Taoism); "He who sees inaction in action and action in inaction, he is wise" (Hinduism); "the phenomena of life are not real phenomena" (Buddhism); "I and the Father are one" and "you are all one in Christ Jesus" (Christianity)]

Since Homo sapiens manifest energy in thoughts and behaviors, they, and all material and spiritual forms, must conform to this principle of necessary opposites. Inner peace and serenity can be found by spending time in the central null, but realistically we must exist for life in some place and time distributed throughout the Universe, as with the air molecules within a balloon. Sometimes this is a happy-healthy-wealthy place, and sometimes it is tragic and painful. When all possible nuclear forces are applied to all sub-atomic events, the result in energy is neutral as they cancel each other out. Every atom is in perfect balance with equal and opposite forces among electrons and protons until some external force unbalances them.

Sheeple create necessary polar opposites by labeling events with value-driven antonyms. There must be predators and prey, peacemakers and warmongers, creators and terminators, up and down, in and out, sweet and sour, joy and sorrow, or it would be different . . . believe it or not. The task in Jungian psychology, as in Buddhism, is to function while holding the opposites, both/and rather than either/or, because they are necessary to have the peaceful center that lies between them. This principle is the most difficult challenge to western thought because it threatens the very existence of ego driven desire for power and control based upon either/or. In no case is this more important than the dichotomy of simultaneous fear and love of God. But, maturity requires that either/or must give way to both/and and then proceed toward "all of the above." If there is only one God it comes with no limitations.

3. Unconscious Decisions: All behavior is driven from unconscious forces driving sheeple who select options presumed to offer more valuable benefits than burdens. Sheeple all basically take in information and make decisions about it. All decisions, though predetermined choices, employ the ranking of benefits and burdens and the values one ascribes to them, even though unconsciously. Stress from conflicts and ambiguity in making decisions is reduced by consciously listing all benefits and burdens for each choice and placing a value on them. All options among choices are selected because the benefits are worth more than the burdens, even though they may be unconscious and seem to be unreasonable or even insane to a rational observer. Behavior can be changed only by changing the benefit/burden ratio of individual decision making in our value system. For example, presumably one who is driven by a compulsion to wash his hands uncontrollably may be induced to stop if the pain of some punishment exceeds the pleasure in washing or the reward

for ceasing is more valuable than benefits of the action. Since most of this process normally is unconscious and beyond conscious control, we can never be fully aware of our deepest drives and motives.

C. G. Jung (1875-1961) instructed, "Man's task is to become conscious of the contents that press upward from the unconscious. Whoever looks outside, dreams; whoever looks inside, awakes." This "awakening" now is being integrated with other theories of mental disorders such as bipolar and schizophrenic episodes when it is more likely some form of spiritual emergence that is described throughout human history. It is nothing less than attempts by the brain to balance the conscious sensing and intellectual functions with its subconscious intuitions. If you ever wake up with some intuitive revelation, that may be evidence of spiritual emergence. It also can be stimulated by some unexpected trauma that changes the assumptions about reality when normal do this—get that no longer works. One may actually feel abandoned by God or a confrontation with death. It has been described like jumping into the ocean from a high cliff. To successfully navigate such an experience one must integrate the rational with the irrational mind, something not often condoned in modern societies which more likely impose repression instead of expression of the normal self in order to make a living. Everyone must live under some restraints of conformity or bear the consequences in mental distress. One who makes this journey into the unconscious may never return to "normal" but rather may enter into a new domain of living in a condition of spiritual freedom.

Roman Emperor and stoic Marcus Aurelius concluded, "He who lives in harmony with himself lives in harmony with the Universe." This phrase implies existence of a subject and object which are beyond consciousness, i.e., repressed to meet the norms of society. As these drives and motives (between he and himself) become conscious, perhaps new contents arise in the unconscious to take their places. They operate through a process, although unknown, as dependable as the rotation of the Earth and its orbit around the Sun . . . until they cease. Science may one day discover the secret to this process lies in the unimaginable complexity of our genes or something even more complex, like morphic energy or maybe even a soul created by God. One may liken this idea to an iceberg, with much more under water than above. The observable top must go where the unseen bottom takes it. Whatever their source, we can assume inevitable decisions and consequences that are not accidents or mistakes rule human life . . . believe it or not. There are no mistakes, only unconscious choices and inevitable consequences.

4. Indefinite Uncertainty: Life does not grant us certainty, only options and probabilities. Nothing about the future can be forecast with accuracy, especially those things that we think we know for sure. Realization of that reality is a stressful situation, and stress is known to cause clogged arteries and ulcers, and other nasty ways of reducing life expectancy. When the world we depended upon from a life time experience of "do this—get that" no longer works, where can we turn for comfort? The famous American philosopher and baseball star, Yogi Berra once said, "Making predictions is hard, especially when it is about the future." That awareness makes humankind feel anxious necessarily.

Existential anxiety is a fundamental, unavoidable, human response resulting from the awareness of universal uncertainty in the human condition. Tolerance for uncertainty is an element of wisdom that is not popular among sheeple who are given to think they have free will and control of their own lives. Sheeple in a state of unconscious incompetence cannot be anxious because they don't know what they don't know. When incompetence becomes conscious, tension begins to demand either competence or return to unconsciousness. When things are out of our control we desperately want them to return to "normal." This awareness commonly is called "the existential predicament" and the "normalcy syndrome." Thinkers have wrestled with it since the dawn of consciousness, whatever that is.

To be anxious is to be human, because it is a normal reaction to the awareness of indefinite uncertainty. Everyone questions eventually where they came from, why they are here, and where they are going without finding any substantial answers. Anxiety is the feeling they get from thinking about it too much. It might even be argued that anyone who knows what is happening and does not feel anxious is practicing denial or is mentally deficient. To have peace of mind is to be less than human or even possibly mentally unhealthy. If you are not scared and confused you just don't know what's happening. Suffering to some extent or other is part of the human experience because no one can know what is coming next. Here and now is all we have for sure and that is a conjunction of past and future that moves through time instant by instant. Life is unpredictable and that is about all one can say about it.

Absolute answers may exist only beyond infinity; among sheeple there are only transient interpretations of inaccurate perceptions. But, there is an opposite idea of course. Some spiritual explorers claim the greatest opportunities for joy, purpose, and personal growth don't happen when we're clinging to security. They happen when we explore what's novel, and when we live in the moment and embrace uncertainty as reality. Life events last longer and we can extract more pleasure and meaning from them when we are open to new experiences and relish the unknown instead of resisting it, so they say. Perhaps it is just this trait of curiosity that enables mankind to survive the shocks of life and to adapt to changing situations. But, it comes with anxiety of indefinite uncertainty.

Although there are apparent causes and effects in science as well as human events, no one can tell which sources the other. No one can step into the same river or situation twice, and in the realm of spirit, there is imagined no beginning or ending; just a continuous flow of now like the roundabout called a mobius. [You can make a mobius by twisting a strip of paper once and gluing the ends together. That makes a continuous loop of both edge and surface.] Everything comes to pass; nothing comes to stay. Human understanding is affected by inevitably imperfect perception and judgment that is scientifically unpredictable with absolute accuracy. Undeveloped sheeple seek avoidance of uncomfortable existential anxiety in transient relations with other sheeple, things, and ideas or pills and drugs. But human nature requires living in an unavoidable state of existential anxiety about the unknown future, instant by instant, including the uncertain application of the other principles in this set. Maturity may be surrendering the need for answers to unanswerable questions and accepting the stimulant of anxiety that creates new discovery. The anxiety of indefinite uncertainty calls sheeple out of unconscious incompetence into conscious incompetence to work through discomfort toward painful growth and development physically, intellectually, emotionally, and spiritually. Supporting each other in that divine process may be the greatest form of human service . . . believe it or not.

5. Immaculate Immanence: God works a very specific plan for each material element and sentient being that forms a unique and necessary part of the whole Universe. Most of human life is like attempting to assemble a jigsaw puzzle without the picture on the box. At first it seems impossible, but the closer to the end you get the easier it gets. As you see the pattern form, the individual pieces are easier to fit into their one and only spot. And as more pieces are placed the fewer there are to assemble, which simplifies the completion.

The best way to begin is by laying down the four corner pieces of human personality, sensing/physical, thinking/intellectual, feeling/emotional, and intuition/spiritual, and from there to build up the pieces in all directions. Only when you are finished does the way all the pieces fit together, each one in its only possible unique place in time and space, actions and consequences, become apparent. In the large jigsaw puzzle in the sky, each individual sentient being may be only one small insignificant piece, but a necessary indispensable piece or we would not be here.

[Jigsaw puzzles were originally created by painting a picture on a flat, rectangular piece of wood, and then cutting that picture into small pieces with a jigsaw, hence the name. John Spilsbury, a London mapmaker and engraver, is credited with commercializing jigsaw puzzles around 1766 as an educational aid for children of the wealthy to help teach them geography. Jigsaw puzzles have since come to be made primarily on cardboard, but you can find many virtual jigsaw puzzles as free shareware on the Internet. Jigsaw puzzle enthusiasts in the Great Depression discovered what many in our own time are rediscovering—that working on a jigsaw puzzle is a great way to reduce stress. Go ahead, amuse yourself. Visit www.jigzone.com.]

"Immaculate" means without flaw or error . . . pure, innocent, and sinless. And "immanence" means operating within, inherent, present throughout the Universe. Of course, this idea comes with several questions. For example; do we get to choose our puzzle for this life before birth? Does God give us a puzzle with a definite beginning and ending with no options? Does God create our puzzle piece by piece as we go for his own enjoyment? Do we create the puzzle as we go as co-creators with God? Are we all necessary pieces in the puzzle of life for each other? Whether we choose the puzzle of life before birth for its growth benefits or whether it is given to us as part of a universal plan we cannot know. Whatever belief you choose about this, it is the one you are given, like entering a labyrinth that has no options but the path just ahead. But, it is that environment in which we live and move and have our being, immaculate immanence, ImIm. Taken together, these are the principles of Theofatalism™. This is the stuff of God.

To continue, retired Episcopal Bishop, John Spong has observed, "There is a difference between the experience of God and the explanation or definition of the experience. Religion tends to assume they are the same but they are not. Theism is a human explanation of the experience of God; it is not God. The experience can be real or delusional. The explanation will never be eternal. Definitions of God have been born, changed and died and that is the process that is going on today. Our knowledge is expanding and our definition of God will expand with it. History teaches us that the word God is never static; it is always in flux and ever changing." So it is that this work clarifies the present image of God with the phrase, God the Almighty One, to distinguish the real from the limited scope of man's present understanding. We cannot yet see the true God because the shock would be too great, like looking directly into the Sun, so we must be content with this limited glimpse into the reality beyond our present boundaries of conscious understanding. If we live in health, wealth, and happiness, we may live without an awareness of our sustaining environment, which includes pain, suffering, and struggle as well as joy, compassion, and charity. But some triggering event of crisis or disaster can give us a new and higher level of ImIm awareness from knowledge of its perfect existence. One example may be fish, who live as though unaware of the water until they are removed from it. Then, we can begin to balance fear, anxiety, and suffering with acceptance, compassion, and detachment.

Sheeple might personalize immaculate immanence in the form of God in their own image, as though reflected in a mirror. But, perhaps it is the morphic energy of the Universe manifested in living genes, which neither can be created nor destroyed, i.e., ImIm. It embraces everything that happens to atoms, to galaxies, and to all forms of matter on Earth. This principle encompasses all that happens among Homo sapiens that we call both good and evil, plus all the polarities in nature, and develops toward a unity of perception that sees the One in all sets of opposites, including the opposing self and ego, body and soul, which comprises each of us . . . believe it or not. Apostle Paul put forward a similar universal idea, saying that God is that in which "we live, and move, and have our being." (Acts 17:28). The state of anyone who reaches this understanding is described in this meditation; "God grants me the serenity to feel good inside no matter what happens outside." After all, if God is in control you better get used to it . . . or not.

Here is a simple example of Theofatalism™ from religious history. Thomas a Kempis (1380-1471) is a revered Doctor of the Church who wrote this instruction he called "The Voice of Christ" in <u>The Imitation of Christ</u>. (1418) "I will teach you the way of peace and true liberty. 1) Seek to do the will of others rather than your own, 2) Always choose to have less rather than more, 3) Look always for the last place and seek to be beneath all others, 4) Always wish and pray that the will of God be fully carried out in you and Behold, such will enter into the realm of peace and rest." But, <u>A Course in Miracles</u> (1975) states, "Disobeying God's will is meaningful only to the insane; in truth it is impossible." . . . soooo . . . Theofatalism™ would say that the above ideas must both exist or they would not, and the logical error of items 1,2,3 being superceded by the will of God in 4 also must be or it would not exist. For examples; suppose that God 1) wants you to do unto yourself rather than others, 2) wants you to have more rather than less and, 3) wants you to be in first place and above all others? Or any combination of the above. Such would be the case . . . get it? God's will be done as there can be no other. God does whatever he wants with whoever he wants whenever he wants. So, the first three instructions by the Doctor of the Church are negated by the fourth. This flaw in Church teaching had to be or it would be different, hence Theofatalism™.

If this is the truth of the matter, then what is the appropriate response from sheeple with egos that want to control, not only themselves but everyone else also? This desire of ego for control is the root cause of all wars and family squabbles. "What causes fights and quarrels among you? Don't they come from your desires that battle within you? [Desires put there by God the Almighty One.] You want something but don't get it. You kill and covet, but you cannot have what you want. You quarrel and fight. You do not have, because you do not ask God. When you ask, you do not receive, because you ask with wrong motives, that you may spend what you get on your own [ego] pleasures." (James 4: 1-3) How shall we reconcile this with the opposite promise of Jesus; ". . . Therefore, I tell you whatever you ask for in prayer, believe that you have received it and it will be yours." (Matthew 17:20, 21: 21-23, Mark 9:23, 11:24) Obviously, such belief has not been granted much lately, especially to the survivors of wars, earthquakes, tsunamis, floods, hurricanes, tornadoes, epidemics, etc. Where could such opposing and confusing beliefs come from, except from God the Almighty One? Perhaps it is time for the ego to be replaced with something that could be called "calm submission" because if anything could be different it would be.

There is a hymn with lyrics by Judson Van Deventer (1896) that carries this attitude to the extreme: "All to Jesus I surrender, all to him I freely give. I will ever love and trust him, in his presence daily live . . . I surrender all, I surrender all." This state is demonstrated in the response of Job to the unjust treatment by God that he suffered along with all his destroyed innocent servants, children, and cattle for no reason except to prove it could be done. "Even though he slay me yet will I trust in him." (Job 2:8-10) When famous actor Charlton Heston (1923-2008) was diagnosed with Alzheimer's disease he mused, "I must reconcile equal measures of courage and surrender." Jesus declared, "Blessed are the meek for they shall inherit the Earth." (Matthew 5:5) But oil mogul and admitted Methodist, J. Paul Getty (1892-1976) appended, ". . . but not the mineral rights." He declared, "Some people find oil and some people don't." Getty amassed a fortune from oil, including a large field in Saudi Arabia, and then left it all to his heirs who lived large on their trust funds while the company was sold and broken up. All in God's will of course . . . AIGWOC. Can you believe that?

Where ever you are and whoever you are here and now must be God's will as there can be no other. [At present, only three churches practice the total pacifism in conflicts and utter dependency upon God that Jesus actually taught. They are the Amish, the Mennonites, and the Church of the Brethren. The meaning of Islam is "submission," so perhaps Muslims are closer to the truth than are hypocritical Christians who think they control their own lives. All the rest put human free will up against God and it always loses.] This does not mean you will not change and your circumstances will not get better or worse. They will. Life is not static, it is dynamic but none of it is yours to control. Some will claim that sheeple all must be broken and convicted of sin before they can be acceptable to God.

After treating hundreds of patients for mental distress, C. G. Jung concluded the bottom line was they all were in a struggle with God that they were losing. Only after they "got right with God" however they did that, were they relieved of their suffering. But, if so, why would God give us the will to sin just so sheeple will not change until it hurts too much not to? It seems that we must learn to trust and obey the will of God the Almighty One because we certainly cannot change it any more than we can change the laws of physics, although we may break them at our own peril. All in God's will of course. Even when you are disobeying you are acting out the will of God the almighty One as there can be no other. So is everyone else. Get it? This attitude was described in the hymn, "Trust and Obey," by John H. Sammis in 1887.

"Not a burden we bear, not a sorrow we share,
but our toil he does richly repay.
Not a grief nor a loss, not a frown or a cross,
but is blest if we trust and obey.
Trust and obey . . . for there's no other way."

This is the relationship of calm submission between a pet dog and its owner, between the slave and the master, between the clay and the potter, between husband and wife (yes) and between man and God the Almighty One. "Slaves, obey your earthly masters in everything; and do it, not only when their eye is on you and to win their favor, but with sincerity of heart and reverence for the Lord." (Colossians 3:22) "Slaves, obey your earthly masters with respect and fear, and with sincerity of heart, just as you would obey Christ." (Ephesians 6:5) "Wives, submit to your husbands as is fitting in the Lord. (Colossians 3:18) "Husbands, love your wives just as Christ loved the Church and gave his life up for her." (Ephesians 5:25) "Let everyone be subject to the governing authorities for there is no authority except that which God has established." (Romans 13:1) But, when he was accosted by the Jewish leaders for teaching about Jesus, Apostle Peter replied, "We must obey God rather than human beings." (Acts 5:29) This relationship between the created and the Creator is one of obedience and fear, tempered with its opposite, the balm of unconditional love or charity. This mindset rules out judging others for their God-given beliefs and behaviors. Jesus declared that judgment was left up to God and that forgiveness was to be expected in the measure that we first forgive others. "Do not judge, and you will not be judged. Do not condemn, and you will not be condemned. Forgive, and you will be forgiven. [Forgive], and it will be [forgiven] to you. A good measure, pressed down, shaken together and running over, will be poured into your lap. For with the measure [of forgiveness] you use, it will be measured to you." (Luke 6:36-38)

However, the one sin he said would not be forgiven either in this life or the life to come is speaking against the Holy Spirit, which is the energy driving his church. "When he comes he will convict the world of guilt in regard to sin and righteousness and judgment. (John 16:6-8) Beware of that. (Matthew 12:32, Luke 12: 10) Thus, it seems we should not judge God for whatever he does, either. You can resist, but you can't win. Life is like one of those staged wrestling matches where the outcome is set before it begins, only you are wrestling with God. And you cannot win. Does not the potter do with the clay whatever he wishes? (Jeremiah 18:2-6, Romans 9:12) "The sacrifices/desires of God are a broken spirit, and a broken and contrite heart." (Psalm 51:17) "Be afflicted and mourn and weep, let your laughter be turned to mourning and your joy to heaviness. Humble yourselves in the sight of the Lord and he shall lift you up." (James 4:9-10) You won't hear many sermons on that attitude in American churches. Since the outcome is certain, the only variable is how much suffering will be needed to break the spirit and heart of his creation by God in order to achieve this end.

The evolution of belief in Theofatalism™ goes like this. First, there is the realization or awareness of the universal God the Almighty One who controls all things, then there is the reluctance to admit that ego has created an illusion of free will, followed by the resistance to divine will. Then comes suffering to break the human belief in free will, and eventually the acceptance of things as they are, with all the confusion and insanity in life. God demands calm submission inside regardless what happens outside under penalty of death. This conclusion may be obtained from the parable told by Jesus in which a king/himself declares, "As for these enemies of mine who did not want me to reign over then, bring them here and slay them before me." (Luke 19:27) Apostle Paul seems to have expressed this condition when he said, "I have been crucified with Christ and I no longer live, but Christ lives in me." (Galatians 2:20) Whether possessed by Christ or Satan, the impact is the same, i.e., replacement of the human ego with a different driving force hopefully from God the Almighty One.

This demand for calm submission also is the lesson from the story of Job's undeserved suffering in the Old Testament from the loss of all that he owned plus his personal health. After Job declares that he will trust God even though he is slain (Job 2:8-10) and argues with his friends over his self-righteousness, God comes in a whirlwind to recount all the forms of his creation and credits Job for his calm submission. (Job 38-41) He finally repents for challenging God in "dust and ashes." (Job 42:1-6) God condemns his accusers for their self righteousness and requires that they do penance for their arrogance. (Job 42:7-9) The Bible says that Job was restored beyond his previous wealth, health, and happiness, but his lost servants, cattle, and children never were resurrected. We are not told whatever happened to the argumentative adversaries. [Note that some scholars think the happy ending for Job was added at some later time to avoid leaving him in the pit of despair and loss at the mercy of God.]

This is far different and opposite to the present assumption of free will and petitions to the God of love for special favors that are the essence of church worship services throughout organized religions. There is always an opposing view. Are you ready? One theologian noted, "God is not your friend, he is your master." The master/slave relationship is described 197 times in the Bible, 67 of them in the New Testament, and Jesus was called "Master" seven times in the book of Luke by his disciples. Whatever the master wants, he gets. So, instead of a "worship service," perhaps there should be a "calm submission service" that emphasizes this relationship between God the Almighty One and his creation. This would require a new type of liturgy and a new form of sacraments. Christians may sing the hymn, "I surrender all . . ." but how many really live like that? The practice of calm submission is glimpsed in certain Bible scriptures that cast a glimmer of light through a small crack in the veneer of religion in modern civilization. One example is the ritual sacrifice of his son Isaac that God demanded of Abraham to prove his worthiness, recounted in Genesis chapter 22. Although Apostle John claimed, "God is love," Jesus declared, "I tell you, my friends, do not be afraid of those who kill the body and after that can do no more. But I will show you whom you should fear: Fear him who, after the killing of the body, has power to throw you into hell. Yes, I tell you, fear him." (Luke 12:4-5) Preachers now seem too afraid of losing their members if they scare the hell out of sheeple. But wait, there is more.

"Fear of the Lord is the beginning of wisdom." (Psalm 111:10, Proverbs 9:10) "Now all has been heard; here is the conclusion of the matter: Fear God and keep his commandments, for this is the whole duty of man. (Ecclesiastes 12: 13) Jesus repeated the commandment from Moses, "Love/fear the Lord your God with all your heart and with all your soul and with all your strength/mind." (Deuteronomy 6:5, Matthew 22:36-38, Mark 12:30, Luke 10:27) The nature of these three elements of humankind—heart—soul—mind—never and the dichotomy of love and fear have not been sufficiently explored nor is the owner of them disclosed in scripture or psychology. But the Bible is clear. "Declare his glory among the nations, his marvelous deeds among all peoples. For great is the Lord and most worthy of praise; he is to be feared above all Gods." (1Chronicles 16:24-26) "Does not the potter have the right/power to make out of the same lump of clay some pottery for noble purposes and some for common use?" (Jeremiah 18: 2-6, Romans 9:21)

The Bible also declares the opposite roles of suffering servant and master that you won't hear in church. "Slaves, submit to/obey your earthly masters with respect and fear and with sincerity of heart, just as you would obey Christ . . . not only to those who are kind and considerate but to those who are harsh. For it is commendable if a man bears up under the pain of unjust suffering because he is conscious of God." (Ephesians 6:5, 1 Peter 2:18) "Submit yourselves for the Lord's sake to every authority instituted among men, whether to the king as supreme authority or to governors who are sent by him to punish those who do wrong and commend those who do right [in the eyes of authorities]." (1 Peter 2: 13-14) It seems what God wants above all else is humility and submission. "Come near to God and he will come near to you. Wash your hands, you sinners, and purify your hearts, you double-minded. Grieve, mourn and wail. Change your laughter to mourning and your joy to gloom. Humble yourselves before the Lord, and he will lift you up." (James 4:8-10) "Whereas you know not what shall be on the morrow. For what is your life? It is even a vapor, which appears for a little time, and then vanishes away. Therefore, you ought to say, if the Lord wills, we shall live and do this or that." (James 4:13-15). "It is no longer I who live but Christ lives in me . . ." (Galatians 2:20) But, recall that Apostle Paul did not choose Christ, but rather Christ chose him on the road to Damascus just as he chose all the apostles. (Acts 9:3-8) The ultimate in calm submission is, of course, the surrender of Jesus as the Son of God on the cross to pay a ransom for the sins of his own creation; ". . . may your will be done." (Matthew 26:42)

So, where is the free will in all that? This is quite a different relationship with God the Almighty One than the present "prosperity preaching" of many churches that would have everyone believe that God only wants sheeple to be healthy, wealthy, and happy, and then to reside with him for eternal bliss in heaven. (John 3:16) Jesus said, "With God, all things are possible." That includes everything, not just the good stuff. (Matthew 19:26, Mark 10:27) And, "My Father is always at his work to this very day, and I too am working." (John 5:17) This text seems to imply that God did not stop in his creating work after his day of rest as described in Genesis 2:1-3. He may have rested but he did not quit. Is this not Theofatalism ™, or what? At the least, it describes God and the Son as verbs, the actions of infinite generation, operation and destruction in the continuous process of change throughout the Universe. Who among the creation can resist such power? Certainly not the feeble Homo sapiens, although they may be given to think they can. Where would they get such an idea from unless from the Source itself? Some will say the Devil makes them do it . . . but Satan has no power not from God.

The principles of Theofatalism™ are mutually inclusive. You can resist them or embrace them but you cannot change them any more than you can change gravity, and they certainly do not need your permission. None is separable from any other, and it seems that all must be taken together in order to feel good inside regardless what happens outside. If any of them is skipped, doubted, or rejected, the whole system will be broken and ineffective because one cannot reach the fifth principle, ImIm, without integrating all the previous ones. This is one example where the whole is worth more than the sum of its parts. Nothing need be added, as the principles of Theofatalism™ describe all that is needed to feel good inside no matter what happens outside. And just as with the law of gravity, it makes no difference whether you know or accept them or not. God the Almighty One does anything he wants, with anyone he wants, anytime he wants. (Daniel 4:35, Isaiah 45:7, Matthew 19:26, Romans 9:14-21) Feel good inside no matter what happens outside. For the full story, visit www.schooloftheofatalism.org and read <u>Voices of Sedona</u> and <u>Lessons From Sedona</u>. Order from www.IUniverse.org, www.amazon.org, and Barnes & Noble book stores.

3. What's Wrong with Fatalism

Many sheeple have the notion that what little they do matters not in the larger scheme of things, while others claim that "God is in the details." Ideas sheeple have about God range from; there is none, to nothing happens outside of his will. These ideas are examples of the necessary opposites in nature; for every thought there is an equal and opposite one. The compatibalists would like to have it both ways . . . the omnipotent God allows mankind free will but he knows what they will do with it. Ever since the dialogues of Plato and Socrates, thinkers have been attempting to reconcile the apparently mutually exclusive ideas of fatalism and free will. The argument favors free will because to accept fatalism Homo sapiens would have to accept the notion of an omnipotent omniscient God the Almighty One of the Universe, not as a person, but rather the Force behind all forces. This is something that organized religion cannot tolerate because it needs a God that can be thwarted by human free will, and petitioned to change his mind through prayer and penance. Such a God must be all-knowing and all-powerful, but one who cannot control its own creation, and willing to change his mind upon appropriate requests, a seeming contradiction and mutually exclusive impossibility. Because, if God is all powerful then he could choose to do something that is unknowable, and if he is all knowing then he could never do anything beyond knowing it a-priori. Such a God would be limited to one or other but could not be both all-knowing and all-powerful. All of the above confusion must be necessary or it would be different.

The Church and Anglo-Saxon courts, plus the Koran, would keep sheeple responsible for disobedience to religious dogma and law by claiming Homo sapiens have the power of free will. That way they can perpetuate the guilt and remorse required to keep their treasuries and prisons full. The obvious contradiction between doctrines of free will and unwilling original sin is conveniently ignored in the dialogue. How could the first creatures

53

commit sin before they had acquired knowledge of good and evil? They were just following the compulsory reasoning of the serpent that God provided to tempt them. How could their disobedience in eating of that tree created by God come before their knowledge of it, except the serpent be the agent of their downfall? And where did he get that knowledge? Was it not God who put the tree in the Garden during his creation? (Genesis 2:9) And if you cannot but be born in sin and are condemned at birth, where is the free will in that? What kind of a God is that? "Make ready to slaughter his sons for the guilt of their fathers; Lest they rise and possess the Earth, and fill the breadth of the world with tyrants." (Isaiah 14:21) "For I the Lord your God am a jealous God, visiting the iniquity of the fathers upon the children." (Exodus 20:5) Apostle Paul declared, ". . . sin entered the world through [Adam] and death through sin, and in this way death came to all men, because all sinned . . ." (Romans 5:12) This argument fails the test of legitimacy because it avoids the action by God of creating man with the ability to sin, which is after all the first cause. It also is voided by other scriptures that give an opposite version.

Actually the Bible also presents this opposing view that very few acknowledge, "Yet you ask, Why does the son not share the guilt of his father? Since the son has done what is just and right and has been careful to keep all my decrees, he will surely live. The one who sins is the one who will die. The child will not share the guilt of the parent, nor will the parent share the guilt of the child. The righteousness of the righteous will be credited to them, and the wickedness of the wicked will be charged against them." (Ezekiel 18:19-20) These different Bible writers obviously do not share the same view of God. And of the blind man healed by Jesus, he explained that his blindness was not caused by sins of his parents nor of him, but so that the power of God could be shown in his healing. (John 9: 2-4) Sooo, God blinds sheeple to show that he can heal them . . . sometimes . . . Hmmm. Did he also not raise up the giant Goliath so that David could kill him to gain the power of a king? Did he not harden the heart of Pharaoh in Egypt and kill all the first born sons so that Moses could show the power of God and free the Jews from slavery? Had he let Pharaoh capitulate, the Jews would not have worshipped Moses as their deliverer. Did he not cause King Herod of Israel to kill all the male children under age of two in Bethlehem to try and execute the baby, Jesus, "King of the Jews?" Did God not create prey so there could be food for carnivorous predators? Of course he did. The Bible says so because he created everything, and we all have been told that it is the Word of God. Doesn't God create losers so there can be winners? Does he not create victims so there can be criminals or does he not create predators so there can be victims? Therefore, maybe A Course in Miracles, (1975) claimed to be channeled from Jesus, is more correct; "Remember that no one is where he is by accident, and chance plays no part in God's plan." However it is one thing to contemplate God's plan if you are a predator and quite another thing if you are the prey.

The Rev. Rick Warren presented the same notion possibly without realizing it in his international best seller, <u>The Purpose Driven Life</u>. (2007) He concluded that it is all God's purpose and not yours/ours. "It is not about you." That must include those who, according to "The Course" are hopelessly imprisoned in this world of illusion by their own volitional rejection of the memory of heaven and seconds the vote of Einstein, "God does not play dice." But, then he could if he wanted to or he would not be God. Thus, a black girl born to a single mother and raised in poverty by a foster parent can grow up to become the rich and famous one known as Oprah Winfrey. Along the way she won a beauty contest, got a scholarship to college, studied communications, starred in a blockbuster movie, "The Color Purple," and hosted news anchor shows before organizing her syndicated talk show. It took actions and choices by a lot of sheeple to make Oprah what she is . . . and still does . . . but she can be given the illusion that she did it all by herself. All in God's will of course . . . AIGWOC. God can do whatever he wants with whoever he wants whenever he wants . . . including blindfolding them to his reality . . . get it?

If you really think the Bible is the Word of God, it presents a grand argument for Theofatalism™. One could begin with words of Jesus; "The Spirit gives life; the flesh counts for nothing. The words I have spoken to you are spirit and they are life. Yet there are some of you who do not believe. For Jesus had known from the beginning which of them did not believe and who would betray him. [So, where is the free will?] He went on to say, This is why I told you that no one can come to me unless the Father has enabled/ caused him." (John 6:63-65) "By myself, I can do nothing . . . but the will of the Father who sent me." (John 5:30) Of course, this is contradicted in John 14:6 where Jesus says, ". . . no man comes to the Father except by me." Go figure. Why would God condemn the descendents of Adam and Eve forever rather than just punish the two of them for their sin of disobedience? Actually, nowhere does it explicitly say that he did. Their son, Cain, killed his brother Abel in a jealous fit because God played favorites with their sacrifices, and God made him the grandfather of a city through his son, Enoch and apparently their polygamous and incestuous wives. (Genesis 4:17) Cain was not punished for his crime of murder. (Genesis 4:15-17) He was actually protected by God. "Anyone who kills Cain will suffer seven times over."

If man cannot choose to be born sinless, then where is the free will? And why did God create the tree of knowledge of good and evil in the first place if he knew what the outcome would be as he surely must since he is God and all? Why would God permit his original creatures to do wrong and then punish all their descendents for it? Apparently, God has two sides, just like that tree of knowledge of good AND evil that he created. The sale of Joseph into Egypt by his jealous brothers was necessary so that he could be in a place to help them when the famine came to threaten the house of Israel and set up their eventual migration into the promised land. (Genesis 45:4-8) Moses was called to lead the house of Israel out of bondage in Egypt, not of his own free will. (Exodus 3: 7-10) Six times in Exodus God "hardens Pharaoh's heart" so he will not let the Israelites go. (Exodus 7:3, 9:12, 10:20, 10:27, 11:10, 14:4) King Saul was repeatedly beset by the "evil spirit from God" to make him insanely jealous of young David. (1 Samuel 18: 10, 19: 9) God confesses to doing "all these things" in Isaiah 45:7.

It goes on. The reported virgin birth, ministry, crucifixion and resurrection of Jesus plus his rejection by the Jews as Messiah all were necessary to fulfill Old Testament prophecies. His selection of the twelve apostles and the conversion of Saul of Tarsus all were acts of God and not their own will. Even Jesus was not his own man. Of his ministry, Jesus said, "By myself I can do nothing; I judge only as I hear, and my judgment is just, for I seek not to please myself but him who sent me." (John 5:30) The role of Judas as betrayer also was necessary for the crucifixion, which was necessary for the redemption and resurrection, etc. Facing the cross, Jesus lamented, "not my will but thine." Apostle Paul reminds us of the story from Malachi 1: 2-3, "Rebekah's children had one and the same father, our father Isaac. Yet, before the twins were born or had done anything good or bad in order that God's purpose in election might stand: not by works but by him who calls, she was told, The older will serve the younger. Just as it is written: Jacob I loved, but Esau I hated." (Romans 9:10-13) "In him we were also chosen, having been predestined according to the plan of him who works out everything in conformity with the purpose of his will . . ." (Ephesians 1:11) [Was he referring to all sheeple for all time, or just the ones in his audience? No one knows.] And the prophecies about end of times in the book of Revelation do not offer any options to mankind. You are either in the Lamb's Book of Life or you are out. (Revelation 20:15)

Christian leaders reference many Bible scriptures which plainly state in great detail what God would, and will do, with and to the major nations of the world. And yet these same leaders also believe that all mankind possesses a God-given free will by which they can thwart the very words, declarations, pronouncements, and detailed prophecies which God has spoken and determined beforehand, that they say absolutely will happen just as he has stated. And even when this total contradiction of logic is pointed out to them, virtually none of them see a problem with it. They say that for God to be in total control of us would be to treat us like robots. They claim it would be evil for God to predetermine us to do sin before he allows good to be done in us, and God can do no evil, as though they can put limits upon God the Almighty One. Many argue that God does not burden himself with the billions of daily details required to run this Universe. Oh really? Is this why Jesus said God knows every bird that falls and every hair on our head? "Are not two sparrows sold for a penny ? Yet not one of them will fall to the ground apart from the will of your Father . . . Indeed, the very hairs of your head are all numbered." (Matthew 10:29, Luke 12:7) It appears that God is in the details, no matter how small from the smallest subatomic particle to the largest interstellar galaxies, and his work never ends. When he was criticized by Jews for healing on the Sabbath day, Jesus said to them, "My Father is always at his work to this very day, and I, too, am working." (John 5:17) God may have rested on the seventh day of creation but he did not quit.

Islam says the same. Sayyid Qutb, (1906-1966) Egyptian sage of conservative Islam wrote in Milestones, (2007) "Life and its allotted span, good and evil are in the hand of Allah and no other" . . . and from the Koran he quoted, "Allah, wielder of the kingly power; thou givest that power to whomever thy will and thou taketh the power from whomever thy will, Thou dost exalt whom thy will and thou doth abase whom thy will . . . Thou over all things are most powerful . . . and if Allah shall help you then none can defeat you, but if He abandon you who will help you?" (3:25, 3:154) [Qutb lived in the U.S. for a couple years getting an MBA degree, which just reinforced his hatred for American culture. He was a founding member of the Muslim Brotherhood and was executed for opposing alliances and cooperation between Egypt and the West. Some claim that he is the role model for Al Qaeda and the mentor of Osama bin Laden.] Apostle Paul wrote much the same idea in his concept of the potter and the clay which he quoted from the Old Testament. "Does not the potter have the right/power to make out of the same lump of clay some pottery for noble purposes and some for common use?" (Jeremiah 18:2-6, Romans 9:21) And we have no power to challenge the power of God . . . just ask Job. Example: God creates both homosexuals and sheeple who hate homosexuals. So, where is the free will in that? Hmmm . . .

It seems the leaders of Christendom do not approve of the God of scripture, so they create their own God in their own image—one that they themselves can control by the power of their own illusory freedom of will. A Course in Miracles, (1975) claimed to be channeled from Jesus declares, "Remember that no one is where he is by accident, and chance plays no part in God's plan . . . Free will is part of the ego's delusional thought system and part of its cherished array of gifts . . . There is no free will in Heaven, for free will implies choice, and choice implies alternatives that can be differentiated among, an impossibility within the Oneness of spirit that Jesus reminds us is our reality . . . what is opposed to God does not exist" . . . [But then it contradicts itself: "the mind which believes it has a separate will that can oppose the will of God also believes that it can succeed. That this can hardly be a fact is obvious. Yet, that it can be believed as a fact also is obvious. Therein lies the birthplace of insanity]." Some very famous modern thinkers expressed similar conflicting views on this matter.

Mega-church pastor The Rev. Dr. Rick Warren wrote in his mega-book, The Purpose Driven Life, (2007) "It's not about you. The purpose of your [pitiful] life is far greater than your own personal fulfillment, your peace of mind, or even your happiness. It's far greater than your family, your career, or even your wildest dreams and ambitions. If you want to know why you were placed on this planet, you must begin with God. You were born by his purpose and for his purpose . . . You are alive today because God chose you to be here. You exist for his benefit, his glory, his purpose, and his delight. Bringing enjoyment to God, living for his pleasure, is the first purpose of your life . . . Because God made you for a reason, he also decided when you would be born and how long you would live. He planned the days of your life in advance, choosing the exact time of your birth and death. The Bible says, 'You saw me before I was born and scheduled each day of my life before I began to breathe. Every day was recorded in your book!' (Psalm 139:16). It is God who directs the lives of his creatures; everyone's life is in his power. (Job 12:10) . . . God also planned where you'd be born and where you'd live for his purpose. Your race and nationality are no accident. God left no detail to chance. He planned it all for his purpose . . . Life is about letting God use you for his purpose, [as though we had any choice] not your using him for your own purposes."

It seems that no one needs to search for his purpose in life according to Pastor Warren because he cannot avoid it. This would include the drug addicts and the criminals as well as the saints and the geniuses, the rich and the poor, the disabled and the athletes, would it not? Is not this a clear claim for Theofatalism™, although not yet called by that name? Was Pastor Warren addressing this conclusion just to sheeple in his church, or did that include all the sheeple in the world? And, why did 30 million sheeple buy his book? Perhaps they had to because it was the will of God the Almighty One because; ". . . it is God who directs the lives of his creatures."

Is this Theofatalism™ of Rick Warren any different from the admonition of Apostle Paul about the potter controlling the clay to form a vessel as he pleases? (Romans 9:21, Isaiah 64:8, Jeremiah 18:2-6) "You created everything, and it is for your pleasure that they exist and were created" (Revelation 4:11)

Where is the free will in that? If this all be true, then everyone is doing exactly what God has willed for their lives. Period. God is in the details whether they be Christian, Mormon, Muslim, Buddhist, Hindu, Republican, Democrat, Communist, neoNazi, or whatever. Think about these scriptures when things seem to be going wrong in your life, whether a little or a lot. Calculated primarily to get sheeple into churches like his, Pastor Rick Warren caught some need for life's meaning among Homo sapiens with his words that made him both rich and famous in a short time by writing them. How different that is from the real life and teachings of Jesus in the Gospels who wrote no books and preached on the hillsides and the plains and beside the lakes to those few who could hear his voice without amplification and became famous but not rich for all time.

On the contrary, Jesus declared the necessary suffering of discipleship even to the point of joining him in crucifixion. "If anyone would come after me, he must deny himself and take up his cross daily and follow me. For whoever wants to save his life will lose it, but whoever loses his life for me will save it." (Luke 9:23-24) "If anyone comes to me and does not hate his father and mother, his wife and children, his brothers and sisters—yes, even his own life—he cannot be my disciple." (Luke 14:26) Contrast that with the Old Testament rule, "Cursed is the man who dishonors his father or his mother." (Deuteronomy 27:16) Are these necessary opposites or both/ and complements? They seem to be opposed to western psychology that emphasizes personal empowerment, free will, and individual autonomy. Which are you given to believe?

Science sees everything as fitted together perfectly according to mathematical equations just like pieces of a giant universal jigsaw puzzle. Albert Einstein (1879-1955) wrote, ". . . the scientist is possessed by the sense of universal causation. His religious feeling takes the form of a rapturous amazement at the harmony of natural law, which reveals an intelligence of such superiority that, compared with it, all the systematic thinking and acting of human beings is an utterly insignificant reflection. **The future, to him, is every whit as necessary and determined as the past . . . God does not throw dice . . .** I do not believe in free will. Schopenhauer's words: 'Man can do what he wants, but he cannot will what he wills,' accompany me in all situations throughout my life and reconcile me with the actions of others, even if they are rather painful to me. This awareness of the lack of free will keeps me from taking myself and my fellow men too seriously as acting and deciding individuals, and from losing my temper . . . a Being, endowed with higher insight and more perfect intelligence, watching man and his doings, must smile about man's illusion that he was acting according to his own free will."

Einstein had some very good company. Read on.

Roman Emperor Marcus Aurelius: (121-180 CE) "How ridiculous and unrealistic is the man who is astonished at anything that happens in life. Everything that happens happens as it should, and if you observe carefully, you will find this to be so. Whatever may befall you, it was preordained for you from everlasting."

Muhammad al-Bukhari: (810-870 CE) "Every created soul has his place written for him either in Paradise or in the hell fire. His happy or miserable fate is predetermined for him . . . People merely carry out what is a foregone conclusion, decided by predestination and written by the Pen. For whoever is destined to be fortunate will join the fortunate, and whoever is destined to be miserable will go to Hell . . . No calamity comes, no affliction comes, except by the decision and preordainment of Allah."

St. Teresa of Avila: (1515-1582) "But when God talks in this way to the soul, I have to listen, whether I like it or not, and my understanding has to devote itself so completely to what God wishes me to understand that whether I want to listen or not makes no difference. For, as he who is all-powerful wills us to understand, we have to do what he wills; and he reveals himself as our true Lord."

Joseph Priestly (1733-1804)—Founder of Unitarianism. ". . . all things, past, present, and to come, are precisely what the Author of nature really intended them to be, and has made provision for."

Friedrich Nietzsche: (1844-1900) "Today we no longer have any tolerance for the idea of free will; we see it only too clearly for what it really is—the foulest of all theological fictions, intended to make mankind responsible in a religious sense—that is, dependent upon priests. Whenever responsibility is assigned, it is usually so that judgment and punishment may follow. All primitive psychology of will arises from the fact that its interpreters, the priests at the head of ancient communities, wanted to create for themselves the right to punish—or wanted to create this right for their God. Men were considered 'free' only so that they might be considered guilty—could be judged and punished; consequently, every act had to be considered as willed, and the origin of every act had to be considered as lying within the consciousness, and thus the most fundamental psychological deception was made the principle of psychology itself."

British philosopher Bertrand Russell: (1872-1970) "When a man acts in ways that annoys us [or breaks our laws] we wish to think him wicked, and we refuse to face the fact that his annoying behavior is the result of antecedent causes which, if you follow them long enough, will take you beyond the moment of his birth, and therefore to events for which he cannot be held responsible by any stretch of imagination."

Spanish philosopher Baruch Spinoza: (1632-1677): "Men believe themselves to be free because they are conscious of their own actions and are ignorant of the causes by which they are determined. The mind is determined to this or that choice by a cause which is also determined by another cause, and this again by another, and so on ad infinitum. This doctrine teaches us to hate no one, to despise no one, to mock no one, to be angry with no one, and to envy no one."

French nobleman and philosopher, Baron D'Holbach: (1723-1789): "The inward persuasion that we are free to do, or not to do a thing, is but a mere illusion. If we trace the true principle of our actions, we shall find that they are always necessary consequences of our volitions and desires, which are never in our power. You think yourself free, because you do what you will; but are you free to will, or not to will; to desire, or not to desire? Are not your volitions and desires necessarily excited by objects or qualities totally independent of you?"

Mark Twain: (1835-1910): "Where there are two desires in a man's heart he has no choice between the two but must obey the strongest, there being no such thing as free will in the composition of any human being that ever lived."

Abraham Lincoln: (1809-1865): "The human mind is impelled to action or held in rest by some power over which the mind itself has no control. I claim not to have controlled events, but confess plainly that events have controlled me."

C. G. Jung: (1875-1961) "Because the search for psychological wholeness— individuation—is an heroic and often tragic task, it involves suffering, a passion of the ego; the ordinary empirical man we once were is burdened with the fate of losing himself in a greater dimension and being robbed of his fancied freedom of will."

Apostle Paul: "So I find this law at work: When I want to do good, evil is right there with me. For in my inner being I delight in God's law; but I see another law at work in the members of my body, waging war against the law of my mind and making me a prisoner of the law of sin at work within my members. What a wretched man I am! Who will rescue me from this body of death? Thanks be to God through Jesus Christ our Lord! So then, I myself in my mind am a slave to God's law, but in the sinful nature a slave to the law of sin." "Romans 7:21:25) "I have been crucified with Christ and I no longer live, but Christ lives in me." (Galatians 2:20)

Martin Luther: (1483-1546) "For by free choice is meant that which one can do and does, in relation to God, whatever it pleases, uninhibited by any law or any sovereign authority. As such, free choice properly belongs to no one but God alone, for God alone is free to do what He desires to be done . . . the term free choice ought to be dropped altogether in the study of man, since such a thing as free choice does not exist in him . . . Scripture, however, represents man as one who is not only bound, wretched, captive, sick and dead, but in addition to his other miseries is afflicted, through the agency of Satan his prince [by the will of God the Almighty One], with this misery of blindness, so that he believes himself to be free, happy, unfettered, able, well and alive."

There is more:

Swami Satyananda Saraswati: (1923-) "Never believe that you are the doer. It was wrong indeed that so far you regarded yourself as the doer. Think that you are not you, that you do not exist, but that it is the power which works through you in all things. Slowly, as this yoga practice matures you will become convinced that you are also the same entity as the doer. In this manner, you will gradually come to realize in experience the knowledge of the doer. Eventually, practice will reveal this secret."

Adolf Hitler: (1889-1945) "Events in the lives of peoples are not expressions of chance, but processes related to the self-preservation and propagation of the species and the race and are subject to the laws of Nature, even if people are not conscious of the inner reason for their actions."

Science writer Michael Brooks: (1958-) "Free will does not exist. Though it is a scary and entirely unwelcome observation, we are brain-driven machines. We do not have what we think of as free will . . . the anomaly, the curiosity, lies in our self-deception, the illusion of free will that we cling to so tightly."

The Apostle James: "Go to now, you that say, today or tomorrow we will go into such a city, and continue there a year, and buy and sell, and make money: Whereas you know not what shall be on the morrow. For what is your life? It is even a vapor, which appears for a little time, and then vanishes away. Therefore, you ought to say, if the Lord wills, we shall live and do this or that." (James 4:13-15).

Apostle Paul: "Everyone must submit himself to the governing authorities, for there is no authority except that which God has established. The authorities that exist have been established by God." (Romans 13:1) [We make plans, and God laughs. So, upon arising each morning it is appropriate to proclaim, "this is a day the Lord has made," because that is the best that can be said for it.]

British analytic philosopher Galen Strawson, author of <u>Mental Reality</u> (1994) concluded, "Almost all human beings believe that they are free to choose what to do in such a way that they can be truly, genuinely responsible for their actions in the strongest possible sense; responsible period; responsible without any qualification; responsible sans phrase, responsible tout court, absolutely, radically, buckstoppingly responsible; ultimately responsible, in a word and so ultimately morally responsible when moral matters are at issue. Free will is the thing you have to have if you're going to be responsible in this all or nothing way. That's what I mean by free will. That's what I think we haven't got and can't have. You cannot make yourself the way you are . . . The facts are clear. One cannot be ultimately responsible for one's character or mental nature in any way at all."

[This assumption is the basis for the first three steps in the effectiveness of twelve-step programs designed originally by Bill W. to aid alcoholics manage their habit of addiction. Abridged, they are: 1) We admitted we were powerless over God and that we cannot manage our own lives; 2) Believed that a power called God is greater than ourselves and controls the whole Universe, 3) Turned our will and our lives over to the power of God . . . think you can handle that?]

Presumably that would include actions taken by sheeple in the U.S. Congress and the White House and all the other capitals of the world as well as the rest of us. History shows that these sheeple are controlled by events and forces they neither create nor control, so they merit neither praise nor blame for the consequences. One of the main issues Strawson addresses is why we so instinctively and stubbornly see ourselves as free and responsible. What is it about human experience that makes it difficult, impossible maybe, to believe something that we can easily demonstrate as true and vice versa? Perhaps it is necessary to believe in free will to offset the belief in absolute predeterminism—both/and. All in God's will of course . . . AIGWOC. Think you can handle that?

Saul Smilansky, a pupil of Strawson, has concluded that belief in the illusion of free will is necessary to maintain order in society through individual responsibility, for without it there could be no morality or ethics. He writes in <u>Free Will and Illusion</u>, (2000) "We are fortunate in being imbued with illusion because we cannot function well [individually and collectively] with a complete realization of the truth on the free will issue . . . in this sense, most sheeple are living in a false world. The important thing however is to grant that this grand illusion is so much of what makes our morality possible and our lives meaningful that overall we must say that illusion is not always a bad thing." He seems to represent the present stage of understanding, i.e., that belief in free will may be an illusion, but it is a necessary one just like Santa Claus or it would not exist. "Our common libertarian assumptions about free will cannot be sustained. All our actions, however an internalized and complex a form they may take, are the result of what we are, and ultimately are beyond our control . . . Revealing the large and mostly positive role of illusion concerning free will not only teaches us a great deal about the free will issue itself but also posits illusion as a pivotal [necessary] factor in human life."

However, Smilansky is not so dogmatic as Strawson because he allows for the necessity of belief in the illusion of free will in order to sustain the current views on morality, justice, and deserts in organized societies. He points out that without belief in free will remorse would make no sense and the whole basis for conscience and jurisprudence would be removed.

Religion only adds more confusion than clarity to this debate. Eminent theologian, Merrill F. Unger (1909-1980) wrote in Biblical Demonology, (1965, 1970, 1994) "It must be obvious that there is something wrong in this world in which there can be such a state of appalling religious confusion and doctrinal jumble. It is ever a matter of amazement that professional Christian people, having one Bible and one Savior and led by one Spirit, can arrive at such diverse and contradictory interpretations and conclusions, even from the same passage of scripture. The lamentable facts of Christian disunity must remain largely an unsolved riddle to those ignorant of the devices of Satan and the reality of the spiritual world of evil because of a lack of elementary knowledge of the power and reality of demonic deception . . . the Holy Spirit of God is the great Unifier whereas the spirit of error is the great divider. Not only is Satan the directing head of the world system, but the system itself is evil. Many believers hate to admit that and unbelievers deny it altogether."

In this he supported Apostle Paul who concluded, "There is none righteous, no not one." (Romans 3:10) This could help explain why so many theologians merely are educated fools. Taken literally, the Bible prophecies that affairs of mankind will grow worse and worse until there is a predestined final battle of Armageddon to destroy evil and eventually to create a "new heaven and new Earth." (2 Peter 3:13, Revelation 21:1) However, the timing of the terminal events is not given, even to Jesus, to know for sure. (Matthew 24:36, Mark 13:32) If even the power of God and his Holy Spirit cannot or will not change this course of events according to the Bible, then what power has mankind to change it? And why should we worry one single minute or devote one single dollar to try and change it? Besides, this prophecy would seem to negate the possibility of any survival of mankind in any present form so that rules out the concept of resurrection of the body because there would be nothing left to resurrect. Anyway, the created cannot tell the Creator what to do with his creation any more than the clay can tell the potter what kind of vessel to make. (Jeremiah 18: 2-6, Romans 9:21) And, that condition must include the illusion that we can. Think you can handle that?

Any competent historian can link previous events in strings of cause and effect, but no one can go back and do any of it differently. Realizing this is true, all the "coulda woulda shoulda" that drives remorse and regrets is immediately disabled. Neither can anyone predict all the future consequences of present actions nor explain the illogical, stupid, and illegal actions of Homo sapiens without some belief in a Higher Power controlling all things. It would be like explaining a motorcycle seen running down the road without a visible rider. Laws of quantum mechanics depend upon indefinite uncertainty of probability, thus leaving everything to some degree of chance. All in God's will of course . . . AIGWOC. Swiss psychiatrist C. G. Jung observed, "In all chaos there is a cosmos, in all disorder a secret order . . . I could not say I believe—I know! I have had the experience of being gripped by something that is stronger than myself, something that people call God." [This experience does not come by seeking it. Apparently it only occurs during a life crisis when you least expect it. For Jung, it was a near-death experience during his heart attack at age 69.]

It took the discovery of fractal geometry to expose the order in chaos. A Fractal is generally "a rough or fragmented geometric shape that can be split into parts, each of which is (at least approximately) a reduced-size copy of the whole," i.e., a property called self-similarity. The term was coined by Benoit Mandelbrot in 1975 and was derived from the Latin fractious meaning "broken" or "fractured." A mathematical fractal is based on an equation that undergoes iteration to infinity, a form of feedback based on recursion. Scientists have learned for example that by using fractals to model any tree at random in a rain forest they can model the entire forest. In other words, one tree represents all trees. That discovery was added to the formula showing that the larger the specific body of any species, the more efficiently it uses energy.

So as one gets larger it takes a larger caloric deficit to lose weight, hence an explanation for the epidemic of obesity. For both Jung and Freud the evidence for existence of psyche/soul was to be found in the stuff of dreams and such intuitive discoveries. But Freud saw dreams as just human phenomena while Jung saw them as beyond time and space, hence evidence for God. Isn't that the goal that everyone seeks, but so very few find, evidence for God? In his view what is seen is driven by the unseen. "Whoever looks outside dreams, but whoever looks inside awakes." So said C.G. Jung.

[Jim Morningstar, self-proclaimed founder of Spiritual Psychology has said, "Since our western scientific heritage has assigned the mind and body to the realm of the measurable and the spirit to the domain of faith, there has been a split in our understanding and approach to these essential aspects of the human phenomenon. The advent of holism as a philosophical tenant in the latter part of 20th century heralded a fundamental shift in consciousness, from linear or causal thinking toward systemic awareness. We can no longer operate with a mechanical model if we are to understand the inter-dimensional realities that allow us so much freedom and expansion of our capabilities. It is critical that we have a psychology that not only admits the existence of the human spirit, but also takes it fully into account in knowing and predicting human behavior. Just as important is for us to have spirituality that incorporates the discoveries we have made about the mind/body connection and how the mind and body mirror and manifest our spiritual intentions. To keep the two realms separate is to keep us split and severely limited in our understanding and treatment of the whole human being." Hence the field called spiritual psychology now seems to be an emerging branch of science. There is even a graduate curriculum with that name at the University of Santa Monica . . . in California of course.]

Like the children enraptured by a puppet show as though the characters were real, most sheeple do not see the puppeteer hidden behind the curtain of life perhaps because that is the way God the Almighty One wants it to be. [Except in Chinese puppet theater where the puppeteers are exposed to plain view on the stage.] It is one thing to be given a view of the puppeteers behind the curtain but quite another to look around and realize we all are just characters in the puppet theater of life, with God pulling the strings as it were. Shakespeare wrote in "As You Like It", "All the world's a stage, and all the men and women merely are players." Now, where could he get that idea from? Everyone is acting out the script they were given by God, the almighty One. Very few sheeple ever get taken backstage to see how God really runs the production because the shock would be too great. It seems that this author was given the grand tour but only as a secret not to be disclosed to anyone else . . . yet. Sheeple who are not ready to absorb the reality of God as writer, producer, director and casting are given to believe in the illusion of free will to protect them from the psychic shock that would be disabling to ego.

Do the unconscious internal neuronal processes of the brain have any controlling role in what we do? If the brain has a spontaneity of its own volition and is capable of making unpredictable choices, as now seems to be discovered, that would make it impossible for an external agent, even consciousness, to control it effectively. Are we just the playthings of internal unconscious forces and their prior imprints in our brain? Is the capability of choices, modified by reasoning and absence of effective external control, what makes every conscious, reasoning, individual responsible for its own actions? If actions come from thoughts, do thoughts exist without some language to manifest them? It would seem so from the actions of pre-lingual infants to seek the needs of survival by very effective communications of their needs. Rational language and reason seem to be centered in the left-brain hemisphere, but we have the more ancient language of emotion and intuition in the right side, and ideally both languages feed back upon one another through the connecting bridge, called the corpus callosum. This area of the human brain consists of some two hundred million fibers. It begins to develop by the tenth week of pregnancy and continues developing perhaps into adolescence. Its ultimate evolution may help determine how well the left and right hemispheres of the brain communicate and coordinate actions and thoughts. How this evolution of thought-action feedback serves to influence human development and decision making of Homo sapiens compared with lower primates is a fertile field for new research in neurology.

If everything we do physically is caused by our brains, which in turn are a product of our genes and our life experiences which are beyond our control, how can we be held responsible for our actions? If God is the Creator of all the Earth and everything in it, then we all are just where God wants us to be. That would have to include those in prisons and those living in huts and those in all manner of suffering as well as those living in splendor and luxury of health, wealth, and happiness for a time. It would have to include both the 15-year old girl murderer and her nine year old female victim, stabbed and cut up "just to see what it feels like." That theory could place every creature of the Universe automatically in the virtual Church of Theofatalism™ right where they are supposed to be; where there are no clergy, buildings, treasury, or dogma. But why must sheeple believe in myths and illusions like free will? It must have a purpose or it would have been removed through natural selection by now . . . if you believe in natural selection. All in the will of God the Almighty One, of course.

4. THE CRUELEST NECESSARY HOAX

The logical conflict between causal determinism and free will has occupied thinkers for centuries. They have all evolved into three possibilities as follows: 1) free will is obvious to anyone who thinks about it because they assume everyone had the power to choose differently, i.e., libertarians, 2) free will is impossible because every event is preceded by a chain of determinants that makes it impossible to do anything differently, and besides God controls everything and, 3) the compatibalists who want it both ways, i.e., things happen for a cause whether from God or not, but sheeple have the freedom of choice in some things if not in all things. Why should these mutually exclusive theories exist and why so do many sheeple adopt one or the other with absolute confidence they are right? Prof. Saul Smilansky set off a modern debate in <u>Free Will and Illusion</u> (2000) with his assumption that the seeming paradox can be accommodated by assuming the presence of necessary illusions in the social affairs of Homo sapiens, including the illusion of belief in free will. He quoted Ludwig Wittgenstein, "When you are philosophizing you have to descend into primeval chaos and feel at home there." The struggle goes on.

The John Templeton Foundation issued a grant for $4.4 million to Prof. Alfred Mele of Florida State University to organize the best minds in the world to determine whether sheeple have free will or not, to be completed in 2013. The Foundation grant states, "The notion that human beings possess free will is fundamental to the world's ethical and religious systems and remains deeply embedded in how we conceive of ourselves. It is assumed free will that allows us to engage in self-directed and intentional activity, which in turn makes us moral agents, susceptible to praise or blame for our actions. Free will allows us to be sources of genuine novelty and creativity, and for some, it is what makes us most resemble the divine. Recent research in a number of fields, however, has challenged the reality of free will. Neuroscientists claim to have shown, for example, that the genesis of action in the brain begins well before conscious awareness of that action. And social psychologists have suggested that human behavior arises not from conscious beliefs but from behavioral scripts activated by particular environmental conditions imposed upon infants from birth without their will. Both scenarios point to free will as an illusion of human self-perception." [Visit www.freewillandscience.com]

For some reason, practically everyone still believes they have free will. Our system of jurisprudence depends on it, and prisons would be empty without it. But beliefs are not always true; in fact new knowledge and theories regularly replace old ones. Sheeple thought no one could run faster than a four minute mile until Roger Bannister actually did it in 1954. The Catholic Church taught the Earth was the center of the solar system and so it was believed until Galileo saw it differently through his telescope. The Vatican did not apologize until 1992 for demanding that he refute what his eyes and intellect told him. The history of science shows that new discoveries that introduce new paradigms can take decades or even centuries to gain acceptance. Anton von Leeuwenhoek saw microbes under magnification in the 17th century, 200 years before the germ theory of Pasteur. He was considered initially a dilletante or an amateur as he was the son of a basket maker. Repeatedly we see that the original discoverers of many phenomena come from simple backgrounds, sometimes with little formal scientific training and most often are not recognized specialists or professionals in their lifetimes. Whenever anything new happens, some sheeple always try to say it's nonsense while others may say, why not. But, why do so many sheeple believe in religious dogma of free will that is centuries old even when new knowledge brings new understanding? So, let's cut to the chase.

Man wants to be free—free to be his own God, free to determine his own destiny, free to override the rule and dominance of God and country, free to rebel or free to obey, and he wants freedom of the will at all cost. But, where does that desire for such freedom come from? It is a real shock when we first come to understand that of ourselves we cannot make one free choice to do good or evil. You see this every day in news that illustrates sheeple doing things that make no sense. Something must cause their choice, but the carnal mind hates to be caused to do anything. Because of this, Apostle Paul lamented that he was a "wretched man" who often did what he shouldn't and omitted what he should. (Romans 7: 15-24) Benjamin Franklin, (1706-1790) whom we can thank for persuading France to aid the American Revolution, laid out thirteen virtues that he had difficulty achieving, "While my care was employed in guarding against one fault, I was often surprised by another; habit took the advantage of inattention; inclination was sometimes too strong for reason. I concluded that the intention to be completely virtuous was not sufficient to prevent our slipping." At least, he was good enough to admit it. It took almost 2,000 years of medical research to discover that much of the human body does what it does through an automatic unconscious nervous system that is beyond logical control. In fact, the human body has a mind of its own when it comes to diseases and such, so why not for all types of choices?

God gave all men free will, the egos shout. And they select Bible scriptures to prove their argument. But, others argue this is an illusion that has plagued mankind since the beginning. All this debate proves is that for every thought there is an equal and opposite thought just as there are equal and opposite forces operating in the laws of physics. How could most of the population of the entire world for the whole history of mankind believe something as fundamental as free will if such a thing does not even exist, although belief in it certainly does, unless God so willed it to be? "Where is the wise? Where is the Scribe? Where is the disputer [debater] of this world? Has not God made foolish [Gk: 'stupid'] the wisdom of this world?" (I Corinthians. 1:20). Notice that it is not the foolishness of this world the Bible says that God made stupid, but rather it is the wisdom of this world that he made stupid! Consider how the banking experts all got it so wrong causing the financial collapse of October, 2008 which still is threatening the world economy. Foolish bankers, who should have known better, loaned mortgages to sheeple who could not afford them and then packaged them into new securities and resold them to even greater fools. Since then more than two million homes have been foreclosed with an estimated four million more in process, and nearly one third of all homes are worth less than their mortgages.

From 2000 through 2007 only 25 banks failed, requiring takeovers by the Federal Deposit Insurance Corporation. But since then, 158 banks failed in 2009 and the pace continues, but no one has yet gone to prison among them. Surveys indicate that nearly 60 percent of American workers lost 40 percent of their retirement savings, and more. But the Social Security Administration reported incomes of the 75 top earners in 2009 rose from 2008 on average from $91 million to more than $518 million while millions of workers were laid off. The median income of all wage earners over age 25 in 2003 reported by the Census Bureau was $33,517 for men and $19,679 for women, including part time workers. As of 2007, the percentage of households that owned $5,000 or more of stock was 35 percent; and only 22 percent owned $25,000 or more. The wealthiest one percent of households had 38 percent of outstanding stock; the wealthiest five percent had 69 percent; the wealthiest 10 percent had 81 percent. The bottom 60 percent of households owned 2.5 percent of the total stock. All these sheeple will come to a rude awakening when it comes their time to retire. All in God's will of course . . . AIGWOC.

The shift of income and wealth from poorer to richer sheeple has been accelerating since the Reagan administration of the 1980s and seems to be unstoppable. It does not seem that either the politicians or the voters know what they are doing. We seem to be in for some grim times ahead. [Politician means "many tongues," so they will say whatever gets them elected, and then re-elected. They know the secret is finding out where their voters are heading and running around to get in front of them. But, there are so many single moms raising boys without fathers we are creating a subculture of violent gang members and drug addicts. More than six million students drop out of high school each year . . . but they can vote . . . and buy guns. If you assume the same drop out rate for the past ten years that could be 60 million uneducated young adults running around . . . or 120 million if you count the past 20 years. No wonder our prisons are full to overflowing.] Now, if God is not the cause of this calamity, then who is? Those who claim it is the Devil cannot explain his source or his power apart from God. If God is God, obviously he can do anything he wants to with anyone he wants to whenever he wants to . . . and that includes using the Devil to put thoughts into their heads or to destroy their health, wealth, and happiness like he did to Job. "Though you build your nest as high as the eagle's, from there I will bring you down, declares the Lord." (Jeremiah 49:16, Obadiah 1:4) If God will pull down the eagle's nest, imagine what he can do to the rest of us. [Consider the politicians and celebrities who sometimes get caught in temptations that they could not resist and ruin their careers.] Throughout history, nations have risen to greatness and fallen into disaster and the process continues, all in God's will of course. There is no example in all history that can be shown to be the exercise of human will that is free from the will of God. There is no power greater than the source of all power.

[Some researchers say there is evidence for at least 20 different species of hominids dating back several million years, all of whom have disappeared. Modern mankind is a very recent form of Homo sapiens that have come and gone several times with changes in climate and geology. Archeology has produced evidence that the present Sahara Desert was a verdant fertile plain 6,000 years ago when a prolonged drought caused by shifts in the currents of the Atlantic Ocean drove a massive human migration eastward to settle the land of Egypt. Artifacts discovered there defy understanding of the way in which they were constructed. Then, 2,000 years afterward again a tragic drought ended the majestic civilization that produced the great pyramids of Egypt and the rival to Rome. Other cataclysmic events, some geological—some manmade, have brought down one great empire after another. All in God's will of course . . . AIGWOC.]

Sheeple are like computers; they do what they are programmed to do. And God is the programmer. That certainly includes all that Jesus himself ever thought, said, or did for he proclaimed, "I do nothing on my own but speak just what the Father has taught me." (John 8:28) Sounds like Jesus thought he was a robot of God, no? Nevertheless, the basis of Christianity rests in ability of mankind to accept Christ as savior . . . or not. (John 3:16) However, this is offset by the scripture that says they do not all have the ability to do so. (Matthew 13:11-17) Check it out.

Nothing is more contentious in society than the wide variety among religious beliefs. Most sheeple, even the professional esteemed theologians, will continue to defend their belief in free will even in the light of a mountain of Bible scriptures that contradict it at every turn. Such is the will of God. Could it be the notion of free will is an obsolete belief that needs to be reconsidered? Take the notion of faith in Christ by personal choice for example. Consider this scripture that established the basis for the Church of Jesus Christ. "But what about you? he asked. Who do you say I am? Simon Peter answered, You are the Christ, the Son of the living God. Jesus replied, Blessed are you, Simon son of Jonah, for this was not revealed to you by man, but by my Father in heaven. And I tell you that you are Peter, and on this rock I will build my church, and the gates of Hades will not overcome it." (Matthew 16: 15-18) He went on to say, "This is why I told you that no one can come to me unless the Father has enabled/caused him." (John 6:63-65) "By myself, I can do nothing . . . but the will of the Father who sent me." (John 5:30) "Believe you not that I am in the Father, and the Father in me? The words that I speak unto you, I speak not of myself, but the Father that dwells in me, he does the works." (John 14:10) Apostle Paul verifies this also; "For by grace are you saved through faith; and that [saving faith] is not of yourselves: it is the gift of God." (Ephesians 2:8)

Jesus told His disciples that they would all forsake him in the end, and they did. In other words, Jesus was foretelling events that would cause (even force, if you will) them to change their wills, against their previously stated volition. They, especially Peter, all denied that Jesus knew what He was talking about. "And Jesus said unto them, all of you shall be offended because of me this night; for it is written, I shall smite the shepherd, and the sheep shall be scattered." (Mark 14:27 & Zechariah 13:7).The disciples, especially Peter, all said that they would remain loyal. But Jesus said that they would all be offended because of him. Was there a reason for God causing the disciples to will loyalty to Jesus and then in the same night to will them to deny Jesus? Does God do anything in vain without a reason? This was apparently a necessary part of their conversion process. God totally humiliated them by proving to them that their own will was not free to do what they wanted. In one theory, since God knows the future he must see to it that it happens, otherwise no prophecy would be fulfilled. Clearly, God brought about circumstances that caused/ made/forced, Peter and the other apostles to do what they didn't want to do. Same with the Jews who rejected Jesus as Messiah. How, then, can such a forced will be free? The reasoning goes like this. If God exists and if God is omniscient, then God creates everything and that means God creates belief in Christ, as well as disbelief, so that means it is not really free now is it. And if man has free will of his own creation then God is not really omniscient and then perhaps God does not really exist, does he. Are these conclusions necessary opposites, or is one right and one wrong? How can we ever know for sure?

Scientists all agree that some processes in the human body are involuntary and some are voluntary. Also, psychology generally agrees to the existence of a subconscious "mind" as well as a conscious "mind," although just what "mind" is still cannot be explained. Dreams appear to be a universal involuntary experience of Homo sapiens that C.G. Jung believed originated in the unconscious and contained valuable insights if they could only be correctly interpreted. Our system of laws is based on the assumption of some ability to understand right from wrong and the exercise of will. But mental illness generally is believed to be outside of conscious control and, therefore, is a legal defense. Everyone agrees that genes control much of who we are, up to the limits set by social boundaries that vary by time and circumstance. But, are social boundaries not created by sheeple in groups driven by their genes? Could there be some energetic forces at work in the genes that are not yet understood? So where is the line that separates the voluntary from the involuntary? This matter has roots deep in physics and metaphysics related to determinism and predictability. Suppose we pit the winning Super Bowl team against a losing high school team and the former wins. We could say the result was deterministic (the Super Bowl team was much better) and predictable (the Super Bowl team was much better). But, suppose the high school team wins. How would you explain that? Such was the case with Muhammad, founder of Islam. Although he was an illiterate camel driver, he vaulted to military, government, and religious leadership far above what his social status would predict. How could that be unless God willed it so to happen?

You may believe you can choose what food to ingest, but obesity is a raging health-threatening pandemic these days that seems beyond control of thinking sheeple. It is easy to say sheeple just eat too much. But when you go looking into it you find there are many theories about its cause and more new ones all the time. All of them raise doubts about free will. Dieting supplements are a $50 billion industry that is 99 percent ineffective. What is wrong here? Some dietitians claim obese sheeple exercise too little, eat too much food high in saturated animal fats, sugars, and calories and too little of fresh fruits and vegetables high in vitamins, minerals, and anti-oxidants. If it were that simple the solution should be easy, but it's not. "It appears that base wiring of the brain is a determinant of one's vulnerability to develop obesity," says Thomas Horvath at Yale University. "These observations add to the argument that it is less about personal will that makes a difference in becoming obese, and it is more related to the connections that emerge in our brain during infant development." Horvath points to other unwanted consequences of these brain mechanisms. "Those who are vulnerable to diet-induced obesity also develop a brain inflammation, while those who are resistant, do not," he says. "This emerging inflammatory response in the brain may also explain why those who once developed obesity have a harder time losing weight."

[Here is a tidbit you will not read in diet books. Science has learned that larger human bodies learn to use the energy in calories more efficiently than smaller sheeple. So if you are gaining weight chances are your body is using food more efficiently and thus needs less than you consume. But the Catch-22 is that to lose weight consumption of food must be below the decreasing level of maintenance as you get bigger but not so low as to deprive the body of needed nutrients. Restaurants have conditioned sheeple to eat too much in order to charge high prices to make profits. (A side effect of the free enterprise system of capitalism.) Another tidbit of aging is that side effects of many drugs cause weight gain . . . Check the wrapper of your pills and look it up on the Internet at www.rxlist.com.]

Fitness guru and television exercise celebrity for 34 years, Jack Lalane (1914-2011) credited a lifestyle of workouts and fresh food diets to his physical prowess and longevity, reaching 96 years before he died. He chortled, "If it tastes good and is man-made, spit it out." But, his older brother lived to age 97 while living a more "normal" lifestyle and his wife is nearly as old and still living. Results of several studies show that obesity often is associated with a mood or anxiety disorder, but the causal relationship and complex interplay between the two is still unclear. Science is learning rapidly that genes may be the strings that God uses to control all living creatures, including your appetite and metabolism. A gene that makes sheeple vulnerable to obesity also produces a protein that may directly modify DNA in a region of the brain known to control food intake. The unexpected finding sheds light on how gene variants can predispose individuals to obesity, say the scientists. Reports also indicate that researchers have isolated a chemical in the brain that seems to control appetite, telling sheeple when they are hungry or full and even what tastes good. The scientists identified the molecule as nesfatin-1, which is produced naturally in the brain. Other studies report finding two hormones that are triggered by the food you eat. One triggers fat storage and the other triggers fat burning. New research is making such discoveries almost every week. Perhaps our choices in food are not so free after all.

Sheeple can be addicted to the taste of sweetness, so merely substituting chemical additives for sugar actually could be inducing more obesity, according to studies at Purdue University. It turns out that artificial sweeteners produce the same increased out put of the dopamine neurotransmitter associated with consumption of real sugar. So, by consuming artificial sweeteners sheeple actually may be increasing obesity while they think they are fighting it. It's possible also that the obesity epidemic could be caused by a flu-like virus. Scientists have long known that viruses can cause obesity in animals such as chickens, dogs and monkeys. Now, they think they're hot on the trail of one that causes obesity in humans. The virus, which needs a host cell to survive and grow, also may trigger immature fat cells to multiply more quickly than normal and signal metabolism to put on the brakes so that the body burns calories more slowly. Could this finding also help to explain why foods that are not healthy for you taste so good? Think about that next time you open a bag of snack food or order up a large helping of ice cream. But there is still more.

You might have a medical endocrine condition like hypothyroid that makes losing weight all but impossible even on a starvation diet. Such sheeple may not lose weight on 1200 calories per day or even less because the body metabolism just slows down for life preservation. If your body metabolism slows down enough there is no amount of free will that will overcome the conditions that make weight loss difficult, if not impossible. Resuming a normal diet then causes it to regain weight even more rapidly in a familiar see-saw pattern.

Additional studies are attempting to relate obesity with hormone production. Excesses or deficits of hormones can lead to obesity. For example, a deficiency of growth hormone may predispose to fat deposition. The endocrine system is made up of glands that secrete hormones into the bloodstream. Hormones are chemical messengers that regulate body processes, all apparently driven by or from the hypothalamus and the pituitary glands located in the brain. Among the favorite hormone suspects are cortisol, leptin, estrogen, obestatin, ghrelin, and growth hormone. Understanding the way such hormones control weight gain could be helpful in developing new treatments, but none has been proven effective as yet. The endocrine system works with the nervous system and the immune system to help the body cope with different events and stresses. The pituitary gland in the brain produces growth hormone, which influences an individual's height and contributes to bone and muscle building. Growth hormone also affects metabolism (the rate at which kilojoules are burned for energy). Researchers have found that growth hormone levels in obese sheeple are lower than those in sheeple of normal weight. These correlations do not prove causation of course. But what is more intriguing is why there seems to be a national pandemic of obesity at this time.

The same could be said for illegal drug addictions and other forms of anti-social behaviors that seem to be out of control. New research indicates that addictions to drugs are linked to chemical changes in the brain identical to out of control behavioral disorders, including gambling. Attempts to control addictive behaviors seem futile because they could be rooted in genetics. Scientists say they have pinpointed a genetic link that makes sheeple more likely to get hooked on tobacco, causing them to smoke more cigarettes, making it harder to quit, and leading more often to deadly lung cancer. The discovery, by three separate teams of scientists in the U.S. and Europe, makes the strongest case so far for the biological underpinnings of the addiction of smoking and sheds light on how genetics and cigarettes join forces to cause cancer. "This is kind of a double whammy gene," said Christopher Amos, a professor of epidemiology at the M.D. Anderson Cancer Center in Houston and author of one of the studies. "It also makes you more likely to be dependent on smoking and less likely to quit smoking."

A smoker who inherits this genetic variation from both parents has an 80 percent greater chance of lung cancer than a smoker without the variants, the researchers reported. And that same smoker on average lights up two extra cigarettes a day and has a much harder time quitting than smokers who don't have these genetic differences. The genetic variations, which encode nicotine receptors on cells, could eventually help explain some of the mysteries of chain smoking, nicotine addiction and lung cancer that can't be chalked up to environmental factors, brain biology and statistics, experts said. "This is really telling us that the vulnerability to smoking and how much you smoke is clearly biologically based," said psychiatry professor Dr. Laura Bierut, of Washington University in St. Louis.

Speaking of the will of God the Almighty One, here is a practical story to illustrate it. A young man from Mexico came to this country illegally, broke and unable to speak English, and got a job at a pet grooming center in San Diego owned by two unnamed women. From there he became rich and famous on the National Geographic cable channel as the "Dog Whisperer" without any formal veterinary training but with an instinctive way of working with distraught dogs. His role is to "rehabilitate dogs and train people." The healthy relationship between dog and owner is one of calm submission, not unlike that between man and God. His name is Cesar Millan. He got inspired about working with dogs on his grandfather's farm and from watching old movies starring *Rin Tin Tin* and *Lassie* on television. In his best selling book, Cesar's Way, (2006) which was ghost written by Melissa Jo Peltier, he credited several celebrities who helped set up his career. There was Oprah Winfrey whose dogs he groomed and got his first television appearance. There was Tony Robins, Dr. Wayne Dyer, Dr. Phil McGraw, and Dr. Deepak Chopra from whom he learned self psychology to achieve success. There was some unnamed editor at the Los Angeles Times who published a favorable review of the business at his Dog Psychology Center and the three producers at the MPH Entertainment Group who sold the idea of a dog-owner training show to the National Geographic Channel. There were the pioneers in dog psychology, Dr. Leon F. Whitney, author of Dog Psychology; The Basics of Dog Training as well as many other books in veterinary science, and Dr. Bruce Fogle, author of The Dog's Mind and more than 50 other pet books, which he says, "saved my sanity and helped me see that I was on the right track." This one example is so complex that to try and diagram all the prerequisites to the television success of Cesar Millan would be impossible. Free will, or the will of God the Almighty One? Shall we say that Cesar's way is his destiny but a criminal locked up in prison for drug dealing is there of his own free will?

These and other such news items occurring almost daily challenge belief in free will among humans as opposed to the divine will of God the Almighty One in all things. If the ideas of divine will and free will are mutually exclusive, which one is true and which one is false, and why do they both exist? It is a very old struggle. Both the Bible and the Koran (holy book of Islam) appear to integrate the impossible opposites of predestination and free will, love and fear, sometimes on the same page. As for the power of nations, ". . . the Most High is sovereign over the kingdoms of men and gives them to anyone he wishes." (Daniel 4:25) The Koran says much the same thing. "Allah, wielder of the kingly power; thou givest that power to whomever thy will and thou taketh the power from whomever thy will, Thou dost exalt whom thy will and thou doth abase whom they will." (3:25) "Don't you know that to Allah alone belongs the dominion of the heavens and the Earth? He punishes whom he pleases and he forgives whom he pleases; Allah has power over all things." (5:40) "Allah has guided by His will those who believe to the truth about which they differed and Allah guides whom He pleases to the right path. (2:213) "Whatever is in the heavens and whatever is in the Earth is Allah's; and whether you manifest what is in your minds or hide it, Allah will call you to account according to it; then He will forgive whom He pleases and chastise whom He pleases, and Allah has power over all things." (2.284) "God sends astray whomever He wills, and directs whomever He wills in the right path." (6:38-39) There are 131 verses just like that in the Koran. The powerful

King, Nebuchadnezzar exclaimed, "His dominion is an eternal dominion; his kingdom endures from generation to generation. All the peoples of the Earth are regarded as nothing. He does as he pleases with the powers of heaven and the peoples of the Earth. No one can hold back his hand or say to him: What have you done?" (Daniel 4:34-36) When Job finally got his meeting with God, the great one exclaimed, "Where were you when I laid the Earth's foundation?" (Job 38:4) And Job was speechless.

Although some scriptures, including the famous John 3:16, imply that salvation through belief in Jesus as the Son of God is available to anyone with free will to choose, it does not appear that everyone has that power because, "many are called/invited but few are chosen." (Matthew 22:14) The Bible also says that Jesus taught his disciples in encoded parables so that the sinners "may not understand lest they should be converted and their sins be forgiven them . . . The knowledge of the secrets of the kingdom of heaven has been given to you, [disciples] but not to them." (Mark 4:12, Matthew 13:11) "For this reason they could not believe, because, as Isaiah says elsewhere: He has blinded their eyes and deadened their hearts, so they can neither see with their eyes, nor understand with their hearts, nor turn and I would heal them." John 12: 39-40) King Solomon thought the same thing; "God has made everything fitting in its season; However, He has put obscurity in their heart so that men may NOT find out his work, that which God does."(Ecclesiastes 3:11).

The apostle Peter seems to restate the same idea, "The stone the builders rejected has become the capstone and a stone that causes men to stumble and a rock that makes them fall. They stumble because they disobey the message, which is also what they were destined for." (1 Peter 2:7-8) It appears that even Jesus could not change the destiny of the Jews who were all but destroyed in the uprising of 69-74 CE that included destruction of their temple by the Romans and dispersal that lasted until Israel was reconstructed by the United Nations in 1947. The land given to them now obviously cannot support its burgeoning population, so Israel must invade its Palestinian neighbors to survive. And yet, they still reject their Messiah. It is written, "What Israel sought so earnestly it did not obtain, but the elect did. The others/Jews were hardened, as it is written: God gave them a spirit of stupor, eyes so that they could not see and ears so that they could not hear, to this very day." (Romans 11:7-8) It appears that Apostle Paul thought God controlled who would accept or reject Jesus as Messiah, "Jews demand miraculous signs and Greeks look for wisdom, but we preach Christ crucified: a stumbling block to Jews and foolishness to Gentiles, but to those whom God has called, both Jews and Greeks, Christ the power of God and the wisdom of God." (1 Corinthians 1:22-24)

Jesus restated the same idea in explaining the parable of the sower of seeds, some to be blown away and some to fall upon fertile ground. "Those [seeds] along the path are the ones who hear, and then the devil comes and takes away the word from their hearts, so that they may not believe and be saved." (Luke 8:12) Jesus was not clear on how the respective selections are made in this instance. It seems to be random. But, Albert Einstein said he could not believe that God just throws dice. Perhaps Jesus cannot change the destiny of those elected to be saved at the end either as he stated, "If the Lord had not cut short those days, no one would survive. But for the sake of the elect, whom he has chosen, he has shortened them." (Mark 13:20) Are some sheeple designated by God to miss out on his eternal life? It would seem so, according to John Calvin and those of the Presbyterian faith who claim they are part of "the elect." But, in order to provide the necessary opposite, the late Rev. Dr. Jerry Falwell, (1933-2007) organizer of the "Moral Majority," declared at the Liberty College convocation on 4/13/07, "We believe that anyone who believes in the birth, death, and resurrection of Jesus will be saved. We believe that whosoever will may come. No one is left out who believes. As a matter of fact, we consider a limited atonement a heresy." Although this idea may feel comforting to many sheeple, the Bible seems to say otherwise. Of course, if you don't believe the Bible contains the word of God, none of this matters very much.

From the choosing of Abraham as the patriarch of Israel to the theme of "the elect" flowing through the Bible it appears that God has chosen who wins and who loses a-priori. That includes his selection of the Jews as his chosen sheeple. "The Lord your God has chosen you out of all the peoples on the face of the Earth to be his people, his treasured possession. " (Deuteronomy 7:6, 14:2, 2 Chronicles 6:6) How come he did not choose some sheeple from China or India or some tribe that would be more obedient? Apostle Paul emphasizes this selection in several letters, "For he chose us in him before the creation of the world to be holy and blameless in his sight. In love he predestined us to be adopted as his sons through Jesus Christ, in accordance with his pleasure and will to the praise of his glorious grace, which he has freely given us in the one he loves." (Romans 8:29-30, 1 Corinthians 2:7, Ephesians 1:4-6) The favored apostle, Peter, says the same, ". . . you are a chosen generation, a royal priesthood, a holy nation, a peculiar people . . ." (1 Peter 2:9-10) This seems to indicate some form of existence before the world was created. As described in the book of Revelation, only those whose names are written in the Book of Life from the foundation of the world, and have not been blotted out by the Lamb, are saved at the Last Judgment; all others are doomed. "And whosoever was not found written in the book of life was cast into the lake of fire" Revelation 20:15). If everyone is born in sin and doomed to hell as claimed by Apostle Paul, (Romans 5:12) except for those who were pre-selected to be chosen, where is the free will in that? If you believe in free will, must you reject the Bible?

To become disillusioned, illusion must first exist; and when illusion is exposed it no longer can exist. But, philosopher Saul Smilansky argues that illusion must have a positive and useful role in society or it would not exist. He claims that without belief in free will, even if it is illusory, society could not exist as we know it because there could be no "just deserts" in this life. Smilansky has no explanation for the ubiquitous disconnects between cause and effect among the affairs of Homo sapiens. When "do this—get that" fails to make any sense and becomes illogical, some higher power must be invoked to account for it. American Poet Laureate Robert Frost (1874-1963) offered this prayer . . . "Forgive, Oh Lord, my little jokes on Thee, and I'll forgive Thy great big one on me." Although he never explained what he meant, perhaps the untimely loss of all his children save one and his wife by his age 62 could be involved. And perhaps he was referring to the illusion of free will laid upon mankind by religious representatives of God.

Of course, claiming that free will is merely illusion is anathema to the leaders of most religions and all those given to agree with them. After all, if there is no free will sheeple cannot be held responsible for their sins, the churches, mosques, synagogues and temples all are out of business, and all the sheeple making a living from law enforcement must seek other work and criminals would roam the land like savage wild dogs. Sheeple who see only the bright side of the moon are unaware of the dark side unless they happen to visit it or take on faith what astronauts say about it. For some sheeple life is full of compassion, love, and charity. For others it is full of disappointment, worry, and suffering. All in God's will of course . . . AIGWOC.

Obviously, a society with so much invested in the illusion of free will is not likely to change its belief until it hurts too much not to. Recall how corrupt the Catholic Church had to get before Martin Luther was able to launch the protestant reformation in Wittenberg, Germany in 1517 on October 31 where he proclaimed the free salvation of faith in Christ is not earned by penance or good works or the purchase of indulgences to forgive sins to raise money for the Pope. The Pope, Leo V, was not pleased. Luther was made an outlaw by the Roman Catholic Church, subject to assassination without punishment, but he translated the Bible from Greek into German, and the inevitable change had begun after 1500 years of religious oppression. When he was finished his work, Luther suffered blindness in one eye and many infirmities and died at age 63. Disagreements ensued and after 100 years of religious wars a treaty in 1648 permitted national governments to adopt either Catholic or Lutheran dogma. Thus it was that many pilgrims sought religious freedom in the New World, called America. Perhaps one day belief in free will also will be replaced when the time is right. All in the will of God the Almighty One, of course.

How many times in life have you done something that turned out harmful or painful, even when you knew better, that you regretted later? The story of God's chosen sheeple is a case in point. It includes the deception that gave to Jacob the inheritance rightly belonging to his brother Esau from their father, Isaac. That was followed by the deception of his uncle Laban that enslaved Jacob and the birth of his twelve sons by polygamous relations with two wives and two maid servants. You can read about the conversion of Jacob into Israel in Genesis, chapters 27-35. You may recall the story of his youngest son Joseph, who was sold into slavery in Egypt by his jealous brothers, patriarchs of the twelve tribes of Israel. And how, when they found him to be a leader with power to save them from famine, they were very afraid. He calmed them by explaining, "Do not be distressed and grieved because you sold me here, because it was God who sent me before you to preserve your life." (Genesis 45:5) The story of Joseph and his brothers may be a parable for the whole plan of God for humanity to those who are given ears to hear and eyes to see. "Let every soul be subject unto the higher powers, for there is no power but of God. The powers that be are ordained of God." (Romans. 13:1). Consider that as the leaders in Saudi Arabia invoke Muslim shari'ah law and still punish adultery by stoning to death.

So, when bad things happen, why do most sheeple deny the notion that God has a plan for their lives that is beyond their own control which includes pain and suffering? The very word "guilt" makes a normal person feel bad. Recalling a guilty deed conjures up judgment and self-condemnation. But C. G. Jung tells us that guilt is necessary for consciousness. If we can suspend judgment, we may find out what our guilty reactions are trying to bring to our lives. They may be like the tiny green shoots of new plants breaking through the soil at winter's end. Guilt creates remorse, and that breeds amends, and amends create balance in life by removing guilt. Belief in free will rests on the unprovable assumption that you could have done it differently. But you can't go back and do it over. Whatever has happened, apparently had to happen. And whatever will happen, apparently must happen. The Infinite Cause of all happenings made all of the effects come into existence. Nothing that has a cause can ever be stopped, for if the cause could be stopped, the effect would have never happened, and we would not have the existence of any such cause to even be talking about in the first place. This is not rocket science. No one can un-ring a bell.

When you realize nothing can be done over again differently, remorse without amends is a terrible thing to live with. Even more terrible/dreadful/

fearful is to "fall into the hands of the living God." (Hebrews 10:30-32) This warning seems to be opposite to the "God is love" that the Apostle John wrote, which most Christians rely upon for comfort. (1 John 4:8) It seems to be such a hollow unreasonable claim with all the suffering and struggle in his creation and the repeated examples of his anger throughout the Old Testament. (1 Chronicles 13: 9-10) God was very brutal and unforgiving to those who disobeyed and broke his covenant. (Deuteronomy 28) But, Jesus the Son of God, instructed sheeple to love their enemies, and to forgive endlessly those who do wrong to you for no good reasons. (Matthew 5: 43-44) If there is only one, the God of love and the God of anger appear to be the same God.

Modern Christians rarely manifest the real teachings of Jesus because they would have to accommodate a gospel of opposites, judgment and mercy, love and fear, suffering and joy, plus a God who controls all things, even their thoughts. They also probably would not accept the lifestyle of first century Christians in which all believers were commanded to sell their property and give all the proceeds to the apostles for equal distribution under penalty of death. "All the believers were one in heart and mind. No one claimed that any of his possessions was his own, but they shared everything they had. With great power the apostles continued to testify to the resurrection of the Lord Jesus, and much grace was upon them all. There were no needy persons among them. For from time to time those who owned lands or houses sold them, brought the money from the sales and put it at the apostles' feet, and it was distributed to anyone as he had need." (Acts 4:32-35) The married couple, Ananias and Sapphira, who attempted deception by withholding some of their wealth, were put to death. (Acts 5:1-10) Today, they would call that a cult. Attempts to live that way in communes seem to always fail.

For the last hundred years, the evidence against free will has piled up higher and higher, for those given eyes to see and ears to hear. Rare, but not unusual, cases show that malfunctions in the brain can cause bizarre physical behaviors in spite of the "will" of the individual to do otherwise. Apostle Paul described how he would do things that "he" did not want to do, which illustrates the splitting of will between spirit and flesh making him a "wretched man." (Romans 7:15-24) Perhaps God provides the illusion of free will to protect sheeple from the disabling fright that would prevail if they assumed he controls even what they think. It may all be in our genes. A recent study reported from researchers in Stockholm shows a direct connection between genes and the way men approach marital commitment. They concluded, "If a man's culture, religion and family background each have a seat at the conference table that determines his attitudes toward marital fidelity and monogamy, his genes might well sit at the head of the table."

Using positronic emissions or radioactive xenon, researchers now can map which individual areas of the brain process mathematics, assemble words, or access visual memory.

It's becoming harder and harder to doubt that our minds are just physical processes occurring as electro-chemical blips in the brain plus elsewhere throughout the body. But, since the discovery of DNA, the makings of human genes, more questions have been raised than answered. The relationship between the observable neuro-physiology and its evidence in behavior is unexplainable with existing theories. Some experts claim that behaviors come from feelings that come from thoughts; so to change behavior one must first change thoughts. But, who is it that changes thoughts? The physical brain does not seem to be adequate to explain how a human being perceives, stores, retrieves, and processes information because it cannot know itself. According to the laws of thermodynamics, energy is indestructible. So consciousness may be indestructible, eternal and infinite. This definition could point to the existence of what the Bible calls "spirit." The "who" or "what" it is that can be aware of its own brain functions as they occur is still a big mystery called the "self." Jesus proclaimed, "The Spirit gives life, the flesh counts for nothing." (John 6:63) Could spirit be another word for mind?

The relationships between reason and emotion are yet to be related to brain functions. Aging dementia and disabling strokes caused by brain malfunctions leave medical science befuddled and as confused as the patients. Whether the brain can be changed by diet, exercise, and even thinking is yet to be proven clinically, although it obviously can be changed by disease, drugs, and accidents plus persuasive advertising. Five centuries before Christ, the Buddha taught, "We are what we think. With our thoughts we make the world." Who it is that "thinks" is beyond knowing, but maybe not. In his hypnotic regressions of clients, Dr. Michael Newton claims to have confirmed reincarnation of souls, although he makes no claims to explain his results. He reports in Journey of Souls (2002), "At some point prior to birth, the soul will carefully touch and join more fully with the impressionable, developing brain of a baby. When a soul decides to enter a baby, apparently that child has no free choice in accepting or rejecting the soul . . . Once birth has taken place, the union of spirit and flesh has been fully solidified into a partnership. The immortal soul then becomes the seat of perception for the developing human ego. The soul brings a spiritual force which is the heritage of infinite consciousness." It seems like the baby is merely a host for the parasite soul that takes over its life and proceeds to live out its karma as planned. Where is the baby's choice to accept or reject the soul? It does not seem much like a partnership; it is more like an involuntary possession such as Apostle Paul lamented as the war between flesh and spirit that made him a "wretched man." (Romans 7.24) If so, the possessor could be either a saint or a demon or anything in between . . . hence the need for criminal law and even exorcism.

Almost weekly, new research is linking more diseases and behavioral disorders with faulty genes in the DNA molecule located in the nucleus of living cells beyond conscious control. The pace of aging appears to be controlled by telemeres, tiny biological clocks at the end of chromosomes that shorten with each cell replication, up to a total of maybe 50 times, a process called cell senescence. The most common causes of death are heart disease, cancer, stroke, lung disease, accidents, Alzheimers, diabetes, pneumonia, kidney failure and bacterial blood poisoning. Normally, each body has its own natural time and way of dying, and too often medical intervention just gets in the way of it. More complex is the mitochondrial DNA that seems to be of separate evolutionary origin and passed on by the mother. Tracing this genetic link backwards in history arrives at a point of origin for present day Homo sapiens about 60,000-100,000 years ago in central-eastern Africa. In comparison, it seems that sharks have been around for four million years. That is about the age of the earliest bipedal hominid pre-human discovered in Ethiopia in 1994 that seems to void the Darwinian bridge supposed with chimpanzees, because "Ardi" was a completely new species. From there in Africa, the human ancestors migrated north, south, and east to populate the Earth. But, why they did no one knows.

If you scale the 4-billion year lifeline of Earth to one year, Homo sapiens in their present form have existed for less than a few seconds. Paleontology has disclosed the transition from a benign nomadic hunter-gatherer way of life to a settled agricultural one began in the Middle East at around 8000 BCE, spreading into Europe and Asia over the following millennia, and also developing independently in some places. Many of the world's cultures have myths that refer to an earlier time when life was much easier, and human beings were less materialistic and lived in harmony with nature and with each other. In ancient Greece and Rome this was known as the Golden Age; in China it was the Age of Perfect Virtue, in India it was the Krita Yuga (Perfect Age); while the Judeo-Christian tradition has the story of the Garden of Eden. These myths tell us that, either as a result of a long degeneration or a sudden and dramatic "Fall," something went wrong. Life among Homo sapiens became much more difficult and full of suffering, and human nature became more corrupt and contentious. It must all be in God's will of course, as there can be no other.

In Taoist terms, whereas the earliest human beings followed the Way of Heaven and were a part of the natural harmony of the Universe, later human beings became separated from the Tao, the Way, and became selfish and calculating. From there sheeple spread throughout the world, seemingly following some irresistible migratory urge to populate the planet and control their neighbors. Along the way, they have continually killed each other by vast numbers in the process, more than 55 million during World War II. Now, it is assumed that human behavior is involuntary, driven by the genes containing DNA in each human cell. Some researchers propose that the driver of DNA is the cell membrane that houses its command and control center . . . or is it all in the brain? If so, what drives that? Perhaps it is some energetic source not yet understood. If we can ever get over the illusion of free will, perhaps we will be more open to the guiding role that God plays through behavioral genetics in the lives of his creatures.

Then perhaps religion will become the sanctuary of God that it can be rather than the chamber of Babel dogma that it has become. Perhaps then churches will accept gay sheeple, poor sheeple, rich sheeple, smart sheeple, dumb sheeple, black, white, yellow and red sheeple, fat sheeple and thin sheeple and even addicts and criminal sheeple just as sheeple that God has made in their own time, no more or less than all the other life species on Earth that have come and gone. [Dr. Michael Eric Dyson earned a Ph.D. degree from Princeton, is a professor at the University of Pennsylvania and is honored as the voice for Black America through his many books. But, he has a brother who is confined to prison for second degree murder.] Perhaps there are no mistakes. Just choices and consequences which have something to teach us . . . like the levees breaking on the Mississippi river under Hurricane Katrina upon sheeple with no flood insurance because the Feds told them it would not be needed . . . after all you can always trust the Feds . . . all controlled by God the Almighty One.

None of the famous patriarchs of the Bible, from Noah to Abraham, to Joseph and Moses, to the prophets, to John the Baptist, to the Virgin Mary and her fiancé Joseph, to the twelve disciples, to Apostle Paul, and even Jesus himself . . . none of them were volunteers. Jesus declared, "You did not choose me, I chose you . . ." (John 15:16) Apostle Paul amplifies this; "In him we were also chosen, having been predestined according to the plan of him who works out everything in conformity with the purpose of his will . . ." (Ephesians 1:11) All of them were drafted into the army of God and many were martyred for his purpose. That would have to include all the infant sons under two years old that were slaughtered under orders of Herod, king of Israel (73-4 BCE) in his outrageous jealous attempt to destroy the new "king of the Jews." (Matthew 2: 12-16) Imagine the grief of all those parents caught up in the will of God who lost their children by the swords of Herod's soldiers.

Infant Jesus was spared the wrath of Herod when Joseph received instructions in a dream to flee to Egypt and wait for the death of Herod before returning, but the other innocent infant victims were killed. All in God's will of course. Much is made about the "betrayal" of Jesus by the disciple called Judas. But it is recorded that "The evening meal was being served, and the devil had already prompted Judas Iscariot, son of Simon, to betray Jesus . . . As soon as Judas took the bread, Satan entered into him." (John 13: 2, 27) Does God control Satan, or not? If he does not, then God is not omnipotent. Perhaps Satan merely is a creation of mankind to avoid seeing God as he really is, good and evil in One, to make up the necessary whole? Where is the free will in any of it, or was it necessary to fulfill the will of God as proclaimed by the prophets?

Some might say that modern theoretical physics seems to accommodate the apparently mutually exclusive randomness of chaos theory and determinism of quantum mechanics in a both/and combination of theories. But Professor Jean Bricmont of the University for Theoretical Physics in Belgium has written, "Not only is a refutation of determinism essentially impossible, but not the slightest argument in favor of that idea is to be found in modern physics, whether in chaos theory or in quantum mechanics." [Deism would say that God wound up the Universe and gave it a push, but then he left the rest up to the laws of physics and the free will of mankind to do as they do. But, Theism would say that God is the omnipotent and omniscient operator and destroyer of the Universe as well as its generator. Such mutually exclusive dichotomies must exist or they would not be. Which you choose is the one that you must believe.] We can assume we all are right on schedule—here and now—no matter how uncomfortable that happens to be, since none of us volunteered to be born into our circumstances either. So lighten up, and let go and let God in calm submission—because he will anyway. Mother Teresa, saint of Calcutta mused, "We must take what he gives and give what he takes."

It must be concluded with present understanding that God provides sheeple the illusion of free will to offset belief in absolute determinism, which he also provides. These must be necessary opposites. Therefore, both one who reads the Bible and finds free will and one who finds predestination must be doing the will of God the Almighty One, as there can be no other. And the clay has no power to tell the potter what kind of vessel to make. Apostle Paul said that, but he was quoting Jeremiah. (Jeremiah 18: 2-6, Romans 9:20-22) Think you can handle that?

5. THE FRAUD OF CHRISTIANITY

Christianity has driven sheeple to some of the greatest accomplishments in the arts, literature, science, and culture for more than 2,000 years. It also has helped many billions of sheeple to navigate great challenges as well as great joy. But, its leaders also have brought great suffering to unbelievers. For example, Charlemagne (768-814 CE) first Holy Roman Emperor, executed everyone that he conquered who disbelieved in Christ. This was about the same time that Muslims were killing anyone they conquered who did not convert to Islam. Go figure. Jesus claimed, "I am the way the truth and the light." (John 14:6) How then could anyone claim it is a fraud? Fraud is defined as an intentional deception. In conducting business it would be a felony offense, but in religion it seems to be the norm. About one third of all sheeple on Earth are given to believe that Jesus Christ is the Lord and Savior of mankind, but only for those who choose to believe in him, including his divine conception and his bodily resurrection. The other two thirds still don't get it. How could this be unless God willed it so?

Not only that, but the Apostle Paul, who claimed to be ordained by Christ himself, proclaimed the resurrection of dead Christians in the fifteenth chapter of his famous letter, 1 Corinthians, which provides basic dogma for Christian belief in an afterlife. Without the bodily resurrection of the Christ there is no hope for some afterlife among humans. ". . . if Christ has not been raised your faith is futile and you are still in your sins." (1 Corinthians 15:17KJV) The fact that so many others believe something different does not deter them from this "truth." Why; that is the mystery to be explored in this essay.

The earliest available copies of the New Testament are in Greek by unknown scribes and date to about 200 CE, although the originals probably were written in Hebrew. The four gospels are thought by scholars to have been written several decades after the death of Jesus, but no original manuscripts remain. The Roman Catholic Church held tight control of its fourth century Vulgate version of the Bible in Latin so that common illiterate sheeple could not read it for themselves. Long before Martin Luther, there was John Wycliff who opposed the Pope's intrusion into secular politics. A resident professor at Oxford, he studied history, law, philosophy, and religion receiving the Doctor of Divinity. He accomplished the first translation of the Bible into English around 1384, but that was before printing so the few issues made had to be copied by hand. The Church reacted by getting the Constitution of Oxford passed in 1408 which prohibited translations of the Bible into English. Then came William Tyndale who was a scholar educated at Cambridge and Oxford. Tyndale worked secretly with aid of some wealthy families and his Bible was first printed and distributed in Cologne, Germany by 1536. Unfortunately for him, Henry VIII had him arrested and executed for sedition when he returned to England. After he was buried, the Church dug up his body and burned it to assure he would not be resurrected at the Second Coming. Only two original copies of the Tyndale Bible remain in museums, although you can buy facsimiles.

King James I authorized an English translation of the Bible that was issued in 1611 with approval of the Church of England. That had been formed by King Henry VIII over rejection by the Roman Catholic Church of his desire to divorce Catherine of Aragon to marry Anne Boleyn in 1533. She became a rousing opponent of the Church and was an active player in the Reformation movement. However, the King had her beheaded under trumped up charges of adultery, incest, and treason. One of her religious advisors, Matthew Parker, would become an architect of the Church of England under her daughter Queen Elizabeth I. During this time there arose in Portugal, France, and Spain, the infamous Inquisition, persecution, torture, and execution by strangulation and burning, of religious dissidents that would not end until the mid 1800s. With this background one may understand why the First Amendment to the U.S. Constitution proclaims that "Congress shall make no law respecting an establishment of religion . . ." Nevertheless, in 1870 it proclaimed Christmas as a Federal employee holiday in Title 5 of the United States Code 5 U.S.C. (6103) [1]. No one has ever challenged its constitutionality. Go figure.

Several attempts have been made to modernize the archaic form of English in the King James Version with later translations. The latest new version of the Bible, the New International Version, (NIV) was issued in 2011 by the Committee on Bible Translation (CBT). It was formed in 1965 to create a modern English Bible translation from the oldest and most reliable biblical manuscripts available after initiatives started by Howard Long, an engineer working for General Electric in Seattle, WA. Its previous edition was published in 1984. Since then, the committee has continued to meet each year to monitor developments in biblical scholarship and English usage and to reflect these developments in periodic updates to the text. The committee "represents the very best in evangelical biblical scholarship. Its members—a self-perpetuating, independent body of 15—are drawn from various denominations and some of the finest academic institutions in the world." A complete list of the CBT members can be found together with brief biographical information at the Committee on Bible Translation's website, www.NIV-CBT.org.

In addition, new attempts at Bible interpretations are published by The Jesus Seminar. This is a group of about 150 biblical scholars and laymen founded in 1985 by Robert Funk and John Dominic Crossan under the auspices of the Westar Institute in Salem, OR. The Jesus Seminar uses votes with color codes to publish their consensus view of the historical truth of the deeds and sayings of Jesus of Nazareth. They published their results in three reports: The Five Gospels (1993), The Acts of Jesus (1998), and The Gospel of Jesus (1999). They also conduct a series of lectures and workshops in various U.S. cities. The Seminar's reconstruction of the historical Jesus portrays him as an itinerant Jewish sage and faith healer who preached a gospel of liberation from religious injustice in startling parables and aphorisms. [Its videos are published on YouTube.]

Consider the dogma that Christian churches all depend upon to recruit sheeple and keep the members they have deluded paying into their treasuries. Fundamentalist Christians say all mankind is declared to be born in the state of sinfulness, i.e., rebellion against God, that dooms them all to eternal punishment after death in a state of burning torment called Hell where there will be incessant weeping and gnashing of teeth. It says so right there in the Bible at six different places in the book of Matthew. [The origin of "God" may predate the Bible by more than a thousand years. Ancient Hinduism included a monotheist belief in one who could be called Generator, Operator, and Destroyer. (GOD)] All human suffering was caused by the original sin of Adam who disobeyed God in the Garden of Eden, according to Apostle Paul. "For just as through the disobedience of the one man the many were made sinners, so also through the obedience of the one man the many will be made righteous." (Romans 5:18-19, 1 Corinthians 15: 20-22). Jesus declared, "Fear him who after killing the body has the power to throw you into hell." (Luke 12:5)

This state of affairs occurred because God created all things as good and he gave the first man and woman free will to disobey him, which they naturally did. All the troubles and suffering they experience during life on Earth and for eternity to come is the result of the sin of disobedience by the original man, Adam, that is inherited by everyone born of a woman for all generations for all time, except for Jesus who was conceived without the seed of a man and possibly his virgin mother also.

However, and here is the good part, God so loved the world that he gave his only begotten son to be born of a virgin and sacrificed through crucifixion upon a Roman cross so that whoever believes on him will not perish but will have everlasting life. (John 3:16) To prove he was the Son of God, [or even God himself as some scholars claim] the man Jesus rose from the dead and showed himself to some 500 witnesses, but not the Roman or Jewish leaders, after which he was lifted into heaven. Now he sits at the right hand of God the Father waiting for the designated time to return to Earth and take all his followers into heaven to be with him for all eternity, after which there is complete destruction of the planet and everyone who disbelieves, and a new one is created in its place. "After the Lord Jesus had spoken to them he was taken up into heaven and sat at the right hand of God." (Mark 16:19) "For the trumpet will sound, the dead will be raised imperishable and we shall all be changed." (1 Corinthians 15:52) "But in keeping with his promise we are looking forward to a new heaven and a new earth . . ." (2 Peter 3:13, Revelation 21:1)

This is what children are taught in Christian Sunday school all over the world: they are born as sinners without any free will condemned to suffer eternity in Hell; God sent his son into the world to suffer for them and to redeem them from consequences of their sin, and exercising free will to believe in Him will turn their lives around and assure they will enjoy eternal life in the utopia of Heaven with him forever and ever if not health, wealth, and happiness on some new Earth as well. With no alternatives, it is understandable that so many of them feel trapped into making a "profession of faith," and take membership in local churches with their families, sometimes at a very young age.

Further, this son of God called Jesus Christ selected twelve apostles to whom he gave the power to save other sinners by going about the world where they lived telling everyone the good news. Note that none of them were volunteers. However, most of them ran away after he was crucified and we hear little more from them. So, he also selected one named Saul of Tarsus, a persecutor of Christians, by a schizophrenic encounter on the road to Damascus and renamed him Paul as the thirteenth apostle to organize and instruct all the churches among Greeks throughout the Middle East to get them started. "This man is my chosen instrument to proclaim my name to the Gentiles and their kings and the people of Israel. I will show him how much he must suffer for my name." (Acts 9: 15-16). Note that Paul was not called to pleasure but to suffering for his allegiance to Jesus. Interesting, isn't it, that a thirteenth apostle was allegedly called by Christ to do that which the original twelve could not do without him. (Acts 9: 3-20) In fact to this day Jews do not officially accept Jesus as the promised Messiah for whom they still wait.

In any event, no one needs to feel abandoned and condemned to Hell anymore. If they just believe that Jesus came to save them from their sins, they can be resurrected sometime and all go to heaven and live with him for eternity, presumably in health, wealth, and happiness. Thus was born the religion called Christianity. Isn't that beautiful? This scenario is repeated over and over again to children in Sunday school classes and is preached from the pulpits of churches all over the world ad nauseam. Countless millions of sheeple believe this story as it is written in their holy book, called the Bible, and God is so good that he just cannot lie. (Titus 1: 2) Of course, if he cannot lie then God would not be omnipotent, would he. Never mind that what happens after we die is never clearly described, except for having a place prepared for us in some "house of many mansions," (John 14:2) and that we should fear him who "after your body has been killed has authority to throw you into hell," (Luke 12:5) and not even Pope Benedict XVI [aka Joseph Cardinal Ratzinger] could provide any definite assurance in his <u>Eschatology, Death and Eternal Life</u>, (1988). Strange that he would use a whole book to say (paraphrased), [I don't know what happens after we die, and I don't think anyone else knows either. The Bible certainly is not clear about it so we will just have to wait until we die to find out since nobody has ever come back to tell us, Jesus notwithstanding. The creation is a work in process and the end is beyond human imagination. It is not just that we don't know what comes after death, but that we cannot know.] Well, if not exactly reassuring at least he was being intellectually honest.

In spite of this admitted indefinite uncertainty about the afterlife, the Catholic Catechism (1023) declares, "By virtue of our apostolic authority, we define the following: According to the general disposition of God, the souls of all the saints and other faithful who died after receiving Christ's holy Baptism (provided they were not in need of purification when they died, or, if they then did need or will need some purification, when they have been purified after death,) already before they take up their bodies again and before the general judgment—and this since the Ascension of our Lord and Savior Jesus Christ into heaven—have been, are and will be in heaven, in the heavenly Kingdom and celestial paradise with Christ . . ." But, then it adds, "The mystery of blessed communion with God and all who are in Christ is beyond all understanding and description." (1027) In addition, the Church claims souls of those in need of additional purification will suffer in temporary housing until they earn their entry into heaven or it is earned for them by loved ones on Earth. "All who die in God's grace and friendship, but still imperfectly purified, are indeed assured of their eternal salvation but after death they undergo purification so as to achieve the necessary holiness to enter the joy of heaven. The Church gives the name Purgatory to this final purification of the elect . . . Immediately after death the souls of those that die in a state of mortal sin descend into the punishments of hell . . . eternal fire." (1030-31, 1035) But this still is not the end. At the second and final return of Christ and the final judgment, ". . . he will place the sheep at the right hand and the goats at the left and they will go away into eternal punishment, but the righteous into eternal life . . . and the Universe itself will be renewed." (1038, 1042)

There is always an opposing view. Retired Episcopal Bishop John Spong has said, "Nobody knows what the afterlife is all about; nobody even knows if there is one. All of these images of bliss and punishment, heaven and hell are not about the afterlife at all. They're about controlling human behavior with fear and guilt and reward on the Earth . . . If our faith is to do anything for us, it is to give us the courage to embrace the anxieties of life and to live with integrity in the midst of those anxieties." Can you believe that?

End of story . . . beginning of fraud. Conveniently overlooked by theologians who would make everyone into sinners who feel threatened and condemned unless they accept church dogma is the fact that the Bible does not claim the sin of disobedience by Adam and Eve in the creation account of Genesis was passed on to their descendents for all generations by God. Go look it up. It is not there. In contrast there are other scriptures that say the opposite. The Bible plainly states that each person will be held responsible for his own sins and those only. "The child will not share the guilt of the parent, nor will the parent share the guilt of the child. The righteousness of the righteous will be credited to them and the wickedness of the wicked will be charged to them." (Ezekiel 18:19-20) and when Jesus healed a man blind since birth, he explained, "Neither this man nor his parents sinned, but this happened so the works of God might be shown in him." (John 9:3.) These counter scriptures never show up in Sunday school classes. Nevertheless, it does appear that some of us reap what we do not sow, whether it is for ill or good. Jesus said so. Where is the justice in that? (Matthew 25:24, Luke 19: 21-22, John 4:36-38) Are these necessary opposites, or what? Somewhere between the God of the Old Testament and that of the New Testament, something obviously changed during the intervening four hundred years of silence. But, nothing much has changed since then, unfortunately. Fundamental theologians claim the Bible is the infallible Word of God, so let's assume that it is and look through it for some enlightenment about the need for a "savior," because it is the primary Christian dogma that begs some resolution for thinking sheeple.

Here is the rest of the story. The word "savior" appears 56 times in the Bible, 32 of them in the Old Testament where the word always refers to God who is saving the Jews from their sufferings on Earth. "I will make your oppressors eat their own flesh; they will be drunk on their own blood as with wine. Then all mankind will know that I, the Lord, am your savior, your redeemer, the mighty one of Jacob." (Isaiah 49:26) "I am the Lord your God who brought you out of Egypt. You shall acknowledge no God but me, no savior except me." (Hosea 13:4) There is not a single Old Testament use of the word "savior" that refers to redemption of sin or promise of eternal life. The whole Christian dogma that claims humankind are all born in sin and condemned to eternal suffering in Hell if they do not accept the sacrifice of Jesus Christ on the cross and believe in his resurrection as Lord and savior is based upon scriptures in the New Testament. The words attributed to Apostle Paul and thought by scholars to precede the Gospels proclaim a link between God the savior and Jesus Christ the savior: ". . . when the kindness and love of God our Savior appeared, he saved us, not because of righteous things we had done, but because of his mercy. He saved us through the washing of rebirth and renewal by the Holy Spirit, whom he poured out on us generously through Jesus Christ our Savior, so that, having been justified by his grace, we might become heirs having the hope of eternal life." (Titus 3:4-7) Notice the promise is one of "hope" and not assurance. Nowhere does Jesus refer to himself as the "savior," although he did claim a kingdom not of this world, and only the writers Paul and Luke seem to do so. Luke does so only once. (Luke 2:11) Nowhere does Jesus claim he was God but rather always refers to God the Father in the second person. So, theologians had to make Jesus into God come to Earth because that is the only way he could be called savior. So we must look elsewhere.

Beginning with the account of creation in the book of Genesis, we find that it was God himself, not Adam, who created the tree of knowledge of good and evil and put it in the garden called Eden because he created everything that was made . . . and it all was good. That would have to include predators and prey, hurricanes, volcanoes, earthquakes, diseases and such. Then he created man and woman with free will and told them to enjoy foods of the garden but to avoid eating the fruit of that particular tree because they would surely die. Nowhere does God tell mankind they can eat animals for food. Along comes the tempter in form of a serpent, one who spoke the same language and convinced Eve, not Adam, to take the first bite because God lied and they would not surely die. So Eve was the first to sin and then she convinced Adam to take a bite. Sin first came into the world by the woman, not the man. So the blame by Apostle Paul upon Adam is not based in fact. Immediately, things changed. When God discovered they did it, by noting they made themselves some clothing because they were immediately ashamed of being naked, he punished them.

First they were expelled from the garden and then they were made to live like human beings. Adam had to farm the soil for food and Eve was made to bear children in pain and suffering from wanting to be a mother. The serpent was made to crawl upon the ground and to be an enemy to the man and woman. No mention of heaven or hell. That is it. No eternal punishment and no mention of passing the sins of these two on to all their descendents who will need a savior in order to avoid the eternal flames of Hell. In fact, it says right there in the Bible that Adam lived more than 900 years, even though mankind was given only 120 years to live. (Genesis 6:3) Even after their son Cain killed their son Abel, because he was jealous when God preferred Abel's animal sacrifice to the farm produce of Cain, still no eternal punishment. In fact, Cain was protected from assault and made the "father of cities." (Genesis 4:15-17) Go ahead, read it for yourself. How, then, to explain all the natural disasters, diseases, wars, crime and pestilence experienced by human beings if they did not bring it upon themselves? If this bothers you, welcome to the thinking part of the human race.

Now, about the part where man caused himself all of his suffering through his disobedience—That is NOT what the Bible says . . . nowhere does it say that, except for the rant by Apostle Paul, who claims that Jesus told him what to say after he was converted from Saul to Paul on the road to Damascus during the schizophrenic encounter with a voice from a blinding light. (Acts 9: 1-15) In fact, the Bible says several times and illustrates over and over that it is God who causes all the troubles for mankind and that often capriciously and maliciously for no reason at all, except possibly his own will.

When President Bill Clinton was asked why he had that affair with Monica he replied, "Because I could." So, it seems, does God. Consider the plight of Apostle Paul as follows: "So I find this law at work: When I want to do good, evil is right there with me. For in my inner being I delight in God's law; but I see another law at work in the members of my body, waging war against the law of my mind and making me a prisoner of the law of sin at work within my members. [I wonder who created that law of sin; is there more than one Creator?] What a wretched man I am! Who will rescue me from this body of death? Thanks be to God through Jesus Christ our Lord! So then, I myself in my mind am a slave to God's law, but in the sinful nature a slave to the law of sin." (Romans 7:21:25) "I have been crucified with Christ and I no longer live, but Christ lives in me." (Galatians 2:20) If he was controlled by Christ how come he still sinned? . . . unless God willed that also . . . he never said the Devil made him do it. Of course one can always take the opposite view of free will as that is one of the Principles of Theofatalism™ . . . for every idea there is an opposite one . . . but that too is the will of God . . . as in physics . . . for every action there is an equal and opposite reaction. Consider the difference between assuming that Jesus Christ paid the price for all our willful sins and assuming that God makes us do whatever we do. Get it?

Check this out. Young David was a perfectly loyal subject to Saul the king of Israel, but the Bible says that an "evil spirit from God" intervened several times to make the king hate David for no reason whatever. (1 Samuel 18: 10, 19:9) God admits to the prophet Isaiah that he is the culprit whenever anything goes wrong. "I make peace and create evil. I the Lord do all these things." (Isaiah 45:7) The prophet Amos got the same idea. "When a disaster comes to a city, has not the Lord caused it?" (Amos 3:6) Muslims also got the same instruction. The Koran says the same thing to Muslims; "No calamity comes, no affliction occurs, except by the decision and preordainment of Allah." (64.11) This would have to include the acts of man as well as the acts of nature. Obviously, God also must create disease and insanity. Why is not for us to know . . . yet.

How much more evidence do you need? Here is more. Read the lament of Job, the most righteous man on Earth, for his unjust treatment by God, "He crushes me with a tempest, and multiplies my wounds without cause; he will not let me get my breath, but fills me with bitterness though I am innocent, my own mouth would condemn me; though I am blameless he would prove me perverse . . . If I wash myself with soap and cleanse my hands with lye, yet he wilt plunge me into a pit, and my own clothes will abhor me . . . I loathe my life. It is all one; therefore I say, he destroys both the blameless and the wicked. When disaster brings sudden death he mocks at the calamity of the innocent." (Job 9) Nice God, huh.

Now, what about the notion that God visits punishment upon the sons for the sins of their fathers . . . for all time? Not so, says the Bible. To repeat; when Jesus healed a man blind since birth and his disciples asked him whose sin was it, his own or his father's, Jesus replied, "Neither this man nor his parents sinned, but this happened so the work of God could be displayed in his life." (John 9:3) Sooo, it appears that God made the man born blind so that Jesus could heal him and appear to be some kind of miracle worker. God works in mysterious ways.

The Old Testament also proclaims again, "Yet you ask, Why does the son not share the guilt of his father? Since the son has done what is just and right and has been careful to keep all my decrees, he will surely live. The one who sins is the one who will die. The child will not share the guilt of the parent, nor will the parent share the guilt of the child. The righteousness of the righteous will be credited to them, and the wickedness of the wicked will be charged against them." (Ezekiel 18:19-20) The law of Moses also stated, "Fathers shall not be put to death for their children, nor children put to death for their fathers; each is to die for his own sin." (Deuteronomy 24:16)

Also, Jesus proclaimed that the Kingdom of Heaven belonged to such as little children so they cannot be born as sinners in order to make this work. (Luke 18:26) Indeed, the Church assumes children are innocent until the age of reason, about the age of twelve. Moreover, if everyone is born a sinner in need of a savior, where is the free will? So, it would appear that the foundation of Christianity is either false or is unsubstantiated by scripture. This position was supported by Pelagianism in the fifth century, but it was successfully defeated by Augustine and the Councils of Carthage in 418 CE and Ephesus in 431 CE.

So, let's get real. The Bible obviously contradicts itself about the very basic dogma of the Church. Little wonder that the Roman Catholic Church wanted to keep sheeple illiterate so they could not read it for themselves. Its claims for original sin and the need of a savior are not supported in its own scriptures. The inconsistency is there for anyone with eyes to see to plainly read. How then can we explain why a couple billion sheeple cannot see it? Perhaps they are not meant to. Although some scriptures, including the famous John 3:16, imply that salvation through belief in Jesus as the Son of God is available to anyone with free will to choose, it does not appear that everyone has that power unless they are given it by the Father. "No one can come to me unless the Father who sent me draws them." (John 6:44) ". . . no one can come to me unless the Father enables them." (John 6:65) The Bible also says that Jesus taught his disciples in encoded parables so that the sinners "may not understand lest they should be converted and their sins be forgiven them . . . The knowledge of the secrets of the kingdom of heaven has been given to you, [disciples] but not to them." (Mark 4:12, Matthew 13:11) "For this reason [the Jews] could not believe, because, as Isaiah says elsewhere: He has blinded their eyes and deadened their hearts, so they can neither see with their eyes, nor understand with their hearts, nor turn and I would heal them." John 12: 39-40) King Solomon thought the same thing; "God has made everything fitting in its season; However, He has put obscurity in their heart so that men may NOT find out his work, that which God does."(Ecclesiastes 3:11).

The Apostle Peter seems to restate the same idea, "The stone the builders rejected has become the capstone and a stone that causes men to stumble and a rock that makes them fall. They stumble because they disobey the message, which is also what they were destined for." (1 Peter 2:7-8) It appears that even Jesus could not change the destiny of the Jews who were all but destroyed in the uprising of 69-74 CE that included destruction of their temple and death of estimated one million by the Romans under Titus, son of Emperor Vepasian and subsequent dispersal that lasted until Israel was reconstructed by the United Nations in 1947. Upon his victory, Titus declared, "There is no merit in vanquishing a people forsaken by their own God." Thus ended the influence of Jesus among the Jews and the beginning of his influence among the Gentiles. If Jesus was the Jewish Messiah and son of God, perhaps even God himself, then why did his own not obey his commandments? Free will or God's will? He raged at the hypocrisy among the Jews and proclaimed, "Snakes . . . vipers . . . how will you escape being condemned to hell? . . . For I did not speak of my own accord, but the Father who sent me commanded me what to say and how to say it." (Matthew 23:23, John 12:49) What about all those cathedrals and churches and tax-exempt real estate, when he plainly commanded not to lay up treasures on Earth but rather treasures in Heaven? (Matthew 6:19)

The only plausible explanation for this fraudulent form of Christianity is that the God of the Universe wants it that way. Get it? This could be one of the missing teachings of Jesus that might clarify it for us. "Jesus did many other things as well and I suppose that if they were all written down the whole world would not have room for all that would be written." (John 21:25) This notion was the essence of Gnostic thought in the first century. It seems that they assumed there were two worlds, this temporary sensory one and the real eternal spiritual one. For Gnostics, man's relation to God was not through his son but by direct revelation and by direct contact as demonstrated by Jesus. ". . . anyone who has faith in me will do what I have been doing . . . he will do even greater things . . ." (John 5:20) Islam proclaims that God had no son and does not need a holy spirit or a concubine to work his will directly among mankind. This form of relationship with God was demonstrated by Jesus in the book of John, possibly the only gospel with Gnostic influence. "The kingdom of heaven is within you." He both spoke directly to the Father and declared that they were one and the same. "If you have seen me you have seen the Father." Although not admitting to Pontius Pilate at his inquisition that he was king of the Jews, he proclaimed to those who could understand, "My kingdom is not of this world." (John 18:36) [Actually, this conversation as recorded probably is fiction because Pilate spoke classical Latin and Jesus spoke peasant Aramaic and maybe Hebrew, so a translator would be needed.]

So why is there so much confusion about Christ in Christianity? Perhaps it was meant to be. Swiss psychiatrist C. G. Jung observed, "In all chaos there is a cosmos, in all disorder a secret order . . . I could not say I believe—I know! I have had the experience of being gripped by something that is stronger than myself, something that people call God." Isn't that the goal that everyone seeks, but so very few find? Jesus included a brief explanation for his relationship with the Father by invoking the Holy Spirit as a counselor who would convict sheeple of their sins after he was gone, leaving them with a subconscious desire to be forgiven. "If you love me, keep my commands.

And I will ask the Father, and he will give you another advocate to help you and be with you forever the Spirit of truth." (John 14-15-16) This notion of self revelation for everyone could not be tolerated by the Roman priests of the Catholic Church after the third century so they destroyed all the Gnostic writings, possibly overlooking the Gnostic teachings in the book of John.

Only recently have some scraps and pieces of other Gnostic gospels been found to describe their view of the scriptures. These are contained principally in the Nag Hammadi texts found in Egypt in 1945. It is found also in the dogma of Islam, which proclaims God is One and only One without the need for a son or any other form including the Holy Spirit that comprises the dogma of a Trinity. That, too, is not found in the Bible but was added later in Church dogma. Jesus always spoke of them as three separately, not as one, and he warned that blasphemy against the Spirit would never be forgiven. (Matthew 12:31)

The rediscovered Gnostic scriptures are so important because they reveal that many early Christians believed Christ's intent was different from what became Christianity. The Orthodox Roman Catholic Church literally defined Christianity politically for their time and it still persists in that form to this day. Christ did not preach a set of such beliefs. His intent was not to establish an all-celibate-male led Church that could dictate rules for faith and morality but rather to open the full relationship with God for all sheeple. He promised, ". . . the counselor, the holy spirit whom the Father will send in my name will teach you all things . . ." (John 14:26) And he proclaimed, "The spirit gives life, the flesh counts for nothing." (John 6:63) His intent was not to establish Christianity as a political power to condemn others or to become a state religion run by a hierarchy of priests, bishops and cardinals. But that is exactly what happened so we must live with the consequences. Perhaps the real God saved us from total fraud by including the book of John in the gospels and preserving a few of the Gnostic writings for us to find when the time was right. Maybe if we consider them absent the writings of the other gospels and the schizophrenic babble of Apostle Paul, we shall be closer to the truth, insofar as sheeple could absorb it in the first century.

In her book, The Gnostic Gospels, (1979) Princeton religion scholar, Elaine Pagels suggested that Christianity could have developed quite differently if Gnostic texts had become part of the Christian canon. Gnosticism celebrates God as both Mother and Father, shows a very human relationship between Jesus and Mary Magdalene. It also suggests the Resurrection is better understood symbolically than literally, and it speaks to self-knowledge as the route to union with God. Pagels argues that Christian orthodoxy grew out of the Roman political considerations of the day three hundred years after Jesus died, serving to legitimize and consolidate early Church leadership while excluding any and all heresies. Roman rule by the sword was replaced with rule by the Word. Her contrast of the developing Roman orthodoxy with Gnostic teachings presents an intriguing option to a world faith as it might have become. The role of Mother/God is missing from the Father/male dominance of Christianity and would more likely be present to the Gnostics that were expelled as heretics by the early church. One can imagine Jesus relying upon his mother and Mary Magdalene for much comfort and encouragement . . . as Adam must have relied upon Eve. Unfortunately, the final truth may never be known for sure. All we can do is look around at the creation and contemplate what the Creator of it all must be like, and we must say with Job, "I am unworthy—how can I reply to you? I put my hand over my mouth. I spoke once, but I have no answer—twice, but I will say no more." (Job 40:3-5).

It is truly amazing that so many Christians can claim absolute confidence in things that are unknowable, like what did Jesus actually teach. Although he did not actually claim to save the entire planet, he did declare that only those who are selected will be allowed to enter the new age of heaven and earth. And recall the claim that each person will have to answer for his/her own life on this one. "Whosoever therefore shall confess me before men, him will I confess also before my Father which is in heaven. But whosoever shall deny me before men, him will I also deny before my Father which is in heaven." (Matthew 10:32-34, Luke 12: 4-5) However, we are told also that the favored Apostle, Peter was made to deny Christ three times before dawn, apparently against his own will. Does this mean the favored Apostle was denied before God? Does it also mean that none of us is really off the hook? The most we can conclude is that, with Apostle Paul, we are the clay and God is the potter, and he makes whatever he wants to with us. (Jeremiah 18: 2-6, Romans 9:21) Shakespeare wrote that the world is a stage and men and women are the actors. But he never said who the playwright was.

Thus some are Christians, some are Muslims, some are Hindus, some are Buddhists, some are Democrats, some are Republicans, some are saints and some are criminals, some are rich and some are poor, some are healthy, wealthy, and happy and some are not, etc. Perhaps the Apostle Paul was right in that work of a potter and us being the clay after all. And God made atheists, too. If there is a God the Almighty One, how could anything that is be otherwise? That would have to include the fraud of Christianity come to think of it. All in God's will of course . . . AIGWOC. Feel good inside no matter what happens outside. And, welcome to the virtual Church of Theofatalism™, where everyone is a member and no one can resign or be expelled. Read the full story in Voices of Sedona, available online at www.amazon.com, www.iUniverse.com and Barnes & Noble book stores.

6. SANTA CLAUS AND OTHER NECESSARY MYTHS

Santa Claus seems to be very important to some sheeple. News from the U.K, says that a grade school teacher in London was sacked for telling kids in third grade that Santa was a myth believed only by the younger kids. Some angry parents said they should be the ones to say when their kids discovered the truth about the myth. They could be the same ones who insist on telling kids the Stork brings babies and Jesus loves them. Do a title search for books about Santa Claus on amazon.com and you get 51,544 hits, all of them written by adults. If you found a book about Santa written by a four-year old child who had seen Santa, sat on his lap, and heard him whisper secrets, and then found all the requested presents under the tree on Christmas morning, the story would no doubt be written quite differently. That is the way it is about the greatest myth of all, written by the children of God, called by many the Holy Bible. It goes like this. Once upon a time about 6,000 years ago God created the heavens and the Earth and all the creatures therein.

[When you dig behind church propaganda, the message appears to be different from the one you probably have been taught in Sunday school. If you take it literally, as many sheeple do, creation of Earth began at nightfall the evening before Sunday, October 23, 4,004 BCE according to some conservative Bible scholars based upon assumptions published in 1654 by Anglican Archbishop James Ussher (1581-1656) of Armagh, now in Ireland. Of course, ever since Charles Darwin published <u>On the Origin of Species</u> in 1859, there have been scientists who think evidence exists for evolution of the Earth that is much older, like maybe 4.54 billion years.]

But, God was lonely so he created a man in his own image and likeness so he could have some company. Realizing that the man was lonely too, he created a woman for him. Also he gave them a perfect, beautiful garden to tend and to enjoy. In that garden he planted two trees he would later come to regret. One was the tree of life and the other was the tree of knowledge of good and evil. You see, God also created good and evil along with free will even though he knew what the outcome would be, dumb as that may seem.

Naturally, the man and woman named Adam and Eve soon were tempted into sampling fruit from the tree of good and evil by a talking serpent, [Some say the Devil made them do it, but God must have created the Devil because he created everything.] and they realized immediately they were naked, which made them feel ashamed for some reason known only to God. For their disobedience, God expelled them from the garden before they could also eat of the tree of life and never die and so become like God. Adam and Eve had two sons named Cain and Abel, although they never got married. Cain was a farmer and Abel was a hunter. God preferred the gifts from Abel to those of Cain, for some unexplained reason, so the latter killed the former in a fit of jealousy. But he was not condemned to hell and became the father of cities. (Genesis 4:15-17) Don't ask where the mother of cities came from.

God also created genes so that all of the heirs of Adam and Eve would inherit the same traits as God, and so mankind became both good and evil. That was the end of free will because everyone born after that carried the sin of their original ancestors along with their guilt and remorse, although they were made to assume that it was all their own fault. After much evil was done by his creation, God regretted his creation of mankind, and he tried a couple fixes that did not work. First, he brought a flood that killed every living thing except for one family of each species that he personally selected to survive in a gigantic boat, because they were mostly good. But, their evil genes prevailed once more and brought much suffering to the whole of creation still again. Honest, I am not making this up.

Then God selected a certain nomadic tribe of one named Abraham for special blessings extending to all his heritage, thinking that would make them behave according to his orders. Abraham became Abram who had Isaac who had Jacob who was converted to Israel, the father of twelve sons that eventually led to the "chosen people." But, having evil genes that God created, they persisted in worshipping other Gods, which made God furious with jealousy, and he created enemies to shed their blood all over the world . . . several times. Still, there was no repentance or remorse among his creation anywhere in the world.

So God, being loving and all, selected a young woman named Mary and sent his son into the world through her by another miracle of creation to be crucified as a blood sacrifice to pay for the sins of mankind that he created. He also promised that anyone who accepted the sacrifice of his son would be saved from punishment for their sins and would enjoy everlasting life with them all in heaven, a place of eternal peace and joy with no suffering, or was that just the ones that he pre selected from before time began. No one knows. But, this happens only after things on Earth must get so bad that he destroys the whole thing in one great conflagration and recreates a new heaven and a new Earth. So the ones who believed this story all lived happily ever after, but the ones who did not were consigned by God to eternal life in hell, which is a burning pit that never goes out.

Still, evil prevailed because mankind could not help themselves. [Some say the Devil, the one God must have created, made them do it.] So, God promised to send his son back sometime again to finally kill all the evil genes in one last and final battle, leaving only the good ones to live forever with him. The ones who believe in him will be saved and those who don't get the message or refuse it will burn in hell for all eternity. [Compare John 3:16 with this; Jesus taught in mystical parables so that the Jews "may not understand lest they should be converted and their sins be forgiven them." (Mark 4:12)] So, it seems that some sheeple God created are intentionally left out of the plan. All this is true because it says so in the Bible, which is the Word of God. And God cannot lie. (Titus 1:2) But, then if God cannot lie, he really would not be God would he? After all, God must be the Creator of lies too because he created everything. This challenge is akin to the debate over whether or not God could create both an immovable object and an irresistible force like a rock too big for him to move. They would seem to be mutually exclusive, thus limiting the power of God. It appears that even God must make choices and, thus, is not omnipotent. And by giving mankind the power to accept or to reject his only son there arises a power greater than his, does it not? Such debates go on and on.

In the process of all this confusion, there arose the myth of Santa Claus to help children realize what God really is like. So good and so kind to obedient little children. Read on. St. Nicholas, fourth-century Bishop of Myra in Asia Minor, has often been represented in paintings, book illustrations, sculpture, mosaics, stained glass, and other forms of art. Born in Patara, Lycia (Turkey), to Christian parents during the late third century, young Nicholas dedicated his life to God and became a priest. Images of St. Nicholas in art often include references to the many legends of his charitable and miraculous acts. When young Nicholas inherited a fortune from his wealthy parents, he decided to share his inheritance with the poor. As the Bishop of Myra, Nicholas was among many Christians persecuted by the Roman Emperor Diocletian during the early fourth century. Fast forward. In the early 1800s, following the American Revolution, St. Nicholas was proclaimed the patron saint of New York City and the newly formed New York Historical Society. His popularity grew even greater with the publication in 1809 of Washington Irving's "Knickerbocker's History of New York," a fictitious account that featured a jolly elf-like St. Nicholas character who suggested a pipe-smoking Dutch citizen of New Amsterdam.

Irving's imaginative "history" launched several new St. Nicholas legends, including the still popular story about St. Nicholas coming down chimneys to bring gifts to good children on Christmas Eve. In 1823 the American image of St. Nicholas gained further popularity with the publication of the poem, "A Visit from St. Nicholas," (or "The Night Before Christmas") attributed to Clement Clark Moore. The new St. Nicholas image was permanently established with drawings by 19th-century political cartoonist and illustrator Thomas Nast (1840-1902) that appeared in "Harper's Weekly" and other publications beginning in 1862 and throughout the late 1800s and with paintings by Haddon Sundblom (1899-1976) for Coca-Cola advertisements in the 1900s. Through their widely published illustrations, the new image of St. Nicholas became better known as Santa Claus, a phonetic derivation of the German Sankt Niklaus and Dutch Sinterklaas. Today the American image of Santa Claus may no longer resemble that of St. Nicholas, Bishop of Myra.

There is another side to the myth you may not know . . . because there is always an opposite. You could look this up. According to mythical history, Saint Nick came from Old Nick. Old Nick was the devil in Geoffrey Chaucer's twenty-eight "Canterbury Tales" from England (1342-1400). If you saw "Beowulf" the movie, it was taken from Chaucer's work. There was a superstition at the time that if you didn't close up your house and windows at night Old Nick, who was the Devil, would get in. He could also get in through the chimney in the winter so you had to light a fire there to keep him out. Somehow the myth evolved into St. Nick being the good guy who brings presents to good kids and coal to bad kids. From there, he evolved into St. Nicholas (duh!) and was well known for leaving gifts of bread, etc. to poorer sheeple on their doorsteps at night. Santa Claus also may be an English bastardization of the Dutch SinterKlass. SinterKlass is the Dutch bastardization of Saint Nicholas as narrated above. Old Nick is a reference to the biblical name Nicodemus, not Nicholas. Santa [which is Spanish for Saint] has not traditionally always worn a red suit; that was an American flourish, sometimes he wears red, sometimes he wears green, and sometimes he wears black. Who knows, maybe he sometimes wears pink and hangs out at gay pride parades. Saint or devil, take your pick.

The wonder of Christmas in western nations is how parents take their kids to sit on the obese geezer's lap and tell him what they want. Parents know where the gifts actually come from, so why does generation after generation insist on repeating this annual fictitious ritual? Common sense proves it is impossible for the chubby guy in red to circumnavigate the Earth with a sleigh driven by eight miniature reindeer between dusk and dawn. Someone calculated Santa would have to make 822 stops per second, travel more than 3,000 times faster than the speed of sound, and drive a sleigh with 333,333 tons capacity. And that does not include the trips to China to pick up the presents at the factories. But, what if your house does not have a chimney or your parents have no money?

Sometime between infancy and puberty most kids outgrow belief in Santa with little or no psychological damage. Or do they? Perhaps when children discover that Santa takes a smoke break and the beard is false they just substitute some other fantasy myth to replace the one that is debunked. Sheeple who would not dare kneel before Santa to pray for health, wealth, and happiness will often do so at the front alter of a church, even if they are otherwise highly educated. The image of God, Jesus, the Virgin Mother, or the saints easily replace the inadequate and disappointing parents and society that do not fulfill desires nearly so well as the imaginary promise of myth does. If there is no substitute myth for Santa then anxiety of indefinite uncertainty prevails, and the human ego runs into the end of its own creation. It seems that believing in myths is a necessary function of Homo sapiens to avoid the anxiety of uncertainty about things we cannot yet explain. Saint Nicholas is dead, long live Santa Claus. God loves you.

America's foremost mythologist, Joseph Campbell, (1904-1987) observed that, "mythology is a control system, on the one hand framing its community in accord with an intuited order of nature and, on the other hand, by means of its symbolic rites, conducting individuals through the ineluctable psycho-physiological stages of transformation during a human lifetime." The power of myths is so great that we must will them to be true, otherwise they would be unbelievable. Campbell saw as few others, except possibly for C.G. Jung, that myths carry stories which serve to permit sheeple to live in their fantasies what would not serve them well in society. Myths also enable sheeple to tolerate the intolerable among relations with the dark and painful elements of themselves. Myths also connect the past with the present, providing a stable foundation for social changes like shifting sand under the tides. Long before recorded history and invention of printing, primitive tribes passed their heritage from generation to generation orally through the myths of their ancestors.

In other words, without myths Homo sapiens would lose their anchor on mental health and flounder in a vast sea of anxiety. For without myths what is left but indefinite uncertainty about everything? Belief in myths provides the needed foundation of psycho-security that is demanded for stable minds. To a query from eight-year old Virginia O'Hanlon who asked if Santa was real or not, Francis P. Church of the New York Sun wrote in his famous response of 1897, "Nobody sees Santa Claus, but that is no sign that there is no Santa Claus. The most real things in the world are those that neither children nor men can see. Did you ever see fairies dancing on the lawn? Of course not, but that's no proof that they are not there. Nobody can conceive or imagine all the wonders there are unseen and unseeable in the world . . . No Santa Claus! Thank God! He lives, and he lives forever. A thousand years from now, Virginia, nay ten times ten thousand years from now, he will continue to make glad the heart of childhood." But what comes after Santa Claus is exposed? And, where do myths first come from?

Kids must give up Santa as they grow older because it would be embarrassing for adults to go sit on Santa's lap, so they substitute God instead and go sit in church to pray to the saints . . . all in the will of God the Almighty One of course. It is as if adults returned to their elementary schools and Sunday school to sit once more in the childhood seats they have now outgrown. Once they learn all the Christmas toys they thought were made by Santa's elves at the North Pole actually come from China, a crisis of faith must be dealt with and going to church is a good solution. There is something of the child remaining in all adults that wishes for the comfort and security of myths in childhood before they became contaminated with the burdens of reality. Jesus said that unless anyone becomes as a child and is "born again" they cannot see the kingdom of heaven. (Matthew 18: 3, Mark 10:15, Luke 18: 15-16) But, this transition comes with much distress as sheeple become aware of the ubiquitous human suffering among Homo sapiens in the world made by God. Who would deny them this comfort of childhood trust if it helps them through the suffering and struggles of life?

For most sheeple religion is not a search for truth, but a search for security based upon faith, i.e. the hope for things unseen. Many sheeple still believe in faith-based myths that are 2,000 years old. Growth requires questioning assumptions about truth and the willingness to leave security behind in search of new knowledge without certainty. Although this is the domain of science, there seems be unconscious neurological blocks in the brain that prohibit this from happening when it comes to religion. Only when the neurons become unblocked can the mind proceed to new levels of investigation. So long as one is living inside a box, what is outside the box is unseen.

The first step to growth is bringing this process into consciousness where it can be digested and manifested by the search for reality. Next comes the need to get outside the box to see what is there, sort of like the astronauts who left planet Earth to see it as it really is from space. Now we must look elsewhere to find heaven because we know it is not above the firmament. A mind that still believes in Santa Claus is not ready for this process to begin. It will persist in its settlement on faith-based security even though it comes with a loss of freedom and the potential fruits of exploring the unknown. But, an exploratory mind proclaims security is not in the absence of danger, but in the presence of God no matter the danger. And its corollary posed by C.G. Jung, "whether called or not, God will be present." "Where can I go from your Spirit? Where can I flee from your presence? If I make my bed in the depths, you are there." (Psalm 139:7-8) The eternal debate seems to be whose God will it be?

Now we face a new resurgence of the conflict between the God/Allah of Islam and the God/Christ of Christianity. On the one hand are those who claim that God enabled mankind as co-creators with him with the full power to oppose and even destroy their divinity if they choose by willful disobedience. On the other are those who claim that if God is truly God, then nothing happens outside his will. One can find scriptures to support both positions, hence the principle of necessary opposites in Theofatalism™.

Indeed, there is the problem; the fruits of growth require just as much faith in their unknown possibility as the faith in security based upon generally accepted myths of God and such. Philosopher and pacifist, Bertrand Russell (1872-1970) wrote in <u>Marriage and Morals,</u> (1929) "The fact that an opinion has been widely held is no evidence whatever that it is not utterly absurd; indeed in view of the silliness of the majority of mankind, a widespread belief is more likely to be foolish than sensible." Russell had it right. The majority of humanity is just spiritually immature so we must not judge them too harshly. American-born English poet, T.S. Eliot (1888-1965) observed that "mankind cannot stand very much reality." Such sheeple are easy to fleece. What is the difference between a child who writes a letter to Santa expecting his wants to be met and a husband who prays to God that his beloved wife will be spared from cancer or a woman who prays for that awful lump in her breast to just go away? If the wish is fulfilled the belief is reinforced and testimonies are given about the power for faith healings in the affairs of Homo sapiens. Humankind seems to never outgrow the need for a hero/friend to bolster their courage when life threatens their existence, be it a doctor, pastor, or myth. But suppose no gifts appear under the tree and the wife dies an untimely death after a decade of suffering?

Fast forward to the thousands of young volunteer soldiers returning from war in Iraq with missing limbs . . . several missing limbs. Now include the families left only with a folded American flag and the sound of "taps" to remember their loved ones forever lost. Why were the many prayers no doubt offered up by family and friends in churches back home answered this way? Indeed, why do professionals who seemingly know better cause deaths and destruction, like the oil spill in the Gulf of Mexico, when they seemingly could be prevented? C. G. Jung believed that faith-based religious myths of all sorts have their necessary place in sustaining mental health when things make no sense. The myth of Christ is no less important to Christians than the myth of Allah is to Muslims or the myth of Santa is to children.

But, what do sheeple do when their religious mythology fails to explain reality and brings pain instead of comfort? [Consider the thousands made homeless in Haiti and Japan by the recent earthquakes and tsunamis that periodically wreck human lives, not to mention all those lost in such "acts of God."] When they realize their myths and rituals have no impact upon God the Almighty One, but are created by him/it, where do they turn for solace from the ensuing depression and apparent futility in life? Moreover, when they conclude that belief in free will merely is an illusion where is the solace of some alternative? Professional therapeutic counseling may be of little help, and the sermons in most churches keep repeating the Santa myth for adults because that is all they have.

That the role of spirituality in mental health has not been developed fully is a curious ambiguity in the field of psychiatry. The line between mystical enlightenment and religious psychosis is very wide and very gray. A few have called for a new integration as did Rabbi Joshua Liebman (1907-1948) in Peace of Mind, (1946) ". . . the time is coming when we have to bring our idea of God into harmony with the new realities of life . . . the mature God idea for our age must end the spiritual and cultural lag which separates our experience from our theological formulas . . . but a religion that emphasizes God's omnipotence will not satisfy the character of America that has made a virtue out of individual initiative and will find it increasingly difficult to submit their [notion of free] will to the idea of a dominant Father." So, many sheeple worship a God substitute instead of the real one.

Sometimes there is little difference between worshipping a modern rock music star, a NASCAR driver, some professional athlete, an actor or actress, even some politician, or a celebrity preacher or a mythical savior upon a cross or the statue of a saint. The psychology is the same, only the object is different. Unless a person seeks treatment because the voice of God is telling them to commit a crime or do harm to themselves, society tolerates enormous variety in religious practice as was noted by William James in his classic Varieties of Religious Experience (1902). There is no preemptive legal recourse for the mentally ill until after a crime is committed. There is no law against being crazy or stupid or making babies in that deplorable state. Adequate training is not provided by most graduate programs and internship sites to prepare professional mental health counselors to deal with these crises in religious issues.

According to Dr. David Lukoff, founder of the Spiritual Competency Resource Center, [www.spiritualcompetency.com] surveys conducted in the

United States consistently show a "religiosity gap" between mental patients who report themselves to be more highly religious and to attend church more frequently than mental health professionals. Lukoff was instrumental in amending the psychiatric diagnostic manual, DSM-IV (1994) to include the diagnosis of "Religious or Spiritual Problem," defined as follows: V62.89: "This category can be used when the focus of clinical attention is a religious or spiritual problem. Examples include distressing experiences that involve loss or questioning of faith, problems associated with conversion to a new faith, or questioning of other spiritual values which may not necessarily be related to an organized church or religious institution."

Lukoff has associated the symptoms of this diagnosis with the Hindu concept of "Kundalini rising" or release of psychic energy from the subconscious from meditation and yoga practice that may produce physical symptoms misdiagnosed in western psychiatry. His treatment modality is available for training of professionals who are interested in treating this diagnosis for clients. Treatment for this diagnosis rarely is covered by insurance, so professionals have rarely ever used it in practice hence there is no standard treatment modality in place. Moreover, symptoms that may appear to be delusional in one culture (e.g., sorcery and witchcraft in Salem, MA) may be commonly accepted in another, (e.g., voodoo in Haiti) so the diagnosis is ambiguous at best.

Auditory and visual hallucinations have played an essential role in religion for thousands of years. Accounts range from Biblical prophets and saints to shamans, as well as Socrates' famous Daemon voice. Some skeptical psychiatrists have retroactively diagnosed all of them as possibly having mental disorders. [But, not always. For example, one could not say that Martin Luther or Galileo were imagining things. But, Catholics who believe in the absolute infallibility of the Pope could be delusional. But, if God made everything perhaps he made delusions and hallucinations too.] Several studies have shown that more than half of the normal population has some experience with voice hallucinations, and approximately 10% of the general population reported hearing a comforting or advising voice that is not perceived as being ones own thoughts. [This writer has heard a silent voice for years saying, "Tell them, tell them" . . . and so he is obeying in this book.] Even the great C. G. Jung claimed the personal presence of one he called Philemon who may have been some apparition from his unconscious self. Hallucinations frequently occur in sheeple during bereavement, life-threatening situations, and stressful traumatic situations such as sensory deprivation, sleep deprivation, illness, and solitary confinement.

Inner voices have played a significant role in their lives reported by many noted individuals including C.G. Jung, Elisabeth Kubler-Ross, Martin

Luther King, Jr., and Winston Churchill. Hearing inner voices often is perceived as helpful by sheeple who are experiencing a spiritual awakening. Lukoff shows that throughout the history of psychiatry there has been an awareness that "visionary spiritual experiences" may drive a person through the "dark night of the soul" to emerge not only well, but "weller" than they ever were. Such an experience has marked the emergence of a shaman in the mythology of primitive healing rituals. Their hallucinations, grandiose and paranoid delusions, and social withdrawal were indistinguishable from those of many schizophrenics. The oft-reported near death experience includes some hallucinations that appear to prepare terminal patients for their permanent departure.

Periodically another book emerges attempting to prove heaven exists with first-hand accounts of near death experiences. Typical is <u>Heaven is for Real</u> (2010) by Todd Burpo, an ordained pastor and garage door contractor, and professional conservative Christian ghost writer, Lynn Vincent. Burpo recounts the events surrounding the near death experience, seven years after the fact, of his son at age four during emergency surgery for a ruptured appendix. In a spiritual voice that belies his age, young Colton allegedly described heavenly encounters while he was unconscious with deceased family members and angels with wings and God himself ("really, really big") that normally only the adults could have imagined. Like, Jesus wore purple and a gold crown and rode a horse, and John the Baptist was "nice." Todd claims that Colton said he also saw dogs, cats, and a friendly lion in heaven too. [The only miracle here is how the pastor in Nebraska met the creative writer in California and found a literary agent in Colorado to get the book published seven years after the fact.]

Human imagination combined with creative writing is a wonderful thing for selling books. But, perhaps Colton was tapping into some reservoir of unconscious information that only emerges under acute crises. Nevertheless, the book is a raging best seller among those poor in spirit who are looking for some evidence for the after life. [The largest data base compiled on near death experiences is that of the Near Death Experience Research Foundation (www.nderf.org) organized by Dr. Jeffrey Long, MD. The reports are all anecdotal and do not provide satisfactory proof for skeptics. Serious researchers into neurotheology are trying to discover exactly what happens during the process of brain dying, which could take several minutes after the heart stops beating. Some, having had such experience and recovered, become powerful religious leaders or mental health professionals, as did Lukoff himself. The mind does indeed seem to exist sans the brain in some reported cases although there is no theory connecting brain, mind, and consciousness. They call it the experience of spiritual emergence but it may be just the normal dysfunctions of a dying brain. Research results are presented in the U.K. by the Horizon Research Foundation, (www.horizonresearch.org.)]

There are no reliable biological markers (lab tests or x-rays) by which to confirm or rule out diagnoses of mental disorders such as schizophrenia or manic-depression, which can resemble religious enlightenment, other than self reporting. Research in neurology is attempting to locate seats of religious experience in the brain, but it is not conclusive yet. Mystical experiences may involve perceptual alterations ranging from heightened sensations to auditory and visual hallucinations. In cases where the individual does not experience distress and may in fact feel positive toward their religious experience, determining whether an individual is psychotic can be a painful responsibility which may fall to family, friends, or mental health professionals. Consider the growing practice of "glossalalia" or speaking in tongues manifested in some main-line churches and those who purposely handle snakes and ingest poisons because the Bible says it is a demonstration of their faith. (Mark 16:18) There is actually no connection between such behavior and the manifestation of Holy Spirit in the Book of Acts that included speaking in actual foreign languages with interpretations. Whether this phenomenon should be classified as a mental disorder is just too hot socially for most psychiatrists to debate. Anyone who claims they were abducted by aliens may cause some raised eyebrows, but one who proclaims a personal relationship with Jesus is not referred for medical treatment, unless they commit some heinous crime that they attribute to a voice of God. After all, Catholic nuns all are given to imagine they are "brides of Christ," are they not?

Lukoff points out that the mental health field has a heritage of either pathologizing spiritual experiences and religion or ignoring them. Sigmund Freud, a lifelong atheist, promoted this view in several of his works, such as in Future of an Illusion (1927) wherein he pathologized religion as: "A system of wishful illusions together with a disavowal of reality, such as we find nowhere else . . . but in a state of blissful hallucinatory confusion." Freud also promoted this view in "Civilization and Its Discontents," where he reduced the "oceanic experience" of mystics to "infantile helplessness" and a "regression to primary narcissism." The 1976 report "Mysticism: Spiritual Quest or Psychic Disturbance," by the Group for the Advancement of Psychiatry (GAP) followed Freud's lead in defining religion as "a regression, an escape, a projection upon the world of a primitive infantile state."

Albert Ellis, creator of Rational Emotive Therapy, the forerunner of cognitive modification approaches now widely used in cognitive-behavioral therapies stated in a 2001 interview, "Spirit and soul is (sic) horseshit of the worst sort. Obviously there are no fairies, no Santa Clauses, no spirits. What there is, is human goals and purposes . . . But a lot of transcendentalists are utter screwballs." In addition to his bias against spirituality as a constructive element in mental health, in many other of his writings Ellis has concluded; "The elegant therapeutic solution to emotional problems is quite unreligious . . . The less religious patients are, the more emotionally healthy they will tend to be." The behaviorist assumes if you act the way you want to feel, soon you will feel the way you act so smile and be happy. However, other reports indicate that regular church attendance and a faith-based belief system accompanies more self reliant mental health, but the results are inconclusive for scientific evidence. Anecdotes are not sufficient proof for the skeptics. Whether firm religious beliefs express a regression to a "primitive infantile state" or a downright mental illness is yet to be determined. So long as any society tolerates the most bizarre of religions as human free will the dilemma will continue.

Historically, the nursing profession has been more receptive to religion and spirituality than psychiatry. "Spiritual Distress" has been a category in the nomenclature of the National Group for the Classification of Nursing Diagnosis since 1983. It is defined as, "The state in which the individual experiences or is at risk of experiencing a disturbance in his or her belief or value system that is his/her source of strength and hope." The mental health nursing journals also include religious and spiritual factors more frequently than psychiatry or psychology journals. There could be a correlation between the spiritual concerns of nurses and the preference of women for the intuitive-feeling sides of personality. Overall, the mental health field is growing more sensitive to religion and spirituality as important factors in health and well-being, but there is a long way to go.

Jesus said there was value in the wonder of a child. "He called a little child and had him stand among them. And he said: I tell you the truth, unless you change and become like little children, you will never enter the kingdom of heaven. Therefore, whoever humbles himself like this child is the greatest in the kingdom of heaven." (Matthew 18:2-4) He was dispelling the arrogance that prompted his disciples to ask who would be the greatest in the kingdom of heaven. Illusions must first exist in order for sheeple to become disillusioned. The wonder and hope that Santa Claus represents is the thing behind the symbol. His suit is no less a symbol than the clothing of high officials of the Church or the empty cross and the crucifix on alters of the churches. But, when the symbol becomes the thing, both are lost.

Retired Episcopal Bishop John Spong has written, "The task of the Christian is to love the least of these our brothers and sisters, [including those who still believe in Santa Claus.] But, protecting them from uncomfortable truth is not just patronizing, it is both demeaning and dehumanizing . . . Faith-based security is not well served by avoiding questions for which there are no answers. A church pastor must accept people where they are. A good pastor, however, does not leave them there forever, for that means they will never grow. One of my professors once said any God who can be killed ought to be killed. To which I would add, any faith that can be undermined should be undermined. A God or a faith that needs you or me to prop it up has already died long ago. You do not need to defend a living God. Only dead Gods seem to require that."

So the next time you see Santa Claus or go to church, ask yourself what myths you live by, and why. Perhaps the answers are in the search. If you are ready, read <u>Voices of Sedona</u> and <u>Lessons From Sedona</u>, the course in Theofatalism™. Buy from www.Iunivese.com, www.amazon.com and Barnes & Noble book stores. Feel good inside no matter what happens outside.

7. To see God, look around.

Possibly the greatest act of hubris given to humankind is attempting to explain what God is like. Some would say it is impossible because we exist in two different realms and our imagination cannot take us there. Mary Baker Eddy, founder of Christian Science, claimed that God is only good so he could not have created this realm of sin, sickness, and death. She makes no claim for its origin if God did not do it. Helen Schucman, scribe of A Course in Miracles (1975) went even further, claiming that Jesus told her this world is only imaginary and does not really exist. "Nothing real can be threatened, nothing unreal exists." Many sheeple believe both of them. Preachers proclaim, "God is . . . God wants . . . God does . . . God does not" . . . as though they had some direct communication from the Almighty One. This dialogue all leads to the universal struggle among thinking sheeple to find the will of God in their lives as though it were some pot of gold at the end of the rainbow if they only could find the map. But thinking sheeple seem to be unable to reconcile the omnipotent, omniscient, benevolent God they created with all the suffering and evil in the world.

Most humans are predatory animals, cruel, and unscrupulous as well as compassionate and charitable. And they live in societies in which if the guilty are occasionally punished, the innocent in great numbers suffer. The wealth of nations is concentrated in control of ten percent of the world's population. The rest live in hunger, darkness, and disease, physically, intellectually, and spiritually. How can such evil and suffering occur if the Creator is infinitely good, infinitely wise, and infinitely powerful? French author, Voltaire [aka Francois-Marie Arouet (1694-1778)] struggled with this dilemma and wrote the religious satire he called, "Candide" (1759) to make fun of the world the Church claims is the best of all possible worlds because it is the creation of God. No matter.

It really is quite simple for those with eyes to see and ears to hear. For the others, it is impossible. In fact, all creation comes from the one source and that source blindfolds many sheeple so they cannot see the truth of it because it would shock them to death. If you think the Bible is the Word of God, consider that it says repeatedly that the creation was "good," (Genesis 1: 4-31) so that must include predator and prey as well as all the various forms of destruction that come with life on planet Earth. It also says that much of what Jesus taught in parables was presented to educate the chosen disciples but to keep others not chosen from understanding and being redeemed. (Matthew 13:10-11, Mark 4: 10-12) Thus, everything must be the will of God or it would be different. In "Candide" there is the utopia of Eldorado, a land of plenty and equality and absolute freedom from want but, alas, it is a fantasy land of merely temporary respite for wanderers from the real world of injustice, horror, calamity, and suffering. "Candide" proclaims, "It is demonstrable that things cannot be otherwise than as they are; for all being is created for an end, all is necessarily for the best end . . . Consequently they who assert that all is well have said a foolish thing, they should have said all is for the best." But, even the best is not sufficient to hold the wandering desire among Homo sapiens for discontent among contentment. Contentment breeds stagnation and happiness, while discontent is necessary to breed change and progress. [The most extreme examples of discontent are those special sheeple who undergo sex-change operations to realign their brains and their bodies that were misaligned at birth. Thus, Chastity the daughter of Cher and Sonny Bono became Chaz, the son of Cher and Sonny. A close second may be the inventors of weapons of mass destruction who are never content with their war making powers. That, too, must be the will of God or it would be different.] A Course in Miracles (1975) states, "Disobeying God's will is meaningful only to the insane. In truth, it is impossible." Even if God gave man free will to disobey the rules, that too was part of the creation that was "good." If you accept this, (no one is asking you to believe it,) then continue reading. If not, go outside and play.

Can anyone internalize this hymn by Maltbie D. Babcock (1858-1901) in the real world? Christians may sing it, but how many really, really believe it?

> "This is my Father's world, and to my listening ears all
>   nature sings,
> and round me rings the music of the spheres.
> This is my Father's world: I rest me in the thought of rocks
>   and trees,
> of skies and seas; his hand the wonders wrought . . .

This is my Father's world, the birds their carols raise,
the morning light, the lily white, declare their maker's
praise.
This is my Father's world: he shines in all that's fair;
in the rustling grass I hear him pass; he speaks to me
everywhere . . .
This is my Father's world. O let me ne'er forget that though
the wrong seems oft so strong, God is the ruler yet.
This is my Father's world: why should my heart be sad?
The Lord is King; let the heavens ring! God reigns; let the
Earth be glad!"

Some sheeple go to great lengths to try and find God. They look in
churches and monasteries and among gurus and cult leaders, among others,
like children playing hide and seek. They read books and take courses and
practice various religious rites and traditions. Some of them renounce the
world of senses and thinking to live alone as a recluse in search of God
inside themselves. Of all this searching, Episcopal Bishop John Spong has
written, "No one has seen God, and the deity about whom most of us speak
is our own creation. Religious systems try to pretend that God has revealed
God to them, but when they describe that God, it is clearly a God in their
own image. Throughout history human beings have perceived of God as an
animating presence, an Earth mother, the sun, the moon, a tribal chief or
shaman, a high priest or guru, and a universal presence. Each image, however,
was shaped by human need and human understanding. That is the first thing
you should embrace. The God you say you cannot see is a deity of some other
human being's creation. As long as you are bound by another's definition,
you may well never see God for yourself. I do not believe that any human
being can ever know who God is; we can only know how we think we have
experienced God. God and my experience of God are not the same thing.
That is a crucial difference. We can experience on some level what we cannot
ultimately define. What we describe in our words, scriptures, creeds and
doctrines is not the reality of God, but our limited human attempt to explain
our experiences of that reality. God is not bound to anyone's definition."

However, Apostle Paul admonished the Roman Jews to take a look around
because all of nature attests to the creation of God. And God reminded
Job that all of creation was his handy work and not that of man. (Romans
1:18:20, Job 38-41) Also, Jesus taught his disciples to pray, ". . . thy will be
done on Earth as it is in Heaven." (Matthew 6:9-11) God being God, how
could it be otherwise? Thomas Paine (1737-1809) concluded in his "Age of
Reason," (1795) "The creation speaks a universal language, independently of

human speech or human language, multiplied and various as they may be. It is an ever-existing original, which every man can read. It cannot be forged; it cannot be counterfeited; it cannot be lost; it cannot be altered; it cannot be suppressed. It does not depend upon the will of man whether it shall be published or not; it publishes itself from one end of the Earth to the other. It preaches to all nations and to all worlds; and this word of God reveals to man all that is necessary for man to know of God." So, if he created it all, just look around at all he created. Some of it stinks pretty badly.

The Dalai Lama, leader of Buddhism, said everybody adopts a lifestyle and then invents a religion to support it. In spite of this outlook, most religions seem to require that God must be displayed in a symbolic form that human senses can perceive, so there are models, crucifixes, statues, paintings, stained glass windows, hymns and poems, and other such displays all about the places of devotees that can be taken for the real thing. Some of them are worshipped as though they are the real thing like, for example, the "miraculous" way in which the cracker dispensed during the Catholic Eucharist becomes the "body" of Christ as he said, "Take, eat. This is my body." (Matthew 26: 26, Mark 14:22). What about that symbol of cannibalism? C.G. Jung observed that there is the thing and the symbol of the thing. The problem is that Homo sapiens cannot seem to rise above the symbols of Gods that they worship so they may never actually experience the real thing. A town in Poland built a stature of Jesus 170 feet tall . . . but it still is not the real Jesus. Think about it.

If God really is omnipotent and omniscient, all this dependence upon symbols should be unnecessary. To see God, just look around, really look around. St. Anthony of the Desert wrote, "My scripture is the world of created things, and any time I wish to read the word of God, the book is there open before me." Ever since recorded history it seems that Homo sapiens have had a yearning to make sense from what they perceive to be mysteries of life they cannot control, be it weather or cancer. Rising from a common trunk like the branches of a tree, their myths and assumptions have taken many forms and directions. As time passed some of the wide variety of beliefs have given way to scientific discoveries that have replaced assumptions proven to be just plain wrong. Take the separation of religion and science, for example. Pierre Teilhard de Chardin (1881-1955) French paleontologist and Jesuit priest, stands among the very few leaders of thought in his century to integrate pure scientific research with a religious vocation. He observed, "All around us, to right and left, in front and behind, above and below, we have only to go a little beyond the frontier of sensible appearances in order to see the divine welling up and showing through. But it is not only close to us, in front of us, that the divine presence has revealed itself. It has sprung up universally, and we find ourselves so surrounded and transfixed by it, that there is no room left to fall down and adore it, even within ourselves. By means of all created things, without exception, the divine assails us, penetrates us and moulds us. We imagined it as distant and inaccessible, whereas in fact we live steeped in its burning layers. This palpable world, which we were wont to treat with the boredom and disrespect with which we habitually regard places with no sacred association for us, is in truth a holy place, and we did not know it."

It is one thing to see God in natural beauty or the performance of a great musician or athlete or artist or some evangelical preacher, but what about including land fills, sewage plants, refugee camps, street gangs, prisons, junk yards, mental hospitals, female and male brothels, opium dens, and industrial effluent that pollutes rivers and lakes plus hurricanes, tornadoes, earthquakes, and all the masses of Homo sapiens seemingly abandoned in their misery and suffering, plus the ones who are causing the suffering. Consider all the drug addicts in America who are creating the carnage in Mexico to get their fixes. Reports indicate that drug cartels operate in 230 U.S. cities and are growing marihuana in national parks. In Mexico, they have infiltrated the police to assure they will not be investigated and arrested.

One would also need to look into diverse religions to see God everywhere. God seems to have many aliases and to wear many costumes. Could you visit a Hindu temple, a Jewish synagogue, a Buddhist shrine, a Catholic cathedral, a Voodoo ritual, a Muslim mosque and an open Bible church, or read both the Bible and the Koran and still say, "Everything is God being God because that is all there is?" Hmmm? And that is only the Homo sapiens. To see God one also needs to look at all the other life forms on the planet both on land and in water, plant and animal included. There also are the geologic processes, both immediate and long term. And beyond this planet one also must look as far as possible out into the vastness of the Universe. If there is only one Creator, is there not only one possible explanation for all things. Hmmm? The voice of God said as much to Job when they finally met face to face. And Job was overwhelmed, "I know that you can do all things. No purpose of yours can be thwarted." [And nothing outside your will can exist.] (Job 42:2)

Many sheeple ask, how can there be a God when war, famine, disaster, child-abuse, starvation, genocide, and all of the other atrocities of life are allowed? What kind of God would allow them? Where is God in all of this? Suppose God IS all of this. Suppose there is Divine Order in every circumstance. A bumper sticker reads: "I screamed at God for all the starving children, and then I realized that all of the starving children were God screaming at me. They were screaming, "Wake up! Get this!" We're showing up in this experience called Life to demonstrate to all of humanity what Life looks like when there is apathy with compassion; hoarding with sharing; taking with giving; separation and oneness. How easily we recognize the Divine behind a gorgeous sunset; a stunning rainbow; a majestic eagle gliding across the sky. But the eagle is on the prowl to catch some food. God is also peering out from behind the eyes of the leper; the starving child orphaned by AIDS, behind the young girl who pierces her arm with a drug-filled needle; the pile of rotting refuse which becomes home to rats and street sheeple; the stench of stale urine piled in hallways labeled as nursing homes and the boarded up homes awaiting foreclosure as well as the mansions and yachts of the rich and famous. Christ said, "I tell you the truth, whatever you did for one of the least of these brothers of mine, you did for me." (Matthew 25:40). God wears infinite disguises, truth comes in many shapes and sizes and is always subject to revision.

Saint of Calcutta, Mother Theresa said, "Each ravished body I hold unto me is Christ. That's all I see, the Beloved in them." Her biographer wrote, "She would embrace those with open, oozing sores, the stench of decay permeating them. Their bloody and festering wounds were invisible to her. She saw only the radiance of Christ, the source of their being, behind the disguise of disease and death. God Is Everything. Everything Is God. All things are God made manifest in the physical realm. Behind the disguise of disease and death, God Is Everything. Everything Is God. Everything is here solely for our awakening and remembering this truth. When we see through our own God eyes, we know this. We remember this." Unless, of course, our human ego still has us blindfolded to reality. All in the will of God the Almighty One, of course.

One of the longest running human needs seems to be searching for a source of all to explain the observable Universe and life forms on Earth that can be assumed to balance the belief in randomness. Present cosmology leans to the creation of the Universe from a "big bang" that converted energy into matter from nothing around 13.7 billion Earth years ago. [Actually the matter in the Universe still can be reduced to nothing because quarks and the other subatomic particles, however many they are, have no gravity and hence no mass. Energy also can be reduced to zero because all the atoms are in perfect balance between the nucleus and its electrons. But, if there really is nothing, then who loves, hates, cheats, steals, eats, invents, etc., nobody?] This notion arose from the discovery by Edwin P. Hubble that objects in the Universe were moving away from each other and, by reversal, must emanate from one original singularity. But, the further away they are the faster they appear to be going. When Hubble looked at the darkest part of the sky he saw untold numbers of galaxies never before known . . . and still racing away at speeds that could exceed that of light. Strange, as no theory accounts for that. What caused the big bang? And what happened before that? Are there any other Universes? On a human time scale, the big bang was very much a sudden, explosive origin of space, time, and matter. But look very, very closely at that first tiny fraction of a second and you find that there was no precise and sudden beginning at all. So here we have a theory of the origin of the Universe that seems to say two contradictory things: First, time did not always exist; and second, there was no first moment of time. Such are the oddities of quantum physics.

Even with these further details thrown in, many sheeple feel cheated by science. They want to ask why these weird things happened, why there is a Universe, and why *this* Universe. Basically, why is there something rather than nothing? This is the fundamental question and mystery of existentialism. They can even ask how many Universes are there, and did they all begin with a similar big bang or some other sources. Perhaps science cannot answer such questions. Science is good at telling us how, but not so good on the why. Maybe there isn't a why. To wonder why is very human, but perhaps there is no answer in human terms to such deep questions of existence. It is easy to say; "everything came from nothing." But it is not so easy to explain why there is something instead of nothing. One argument even claims that nothing cannot exist, so there must be something. If you look it up, the history and applications of nothing could be quite interesting. Space science experimenters seek nothing less than discovery of the ultimate source. Among the oldest Vedic Hindu culture of India dating back to 2500 BCE, there is one Supreme Being with no beginning or ending depicted as in a "mobius." Since modern physics assumes no beginning or ending to time and space, that idea still exists. [The vast volume of Vedic literature in the Sanskrit language contains the world's richest mythology and predates that of the Hebrews, Greeks, and Romans by hundreds of centuries. Possibly the best known Vedic work in the West is the Bhagavad-gita, literally meaning "conversation" between a warrior-prince named Arjuna and his demiGod, Lord Krishna.] God is seen in three parts, Brahma, Vishnu, and Shiva, as a precursor to the concept of trinity in Christianity. They are the merger of all souls combined into one spiritual energy, the individual super-soul in the heart of everyone, and the divine personality with whom mankind is sustained by supreme love.

God is a universal construct of human imagination. Even atheists must have a God not to believe in to refute it. The most vocal among atheists are no less fervent in their evangelism than conservative religionists. Each is expressing a form of faith that cannot rationally be proven, God is and God is not, necessary opposites for sure. Indeed, one could speak of a secular fundamentalism that resembles religious fundamentalism of an opposite nature. This may be one of those cases where opposites eventually converge into both/and rather than either/or. Some cultures have many Gods, but the common element seems to be acknowledgment that man is not the master of his fate, although he is given the illusion that he is. This is the necessary opposite complement to belief in humanism which assumes that man is the crown of creation and controls his own destiny as the "captain of his soul," the way William Ernest Henley expressed in his poem, "Invictus." But, who is it that is captain of "his" own soul? How can the soul have an owner? The Bible myth of creation claims that God made man in his own image and likeness. If that is true, then all the evil and brutal forms and criminal behaviors of Homo sapiens are manifestations of God, not just the good and compassionate and lovely parts. In fact, everything in the Universe is a manifestation of God in some way to those who believe in creationism and the evolution of a grand divine design. To those who don't believe, there are only more and more questions with no answers.

If one could take the time out of a life full of busy-ness long enough to look around, it might be noticed that life on Earth seems to be a complex mesh of interactions among and within species which are so interrelated that chance could scarcely be assumed to explain it. And Homo sapiens are but one of many species to be seen, maybe not the smartest or most durable either. One of the benefits of new video technology is the display of life forms in High Definition provided by educational resources now viewable in households that before were unavailable to most everyone. Instead of practicing eye-hand coordination with mindless, ubiquitous video games, perhaps a more helpful use of imagination would be viewing the many forms of life, plant and animal, now available to everyone from educational television. For example, there is a species of cactus that blooms only once each hundred years. At that precise time a special moth shows up to distribute its pollen to other cactus plants to assure that it will be reproduced. Air France flight 447 went down in the Pacific Ocean killing all 228 souls on board. But, four sheeple missed the flight and were spared. Whether by intelligent creation or random natural selection, or evolution by design, the human imagination is challenged to look around at the awesome life on Earth and not see God. Perhaps after a little wonder, you might conclude as did C. G. Jung, "I could not say I believe—I know! I have had the experience of being gripped by something that is stronger than myself, something that people call God . . . In all chaos there is a cosmos, in all disorder a secret order." If you experience that order, you will have no difficulty seeing God in all things, because maybe that is all there is.

You cannot fight reality; well, you may fight it but you cannot win. Life includes the celebration of sexuality, birth, growth, compassion and enjoyment. But it also includes disease, decay, violence, aging, loss, and death. To focus upon the former is to love God only for his goodness. To focus on the latter is to fear God for his wrath. Many sheeple worship the one but ignore the other until it is forced upon them. Both are the One. God did not make any one-sided coins. Of course, to see God all around you would need to peer into not only churches and hospitals, but unseemly places too, whore houses, drug dens, prisons, battlefields, mortuaries, political campaigns, gambling casinos, used car lots, garbage dumps . . . homeless shelters . . . mental institutions . . . primitive tribes . . . deserts and rain forests . . . hurricanes, earthquakes and rainbows . . . beaches and tsunamis . . . for you cannot have one side of God without the other. Lastly, if you believe the Bible is literally the word of God, then look into a mirror because it is written, "When God created man, he made him in the likeness of God. He created them male and female and blessed them. And when they were created, he called them man." (Genesis 5: 1-5) The enlightened one recognizes that everything manifests the energy of God, because there can be no other. "There are different kinds of working, but the same God works all of them in all men." (1 Corinthians 12:6) The truly liberated person does not worry about returning to God. He knows that he is already there because he never left. It is impossible, although when he takes on human personae it may appear that he has lost the way.

King David sings the praises of God, "The Earth is the Lord's, and everything in it, the world, and all who live in it." (Psalm 24:1) But, the prophet sees this power in a different light. "See, the Lord is going to lay waste the Earth and devastate it; he will ruin its face and scatter its inhabitants . . . The Earth will be completely laid waste and totally plundered. The Lord has spoken this word." (Isaiah 24:1-3) If you look around with clarity, you may conclude that everything is God being God the Almighty One. When the blindfold comes off and you see God the Almighty One as it is, you may be scared to death. That is why we are given only one small peak at a time. There is a hadith [a saying of the Prophet Muhammad] that tells us: "The world is your friend if it reminds you of God, and it is your enemy if it makes you forget God." But, it takes special eyes to see God the Almighty One everywhere in everything, otherwise the shock would be too great.

There is a form of deism called pantheism in which God got the Universe started and then let it go on its own, being uninvolved in the daily lives of his creation. In this belief, the Universe is like a wind-up toy while God sits back and waits for it all to wind down. Pantheism says that once God formed natural laws they work without any continued intelligence or consciousness as the true mindless governors of an inert and dumb Universe. The message from the Bible, from Christian mystics, and lately even from science, is quite different for some. The opposing view is called panEntheism. In this view, God may have rested on the seventh day, but then he got right back to work again. The Bible states that the heavens are alive, declaring the glory of God (Ps. 19), and that Christ is the One who holds all things together. (Col.

1.17). Christian Universalists often point to Bible verses such as Ephesians 4:6 "[God] is over all and through all and in all" and Romans 11:36 "from [God] and through him and to him are all things" to justify both panentheism and Universalism.

In panentheism, creation is seen as the ongoing expression of God's will in the contingent world, and every created thing is seen as a sign of God's sovereignty and leads to knowledge of him. The signs of God are most particularly revealed in human beings but also through nature and the laws of physics. Panentheism lacked a clear label in philosophical and religious reflection about God until Karl Krause (1781-1832) created the term in the eighteenth century. Various advocates and critics of panentheism find evidence of incipient or implicit forms of panentheism present in religious thought as early as 1300 BCE. Panentheism seeks to avoid both isolating God from the world as traditional Deism often does and identifying God only with the natural world as pantheism does. Traditional deistic systems emphasize the difference between God and the world while theistic panentheism stresses God's active presence in the world.

Ever since the double-slit experiment demonstrated that individual photons of light seem to be aware of the experimenter, some scientists assume that God consciousness permeates the Universe at some subatomic level through energetic influence. A Universe in which not just plants, animals, and humans, but subatomic particles, and the rocks and stars composed of them are also aware of God, is a Universe which be unfamiliar to Christians. The late mystic and grief-work psychiatrist, Elisabeth Kubler-Ross (1926-2004) claimed that rocks under her feet "spoke" to her and cried out when she was hurting them. Jesus said that even if the crowd kept silent when he entered Jerusalem, the rocks and stones themselves would start to sing (Luke: 19.40), and David described all heavenly bodies singing for joy in his Psalms. The important theological implication is that perhaps Creation did not end on the sixth day, but is continually flowing forth from God. When Jesus encountered criticism for healing on the Sabbath, he responded, "My Father is always at his work to this very day, and I, too, am working." (John 5:17) Note the present tense.

Countless times every second, perhaps every subatomic particle in the entire Universe is being re-created from energy to matter according the Einstein's law of nuclear physics. Panentheism offers the potential for greater dialogue and communication between Christians and all those of other religious views because nothing may exist outside the immaculate immanence of God the Almighty One. We must then realize that "God" as personality is a metaphor, (he? she? it?) for all personal pronouns fail when contemplating this magnificence! IT is as infinitely beyond being a person as the One who created light is beyond being light. All other theisms (deism, theism, polytheism, animism, pantheism, atheism) are fragmented theologies compared to panentheism. The principles of Theofatalism™ apply panentheism to the world of mankind through discussions of daily living. No view of God is larger than the view of Theofatalism™ because it contains all other views. Perhaps this thought is captured in <u>A Course in Miracles</u> (1975) which claims; "Disobeying God's will is meaningful only to the insane. In truth, it is impossible." Its writer, Helen Shucman perceived a banner declaring simply, "God IS." It seems that every part of the Universe is aware in some way of the immanent presence of God. And since it comes from God the Almighty One it is perfection in existence; immaculate immanence. (ImIm) Is this the truth? Who knows? We must live with the existential anxiety of indefinite uncertainty.

The human ego cannot bear the sight of God in everything because it means loss of control, so it substitutes fear and confusion to block the view. If what the senses detect is all an illusion, why? Why would the Creator of the Universe give its creatures the power and free will to thwart his plan? It boggles the mind to ponder such mysteries. However, India guru Neem Karoli Baba said, "It is better to see God in everything than to try to figure it out." If God is God, he could have created any world he wanted to . . . and this is the one we got. God is in control, really, so get used to it. Read the full story in <u>Voices of Sedona</u> and <u>Lessons From Sedona</u> available from www.Iuniverse.com, www.amazon.com, and Barnes & Noble book stores. Feel good inside no matter what happens outside.

8. GOD WORKS IN MYSTERIOUS WAYS

In the news one day was a report that more than a hundred devotees were killed in a stampede among the crowd of several hundred thousand attending a special ceremony at a remote Hindu shrine in India, while the stock of Apple computer had risen to new highs. Did you know that unless you call 888-382-1222 to opt out of the system you will be charged for time used to receive unsolicited advertising sent to your cell phone? That is a common rumor or urban legend that is not true in fact. It is a hoax. There are others. Set off on a page by itself in his last book of poems titled, <u>In The Clearing</u> (1962), is this short couplet penned by the late Poet Laureate Robert Frost, "Forgive, O Lord, my little jokes on Thee and I'll forgive Thy great big one on me." The same goes for all of us. It seems that God likes to play jokes, small and large, on his creation. Frost lost his wife and five of his six children by his age 62 and then he lived until age 89 to think about it. But his sense of humor leaves a lot to be desired. Frost never clearly described his outlook on religion, but this review of his family biography may provide a clue about his motivation for this rhyme. It may also help to expose the will of God the Almighty One in the life of this one solitary man.

Robert Lee Frost won the Pulitzer prize for poetry four times and received more than forty honorary degrees. But, the famous poet's home life was anything but pleasant. Born in San Francisco in 1874, his father was an abusive drunkard and his mother a mystic and sometimes school teacher. Frost described her as "a queer woman with incipient insanity." After his father died when he was eleven, they moved to Lawrence, MA to live with his paternal grandparents. His only sibling, Jeanie, was eventually sent to a mental institution, where she wrote her brother, "I am very peculiar and did not start right. If I ever was well and natural it was before I can remember." Frost attended Dartmouth and Harvard but never graduated. His first attempts to sell his poetry in America failed so he moved to London where he received international acclaim for his first book of poetry.

Frost settled in Vermont and became a mediocre school teacher and mediocre farmer. His wife, Elinor, bore six children but tragedies stalked five of them: the oldest, Elliott, died of typhoid fever when three; a daughter, Elinor Bettina, died soon after she was born; son Carol killed himself with a deer rifle when thirty-eight after failing as a poet; Marjorie died of a postpartum infection; Irma had an unhappy marriage and was eventually committed to an insane asylum. Frost's wife, two years before Carol's suicide, died of a heart attack—after her untimely death in 1938 he wrote to a friend, "God damn me when he gets around to it." Alone and grieving, the poet asked his remaining daughter Lesley to let him live with her, but she refused. According to biographer Lawrance Thompson, "She said she had seen him cause so much injury to the lives of his own children [and her mother] that she would not permit him to move into her home, where he might also injure the lives of her two daughters. Then she hurt him most by concluding that he was the kind of artist who never should have married, or at least never should have had a family."

Robert Frost lived alone then with domestic help from his secretary until age 89. He did not issue another book of poetry for fifteen years. Frost was commissioned to write a special poem for the presidential inauguration of J.F. Kennedy, but he left his reading glasses in the hotel and so he had to recite a previous poem from memory at the ceremony. He died unexpectedly soon after. When Frost entered a hospital for the final time, he told a reporter, "I don't take life very seriously. It's hard to get into this world and hard to get out of it. And what's in between doesn't make much sense. If that sounds pessimistic, let it stand." One may say the only reality is reproduction and death while all else is moot. It may seem that God just likes to make babies and kill sheeple, and leaves the rest up to us. And so it seems to be with all species on Earth. Birthing and dying. But wait. There is more.

Back in 1949 there was a successful radio host/actor/western song writer in Hollywood named Carl Stuart Hamblen (1908-1989) who was noted for his drinking, womanizing, and partying. Here is his story from an online biographer. A young preacher was holding a tent revival, and Hamblen had him on his radio show to poke fun at him. To gather more material, Hamblen showed up at one of the revival meetings. The words from the preacher haunted him until a couple of nights later he showed up drunk at the preacher's hotel door around 2 AM. He invited Stuart in and they talked until about 5 AM at which point Stuart dropped to his knees and with tears, cried out to God for forgiveness. But that is not the end of the story. He quit drinking, quit chasing women, quit everything that was fun, and he began to lose favor with the Hollywood crowd. He was fired by the radio station when he refused to accept a beer company as a sponsor. Hard times were upon him. He tried writing a couple of gospel songs but the only one that had much success was "This Ole House," written after he discovered the corpse of a dead man in an abandoned farm house on a hunting venture.

As he continued to struggle, an old friend named John took him aside at a party and told him "all your troubles started when you got religion," and asked if it was worth it all. Stuart answered simply, "Yes." Then his friend said, "You liked your booze so much. Don't you ever miss it?" And the answer was, "No." John then said, "I don't understand how you could give it up so easily." And Stuart's response was, "It's no big secret. All things are possible with God." To this John said, "That sounds like a song." The rest is history. The song Stuart Hamblen wrote was "It Is No Secret"—"It is no secret, what God can do. What He's done for others, He'll do for you. With arms wide open, He'll welcome you. It is no secret, what God can do." It became one of the most widely recorded songs ever in country music and was translated into more than 50 languages. Stuart Hamblen went on to write more than 200 gospel songs. The friend was actor John Wayne, and the young preacher in the tent revival was the Rev. Billy Graham. Of course, the whole thing would be much different if the song said, "What He's done to others, he'll do to you." Some folks who are experiencing painful losses might say that would be more realistic. All benefits come with burdens, and what God gives he also takes away, often with great suffering. Go figure.

Francis "Mickey" Featherstone is an Irish-American mobster and ex-member of the Westies, an organized crime gang from the "Hells Kitchen" section of upper western Manhattan in New York City that plagued the city from around 1965 until 1988. Born in 1947, the youngest of a large Irish family, young Mickey was a brooding and introverted shy kid with no particular goals in life. He enlisted in the Army at age 17, hoping to find his calling in combat. But, the army assigned him as a supply clerk and, although stationed in Vietnam, he never actually served in combat. One night while he was drinking with some army medics, they got him drunk and attempted to circumcise him. But they botched the operation and left him scarred emotionally and physically.

After returning to his old neighborhood he soon got involved with the organized Irish crime group called "The Westies." He became the right hand man for its leader, Jimmy Coonan. Mickey was 5'8", 160 lbs and fearless, never backing down from a fight. Under their reign, the trigger-happy Westies committed many alleged murders in addition to engaging in loan-sharking, drug trafficking and protection rackets. With Coonan's cunning and

Featherstone's reputation, the two young men ensured a notoriously vicious stranglehold on the already brutal racketeering circles of Hell's Kitchen. He was accused of several murders but was never convicted, although he served time for various drug offenses. During this time period, organized crime experts believe that the Westies probably murdered 60-100 sheeple. Westies victims often were dismembered and in some cases tortured to death. Organized crime experts consider the Westies to have been one of the most violent and feared crime groups in New York City during the time of their operation.

Eventually, bad blood between Coonan and Featherstone led to Featherstone being framed for the 1986 murder of Michael Holly, a construction worker and neighborhood bar owner who refused to give the Westies "protection money." He initially tried to use his claim of suffering from post traumatic stress related to his experiences in Vietnam as a defense. However, because the prosecution revealed that he only had a non-combat role during the war, plus the testimony of two eyewitnesses who identified Featherstone, Mickey was convicted and sentenced to life in prison. The prosecutor who oversaw Featherstone's conviction in the Holly frame-up told the presiding judge that post-conviction investigation had revealed Featherstone was innocent of that particular crime. The judge immediately overturned the verdict.

Believing that Coonan had deliberately framed him, Featherstone became an informant and testified against fellow Westies, including Coonan, and during the later trial of Mafia crime boss, John Gotti. The information provided by Featherstone resulted in the conviction of Coonan and several other Westies on charges of murder and other crimes. The defense lawyers in the respective trials unsuccessfully tried to have Featherstone's testimony invalidated because he had previously been diagnosed by the Army with schizophrenia. Cleanup of the Westies was accelerated by the dedication of a Federal prosecutor named Rudolph Giuliani, aided by the Racketeer Influenced and Corrupt Organizations Act (RICO) of 1970. He later became Mayor of New York City and ran for President in 2008. Featherstone lives under an alias supported by the Witness Protection Program with his wife, Sissy, and their four children. The neighborhood known as Hells Kitchen has been redeveloped with more white color professional residents and was renamed "Clinton."

The famous English author and theologian C. S. Lewis (1898-1963) remained a bachelor until he fell in love and married an American divorcee. She died of breast cancer soon after. He wrote this theodicy in A Grief Observed (1961) after untimely death of his wife: "Tortures occur. If they are unnecessary then there is no God, or a bad one. If there is a good God, then these tortures are necessary. For no even moderately good Being could possibly inflict or permit them if they were not." It seems that Lewis lost his will to live and died only a couple years later. Dana Reeve, surviving wife of actor Christopher Reeve also died soon after her husband who, you may recall, was paralyzed in a horse riding accident. She got lung cancer although she never smoked and died sooner after leaving a ten year old son. She disclaimed, "It is another journey and I tell you I am through with the journeys." It seems that loss can trigger a grief that is life threatening if not navigated successfully. Letting go of the attempt to control the uncontrollable seems to be necessary for healthy living.

California therapist, David Richo relies upon Buddhist philosophy to explain in Five Things We Cannot Change (2005) five facts of life that are uncontrollable—the unavoidable "givens" of human existence: (1) everything changes and ends, (2) things do not always go according to plan, (3) life is not always fair, (4) pain is a part of life, and (5) sheeple can be cruel and unloving some of the time. He claims by embracing these givens they teach us courage, compassion, and wisdom. He claims that only after we admit we are defenseless against the overwhelming will of God and give up our attachment to ego control can we begin to grow. Richo recommends that by dropping our ego-seated resistance to these givens, we can find liberation and discover the true richness that life has to offer.

Jesus actually taught the same thing. In all four gospels, he says, "If anyone would come after me, he must deny himself and take up his cross and follow me. For whoever wants to save his life will lose it, but whoever loses his life for me and for the gospel will save it. What good is it for a man to gain the whole world, yet forfeit his soul?" (Mark 8:34-36) This is a bit like saying if rape is inevitable, you might as well relax and enjoy it. Another metaphor is a fish on a hook. Resisting the inevitable can only cause more pain and suffering without changing the outcome. If God is omnipotent it seems that he could have done a better job of creation than that. To paraphrase the Queen, "We have seen his creation, and we are not impressed." Mother Teresa concluded, "God can do anything he wants with whoever he wants whenever he wants." And he does.

St. Thomas Aquinas (1225-1274) provided a Catholic explanation of what are generally considered to be the two main difficulties with God, the Divine permission of foreseen moral evil and why God chose to create anything at all. First, one may ask why God, foreseeing that his creatures would use the gift of free will to injure themselves and others, did not either abstain from creating them, or in some way safeguard their free will from misuse, or else deny them the gift altogether? St. Thomas replies that, "Fire could not exist without the corruption of what it consumes; the lion must slay the ass in order to live, and if there were no wrong doing, there would be no sphere for the patience and justice of God. Divine will is free from the defect of weakness or mutability. Such mutability would be a defect in the Divine nature (and therefore impossible), because if God's purpose were made dependent on the foreseen free act of any creature, God would thereby sacrifice His own freedom, and would submit Himself to His creatures, [as in answering all their prayers] thus abdicating His essential supremacy which is, of course, utterly inconceivable." It seems that God's freedom trumps that of his creation. As to why he bothered to create anything at all, St. Thomas Aquinas is silent. It is a mystery.

In the New Testament, the writer of Matthew speaks of the world as populated with broken human beings who are harassed and helpless like sheep without a shepherd. (Matthew 9:35-10:4) It is to these sheeple subject to sin, sickness, death, evil and injustice that Jesus came to be the shepherd who will feed, heal, and nourish not to mention, save them from hell for eternal bliss in heaven, but only if they believe. Not in the way that was expected by Jews or in the way of material health, wealth, and happiness because he promised none of these things. The wisdom of Chinese Tao te Ching says spiritual health requires nothing that money can buy. But what an odd lot of men Jesus chose to carry out his mission. We read that he chose twelve apostles, thirteen if you count Apostle Paul. By the world's standards, none of them belonged to the rich and famous. In fact, some of the apostles like Andrew, Bartholomew or Jude and Thaddeus we know almost nothing about. The rest are no impressive bunch of men, for sure.

There was Peter, impulsive and rigid in character, whom we know denied his Lord and, yet, was chosen as the pier of his church. In the list was doubting Thomas. There were the hot-headed Zebedee brothers, James and John, who saw themselves as superior to the rest of the apostles. And there was Matthew the tax collector, despised by the Jews as a collaborator with the oppressive Romans. There was Simon the Zealot, who would have been considered by the Romans as a "terrorist", (or a "freedom fighter" by the Jews, depending on one's own political allegiance), for zealots were armed militants against Rome. There was Judas Iscariot who was like Simon the Zealot, and thus could not accept Jesus' way of non-violence. [Neither can most Christians today enact the teachings of Jesus. Read the instructions in Luke 6:20-49 and ask how many Christians actually practice their religion.]

Because of his violent leanings, we know that Judas betrayed his Shepherd, as he was called to do, the one who preached peace and advocated response to injustice not by violence but the power of love, forgiveness, and tolerance. It was these men whom, for better or for worse, Jesus called to be the foundation of his kingdom not of this world. The Jewish sheeple he came to serve rejected him and within a generation they were routed, their temple was destroyed by the Romans, and their culture was all but abolished for two millennia. The Bible claims it was their destiny. (1 Peter 2; 8) Bet you did not know that. It would be the persecutor of Christians, Saul of Tarsus, and not the disciples, who was chosen to spread the message throughout the Greek culture from about 34 CE until he was (assumed) beheaded in Rome about 67 CE. He was converted to Apostle Paul who left the letters to newborn churches which serve to this day as the record and dogma of first century Christianity. Christians still do not understand his message nor believe in all his teachings. But, they like to pretend that they do. All in the will of God the Almighty One, of course.

Someone observed, "The harder I work, the luckier I get." But not always. Some sheeple seem be more blessed than others, and "working smarter" pays off more than does simple hard work. For some, neither hard work nor being smart apply as they inherit theirs from the efforts of previous ancestors. Being in the right places at the right times helps also. No one gets off without suffering though. Jesus observed that God prunes his creation to improve its fruits and to remove the unfruitful, sort of like Homo sapiens being the vines in a vineyard that the winemaker must prune back every season in order to replenish the growth for next season. (John 15:1)

So, who do you forgive when you feel pruned and you realize it is God who is doing the pruning? Human egos need to feel in control of their lives, and when the realization that God the Almighty One really is in control takes over, the shock can be overwhelming. The Bible claims that God works all things for good to those who love him and are called to his purpose. (Romans 8:28, 9:11) But, what if you are not one of them? Mother Teresa said we must take what he gives and give what he takes . . . with a smile. If God is omnipotent, all powerful, what choices do we have but calm submission or reluctant resistance to his will? And if we resist, is that not the will of God the Almighty One? We need not worry about our own inadequacies for the work we are given, because as scripture says, God the Almighty One ultimately is the shepherd and harvest master; we are simply his hirelings, his servants, his puppets no less than was Jesus and the twelve apostles. (John 10: 14-16)

History is full of events that seem to make no sense using applied logic. It is not for the created to challenge the Creator. After all, we are the clay and he is the potter who makes some pots for royal use and some for chamber waste. (Isaiah 64:8, Romans 9: 21) Like Job, all we can do is trust in the assumed existence of him who, after killing the body, can cast the remainder into hell. (Luke 12:5) Heaven is populated by those who as little children leave their adult assumptions that no longer work and walk fearlessly wherever the Lord their God asks them to go without knowing the unknowables in what comes next. (Matthew 19:14) Feel good inside no matter what happens outside.

9. OF PAPARAZZI, FAMILY SECRETS,
AND CHRISTMAS

Every family has some dirty little secrets. Things everyone knows but no one mentions in public, or even in private. Scarcely any politician seeking public office or movie star is above discovery of some latent little or not so little skeleton in the closet that sometimes comes out to mar the otherwise noble persona of a public man or woman. There is a name for sheeple who make a career out of discovering and publicizing their dirty little secrets. The word "paparazzi" was popularized after the Frederico Fellini film, "La Dolce Vita." One of the characters in the film is a news photographer named "Signore Paparazzo." In his book, Word and Phrase Origins, (2008) author Robert Hendrickson writes that Fellini took the name paparazzi from an Italian dialect word for a particularly noisy, buzzing mosquito. In his school days, Fellini remembered a boy who was nicknamed "Paparazzo" (Mosquito), because of his fast talking and constant movements, a name Fellini later applied to the fictional character in "La Dolce Vita." Now, the paparazzi serve a useful purpose in two directions, since the opposites must be necessary. They inform the public about dirty little secrets of the rich and famous, and they help to make the rich and famous even more so with all that free publicity. They must be necessary or they would not exist.

Sometimes little family secrets are exposed when their energy can no longer be contained in private by public characters. Scarcely anyone is immune from being exposed for some latent misbehavior or character slip better left in the closet. No less than presidents of the United States and religious leaders, including Catholic priests, have had to contend with slips in ethics or morality that they no doubt wish had never happened or at least wish could be kept a secret throughout their lifetimes. Sometimes the exposure damages a career so badly it cannot be recovered and the perpetrator loses all public acclaim and fades into obscurity. [Think President Richard M. Nixon.] But sometimes forces that scarcely are understandable propel them into excellence in spite of the skeletons hanging there in plain view. [Think President Bill Clinton and golfer Tiger Woods and CA governor Arnold Schwarzenegger plus Senator John Edwards and the popular advice expert, Dr. Laura Schlesinger. We can only wonder what subconscious forces drive public sheeple to ruin their reputations . . . but we can assume that the benefits of their behavior always must outweigh the burdens if only subconsciously. All in God's will of course . . . AIGWOC.] In certain rare situations, the benefits of the roles sheeple play are valued so highly that the public just covers up the dirty little secrets behind a curtain and goes on admiring and rewarding the individuals no matter what. Sometimes a tearful apologetic act of contrition and pleading for forgiveness, while not erasing the stigma, enables the individual to go on with public acceptance, if not downright approval.

Occasionally a respected religious leader is found with his/her hand or other body parts in places they should not be. [Think television evangelists Jimmy Swaggert and Jim Bakker, and all those pedophilic Catholic priests.] Some such careers are so broken they cannot be repaired, but some find forgiveness and even enthusiasm among their fans . . . possibly because they realize that except for the grace of God, they could be next. However, forgiveness from God apparently is conditioned upon how well we forgive others because Jesus taught us to pray, ". . . and forgive us our debts/trespasses, as we forgive others . . ." (Matthew 6:12, 15, Luke 6:37).

Speaking of God, it seems very odd, even incredible, that he would come to Earth as his own son to save sinners (whom he created by putting the tree of knowledge of good and evil in the Garden) through an act of questionable moral integrity i.e., the rape of a young virgin girl, even tracing his lineage to King David, an infamous adulterer and murderer. [By the way, the Jesus story is thought by some scholars to be a rehash of the birth of Egyptian God Horus, an ancient mythical deity, who was born to the virgin Meri/Isis by the resurrected sun God Osiris described in 3000 BCE literature. The Egyptian God Osiris was killed and reputed to be resurrected and taken to heaven where he lived eternally. There are many parallels between the mythical life of Horus and his several incarnations and that of Jesus. Other similarities also exist among the fragments of epics left about the life of Persian prophet, Zororaster about 600 BCE. The birth of Jesus is referred back to Isaiah who prophesized his mother to be a "young woman" in the Masoretic Hebrew or a "virgin" as in the Septuagint Greek. (Isaiah 7:14) Neither version claims it was to be a miracle sired by the Holy Spirit.]

In any event, it is very unlikely that the story of Christmas presented in the Gospels is anywhere close to historical reality as it was written decades after the fact from oral history. The gospels of Matthew, Mark and John are attributed to actual apostles but no original manuscripts exist so there is no way of telling how accurate the copies are. Retired Episcopal Bishop, John Spong has written, "As far as I know, adults don't believe there is a literal North Pole workhouse inhabited by a jolly elf named Santa Claus, who harnesses his toy-laden sled to his eight miniature reindeer in order to bring gifts to all of the children of the world on Christmas Eve. Yet we still sing, 'Rudolf, the red-nosed reindeer' and 'Santa Claus is coming to town' without twisting our minds into intellectual pretzels." What then are we left with when it comes to the Christmas story?

Consider this possible alternative. Suppose that you were a parent of the betrothed couple described in the New Testament gospels of Matthew and Luke as Joseph and Mary. Suppose that you discovered the female of the couple to be pregnant in the usual manner before the scheduled nuptials, in a land and culture where such behavior was scorned and where harlots were stoned to death in public. What would you do? Perhaps you might go to your spiritual advisor, in this case a Rabbi, for advice. He might say, "We cannot come out and say that God is the son of an unwed mother . . . that could get her stoned to death. The prophets have been silent now for 400 years. It is time we Jews had our Messiah. So why not put out the word that an angel of the Lord came unto Mary and Joseph in dreams and told them not to worry because there was a miracle happening before their very eyes." After all God being God, he can do whatever he pleases, right? No parents want to see their pregnant kid stoned to death and there could be no witnesses to such a thing, so it might just work, sheeple being so gullible and all. The paparazzi of the day might even pick up the story and run with it. [Among the gospels, only the writers of Matthew and Luke record a visit from angels and the virgin birth. One can only wonder why such a momentus event would not be recorded by the writers of Mark and John also. How could it be that half of the gospel writers did not include the virgin birth of Jesus?]

The Rabbi could have continued, "And if we all keep telling the child that he was the son of God, he might just come to believe it and act like it. And then other people might consider him to be God made flesh and no one knows where it will go." After all, the human mind is a powerful creative force that often turns imagination into reality, and this version certainly is better than the one about the stork bringing babies or the decree by Pope Pius IX in 1854 that Mary was conceived without original sin by the "immaculate conception" of her parents. At a subsequent Vatican Council, Pius IX got the assembled bishops to adopt his decree of Papal Infallibility in 1870. There is this twist to the "Lincoln rule" in politics: You can fool some of the sheeple all of the time, and all of the sheeple some of the time, and that's enough. Just a thought. "And if it works," perhaps said the Rabbi, "we can just keep this conversation to ourselves. It will be our little secret." But Mary, being a young girl with a big secret, had to share it with her cousin Elizabeth who trained up her own child, John, to aid in the conspiracy. By the way, the father of John is never mentioned in the Bible so perhaps he was born of a single mother also. Perhaps the writers of books called Matthew and Luke let the cat out of the bag by tracing the lineage of Jesus from King David to his real father, Joseph. Joseph did all he could to raise the child as his own because, perhaps, it was. [Curiously, there is no Biblical record of Joseph and Mary ever getting married.]

The family of Jesus included at least four brothers, James, Joseph, Simon, and Judas. (Matthew 13:55) Some religious claim the only way to account for this and still maintain the eternal virginity of mother Mary is to assume that Joseph was an older widower with children from a previous wife. The Rabbi could not tell a lie, but he never informed his leadership of the plan and the Jews called Jesus "the carpenter's son," even to this day, so he could do no magic miracles among his own neighborhood. Then along came twelve involuntary inductees including fishermen, tax collectors, and a publican plus Saul of Tarsus, and the rest, as they say, is history. If Jesus was to be Messiah, of course he must perform miracles and be resurrected from death, so that is what the paparazzi said and the chroniclers wrote about him. As to all that Jesus really said and did, no one knows because none of the Gospel writers were eye witnesses to his many private discourses. Consider, for example, his private dialogue with the "woman at the well," in which the writer claims that he declared he is the Messiah promised to the Jews. (John 4:25-26)

As for the father and mother, Joseph and Mary, the other two principles in this tale, they seem to have been absent witnesses. They do not appear in the gospels as advocates for the divinity of Jesus when he debates the source of his fatherhood with Jews (John 8: 19-20) and they actually seem confused when he took up his mission at the age of twelve and they found him teaching in the Temple. (Luke 2:46-50) Except for the role of his mother Mary at the wedding feast, his parents are absent in his ministry. (John 2:1-5) Their silence is curious to say the least seeing as how his coming was foretold to Mary and Joseph by angels of God. Taken all together, the teachings reported of Jesus show him to any thinking person as a two-faced bastard, i.e. born out of wedlock to a single mother. Only God could make him into the eternal Messiah. Moreover, none of the original manuscripts of the New Testament have survived so no one knows exactly what they contained. Imagine some writers today trying to describe details of what General Eisenhower did and said during his command of the allies in Europe during WWII from hearsay accounts. But, many sheeple believe it is literally true nevertheless. And among professional Catholics, more than 10,000 have achieved sainthood by edict of the Pope after devoting their lives for his cause. AIGWOC . . . all in God's will of course. Think you can handle that?

Scholars think that Jesus probably was born in the spring when shepherds would be out grazing their flocks, not in the middle of winter when the feast of lights was celebrated to drive out the darkness. Astrologers estimate the most likely date was April 17, in the year 6 BCE. However, Pope Julius I chose December 25 for celebration of Christmas in 336 CE to help it absorb a pagan holiday celebrating the winter solstice. It is commonly believed that the Roman Catholic Church chose this date in an effort to adopt and absorb the traditions of the pagan Saturnalia festival and the celebration of Mithra, the God of the unconquerable sun. First called the Feast of the Nativity, the custom spread to Egypt by 432 CE and to England by the end of the sixth century. By the end of the eighth century, the celebration of Christmas had spread all the way to Scandinavia. But, it was more like a runaway "trick or treat" celebration than a solemn religious event. The poor were allowed to invade properties of the rich and demand a large measure of charity during a full month of revelry. In the early 17th century, a wave of religious reform changed the way Christmas was celebrated in Europe. When Oliver Cromwell, dictatorial protestant leader of a short-lived revolutionary attempt at republican government and his Puritan forces took over England in 1645, they vowed to rid England of decadence and as part of their effort, they cancelled Christmas. By popular demand, Charles II was restored to the throne after Cromwell died and with him came the return of the popular holiday.

The pilgrims, English separatists that came to America in 1620, were even more orthodox in their Puritan beliefs than Cromwell. As a result, Christmas was not a holiday in early America. From 1659 to 1681, the celebration of Christmas was actually outlawed in Boston. Anyone exhibiting the Christmas spirit was fined five shillings. By contrast, in the Jamestown settlement of Virginia, Captain John Smith reported that Christmas was enjoyed by all and passed without incident. After the American Revolution, English customs fell out of favor, including Christmas. In fact, Congress was in session on December 25, 1789, the first Christmas under America's new constitution. Christmas wasn't declared a federal holiday until June 26, 1870. Some sheeple believe that this is a violation of the First Amendment that prohibits Congress from making "any law respecting the establishment of religion . . ." After all, there is no similar Federal holiday for Muslims and Jews.

Many sheeple seem to feel so guilty about their behavior that they need a Savior to absorb their remorse and protect them from the eternal punishment they think is their due. Where would they ever get such a notion unless God implanted it in their genes? So they attempt to make up for it by buying gifts to make peace and donating to charity at Christmas for all those they have ignored or harmed throughout the year. We all do our emotional penance in our own way. And retailers take good advantage of the desire to make amends. Nevertheless, retired Episcopal Bishop, John Spong recommends, "My suggestion is that you separate fantasy from history and then enter into and enjoy the fantasy of the season. Dream of peace on Earth and good will among men and women, and then dedicate your self to bringing that vision into being." It may be the least we can do as the world of Homo sapiens seems poised on the verge of another great international conflict over the necessary opposites in religious beliefs between Christians and Muslims. All of it occurring according to the will of God the Almighty One of course, as there can be no other.

10. Acts of God

If you are not scared and confused, you just don't know what is happening. Consider the following true events from actual news stories. A mentally disabled student shot and killed 31 faculty members and fellow students during a rage on the campus of Virginia Polytechnic Institute, then killed himself. Also in northern Virgina, a drunken illegal immigrant with three previous DUI arrests and fake ID who was out on bond awaiting a deportation hearing ran into and killed a Catholic nun and injured two others at 8 AM on a Sunday morning. A single mother and her boyfriend in Idaho were charged with first degree murder after allegedly torturing and killing her eight year old son. Another single mother suffocated her two infant sons before loading their bodies into her car and sinking it into a river because she said she wanted her freedom back. A man driving his family home from vacation in Colorado was killed instantly when a large boulder fell from the mountainside and crashed through the windshield of their car. A retired couple taking a walk along a country road was killed in a grisly attack by a pack of feral dogs. A pregnant mother died of the H1N1 virus but they saved the infant, so now the father has a two-year old and an infant and no job. Children and pregnant women seem to be the main targets of this new epidemic, called swine flu. A fellow named Bernie Madoff made off with about $60 billion of investors' money in a giant Ponzi fraud investment scheme that he ran for more than 20 years until it finally collapsed, but only after his own sons turned him in. Now, one can respond to such news only two ways. In one way, such events are to be overcome with some corrective social actions by Homo sapiens. In the other, they are to be accepted with contentment and calm submission as the will of God the Almighty One. How many such events must be documented for sheeple to make this confrontation with reality?

Natural disasters recently remind us that the Earth is a dangerous place to live. A great earthquake deep in the Indian Ocean on December 26, 2004, which was the second worst ever recorded, caused a gigantic tidal wave to sweep across coastal areas in all directions killing 220,000 sheeple. Worse than that was a later deep sea earthquake off the coast of Japan on March 11, 2011 that caused a giant tsunami which leveled coastal towns and moved the entire island eight feet and changed the orbit of Earth. It also damaged a nuclear power plant that will cause dangerous radiation for years to come. That may not affect you unless you are one of the surviving family members with nothing left but splinters of wood remaining from their homes. The great hurricane labeled "Katrina" caused terrible unexpected flooding and property damage to New Orleans and the Mississippi Gulf coast in late August, 2005. It was the costliest hurricane ever, exceeding $100 billion in damages and loss of more than 2,000 lives. Thousands lost their homes, many never to be reconstructed. An earthquake destroyed much of Haiti in 2010, killing thousands and leaving 200,000 sheeple homeless. Such tragedies are called acts of God.

But, when sheeple cause damage and suffering it is something else. Annually, more than 16,000 sheeple are killed on America's highways in auto accidents. In New Jersey, a 40 year old man was found guilty of drunk driving for the 15th time and was still driving without a license. You never know who is sharing the road with you or what idiot is a local judge. After their high school graduation in 2009, some students were hanging out near their homes in Prince Georges County, MD. Shots rang out from the darkness and three students were wounded and one was killed. She was the mother of a 15 month-old child. Every day, tragedies happen to innocent sheeple who just seemed to be in the wrong place at the wrong time. Or, could that be the right place and the right time? Like the 69 year old retired Marine in Chicago who shot and killed his 23 year old neighbor for letting his dog urinate on the award-winning lawn. Both of them had a choice . . . or did they? The fact is that violence and destruction are part of God's creation, and that does not include the shedding of blood to support the food chain, with one species preying upon another in order to live . . . all of which was labeled "good" in the book of Genesis.

Exceptions often are made in insurance policies for "acts of God" so that harms of this kind will be uncompensated. Typical are weather and geological events such as tornadoes, hurricanes, earthquakes, floods, forest fires, droughts and such. The survivor of a tornado exclaimed, "You don't really think it's going to hit you until you realize it's on top of you; by then it's too late." That is an apt description of many events that come along unpredictably in life. Sometimes included are accidents among humans that seem to have no intentional precedents as well as pandemics caused by viral and bacteria life forms. Life threatening disasters seem to come in two flavors, those that are preventable and those that are not, those that are acts of God and acts of man. This distinction presupposes that some events are man-made and some are not. It also presumes that Homo sapiens have some control over their actions sometimes and sometimes not. That assumption raises many issues and questions that have plagued philosophers forever. Deciding which is which, acts of God and acts of men, is left up to the courts of law.

We expect sheeple with free will to suffer the consequence of their actions, but what of children born with chronic disabilities and those orphaned by AIDS. Jesus said the man who was blind from birth was made so just to prove the power of God to heal him. (John 9:1-3) But, what about all the other blind sheeple who are never healed? And there is that repeated theme in both the Bible and the Koran that God does what he will just to show off his power. (Ezekiel 36:21-23; Romans 9:15-18) Apostle Paul seemed to think that he was called involuntarily by God for the work that he did just as were the others who were called into the service of God. (Hebrews 5:1-6; 9:15; 11:8) The favored apostle thought the same (1 Peter 1:15; 2:21; 3:9; 5:10) But, shall we assume the same thing about criminals and warmongers?

Psychology and neurology now assume that sheeple are driven to do what they do by thoughts not of their own conscious making. How else can one explain why Tiger Woods, the world's best golfer, would threaten his reputation and his financial empire by multiple affairs with various females, just because they were available and willing? Or why academy award actress, Sandra Bullock, would marry and then divorce Jesse James, who had a long reputation for womanizing. Thoughts come before actions, but no one knows where thoughts come from. [It appears that thoughts occur in the brain about 300 milliseconds before they become conscious. But, where thoughts come from is unknown.] It is clear from their writing that the apostles thought God the Almighty One himself had called them to their vocations. If so, one must also assume the same about their Roman conquerors. None of them were volunteers. This must also apply to the Islamic warriors who commit suicide bombings to kill the enemy infidels. Altogether, it just seems that God really likes to show off, and one must wonder at the awesome power and willingness of God the Almighty One to destroy his own creation. And he never asks permission first.

Take the great ship "Titanic" that was touted as being unsinkable that sunk on its first voyage in 1912 from hitting an iceberg in the North Atlantic taking the lives of 1250 rich and famous sheeple. Consider flooding of vast farmlands by the raging Mississippi River in the spring of 2011 that destroyed much of the economy of the south. Meantime, the "war against terrorism" pits Christians against Muslims in the cause of peace. Sometimes God the Almighty One uses forces of nature and at other times he brings one species against another, and perhaps most implausible is when he drives tribes of the same species against each other. Still, there is always an opposite idea and Apostle James provides it as he says that sheeple bring death upon themselves through sin as the loving God of all good could never do such a thing. (James 1:13-15) But, reason would say that God would not be God the Almighty One unless he can do as he wishes without limitations. It seems that often God brings tragedies and disasters, including disease and wars, to refocus human attention onto him and him alone. The Bible says he is a jealous God who will punish for worshiping any idol, human or material, that would be set up in his place. (Exodus 34:14, Deuteronomy 6:14-16) He also prunes his chosen ones like a vineyard to make them more spiritually productive. (John 15:1-2) It seems that God does whatever he wants with whoever he wants whenever he wants. Get it?

Thinking sheeple, such as American revolutionary patriot Thomas Paine, (1737-1809) have chosen reason over faith to explain human events and reliance upon the nature of science. That approach leads to probing questions about God, as it did in his essay in 1795 titled "Age of Reason," in which he debunks the Bible and supports the logic of Deism. Modern humanists disclaim any reliance upon faith and put all their trust into human ability to reason. In effect, they make reason their God. However, Deism requires as much faith as reason, if only the faith in reason that postulates an omnipotent God who started it all and then left the rest up to us. Reason fails to reconcile a loving God with all the suffering in the world.

Suffering in the world can be seen in several categories; natural geological events, biological diseases, immoral human behavior, satanic possession, animal predators, and accidental inflictions to name a few. To focus responsibility upon only those of immoral human behavior would seem to limit the evil creativity of God the Almighty One who is, after all, omnipotent and does anything he wishes without limitations. Nevertheless, theologians have composed a wide literature to make Homo sapiens singularly and solely responsible agents through the illusion of free will. If there is only one God the Almighty One, then are not all things his creation? If man was made in his image and likeness are we not a manifestation of God, good and evil combined, faith and reason included? Among questions about God regarding Homo sapiens posed by thinking sheeple could be the following, in no particular order.

If the Bible is the Word of God, how come it is so flawed historically and is so factually inconsistent and self contradictory? It begins with the book of Genesis and the account of creation. For example, who was the wife of Cain, the second generation man, with whom he begat children? There are only two options and both are incest. Hmmm. And why did God reject his sacrifice of garden produce offered by Cain in favor of some blood sacrifice from his brother, Abel, which provoked the first murder? Then, why was Cain not punished by death but instead was made the father of cities? You could look it up. And how come most religious sheeple differ on which dogma in the Bible they should live by? Why do Muslim sheeple of the Koran think that Jews and Christian sheeple of the Bible are misled and we should all live under the shari'ah law of Moses where the penalty for adultery was stoning to death and an eye for an eye and a tooth for a tooth, etc.? If the God of creation is only completely good, why must sheeple suffer and struggle so much with disease and calamities and criminals? Where did the "evil spirit from God" that bedeviled King Saul come from? (I Samuel 18:10) If the Bible is the Word of God, what about this: "I make peace and create evil. I the Lord do all these things." (Isaiah 45:7) "When a disaster comes to a city, has not the Lord caused it?" (Amos 3:6)

If sin causes all the troubles of man why did the all knowing all powerful Creator include sin in his creation? If he did not, then where did it come from? If sin comes only from Satan and not God then who created Satan? [By the way, is Devil a contraction of Deism and Evil?] If all sheeple are born in sin (except Jesus and his mother Mary) where is free will? Why did God put the tree of knowledge of good and evil in the middle of the garden in the first place? (Genesis 2:9) Surely, we could have done without that. If Jesus came to save sinners why did he teach them in parables so that the common Jewish sheeple "may not understand lest they should be converted and their sins be forgiven them." (Mark 4:12)

Are some sheeple destined by God to miss out on his blessings? It seems so because this was predicted in Isaiah 6:10 and quoted by Apostle Paul. "In him we were also chosen, having been predestined according to the plan of him who works out everything in conformity with the purpose of his will . . ." (Ephesians 1:11) As described in the book of Revelation, only those whose names are written in the Book of Life from the foundation of the world, and have not been blotted out by the Lamb are saved at the Last Judgment; all others are doomed. "And whosoever was not found written in the book of life was cast into the lake of fire" (Revelation 20:15). Is salvation provided for anyone who believes (John 3:16) or is it reserved for a select few who were elected before time began, maybe as few as 144,000? (Matthew 24: 22-31, Revelation 14:3-5)

The Bible and the Koran both relate God only to planet Earth and to the destiny of Homo sapiens. What about the rest of life on Earth as well as the whole Universe? Why does the Universe seem to include a dichotomy in all things like sweet and sour, hot and cold, light and dark, rich and poor, sick and well, life and death, faith and reason, etc. Why must one form of life eat another, sometimes while they are still alive, In order to survive? Why are sheeple made to equally desire health, wealth, and happiness, but also made to so unequally attain them? Contrary to modern Christian common sense, our lives are not our own to live as we choose but rather to live as God chooses for us. For it is he who has the power to make from the same lump of clay "some pottery for noble use and some for common use." And we are in no position to argue with him. (Jeremiah 18: 2-6, Romans 9: 20-22) If all sheeple are created equal why is their power so unequally distributed with the few controlling the many? In the U.S., sheeple at the top one percent of income receive as much as the whole bottom half combined. Why is religion the cause of more wars and atrocities than of peace and brotherhood?

[Take a look at the historical conditions within the Roman Catholic Church that motivated German monk Martin Luther to initiate the Reformation in 1517. The Bible then was available only in Latin to educated priests who swore obedience to the Pope. But King James and the printing press changed all that. Consider now the role of Islam in world conflicts. Nothing is more opposite to the Christian New Testament than the Koran. If you doubt that God destroys his own creation, interview some of the disabled troops at Walter Reed Hospital returning from Iraq sans limbs [one of them returned blind and missing both legs] and the refugees of Darfur or the AIDS orphans in Africa or the tsunami that wrecked Sri Lanka and the victims of Hurricane Katrina who still live in FEMA trailers. Jesus said he came not to bring peace but a sword even though he also taught pacifism. The declaration of peace on Earth by the angels at his birth was farcical then as it has been ever since. Sheeple pray for peace on Earth and good will towards all men while they invent ever more lethal weapons of mass destruction. So, if the Bible is the word of God why is it based upon doctrines that are diametric opposites? Perhaps they are necessary acts of God to make up the whole.]

If the Ten Commandments were given to Moses by God, why did he and the prophets and judges of Israel add hundreds more rules to their code of behavior? [Retired Episcopal Bishop John Spong claims there really are four versions of the Ten Commandments: "the primitive Exodus 34 version from the "J" writer in the 10th century BCE; the familiar one from Exodus 20, which is originally from the "E" writer in the 9th century BCE but has been substantially edited by the "P" writer in the 6th century BCE; and the Deuteronomy 5 version, which is from the 7th century BCE and from the hand of the Deuteronomy writer." The biblical writers accounted for these several versions by suggesting that because Moses broke the tablets, God had to redo them and God did not redo them in the same way.] And why do the Jews of this day obey so few of them while the orthodox Muslims require they be wholly integrated with society?

Jesus taught to "render unto Caesar what is Caesar's and unto God what is God's," but why did he provide no instructions on reconciling the two? This dichotomy is unresolved in scripture. [Compare Romans 13:1-7 with Acts 5:29.] Why did the Gods prevent sheeple from collaborating by creating so many different languages at the Tower of Babel? If the Gods could anticipate the ubiquitous power of the Internet yet to be created that expands the babel infinitely without perceived limits, they would be quaking in their boots. Nowadays, information exchange is doubling every two years or less, but wisdom of humans for using it is lagging far behind. When dialogue is reduced to 140 characters on Twitter and thirty-second television commercials, what can we expect of human understanding in the future? Why are sheeple created to believe in things that are unbelievable and to achieve growth, whether physical, intellectual, emotional, or spiritual, only by suffering and struggle? What is belief and what relationship has it with reality? Who is it that believes? What is the relationship between mind and neurons in the brain?

Roman Emperor Marcus Aurelius (121-180 CE) learned, "Nowhere can man find a quieter or more untroubled retreat than in his own soul." There is a Buddhist proverb that says, "The right man sitting in his house thinking the right thoughts will be heard a hundred miles away." Experiments at scientific centers, including those of Dr. Russell Targ at Stanford Research Institute, seem to prove that thoughts can indeed be induced at a distance between human subjects, possibly like sending a wireless television signal. If all actions are driven by thoughts, where do thoughts come from and why? Thoughts now are assumed to be preceded in milliseconds by detectable neuron activity in the brain. If you think you control your own thoughts you might have another think coming. Who is the "you" doing the thinking? The psalmist said simply, "Be still and know that I am God." (Psalms 46:10)

Try this Zen meditation experiment. Sit quietly with your eyes closed; concentrate on your breathing and during each exhale count backwards from fifty, what Buddhists call Mindfulness of Breathing—anapanasati. Few sheeple can complete the counting to zero in one attempt before involuntary thoughts intrude like a river flowing past. Where do such thoughts come from? If your mind wanders off into thinking various thoughts just begin again . . . and again. Meditation is a release of ego identity when all attempts to meditate, all striving, all doing stops, when there is no past or future, just radiant emptiness. It is being present in surrender to the moment - fully aware and present - and we can do that whatever we are doing and wherever we are.

Buddhists claim this is like cleaning off a blackboard in school so the teacher can write a new lesson on it, or beginners mind. Perhaps it also may help one to gain contact with the counselor, comforter, and friend—even the Holy Spirit that Jesus promised to send his disciples that energized their ministry after his departure. (John 14: 25-27) As such, meditation may be required 30 minutes each day except when you are very busy, and then it takes an hour. You may feel the energy shifting into a deeper and more mysterious space as you meditate—and you are quite fascinated yet also frightened by the unknown. If nothing else, it would put your mind in the here and now, leaving the past back there and avoiding anxiety about the future, at least for the moment.

But, beware too much of a good thing. French philosopher, Blaise Pascal (1623-1662) discovered, "Man finds nothing so intolerable as to be in a state of complete rest, without passions, without occupation, without diversion, without effort. Then he feels his nullity, loneliness, inadequacy, dependence, helplessness, emptiness." If meditation is the pathway to tranquility and enlightenment for Hindus and Buddhists, for German man of letters, Johann Wolfgang von Goethe (1749-1832) it was a pathway to madness; "Where a man has a passion for meditation without the capacity for thinking, a particular idea fixes itself fast, and soon creates a mental disease." Goethe was a literary genius of his time and should be given due consideration. Perhaps here one could apply the four functions of personality presented by C. G. Jung, and described by the Myers-Briggs Type Indicator, i.e., sensing, thinking, feeling and intuition, one of which is preferred more than the others in most normal sheeple. Personality functions like a filter, passing some things and prohibiting others from entering the psyche, uniquely for each person as they were born. What we see is what we are given to perceive. C.G. Jung declared, "If one does not understand another person, one tends to regard him as a fool...Every man is so imprisoned in his own type that he is simply incapable of fully understanding another standpoint." What is perceived as genius for one may be perceived as insanity by another. Human minds do not like new ideas if they make them feel uncomfortable or insecure or refute accepted assumptions so they often are automatically rejected.

If something springs into your thoughts that surprises you when meditating, don't push it away but rather just pay attention. Faith in God the Almighty One will find the best way to nudge you along as you strive for that growth which arises through discomfort. If you cannot control your thoughts or the organs and genetics of your body, why do you think you control anything at all? Who is the you doing the thinking? Could it all be in the stars as astrologers have been claiming for centuries? After all, if the moon controls the tides what else could be controlled from space? How come the physical laws derived by Isaac Newton stood firm for 200 years before they had to be replaced with the quantum physics of Albert Einstein? What new discoveries lie in the future to be exposed by souls not yet born? Are we all just the acts of God the Almighty One? Would that include sinners as well as saints, criminals as well as judges, and all the species of life on Earth, predator and prey alike?

For C.G. Jung, Christianity's focus on "God is love" left mankind helpless in reconciling the dark side of his own nature and left him constantly at war, projecting evil upon and seeking to eradicate it from, his neighbors. Jung explored the depths of what it means to be human, taking on the challenge of becoming fully conscious, and reconciling the oppositions within human nature as it is manifested by God. There is something mentally unhealthy about seeing only the bright side of the moon, although its dark side seems hidden from view on purpose. Jung's psychology is a far cry from ego psychology with its concentration on judgment and control. For Jung the purpose of life is to fully discover and embrace the totality of the self, to find completion in wholeness. But, it requires a certain worthiness to explore the dark side. Worthiness, not in terms of ego achievements, but in a readiness to leave behind the world of judgments that both torture us yet comfort us by keeping us securely nestled in the womb of an assumed life, a world we can function in however wounded and insecure we are.

C. G. Jung said that he was deterred from following his father and grandfather into theology when at age ten he had a dream in which he saw God sitting on his throne and dropping a "giant turd" (sic) upon the symbol of his creation, a Roman Cathedral, which was crushed by the blow. The awesome power and willingness of the Creator to destroy his own creation so impressed him, the pastor's son came to the painful recognition that his father's religion could give him no answers to the existential questions about life because God shits on whomever he pleases. So he went on to develop some of the most profound contributions to psychology of religion for mental health. One of his ideas was the existence of a universal subconscious that contains all the memories of all the pasts of all living things, the "collective unconscious." Among Homo sapiens, this realm contains memories of social role models, archetypes, of all it means to be human; examples include mother, father, cad, etc., that are transmitted from generation to generation through the genes.

Near the end of his life, C.G. Jung (1875-1961) explained, "To this day, God is the name by which I designate all things which cross my path violently and recklessly, all things which upset my subjective views, plans and intentions, and change the course of my life for better or for worse. Man's suffering does not derive from his sins but from the maker of his imperfection, the paradoxical God. Now that is a shocking dilemma, I admit, but when you think consistently and logically, you come to the conclusion that God is a most shocking problem. And that is the truth. God has shocked people out of their wits." Jung is saying the capacity for murder, for example, is a given in human nature, and as such is an act of God. A man from Naples, Fl was charged with killing his wife and their five children ages nine to eleven months after he fled to Haiti. A divorced mother was charged with stabbing to death all of her four children before attempting suicide that failed. About the same time, two American soldiers manning a road stop in Iraq were attacked and beheaded by Islamic terrorists. The body of a musician and school teacher working part time as a census taker in Kentucky was found naked and lashed to a tree in rural Kentucky, a county known as a drug haven. A 16-year old neutral high school honor student was stomped to death trying to mediate a fight between two street gangs in Chicago. [Jesus said, "Blessed are the peacemakers for they will be called sons of God. (Matthew 5:9)] And in Texas a teacher, who was a father and grandfather, was stabbed to death by one of his special needs students in the classroom with a paraprofessional aid present. Such news occurs every day, several times.

The late Episcopal priest, Prof. Dr. Cliff Stanley (1902-1994) shocked his Virginia divinity students in a lecture by declaring, "My friends, God is acting in the hand of the murderer as he plunges a knife into his victim's body!" One of his students hanged himself after that. There is nothing outside the will of God the Almighty One. Jesus taught us to pray, ". . . lead us not into temptation and deliver us from evil," (Matthew 6:12-14) but as you can see from these events, he left plenty of both to go around. Think you can handle that? British biologist, Rupert Sheldrake has carried this idea further with his concept of impersonal *morphic* energy. His basic argument is that natural systems, or morphic units, at all levels of complexity—atoms, molecules, crystals, cells, tissues, organs, organisms, and societies of organisms—are animated, organized, and coordinated by *morphic fields,* which contain an inherent memory, maybe what C.G. Jung called the "collective unconscious." Natural systems inherit this collective memory from all previous things of their kind by a process called *morphic resonance,* with the result that patterns of development and behavior become increasingly habitual through repetition within species throughout the generations. Sheldrake suggests that there is a continuous spectrum of morphic fields, including morphogenetic fields, behavioral fields, mental fields, and social and cultural fields. Morphogenesis—literally, the "coming into being" *(genesis)* of "form" *(morphe)*—is more than something of a mystery. It is THE mystery.

In recent years a number of leading developmental biologists have suggested that the concept of genetic programming should be abandoned in favor of terms such as "internal representation" or "internal description." How do complex living organisms arise from much simpler structures such as seeds or eggs? How does an acorn manage to grow into an oak tree, or a fertilized human egg into an adult human being? Such questions are being asked by researchers at the Center for Alternative Medicine at the National Institutes of Health, but they have not yet developed a way to find out if claims for bio-energy fields have any validity. Studies of putative [undetectable] energies suggest that energy fields from one person can overlap and interact with energy fields of other sheeple. For example, when individuals touch, one person's electrocardiographic signal (ECG) is registered in the other person's electroencephalogram (EEG) and elsewhere on the other person's body. In addition, one individual's cardiac signal can be registered in another's EEG recording when two sheeple sit quietly opposite one another. This discovery could be one small step towards validating the hands-on healing reported of Jesus and practiced by Asian energy healers and modern western "therapeutic touch" nurses. Exactly what these representations and descriptions are supposed to be has still to be explained.

The role of genes may be vastly overrated by mechanistic biologists. The genetic code in the DNA molecules determines the sequence of amino acids in proteins; it does *not* specify the way the proteins are arranged in cells, cells in tissues, tissues in organs, and organs in organisms. As biologist, Rupert Sheldrake remarks, "Given the right genes and hence the right proteins, and the right systems by which protein synthesis is controlled, the organism is somehow supposed to assemble itself automatically. This is rather like delivering the right materials to a building site at the right times and expecting a house to grow spontaneously . . . An enormous gulf of ignorance lies between all these phenomena and the accepted theories of molecular biology, biochemistry, genetics and neurophysiology." The fact that all the stem cells of an organism have the same genetic code yet somehow behave differently and form tissues and organs of different structures and functions including hearts, lungs, kidney, and livers, clearly indicates that some form of intelligence other than DNA must be forming the developing organs and limbs. Anyone can count the seeds in an apple, but only God knows the number of apples in a seed.

There are many examples of common inventions that only can be described as acts of God. Among them could be the microwave oven, vulcanized rubber, penicillin, safety glass, and Krazy-glue, gunpowder, space rockets, cell phones, anesthesiology, concrete, and such. If one stops the pursuit of health, wealth, and happiness even momentarily to question their origins, things we take for granted may seem to be quite unusual, even unimaginable before their creation. But, where do they come from? Where are the answers? Why bother? Near his death C. G. Jung exclaimed, "I do not have to believe. I know . . . I have had the experience of being touched by something that people call God . . . I loved it and hated it. But delivering myself over to it was the only way I could endure my existence and live it as fully as possible." To one who knows, no further explanation is needed and for one who does not know, no explanation will suffice. It seems that catastrophes are inevitable. Some things that are broken can never be fixed.

Mother Teresa (1910-1997) concluded that God does whatever he wants with whoever he wants whenever he wants. "We must give what he takes and take what he gives." As Jung observed, most of the problems one encounters in life are unsolvable; they just must be outgrown. Every event that happens is the precise conclusion of all its precedent events, over which we have no control. Jesus did not promise everyone a rose garden. "It has been granted to you on behalf of Christ not only to believe in him but also to suffer for him." (Philippians 1:29) When the student is ready a teacher comes and when the teacher is ready, the student comes. Read the full story in Voices of Sedona and Lessons From Sedona. Feel good inside no matter what happens outside.

11. DIET, REST, EXERCISE, ACQUIRE, DIE

That list seems to sum up life for all mankind. DREAD. Movie maker, Woody Allen said, "I don't mind the thought of dying; but I don't want to be there when it happens." While most animal species just do it, some Homo sapiens seem to analyze it endlessly and even try to change it. Sheeple may spend a lifetime engaged in recreation and entertainment to avoid it as human doings, but in the end they will be confronted with death as human beings. Much as they have tried for centuries to make things different, that is the way life still is. Of course, there are variations. Depending on the latitude and longitude of your homeland on Earth and the values of your culture, things vary from place to place and time to time and individual to individual. But the general pattern prevails. DREAD. Although the human ego wants to control everything, no matter how much we try there seems to be a steady repeatedly predictable pattern to the life cycle among Homo sapiens. We could begin with the frailty of human bodies.

When he was asked how he stayed in shape, astronaut Neil Armstrong, first man on the moon, quipped, "I don't exercise. I believe my heart was given so many beats at birth and I don't intend to use them up any faster than necessary." It seems that everyone wants to make it last as long as possible. But, life always ends. What happens after is unknown, even though everyone seems to have an opinion. C. G. Jung consoled his older patients facing death with his near death experience during a heart attack at age 69; "The psyche/soul, in its deepest reaches, participates in a form of existence beyond space and time, and thus partakes of what is inadequately and symbolically described as eternity . . . For the psyche this means a relative eternality and a relative non-separation from other psyches, or a oneness with them . . . what happens after death is so unspeakably glorious that our imagination and our feelings do not suffice to form even an approximate conception of it." So, why do we "dread" it so much?

Sheeple all over, but especially in western developed countries, seem to thrive on being in control of their lives . . . until they lose it. No matter what type of diet they eat, or what they do for rest, or how they get their exercise, or what motivates them to acquire things, heirs, relationships, knowledge or whatever, all species inevitably meet death. Since death seems to require some cause or other, it poses a seminal question. What is there about life that is collectively self-sustaining, but individually unsustainable? Actually, most sheeple who survive a near-death experience report it to be very pleasant and comforting. But if Heaven awaits, why are sheeple so reluctant to go there? If Heaven is so desirable, how come mourners are made to grieve instead of rejoice at the new home of the departed? We grow, we blossom, we wilt, and then we die. When the awareness of death comes into consciousness, why do sheeple fear it so much? Could it be that we are made to reproduce and if you die, you cannot do that?

Perhaps it is because of something called ego, which was described as one part of a tri-partite model of personality by Sigmund Freud, (1856-1939) his daughter Anna, and Heinz Hartmann. Id, ego, and super-ego are the three parts of the "psychic apparatus" defined in Freud's structural model of the psyche; they are three theoretical constructs he used to describe mental life. According to this model, the uncoordinated instinctual trends are the "id"; [id says just do it] the organized realistic part of the psyche is the "ego," and the critical and moralizing function is the "super-ego." [super-ego says just say no] The purpose of ego is apparent in its absence among sheeple who lose self control and easily become addicted to substances and to behaviors that are self-destructive, even to the point of death. Neurology seems to have found a basis for locating actions of the ego in the frontal lobe of the brain as tumors in that area have been linked with a faulty or disabled reasoning. An insufficiently developed ego may exhibit infantile or primitive behavior tilted towards either id or super-ego if it is stressed beyond its security limits by social events beyond its control.

Someday, "faulty ego" may become a legal defense for many of the criminal activities that get sheeple in trouble with the law. [A young soldier was accused of murder after he shot and killed an Afghan Taliban fighter who was confined in a prison cell. In contrast, the anonymous Navy Seal who shot and killed unarmed Al Qaeda leader, Usama bin Laden in his bedroom was honored for obeying orders, while this soldier was imprisoned for disobeying his orders to guard the prisoner. Apparently, his id overcame his superego while his ego was disabled. All in God's will of course...AIGWOC. Get it?]

The word "ego" was coined from ancient Greek ideas, preceded in Hindu thought, by Sigmund Freud to identify some force of life that wants control and safety and immortality. Parents all know that the ego begins to show itself about the age of two in children when they are so pleased to gain bladder and bowel control, and it grows on from there, screaming "but I want, but I want." Other ego markers occur about age eight with social peer networking, age 13 with sexual maturity, and age 18 when sheeple seek fame and fortune independent of family security, then at midlife when the realization of immortality begins to set in. Life becomes mostly a struggle between ego and conformity to make a living, and in the end reality wins unless some religious experience replaces ego with the numinous figure, as in Jesus with Apostle Paul, "I have been crucified with Christ and I (ego) no longer live but Christ lives in me." (Galatians 2:20) Once a normal child realizes that its behavior produces good and bad consequences, naturally it learns to seek control of the outcome. This reaction comes from realization that the unconditional security enjoyed in the womb and the suckle of mother no longer are available.

The normal infantile ego soon learns defensive tactics for self protection and offensive tactics for personal gain. This is why most sheeple recoil at seeing disabled or broken bodies and minds; the ego is protecting its own illusion of control and desire for safety and security. A person with weak ego may have few coping resources to deal with the challenges of life making them dependent upon others and susceptible to control and manipulation, while a strong ego may be over controlling and cause relationship ruptures for insufficient reasons. Unfortunately, such drives usually are subconscious, and not until a crisis develops does the situation evoke professional intervention. However, how ego defines "good" and "bad" or "acceptable" and "unacceptable," and "satisfying" and "unsatisfying," are debated with no simple conclusions. Why some sheeple are docile law abiding citizens and others habitually break the laws and escalate their behavior until they end up in prison for life still is debated among social scientists. Some researchers focus on the inner locus of control, called free will, while others assign power to the influence of social and environmental factors . . . inner versus outer as it were. As with everything, there are both benefits and burdens to ego. The ego commonly is misconstrued as a self-serving force that causes much suffering, without compassion or charity, but there is another possible explanation.

The ego seeks immortality, if not continued physical existence, then a form of afterlife that is infinitely blissful. Needs for control and safety arise from natural selection and survival of the species, but the desire for immortality is unexplainable, unless God the Almighty One wills it so. This desire for immortality among Homo sapiens is traceable back to the oldest written story of 2200 BCE in the *"Epic of Gilgamesh,"* fifth king of Uruk in Mesopotamia. The threat of annihilation makes the ego susceptible to all manner of religious beliefs and practices that will assure its eternal survival.

Many sheeple are so disabled by the thought of their possible extinction they avoid making plans for their estates and terminal medical decisions, and then they often leave a mess behind for the family heirs to sort out. Religion only confuses the matter and leaves most thinking sheeple in a muddle.

A typical example is the Catholic "mystery" which says the bread consumed in the Mass converts actually to the body of Christ in an act of divine cannibalism that defies reason but also unites sheeple with the immortal savior. The Catholic Catechism declares: "The Council of Trent summarizes the Catholic faith by declaring: Because Christ our Redeemer said that it was truly his body that he was offering under the species of bread, it has always been the conviction of the Church of God, and this holy Council now declares again, that by the consecration of the bread and wine there takes place a change of the whole substance of the bread into the substance of the body of Christ our Lord and of the whole substance of the wine into the substance of his blood. This change the holy Catholic Church has fittingly and properly called transubstantiation." (1376) (Matthew 26:26, Luke 22:19) Most sheeple who believe in God, heaven and hell, do so because it is logically beneficial just in case it may be true. If we believe and it turns out to be false we have lost little. But if we disbelieve and it turns out to be true we may gain or lose a lot. It does not seem to matter so much what we believe so long as we have some kind of myth that transcends the human condition. Of course, there are exceptions called atheists but they seem to be less than five percent of the species Homo sapiens. But atheists need a God not to believe in, and God made them, too.

Sigmund Freud claimed the ego was necessary to provide balance between the other two elements of self, an opposing force of id and the force of superego, to assure order in relation to the social and cultural environment. The id is a self-indulgent force that seeks gratification without regard for that of others or the consequences of actions. It is the self-preservation instinct of the infant and the spontaneous "to hell with the consequences" indulgence of the irresponsible adult. The superego is just the opposite, and would restrain or prevent the id from any action it does not confirm as right or just. The id says, "Just do it," and the superego says, "Just say no." Perhaps the id is best represented by the Church of Satan, an organization for those who practice self-preservation as articulated in The Satanic Bible, written in 1969 by Anton LeVey. The superego could be represented by isolated monks and nuns who leave society to seek a life of self denial including chastity and poverty in order to touch God within while the id is manifested in criminals and sinners running amuck. Reconciling these opposing forces in life may be what living is all about, as in the wolf and the lamb lying down together in spite of their natural roles of predator and prey. That is the job of ego in normal sheeple. The ego is the negotiator between the inner instinctual drives and relations with the changing outer social world of relationships, rules, and morals. There needs to be some balance between conformity with group and social standards and anarchy among individual behavior if a nation is to survive . . . personal freedom has its limitations . . . and some sheeple choose security over freedom . . . as in marriage, the military, and government jobs.

From his experience with neurotic patients, Freud was pessimistic about the ability of mankind to control their unconscious impulses. He saw mankind as doomed to suffer and to destroy. If man is created in the image and likeness of God, what does that say about the Creator God? The instincts that drive human pathology behavior can only be repressed or at best sublimated but never controlled, so there will always be criminals and prisons. The normal ego enables one to be joyful and spontaneous while restricting behavior that is illegal, immoral, and harmful. If the id and super ego are not integrated and controlled by the ego, they can be split off when the id drives some sheeple into sin and criminality and the super ego drives others into monasteries and convents. It appears now from neurology that the id and superego may be functions of the amygdala, a primitive element of the central brain. The ego may be housed in the frontal lobe that evolves slowly until age 20 or so.

[A military unit must translate competition among individual egos into sacrificial cooperation as it pursues a common goal or mission in combat. Once a soldier is trained for such unit cooperation it may be difficult to adjust to normal civilian living again. In Chicago, a 69-year old retired Marine shot and killed his 23-year old neighbor whose dog urinated on the award-winning lawn. Clearly the superego that just says no and the id that just says do it clashed without sufficient modulation from the egos of both to prevent this tragedy. In a related case, a woman jumped onto the subway tracks in NYC to retrieve a fallen jacket. Her companion jumped on to help her and both were hit by an oncoming train. He was killed but she survived to think about it. Both were driven by the id that overcame the superego as the ego was disabled . . . . get it? AIGWOC . . . all in God's will of course.]

Thus we have Muslims and Jews and Christians in constant wars and rumors of wars and prisons that are bursting beyond their capacity. C. G. Jung observed . . . "how important it is to affirm one's own destiny. In this way we forge an ego that does not break down when incomprehensible things happen; an ego that endures and that is capable of coping with the world and with fate . . . when we accept human nature, there is hope." Hope for what, he did not explain.

Someone said that Homo sapiens are 99 percent animal and one percent human, and it is the human part that causes all the trouble. Perhaps this is all due to dysfunctional ego. Both the id and the superego are irrational compared with the ego, which should be rational in this Freudian model of personality. The ego seems to be needed to enable sheeple to navigate and adapt to the inevitable changes that one encounters in a lifetime of challenges. It attempts to predict consequences of actions and to provide balanced control of the id and superego to achieve safety for survival of the species and its function in society. A perfect ego would make perfect choices, but such does not seem to exist. The ego must learn that the only task done perfectly is one that is not attempted at all, which may require several lifetimes, because all outcomes are indefinitely uncertain. All conflicts among individuals appear to be clashes of egos attempting to control other egos.

Consider the dangerous rush by sheeple to retrieve their luggage from the overhead bins in airplanes before the plane stops at the gate, which is against the safety rules. After one too many encounters with unruly flyers a male flight attendant with 20 years service got himself a beer from the cooler, popped the emergency chute and exited the plane along with his career. The ego knows no limits and wants to control all the ids and superegos that it encounters. A person so endowed is termed egotistical. In the extreme case, an ego run amuck may rape and kill to gain control of others. All great leaders appear to have an ego stronger than their followers. [Of course, employees must subordinate their egos to employers if they are to sustain secure employment. You can only violate the rules so many times before you get fired. During working hours your ego belongs to your employer. This may help explain why sheeple with strong egos prefer to be employers rather than employees.]

The essence of ego is to maintain control while the essence of human life is to lose control in the end. When life overcomes the ego, mental illness can result if there is not some spiritual foundation to preserve its anchor in reality. The ego will not volunteer to die so it must be crucified in the end. Jesus warned, "Whoever tries to keep his life will lose it, and whoever loses his life will preserve it." (Luke 17:33) Eda G. Goldstein, who devoted her career to teaching at New York University and practicing ego psychology among troubled clients questioned, "Suppose the purpose of life is to abandon the ego rather than to feed it?" Among spiritual self-help books it is popular to proclaim defeat of the ego as the pathway to happiness and inner peace. In his international best seller, The Purpose Driven Life, (2007) pastor Rick Warren declared, "It is not about you . . . [or your ego] . . . it is about doing God's will." Defeat of the ego in some sheeple may require its complete involuntary crucifixion. One cannot help but realize once again how the creations of God all seem to come with both benefits and burdens, and ego is no exception. When the ego is threatened, optional responses among Homo sapiens include fight, flight, avoid, negotiate, or submit just like other pack animals. That is why we have labor unions . . . or not.

[Researchers in London have discovered that the amygdala, the emotional primitive part of the brain, is larger in sheeple with tendencies to fight and flight responses to stress, compared with those who prefer negotiated settlements to disputes. They also suggest that this brain structure may account for why some are conservatives and some are liberals. The higher order sections of human brains are larger than the amygdala in the liberals than conservatives, possibly accounting for the liberal tendency of more highly educated sheeple. Of course, skeptics will claim that such correlation does not prove causation but, perhaps, it does. All in God's will of course . . . AIGWOC.]

When two uncompromising and controlling egos are married, divorces may result, when they are company managers and unions strikes may result, and when they are national leaders wars may result. So long as egos want to control each other there can be no lasting peace at work, at home, at play. Sheeple need to feel freedom of choice and confident in their personal autonomy, but societies need rules, boundaries, and limitations, so clashes are inevitable. AIGWOC . . . all in God's will of course. Think you can handle that?

World peace does not seem to be a natural state of existence among Homo sapiens. When the egos of teenagers are captured by criminal gangs, it is difficult to regain them even by military organizations. The basic difference between a criminal gang and a military unit is that taxpayers fund the latter and victims fund the former. The group psychology is identical. Research shows that whenever overwhelmed with perceived superior authority, the rational decision making part of the human brain actually shuts down. Military discipline during battle is obtained by suspending the egos of soldiers and assigning their function to superior officers in the line of rank. The most impressive and appalling studies in this area were done by Stanley Milgram (1974). They are famous experiments. Milgram's intent was to see how much harm ordinary sheeple would do to another person if directed and urged to do so by an authority (a psychologist) asking them to electrically shock a person (actor) when he/she gave a wrong answer in a learning experiment. No one was actually shocked although they acted hurt, but the subjects obviously believed they were hurting another participant in the experiment. More than 60 percent of the subjects carried the experiment all the way to "executing" their victims by following orders. Only Homo sapiens among all life forms torture others in the process of warfare and sociopathic criminal acts. Sheeple with weaker egos make better soldiers and gang members because they are more easily commanded by higher authority.

Normal sheeple do not shoot each other, so something must change in order to get soldiers to kill others on command or gang members to kill rivals for the fun of it. Run that idea up to God and you get some interesting concepts about the will of God in affairs of mankind. The clash between personal ego and military discipline exploded on November 5, 2009 when Maj. Nidal Hasan, an army psychiatrist and a Muslim, stormed into the deployment center at Fort Hood, TX and shot and killed 13 soldiers and wounded 29 others because he was vehemently opposed to the wars in Iraq and Afghanistan. Military discipline includes rules, boundaries, and limitations that criminal and religious egos cannot tolerate. Lack of such discipline has contributed to the failures among families and schools in western societies, and it could erode the war against terrorism if enough radical Muslims enter the U.S. Army. All sheeple seem to need a pack leader who serves as head of a family unit for safety and security, no matter whether the family is civilian or military. Where the role of pack leader is missing, the unit culture disintegrates or is replaced with socio-pathic gangs of roaming feral youths, of which the army is a legalized form. Here is the catch; sheeple can only serve one pack leader at a time, according to Jesus. "No one can serve two masters. Either he will hate the one and love the other, or he will be devoted to one and despise the other . . ." (Matthew 6:24) All in the will of God the Almighty One, of course. The question is who is your pack leader?

It is curious that those who fight the wars for personal freedom must give up theirs and suspend their egos in battles to do so. They must convey ego control over to their superiors and obey orders to the point of killing others who are labeled, "enemy." They are told what to wear, how to behave, and where to sleep and what to do 24/7. Perhaps this is why criminals and sociopaths with unyielding egos are not suitable for military service. Killing the enemy becomes heroism and justifiable self defense to well-trained soldiers, as well as gang members. They fight for the preservation of their unit, not unlike a tribe of animals or primates protects its territory. Napoleon Bonaparte (1769-1821) discovered that "a soldier will fight long and hard for a small piece of colored ribbon," and international consultant and former Secretary of State, Henry Kissinger reportedly concluded, "(Soldiers are) dumb, stupid animals to be used as pawns for foreign policy." The essence of the role of the soldier is obedience, submission and abandonment of one's own ego/will in the name of executing the ego/will of an authority. Presumably that includes generals and admirals too.

We convert civilians into professional warriors by disabling their egos and when they return from the killing fields, we expect them to act as though nothing happened. It just doesn't work that way. When conflicts develop between id and superego anxiety emerges to signal the ego that some type of mediation is needed to reduce stress. If not completed, some form of conversion reaction is likely to occur. Many soldiers are emotionally scarred for life for this reason and cannot return to the personal freedom and responsibility of civilian life. The increasing number of suicides among soldiers [more than were killed in combat during 2009 and 2010] could be caused by conflicts they cannot resolve between being an obedient killer at war with ego replaced by the Uniform Code of Military Justice and a responsible citizen at home under civil laws with ego intact. Ego cannot resolve between being an obedient killer at war with disabled ego and a responsible citizen at home with ego intact. After recycling in and out of combat several times they hardly know who they are.

Such mental dichotomies are called "cognitive dissonance," and it takes some very careful navigation to play out both roles of civilian and soldier without permanent damage. The ability of its professional soldiers to do this without emotional scarring is being labeled as "resiliency" by the U.S. Army. Normal sheeple are born with a conscience that uses remorse to prick them into making amends when they do something wrong, But, military training must disable this conscience in order to obey commanders and kill the "enemy." Without any training to re-enable the conscience some of them find it difficult to adjust back to civilian life with family and friends who have not had their experience. The professional soldier of today must make that transition repeatedly and the Veterans Administration just does not seem to understand the problem.

Adolf Hitler (1889-1945) understood this psychology as he wrote in Mein Kampf, (1926) "When two bodies of troops are arrayed in mutual combat, victory will not fall to that side in which every soldier has an expert knowledge of the rules of strategy, but rather to that side which has the best leaders and at the same time the best disciplined, most blindly obedient and best drilled troops." Some warriors returning from the war in Iraq with disabling wounds still cling to their units and wish to return to duty, including one Marine corporal blinded and minus both of his legs. The main difference between an army and a mob is the discipline that requires disabling and suspending the ego. Any soldier who has had his normal ego suspended and replaced by the chain of command needs a total remake to reenter normal society, but few of them get the needed treatment to make the transition. Many of them never make the readjustment, and that must have troubled Maj. Hasan to the point of murderous violence.

In contrast to the notion presented in Plato's "Republic" where soldiers were assigned to the lowest level of society, Adolf Hitler wooed soldiers as the highest form of contribution to a culture through its preservation at the expense of ego. "Our own German language possesses a word which magnificently designates this kind of activity: (fulfillment of duty); it means not to be self-sufficient but to serve the community. The basic attitude from which such activity arises we call "pflichterfullung," to distinguish it from egoism and selfishness idealism. By this we understand the individual's capacity to make sacrifices for the community, for his fellow men." In the end, it is said that Hitler detached from his commanders who he thought were unable and therefore undeserving to win the war.

War brings out extremes of both cruelty and nobility among its soldiers. It is difficult to make the reconciliation with civilian family life and work after they return home from killing sheeple labeled "enemy," and many take alcohol and drugs to stifle the pain; some commit suicide, a well kept secret. The line between murder and military defense often is almost invisible. To help them readjust, in 1855 the U.S. Army created the United States Government Hospital for the Insane, later called St. Elizabeths, near Washington, D.C. to care for its psychiatric patients. But, "combat fatigue" and "post trauma shock disorder" (PTSD) scarcely get the attention they deserve because they are social taboos and returning soldiers are expected to tough it up and get on with life. Psychologists call that "reintegration." But when the psyche of a person has been scrambled and the ego becomes disabled "disintegration" is a more realistic term that illustrates the necessary opposites. It is aptly described by the child's nursery rhyme...

> Humpty Dumpty sat on a wall
> Humpty Dumpty had a great fall
> All the king's horses and all the king's men
> Could not put Humpty Dumpty together again.

Soldiers returning from combat in Iraq and Afghanistan are committing murders at nearly twice the normal rate among the population. These soldiers, who are fighting for the sheeple back home who have no clue about their stress, pay a price not only in terms of endangering their lives but also pay a heavy psychological price, both in coming and going, and Dr. Hasan knew that all too well from his work with them as a psychiatrist. It all starts off with mild anxiety and passing irritability, difficulty in sleeping and increasing feelings of pessimism and apathy. As it worsens, these feelings last longer and the soldier becomes panicky and angry, unsuitable for employment. These symptoms are not restricted to the battlefield and continue even when these soldiers go back home, which affects their personal lives and results in broken marriages, breakdowns, suicides, and murders. It is tragic that soldiers are not trained to reactivate their egos for individual consciousness in civilian life when they return from combat, so many of them are troubled all their lives because of the conflicted values they have to live with. And that does not mention the lifetime physical disabilities that many of them carry as visible evidence of their sacrifice. Perhaps the ones who lose their lives in war really are the lucky ones.

Everything comes with burdens as well as benefits, and the ego is no exception. It is given to think it is immortal and omnipotent, possibly even the eternal life force posed by French philosopher Henri Bergson, (1859-1941) or even the manifestation of God. Only by restraint of nature and other egos, at the level of individual, group, and society or nation, can it be held in check. If the ego cannot give up attempts to control its host as well as others, it must be crucified if it is ever to be enlightened. Perhaps this is an event to be celebrated rather than feared, because it is a necessary transformational experience. God has done that countless times throughout history to prove who is in charge, including sacrificing his only son. (Romans, chapter 9) Perhaps that is why we call the day Jesus was crucified, "good" Friday. We are not made to like it, so aging and death happens without our permission . . . on the scale of time and space we all are insignificant zits in history of the Universe, and the ego does not like that.

Getting Homo sapiens to let go of the will to control may require the will of God the Almighty One to overcome each person, one at a time. For some who cannot let go of the need for control, this experience is fearful, depressing, and may even result in suicide; the last act of self control. It is the eventual universal struggle of all sheeple to confront the fears of existential anxiety, described by Soren Kierkegaard, and surrender their will to their Creator. For others who can substitute Christ from ego control, it is a renewal and possibly even rebirth into becoming a different person, transformed by the will of God the Almighty One. The payoff for this condition for Apostle Paul was contentment with his circumstance whatever they may be. "I have learned the secret of being content in every and any situation, whether well fed or hungry, whether living in plenty or in want." (Philippians 4: 12). One can only wonder how he accommodated his execution.

That kind of growth takes struggle and suffering and maybe meditation as practiced in Buddhism, and maybe a personal crisis beyond control. In Zen Buddhism, one of the eight main branches, it is not that the ego has a problem, but that the ego IS the problem. No matter what the ego does and no matter what happens to the ego, as long as the ego remains, the tensions of opposites must also remain. It is not enough to raise the ego to a higher synthesis; it is necessary to transcend the ego altogether, that is, to break out of the dualistic matrix which the ego itself embodies. Unless the I/Self dies, God cannot live within. This goal is sought through intense practice of meditation and yoga by the Hindu and Buddhist devotees. And it is accomplished by Christians in total loss of self in Christ.

Apostle Paul remarked, "It is no longer I who live but Christ lives in me . . ." (Galatians 2:20) But, recall that he did not choose Christ, but rather Christ chose him on the road to Damascus . . . so where was the free will? (Acts 9:3-8) Many sheeple find this idea difficult to understand and very depressing, but it is like the seed that must die in order to make a tree, or the crucifixion and resurrection needed to liberate the everlasting Christ in Jesus. Jesus struggled as he prayed, "My soul is overwhelmed with sorrow to the point of death . . . My Father, if it is possible, may this cup be taken from me. Yet not as I will, but as you will." (Matthew 26-38-39) He sweat as though it were blood oozing from his pores. His humanity had to be sacrificed to gain eternal life, but where was the free will? For most of us, trust in God only occurs when we have nowhere else to turn, when our basket of resources is empty and there is no one who can help us escape death of ego.

The law of opposites says for every action there is an equal and opposite reaction. After all, the first law of thermodynamics says energy can neither be created nor destroyed, so it must go somewhere whether it is positive or negative. The same goes for information . . . it also possibly cannot be created, only discovered. So perhaps the human genome code of DNA was there all the time just waiting for the moment of its discovery. So perhaps hopelessness marks the beginning of wisdom, and death is a necessary opposite to life and pleasure that must be balanced with suffering. The wise King Solomon observed that everything comes with benefits and burdens, even wisdom. There just is no free lunch. "Then I applied myself to the understanding of wisdom, and also of madness and folly, but I learned that this, too, is chasing after the wind. For with much wisdom comes much sorrow; the more knowledge, the more grief . . . I saw that wisdom is better than folly, just as light is better than darkness. The wise man has eyes in his head, while the fool walks in the darkness; but I came to realize that the same fate overtakes them both. Then I thought in my heart, the fate of the fool will overtake me also. What then do I gain by being wise? I said in my heart, this too is meaningless. For the wise man, like the fool, will not be long remembered; in days to come both will be forgotten. Like the fool, the wise man too must die . . . Man's fate is like that of the animals; the same fate awaits them both; As one dies, so dies the other. All have the same breath; man has no advantage over the animal. Everything is meaningless. All go to the same place; all come from dust, and to dust all return. Who knows if the spirit of man rises upward and if the spirit of the animal goes down into the Earth?" (Ecclesiastes 1:17-18, 2:13-16, 3: 18-21) Is this not indefinite uncertainty, or what?

More than 2,000 years later, Russian author Alexander Solzhenitsyn (1918-2008) came to a similar conclusion. "Do not pursue what is illusory—property and position: all that is gained at the expense of your nerves decade after decade and can be confiscated in one fell night. Live with a steady superiority over life—don't be afraid of misfortune, and do not yearn after happiness; it is after all, all the same: the bitter doesn't last forever, and the sweet never fills the cup to overflowing." Think you can handle that?

Perhaps the sacrificial suffering and death of Jesus of Nazareth were symbolic of crucifying the ego to obtain its submission to a higher power. "Nevertheless, not my will but thine be done." However, ego-driven writers had to invoke the resurrection to reinstate his immortality and rule over death. Mother Teresa expressed this purification of ego through her struggle and suffering among the abandoned outcasts of Calcutta. She lamented suffering but reveled in giving all that Jesus wanted to take and taking all that he gives, always with a smile. She saw Jesus in the sheeple of the slums and understood him to say, "When you did not do it for them, you did not do it for me." (Matthew 25:45) She wrote, "Heaven is full of slum people."

Everyone has some approach to longevity. For some it resides in perpetual activity and for others in pursuit of wisdom. A wise sage wrote, "The exercise of will consumes us; the exercise of power destroys us; but the pursuit of knowledge leaves our infirm constitution in a state of perpetual calm. So, desire or volition is dead in me, killed by thought." A Chinese proverb states, "To gain knowledge add something everyday; to obtain wisdom remove something everyday." The word "wisdom" is discussed thirty-seven times in Voices of Sedona. The only problem with wisdom is by the time you get it there is little time left to use it. The capacity for true wisdom does not develop before experiences arising from polarities of success and failure, gain and loss, love and fear, sickness and health, and life and death.

Psychologist, M. Scott Peck (1936-2005) in his award winning book on psychotherapy, The Road Less Traveled, (1978, 2003) observed that becoming aware of being powerless to change things leads to "therapeutic depression" often found in older sheeple. To be aware of how we think things could be, should be, ought to be, and not having the power to make it happen is a personal tragedy because that awareness fills some of us with sadness, helplessness, and loneliness. That's why they say that ignorance is bliss, because if we didn't know any better it wouldn't bother us, so when we do know and can't do anything about it we feel depressed. And yet, this too is a part of human life. So, medicating it to avoid the feelings deprives one of this human growth experience.

The only options in aging seem to be the depressive role of useless baggage or the pseudo gusto of gray-haired imaginary youth seen in the air-brushed models used to sell everything from assisted living to golf clubs to vacation trips and pills for erectile dysfunction. It might be preferable to recapture the traditional role of Chinese elders, that of the wise old sage, but modern technology moves too rapidly for aging elders to keep pace. The ancient <u>Tao te Ching</u> teaches, "The great task of the sage is to see into the darkness and not be afraid because therein lies the greatest truths amidst infirmity and death, fears and frustrations . . . The sage has experienced all opposites and lets them go without clinging or fretting. Therefore, the sage can talk without lecturing, act without worrying, and live in contentment with all events. The sage releases things, thoughts, fears, and expectations to make room for growth . . . The sage lays down the burdens of resentments, regrets, slights, injuries, grudges, and disappointments as they are much too cumbersome for a person of wisdom and contentment . . . the sage must travel light."

The Bible offers some similar aging wisdom. "The fear of the Lord leads to life: Then one rests content, untouched by trouble." (Proverbs 19:23) "I know what it is to be in need, and I know what it is to have plenty. I have learned the secret of being content in any and every situation, whether well fed or hungry, whether living in plenty or in want." (Philippians 4:12) Perhaps we all need to search deeply for that secret. Things came and went in the past without our permission and control, and the future will unfold in the same way. All that exists is NOW and hope for the future. Life is not over until it's over, but God is in control, so you better get used to it. Perhaps a read of the Principles of Theofatalism™ could help support the "D.R.E.A.D." of life with something more . . . wise . . . or not (Chapter 2). Maybe the opposite is just curiosity and the wonder at what will happen next if one can only survive another day. Feel good inside no matter what happens outside. That's an order.

12. The unreasonable power of faith

[Fair warning: This essay is long and as challenging to read as it was for me to write. So give your self time to really understand it.] Anyone who relies upon faith-based beliefs may be driven by some form of insanity, i.e., the necessary opposite to reason. But, faith is not a free choice so don't be so quick to judge. For example, anyone who claims the United States was founded in freedom upon faith in Christian principles is deluded . . . by God of course. The British pamphleteer recruited by Benjamin Franklin who helped George Washington obtain support for the American revolution with his persuasive arguments, Thomas Paine (1737-1809) wrote, "We can only reason from what is; we can reason on actualities, but not on possibilities." It seems that reason can only take us where logic will, while faith can take us anywhere it wants us to go. But, if reason points to a black hole in cosmology and to the ultimate extinction of our solar system, who would not prefer to contemplate the stars instead?

Our nation was founded upon faith more than reason. It seems that only about one third of colonists supported the revolution, one third opposed it and one third were neutral. Nevertheless, the Continental Congress declared independence anyway, and some say it was based upon doctrines in free masonry. However, the American revolutionaries who signed the Declaration of Independence had to void faith in their own scriptures in order to take up arms against their king, replacing faith in God with faith in themselves. Nevertheless, they proclaimed, "We declare these truths to be self-evident; that all men are created equal and are endowed by their creator with certain inalienable rights . . ." except for women and slaves of course.

In writing his declaration of independence, Thomas Jefferson was disobeying the instructions of Apostle Paul to obey those in authority and to pay their taxes; ". . . whoever rebels against authority is rebelling against what God has instituted and those who do so will bring judgment upon themselves." (Romans 13: 1 7) Jefferson's premise that governments "derive their just power from consent of the governed" voids the instruction of St. Paul; "The authorities that exist have been established by God . . . if you owe taxes then pay your taxes." Who you gonna believe? Jefferson was obviously a reader of Paine and a humanist who would later write his own edited version of the teachings by Jesus called, The Jefferson Bible. (1819) Although Paine definitely influenced the founding fathers, after he used logical reasoning to debunk faith in the Bible in his infamous pamphlet, "The Age of Reason," (1795) he was abandoned by all his friends, including George Washington, so he died bereft and alone and his beheaded body was scattered about Europe. No one knows whatever became of his wife. It seems that political correctness trumped reason even then. Ironically, the faith used by Paine to gain support for the American Revolution defeated the reason that he used later to criticize religion . . . and in the end faith trumped reason as all of his friends abandoned him. It may be as Jesus said, "The spirit gives life, the flesh counts for nothing." (John 6:63)

St. Augustine said faith requires no explanation and without it no explanation will do. Such is the mind of mankind created by God. Jesus declared, "No one can come to me unless it is granted him by the Father," (John 6:65) and also, "All that the Father gives to me will come to me." (John 6:37) Taken together Jesus is stating that no one can believe in him unless God grants it, and all to whom God grants it will believe. According to this passage, then, God grants faith to whomever he wills, and they cannot refuse to accept it. That leads to some very strange beliefs. Jesus taught that anyone with faith the size of a mustard seed could move mountains and "nothing will be impossible for you." (Matthew 17:20) Believe it, or not. Whether it is true and factual or not does not seem to matter to those who by faith find comfort and security in his teachings. During the Great Depression, empirical psychologist Henry Link wrote in his best selling, The Return to Religion, (1936) ". . . religion does not promise you a perfect life on Earth nor freedom from suffering; it does guarantee you the strength to bear suffering. The basic values of life and character are religious, often unreasonable and in the last analysis beyond reason . . . the strategic time to teach children the higher values is when they are too young to understand, but not too young to accept." So it was that Jesus taught the kingdom of God belonged to little children presumably because their imagination and trust is still maleable.

[But, why do some sheeple commit suicide and worse? Tragedies occur almost daily if you have the right internet connection. Just google "murder-suicide" to get the latest reports. A mother, age 25, drove herself and three small children into the Hudson River and drowned them all to escape a life she could no longer justify. Obviously in her mind, the benefits of murder-suicide outweighed the burdens of living at that moment. Her ten-year old son escaped to think about it the rest of his life. He reported the last words his mother said as the car sank were, "I made a mistake." Whether she meant making four kids she could not support with a deadbeat dad or committing murder-suicide is not known. Her dredged up car was found in reverse. The one thing that is certain is she cannot go back and do anything differently. In Ohio a man killed his wife and three infant children and then committed suicide while a mother of two killed her children and then herself also. A man killed himself in a car "accident" the day after his most beloved wife died. A freshman violinist at Rutgers University threw himself to death off the George Washington Bridge after his brief tryst with a male subject was secretly taped and posted on the Internet. About the same time, a vivacious and popular young student about to graduate from Yale was killed in an accident when her long hair got stuck in a rapidly spinning lathe machine during a lab experiment. A man in Australia threw his four-year old daughter off a highway bridge to punish his wife who was divorcing him. A 15-year old boy was lured to a grizzly death in Florida by his ex-girlfriend and other teenagers who burned his body and disposed of the remnants in a dumpster while her stepfather tried to hide the facts. Such tragedies occur in the news almost daily. Death is a permanent solution to a temporary problem called life. Sheeple make decisions all the time they may later come to regret when the subconscious benefits exceed the burdens of doing something . . . anything . . . often in the blink of an eye. If nothing happens outside the will of God, such things must be necessary or they would be different. So maybe there are no mistakes, only God-given choices and inevitable consequences. Think you can handle that?]

Abd-ru-shin [aka Oskar Bernhardt (1875-1941)] wrote in "In the Light of Truth—The Grail Message," that ". . . all teachings/thoughts were at one time willed by God precisely adapted to the individual peoples and countries . . ." When you overlay the research in neurology and the new theory of memetics, i.e., contagious ideas, with this assumption about God, one may conclude that mankind thinks what God wants them to think—including murder-suicide—difficult as that may be to accept. Most sheeple feel the need to believe in something more powerful than they are even though it may conflict with their insistence upon having free will or the laws of nature, no matter how unreasonable that obviously is. Only those given unbridled egos can think they are more powerful than God.

There are many folks trying to accommodate faith and reason in the same sentence, up to and including the Pope. Faith is an unproven hypothesis, the hope of unseen things, and when it becomes accepted it is a belief, still subject to challenge and adaptation but capable of driving behavior until overturned.

Faith and reason seem to be mutually exclusive; reason is driven by the senses and intellect, and faith is driven by intuition and feelings in the terms of C.G. Jung. Both faith and reason seem to be a necessary aspect of human psyche. But the belief in existence of human free will and the omnipotent God is a mutually exclusive dichotomy that mankind has not reconciled after trying for 2,000 years. All in God's will of course . . . AIGWOC.

Reason is based upon a rationally developed body of formal logic, but faith is a non-discriminating function of mind that is directed by ego to a given object, often depending on social norms and focused upon authority figures, real or imagined. This is why Catholics worship their patron saints, and children write to Santa Claus. Faith seems to be based upon outrageous declarations without any basis in fact, the more the better, which makes its power all the more baffling. If it were not for the social pressures against it, psychiatry might well label faith a mental disorder. Faith and belief seem to be used as synonyms related to teachings of Jesus 229 times in the New Testament. In each case, it appears that such belief is within the power of the believer, except for those to whom it is not given. (Luke 8:12, John 12:39-40) Apostle Paul said faith is "being sure of what we hope for and certain of what we do not see." (Hebrews 11:1)

The world changed with this declaration of faith, "Therefore let all Israel be assured of this: God has made this Jesus, whom you crucified, both Lord and Christ." (Acts 2:36) In science, we progress from hypothesis to conviction bolstered by reason, and finally to certainty forged in the fires of personal experience. But, the challenge of faith is to believe what you do not see, and the reward of faith is to see what you believe. The Church teaches that faith is both an act of God and an act of Man, the ultimate in both/and duality. Jesus proclaimed the duality of faith after he asked his disciples who they thought he was. "Simon Peter answered, You are the Christ, the Son of the living God. Jesus replied, Blessed are you, Simon son of Jonah, for this was not revealed to you by man, but by my Father in heaven. And I tell you that you are Peter, and on this rock [of faith] I will build my church, and the gates of Hades will not overcome it." (Matthew 16: 16-18)

From that declaration of mutual faith there has arisen a presumed dual nature of mankind, spirit and flesh, those who are born-again Christians and those who are not. Prior to that time Homo sapiens had invented all manner of different beliefs to help explain to each other the unknown and the unknowable. From beliefs in the roaming spirits of animals and inanimate objects to the projection of human-like behavior onto Gods of many different names, there was no general belief in a universal monistic God until he allegedly took form as a human and lived among the Jews and Romans of antiquity. Faith did not mature until it was focused upon belief in that one single solitary life. But, that is not the end of the story.

There continue to be unlimited new versions and interpretations among Homo sapiens. Take, for example, the Catholic beliefs about the immaculate conception of Mary by the "Virgin Mother" that are not Biblical, but are taken as gospel because the Pope says so, and he ought to know because God told him so and the Council of Trent made it official in 1564. The problem with all faith-based religious beliefs is that they are so irrelevant to the problems facing sheeple daily that require reason for solutions. Faith and reason seem to be necessary either/or opposites unless they can merge into both/and complements. The human intellect seems unable to reconcile the difference without some external force or power of intervention . . . called God.

In order to accept the first century Christian faith, sheeple had to suspend the reason they depended upon to function in the society they had created. It is not much different today. Faith must exist in order for disbelievers to refute it. You can't have the ability and freedom to believe without the ability and freedom to disbelieve. Sheeple, from atheists and agnostics to Buddhists and Baptists, Catholics, Deists, Jews, Muslims or Mormons, Scientologists and Zoroasters all think they have it figured out, but none of them can be sure what they believe is true. Everyone must believe what they are given. But, why do sheeple want to believe so badly that they are willing to suspend their common sense and believe unbelievable things with no real proof? Answer: Sheeple seem to be born with the need to believe in things that are unprovable. It is from the seeds of imagination and faith that knowledge seems to grow. However, knowing for sure that what we know is true may be universally impossible. All we have are assumptions and probabilities . . . indefinite uncertainty.

Neurologist, Robert A. Burton has shown in <u>On Being Certain</u>, (2008) from experiments with the human brain that sheeple often believe they are right when they are not. According to him, certainty is indefinitely uncertain. This is true in science, government, business, and most often in religion. But, billions of sheeple believe that a resurrected Jesus is real and walks and talks with them, like it says in the hymn titled, "In The Garden" . . . "and he walks with me and he talks with me, and he tells me I am his own." Is that human imagination or what? If atheists can "prove" by logical reasoning that God cannot exist, as he is described in the Bible, then why do so many sheeple still believe that he does?

[Written in 1912 by C. Austin Miles, as a commission by a music publisher, "In the Garden" was no less spiritually inspired for all its secular beginnings. Miles left an accounting of the writing of it. He described sitting in a darkened room and taking up the Bible for inspiration. "My hands were resting on the Bible while I stared at the light blue wall. As the light faded, I seemed to be standing at the entrance of a garden, looking down a gently winding path, shaded by olive branches. A woman in white, with head bowed, hand clasping her throat, as if to choke back her sobs, walked slowly into the shadows. It was Mary. As she came to the tomb, upon which she place her hand, she bent over to look in, and hurried away . . . Mary reappeared; leaning her head upon her arm at the tomb, she wept. Turning herself, she saw Jesus standing, and so did I."]

The image of Mary arises out of the initial stanza, as she seeks her lost son. Sheeple who are bereaved take comfort and succor from the lyrics of the refrain, in which it becomes clear that the loved one's spirit is yet alive and ever present. The stanza is generally sung in a sweet, almost unsure, light and wistful tone, while the refrain is sung joyfully with great strength and conviction.

> And He walks with me, and he talks with me
> And He tells me I am His own,
> And the Joy we share as we tarry there
> none other has ever known.

"I awakened in full light," finished Miles in his accounting, "gripping the Bible, with muscles tense and nerves vibrating. Under the inspiration of this vision I wrote as quickly as the words could be formed the poem exactly as it has since appeared. That same evening I wrote the music." It does not take a terribly religious individual to grasp in the hearing of the song its seamless content and timeless power to tame grief. This can only have come of Miles' astonishing spiritual experience the night he wrote it whole of one piece. It is a hymn that eases pain for all who sing it or hear it sung.

What is amazing about Homo sapiens is how they grant authority to so many different religious sources that vary with time and situation. Among the most curious are the "psychic readers" who claim they have direct access to the library of "Akashic Records" that contains the complete file on everyone for all past and future lives to come. The term "akasha," along with the concept of an aetheric library, originated with Hindu philosophy and was incorporated into the 19th century movement of theosophy called the New Age originating with Russian mystic, Helena Blavatsky and her partners. The idea is comparable to the biblical "Book of Life" which is consulted to see whether or not the dead are admitted to heaven. (Revelation 20:12) Now it is a principle of physics that information is never lost even though it may be dispersed throughout the Universe. It may have been there all the time just waiting for the right time to be discovered and applied . . . just like energy. So, maybe there is some truth to the odd beliefs among mystics and psychics who claim they can access the "collective unconscious" proposed by C.G. Jung and practiced by the late clairvoyant mystic, Edgar Cayce.

Following a charismatic leader or wanting to lead willing followers is part and parcel of the human condition. But no leader can exist without willing followers. In fact, it is followers who make leaders. One is reminded of the genetic setup of ants or bees who are born to act as is best for the survival of the tribe with no regard for individuals. In the case of humans there are the lust for power on the side of the leader and the fear of standing on one's own insecure feet on the side of the follower. There is also the longing for the grand feeling of security and identity by belonging to a faith-based group, to be one with a crowd under one common theme, the sense of unity with others under one aim even if it is fraudulent. This unity is a necessary prerequisite for an army or a corporate unit or a church to succeed. Many sheeple would rather be wrong in a crowd than to be right all alone. It is basic to human psychology.

Consider followers of the Beetles rock group, for example, or the fans of Lady Gaga and Bruce Springsteen, "The Boss," or the not Rev. Joel Osteen and his "prosperity preaching," even though it conflicts with the teaching of Jesus about hoarding personal wealth. (Matthew 6:19) [Osteen proclaims that his success was ordained by God, and those church members who disagreed with his vision were replaced by thousands more who agree with him . . . and who are we to say it isn't so. He ignored his critics and followed the call of his spirit/intuition to become what God called him to be. Is it not so for everyone?] What is the difference between the rocketing success of Osteen and President Barack Obama? Neither of them could occupy their lofty positions unless a camp of followers were driven [by what force?] to call them "my pastor" or "my president." Napoleon de Bonaparte caused the deaths of more than a million sheeple during his conquest of Europe, but that was peanuts compared with the 55 million sheeple who were killed in WWII, thanks to Adolf Hitler. The Bible says there will be false prophets so who are we to make it otherwise? Jesus said so; ". . . many false prophets will appear and deceive many people." (Matthew 24:11) The problem is we cannot tell the real from the false prophets as it all definitely is indefinitely uncertain. That is the fact, Jack.

Some researchers are calling this phenomenon evidence for a "God gene" existing in all Homo sapiens. But, perhaps there is no need for religion if we have faith in science. British Oxford professor and zoologist, Richard Dawkins has become wealthy and famous trying to explain biology sans a God for his fellow atheists. His books, <u>The God Delusion</u> (2008) and <u>The Selfish Gene</u>

(2006) are worldwide best sellers, so perhaps something new is developing. Extending the work of Charles Darwin, Dawkins proposes that sheeple may have developed the God gene as a means of survival among the fittest who feared the powers of nature that are life threatening and respected the nurturing aspects of Earth that sustains them. From this evolution, sheeple developed fear and respect for the warrior/protector in the father of the primitive family and love for the nurturing mother image that cared for the young until they became self supporting. As the children grew to adults they never left behind all the images of parenting and created idols as substitutes.

When feeling distress, it would seem natural for sheeple to seek comfort and solace from the mothering figure or archetype imbedded in the brain as an "engram," i.e., a fixed pattern in the neuron cells that C.G Jung labeled archetypes. Although the parent relationship is outgrown, the mental substitute prevails. Thus, there developed the Greek and Roman Gods of mythology who acted much like sheeple and, eventually, a savior of his tribe in a family of God on Earth. The earliest form of such a God is from ancient Hinduism that had words in Sanskrit which translated mean, Generator, Operator, and Destroyer. (G.O.D.) The notion of a single God as Father of all, to be feared and loved simultaneously, is the present manifestation among western cultures of the genetic evolution up to this time with all its many variations. This may help explain why the Catholic Church calls their priests, "Father," even though Jesus expressly forbade it. (Matthew 23:9) Of course, the Eastern cultures developed a genetic strain somewhat differently to help them cope with the challenges of life not based upon a monistic God from the teachings of the Buddha. However, this does not help explain why some are Catholic, some Protestant, some Mormon, some Muslim, some Hindu, some Buddhist, etc. unless God wills it so. Although family faith is most often an accident of birth, how can one explain the occasional conversions from one faith to another? God's will, of course.

The fact is that life is dangerous on planet Earth and most sheeple can't face the harsh realities of suffering and death without a sedative to keep them from thinking rationally, and faith in faith emerged as that sedative. When the Roman Empire was starting to disintegrate, Augustine of Hippo, possibly the originator of Catholic dogma, (354-430 CE) developed the concept of the Church as a spiritual City of God distinct from the material City of Man. The rule of Rome by the sword was replaced with rule of Rome by the Word. His faith was late in coming after he fathered a son with his concubine and prayed, "Lord, give me chastity and continence, but not yet." After he was converted, his pen and voice were able to put down all the rising "heresies" of his time in the fourth century with which he was given to disagree. St. Augustine, possibly the father of Catholicism observed, "To one who has faith, no explanation is necessary. To one without faith, no explanation is possible. We must start by believing; then afterwards we may be led on to master the evidence for ourselves." The question for thinking sheeple is where does that need to believe come from? Augustine answers; "God has made us restless until we find our rest in him." What purpose does this hunger serve and why does it continue to exist? History provides many examples, but few answers.

The Bible as we know it was not formalized by the Church until the Council of Trent in 1564 to counter the Reformation. Perhaps one can only say that mortal ego, which serves us so well in life, must give way to surrender because God created it that way. Perhaps Apostle Paul was expressing such a hope as he wrote, "So when this corruptible shall have put on incorruption, and this mortal shall have put on immortality, then shall be brought to pass the saying that is written, Death is swallowed up in victory. O death, where is thy sting? O grave, where is thy victory?" (1 Corinthians 15: 54-55)

Those without faith must rely upon logic and reason that often fails to justify reality. Sage of the "Baltimore Sun," H.L. Mencken (1880-1956) wrote that "the most common of all follies is to believe passionately in the palpably not true. It's the chief occupation of humankind." St. Paul foresaw the need for sheeple to prefer fantasy to truth. "For the time will come when men will not put up with sound doctrine. Instead, to suit their own desires, they will gather around them a great number of teachers to say what their itching ears want to hear. They will turn their ears away from the truth and turn aside to myths." (2 Timothy 4: 3-4) Joel Osteen and those preachers of his ilk prove the power of giving sheeple what they want to hear. How sad to have to live an illusion just because sheeple can't handle the existential anxiety of indefinite uncertainty. The opposite, of course, is faith in reason and the acceptance of indefinite uncertainty about knowing what we know. Mark Twain said it is not what we don't know that causes all the trouble. Rather it is what we think we know for sure.

Among the modern nations of Europe, sheeple appear to be evolving some new genes as half or more of them claim they do not believe in a monistic God. But, the opposite is a developing war between Islam and Christianity that is based totally upon their understanding of God as it is taught by their religious leaders and affirmed by their observations. At the root of it is determination by Jews to take the land they believe that God promised to them and equal determination by the Arabs to keep the land they occupied before the Jews arrived. Of course, killing each other over faith-based beliefs among Homo sapiens is nothing new. God has many disguises. No one knows where we came from, why we are here, or where we are going. No one knows whether God made man or man made God. Viewed from a wide variety of perspectives one could conclude that life itself is a pointless enterprise. So we must live with the existential anxiety of indefinite uncertainty. Apparently, things are evolving as they must or they would be different. Nevertheless, faith makes an interesting study because it appears to be a necessary complement to doubt.

The more committed we become to a belief the harder it is to relinquish it even with overwhelming evidence to the contrary. Kurt Wise, with a Ph.D. in geology from Harvard gave this testimony; "I had to make a decision between evolution and Scripture . . . . If all the evidence in the Universe turns against it, I would be the first to admit it, but I would still be a creationist because that is what the Word of God seems to indicate." Faith is very powerful stuff and acts like a drug addiction; Denial when challenged; Irritability when confronted; Using it to avoid real issues; Temporary feeling of well being; Crutch syndrome. Jesus said if you have only so much faith as a mustard seed you could order a mountain to move and it would and "nothing would be impossible to you." (Matthew 17:20) He repeated this same promise to his disciples in several forms in other texts too. (Matthew 21:21-22, Matthew 7:7-8, Matthew 18: 19-20, Mark 11: 24-25, Luke 11: 9-13, Luke 17: 4-6, John 14: 13-14, John 15:7, John 15:16, John 16: 23-24) This is pretty fantastic stuff. The only problem is that none of these promises was fulfilled in the Bible nor since then, and yet each generation seems to produce a new wave of preachers who claim it is all true followed by a flock of sheeple who believe them. Even Jesus seemed to have his doubts as he said the opposite; "Which of you by taking thought can add one cubit unto his stature?" [or by worrying can add a single hour to your life?] (Matthew 6:27, Luke 12:25) From time to time a new guru arrives and finds no shortage of followers on the path to enlightenment.

Everything has its opposite and religion is no exception. Two opposing incompatible beliefs are the basis of Christianity and Islam. It is written in the Old Testament, "But I am the Lord your God, who brought you out of Egypt. You shall acknowledge no God but me, no Savior except me." (Hosea 13:3-5) The Koran, holy book of Islam, relies upon that idea to this day. But, the New Testament says, ". . . the angel said to them, Do not be afraid. I bring you good news of great joy that will be for all the sheeple. Today in the town of David a Savior has been born to you; he is Christ the Lord. This will be a sign to you: You will find a baby wrapped in cloths and lying in a manger. (Luke 2:10-12) The Koran proclaims the opposite, "Allah is only one God. Far be it from his glory that he should have a son." (4:171) "How could he have a son when he has no consort and he himself created all things?" (6:101) "Never did Allah take to himself a son and never was there with him any other God." (23:91)

Maybe these opposite ideas are leading the world into its next great religious conflict between Christians and Muslims. In the gospel of John, Jesus is quoted in opposites also; "No one has seen the Father except the one who is from God; only he has seen the Father." (John 6:46) "If you really knew me, you would know my Father as well. From now on, you do know him and have seen him." (John 14:7) So, let's take him at his word. Jesus describes the kingdom of heaven/God 18 times in all the gospels as a place that can be literally entered and seen. "I tell you the truth, anyone who will not receive the kingdom of God like a little child will never enter it." (Mark 10:15) "I tell you the truth, some who are standing here will not taste death before they see the kingdom of God." (Luke 9:27) But, then he says, "The kingdom of God does not come with your careful observation, nor will sheeple say, Here it is, or There it is, because the kingdom of God is within you." (Luke 17: 20-21) Such obvious contradictions in the Bible are conveniently ignored by sheeple of faith and their trusted leaders. If the Bible actually is the Word of God, why did he include stumbling blocks so that some sheeple disbelieve and will be condemned for eternity while others accept by faith and will be saved? How can this be unless it is the will of God the Almighty One? Muslims and Jews prefer the Old Testament while Christians prefer the New Testament. So, who you gonna believe?

Every religion seems to be based in some revelations of its founders whose followers think they got it from God. There was an illiterate camel driver named Muhammad (570-632 CE) in what is now Saudi Arabia whose life was interrupted by strange revelations that occurred over a period of years while he meditated in a cave for relaxation near Mecca. Today they call that schizophrenia for sure. His wife encouraged him to share what he was given to others and soon there developed enough converts to defend his faith and to conquer a large part of the world for Islam. Although the earliest text of the Koran appears to be dated some 70 years after his death, Muslim devotees claim the authenticity of present versions must not be questioned. But, they immediately split into two factions, Sunni and Shiite, over which should be the supreme rulers, a fight that continues to this day. Limitations of the written Koran eventually were realized, so one Muhammad al-Bukhari (1810-1870) devoted his life to compiling the essence of truths in Islam in the form of oral sayings called the "Hadith."

Emerging from early Islam is the mystical version called Sufism, meaning wisdom. It spans cultures and languages and seeks for its devotees a "science whose objective is reparation of the heart by turning it away from all except God." Scholars believe that Arab Muslims are descended from Ishmael, the bastard son of Abraham and his wife's slave girl, Hagar as described in Genesis 16-19. Note that God promised to protect Ishmael and to make him a mighty nation of twelve tribes also, but his descendents are lost in history. (Genesis 17:20) So those who support Israel against the Arabs are not being fair to the Muslims now are they. The Muslim belief in the Torah (first five books of the Bible) as well as the prophet-hood of Moses are fundamental tenants of Islam and are codified into Shar'ia law. Mere public threats of burning the Koran can set off riots all over the Muslim world proclaiming death to the unbelieving infidels. They regard Muhammad as the restorer of the original monotheism of Abraham, Moses, Isaac, and Jacob which they claim became distorted over time either in interpretation, in text, or both. So they condemn the Jews for abandoning their common father Abraham and disobeying the 613 laws of Moses—365 don'ts and 248 do's. [Notre Dame Professor Joseph Blenkinsopp queried, (1992) "One would think that what calls for an explanation is not why most people stopped believing in the dogma of Mosaic authorship, but rather why anyone believed it in the first place."]

Muslim devotees of Islam are required to observe Five Pillars which unite Muslims into a social community no matter their nationality. In addition, Islamic law (shari'ah) has developed into a system of rules that direct virtually all aspects of life and society for Muslims as it was in the day of Moses. For example, under shari'ah law the penalty for adultery is death by stoning. Muslims also are directed to fight off invaders and to convert infidels by force if necessary, apparent opposites to the pacifism of Jesus. Muhammad (570-632) proclaimed, "I am commanded to fight all people until they believe there is no God but Allah, and Muhammad is his messenger." The basis for Jihad or holy war in the Koran could be this verse; "Fight those who believe not in Allah nor the last day, nor hold that forbidden which hath been forbidden by Allah and his apostle, nor acknowledge the religion of truth even if they are the people of the book, until they pay the Jizya tax with willing submission, and feel themselves subdued." (9:29). Until September 11, 2001 few westerners had ever heard of "Wahhabism." Now some recognize the word as describing an austere and puritanical type of Islam, mentioned frequently in connection with Osama bin Laden and Saudi Arabia and often named as the inspiration behind the 9/11 terror attacks in New York City. The word "Wahhabi" stems from the name of the founder of this conservative system of Islamic thought, Muhammad Ibn Abd al-Wahhab (1702-1791), companion and religious adviser to Muhammad Ibn Saud, founder of the House of Saud.

Adolf Hitler (1889-1945) had some profound insight that fits the Islamic threat now facing all Christian-based nations. He wrote in Mein Kampf (1926), "Any philosophy, whether of a religious or political nature—and sometimes the dividing line is hard to determine—fights less for the negative destruction of the opposing ideology than for the positive promotion of its own. Hence its struggle is less defensive than offensive. For this reason alone, the philosophy's offensive will be more systematic and also more powerful than the defensive against a philosophy, since here, too, as always, the attack and not the defense makes the decision. The fight against a spiritual power with methods of violence remains defensive, however, until the sword becomes the support, the herald and disseminator, of a new spiritual doctrine . . . Good care should be taken not to deny things that just happen to be true." In other words, Hitler thought sheeple always are more inclined to fight for something than against something. The question facing Christians now is whether they are driven to fight for their way of life against the onslaught of radical Islam, for they are mutually exclusive religions and are impossible of compromise. If they are truly Christians, pacifism must govern, and Islam wins. (Luke 6:20-47) All in God's will of course . . . AIGWOC.

Any moderately thinking person who takes the time can find many contradictions and downright falsehoods in every holy religious text, the Bible probably chief among them, but the faithful believe in them anyway. Jesus claimed that with enough faith, (as a much as a mustard seed) one could move mountains, throw trees into the sea, handle snakes and drink poison with no harm, and do greater miracles than he did. The question again is, where does such faith come from? Sheeple seem to need some object of worship outside themselves to get through the day. If it is not a God or savior or mythical warrior hero, it is a celebrity such as a professional athlete or a rock star or actor and actress, a super-wealthy icon, even a politician. Especially a politician. Think how they are chosen by the voters who know very little about them and nothing about how they will perform. Anyone who has gained celebrity status will do for faithful worship, including celebrity preachers. This need to worship something/someone accounts for the sales of those celebrity magazines at the checkout counter in your grocery store and the hyperventilating crowds that follow sports and movie idols.

Such celebrity idol worship has economic, political, and religious aspects. This could be a distortion of what is called in Vedic yoga the "ishta deva" or mental image of God incarnate. In Hinduism, spiritual celebrity is reserved for the ascetics, who are called the sadhu or the sannyasin. Theirs is a rejection of life and all that it means in exchange for a search to attain moksha, that is, release from the cycle of rebirth or samsara. It requires rejection of the household duties and responsibilities of all stages of life. It also requires the rejection of the religious beliefs. Indeed, the ceremony making one a sannyasin includes the burning of copies of the Vedas, a symbolic rejection even of one's role in maintaining the cosmos. The sannyasins become wandering hermits, living life without any shelter or possessions. They eat when they can acquire food, but never enter into any work to acquire it; it must be given or found. They become holy men, seeking spiritual enlightenment and power, striving to achieve the true wisdom of the cosmos. When such idol worship through a fantasy life embedded in the subject replaces reality and consumes normal life it becomes a Celebrity Worship Syndrome, now recognized as a mental disorder.

Churches are not immune to celebrity worship as religious leaders sometimes assume the celebrity role for the members who seem to need an object of worship to complete their lives. Television and now the Internet have provided a communications venue that brings fame as well as fortune to a new generation of celebrity preachers who are little more than entertainers with their prosperity gospel. When faith in one's self fails, sheeple turn to some external object of faith. When flooded by the media attention paid to such idols, the mundane tasks of living and dying pale into the shadows, but only temporarily. You cannot reason with a person who is under the influence of such faith. In fact, such a person has lost the power to reason and is mentally ill. Mark Twain observed that faith is "believing something that you know ain't so." But, sheeple still must believe.

This popular aspect of human culture is reported by psychologist John F. Schumaker in his book, The Age of Insanity. (2001) His innovative approach to mental health seeks to explain a variety of psychological trends, including the steep rise in depression, the sharp increase in the prevalence of existential disorders, and the emergence of consumption disorders. Sheeple living in modern cultures are desperately hanging onto legacy beliefs that no longer work in the age of Ipod marketing, weapons of mass destruction, and Internet communications. The urge to believe in something is making fools of many sheeple and contributing to a pandemic of mental illness. Muslim writer Ziauddin Sardar adds, "Nothing moves in our Universe without the imprint of celebrity. There is no boundary that celebrity does not transcend." Consider the exalted role of Muhammad in the Muslim faith. We have met the zoo, and it is us. Whether it is worshipping a crucifix or a celebrity logo or a Christmas nativity, the mental neurosis is the same.

Every human culture seems to have a system of myths, legends, and religions going back some 5,000 years to the Vedic culture of India that are bigger than life. In His holy book, Bhagavad-gita, the Lord Krishna, destroyer of evil claims, "Whenever and wherever there is a decline in religious practice, O descendant of Bharata, and a predominant rise of irreligion—at that time I descend Myself. To deliver the pious and to annihilate the miscreants, as well as to reestablish the principles of religion, I Myself reappear millennium after millennium." In spite of lacking scientific evidence, sheeple seem to need to believe in such things. Those sections of the ten billion or more neuron cells in the human brain that perform the functions of logic apparently are disabled when faith takes over. Nowadays, anyone claiming to speak with

God like the ancient Hebrew prophets did might be labeled as schizophrenic. But such sheeple are the basis of faith in the Bible and the Koran, plus the Book of Mormon.

Religious imagination offers a way for schizophrenics to express their delusions in a way that is socially acceptable. Common sense is no match for the voice of God the Almighty One. Sheeple of faith could be classified with delusional mental disorder if it were not politically incorrect. They certainly are guilty of the most common error in logical judgment, that of over-generalizing from a specific scripture given in a certain context at a certain time that does not apply to all circumstances all the time. Unless sheeple learn formal logic and the mathematics of probability, they often must abandon logical reasoning in order to sustain their beliefs. Poor things; they just cannot help themselves. It is inevitable. As such, sheeple of faith should not be judged for that which they do not control. How else can a reasonable person explain the strange ways of faith?

Zoroaster apparently was the first to teach the doctrines of an individual judgment, Heaven and Hell, the future resurrection of the body, the general last judgment, and life everlasting for the reunited soul and body. The religion was founded about 600 BCE by Zarathushtra in Persia—modern-day Iran. It may have been the world's first monotheistic faith. It was once the religion of the Persian Empire, but has since been reduced in numbers to fewer than 200,000 today living in India and Iran because they do not accept converts and they do not permit intermarriage with other faiths. The Zoroastrian holy book is called the Avesta. This includes the original words of their founder, Zarathushtra preserved in a series of five hymns, called the Gathas, abstract sacred poetry, directed towards the worship of the One God, understanding of righteousness and cosmic order, promotion of social justice and individual choice between good and evil.

At some later date (most scholars say many centuries after his death), the remaining parts of the Avestas were written. These deal with laws of ritual and practice, with the traditions of the faith. Elements of Christianity are included in its tenants: The Universe will go through a total of three eras: 1) Creation; 2) The present world where good and evil are mixed, and a final time of 3) reconstruction where evil is banished forever. Sheeple's good works are seen as gradually transforming the world towards its heavenly ideal; and a final state after this renovation when good and evil will be separated and only good remains. A Saoshyant (savior) will be born of a virgin, of the lineage of the Prophet Zoroaster, [aka Zarathustra] who will raise the dead and judge everyone in a final judgment. Eventually, everything will be purified and even the occupants of hell will be forgiven and released if you can believe that.

These doctrines were to become familiar articles of faith to much of mankind, through borrowings by Judaism, Christianity and Islam.

But, that's not all. There is a Bible story in Genesis about Noah who "found favor with the Lord." He was instructed by God to build an ark the size of two football fields and collect two of each species and enough supplies to survive a flood of such proportions to kill all the sinful members of his race. This story is so absurd as to be laughable. There are an estimated thirty million species of life on Earth, and many of them eat each other for food. They don't all live in the same areas either, so rounding them up would require searching the entire planet. How this menagerie could be corralled, loaded, fed, and sustained for forty days during the flood and at least one growing season past its end is beyond imagination, even if the ark was large enough to contain them all. But, of course, all things are possible with God. The Bible says so. (Matthew 19:26, Mark 10:27)

Legends of a flood can be found in the folklore of such diverse places as the Middle East, India, China, Australia, southern Asia, the islands of the Pacific, Europe, and the Americas. But the best-known flood legend—that on which the story of Noah is based—had its origins among the sheeple of ancient Mesopotamia in the Tigris-Euphrates river valley in southern Iraq. The first true literature on planet Earth of which we are aware developed in Mesopotamia, and the sheeple who built this first civilization are known as the Sumerians. Around 3000 BCE the Sumerians, who lived along the Euphrates and Tigris rivers, invented the skill of writing which spread to other cultures and races. To explain the mysteries of the world, the Sumerians created thousands of deities. So did the Egyptians, the Babylonians, and the Assyrians. The first sheeple to seek non-divine explanations for natural phenomena were Greek thinkers, such as Thales (547 BCE), Anaximander (547 BCE), Socrates (399 BCE), Plato (348 BCE), and Aristotle (322 BCE). According to Plato, the Universe reveals design, purpose, and therefore a supreme architect. Aristotle observed that nothing starts to exist by itself. Its existence depends on something or someone else, i.e., a previous cause. An infinite series of beings, each depending on another for existence, could never get started except by a being who needs no one or nothing for existence, i.e., the first cause. We call that self-sufficient being God the Almighty One.

Ironically, until little more than a century ago, nothing was known of the Sumerians. The first civilization in history had been lost to history. Slowly, over the past hundred years, and largely due to the efforts by archeologists of the Universities of Chicago and Pennsylvania, the puzzle has been slowly pieced together. Excavations in Mesopotamia have led archaeologists and other scientists to conclude that a number of serious floods occurred there between 4000 and 2000 BC. It is possible that one of these floods was so destructive that it made a lasting impression on the population and became a subject for the ancient literature of the period. In its fully developed form, the Mesopotamian flood myth appeared in the "Epic of Gilgamesh," one of the first literary masterpieces, which relates the adventures of a hero, King of Sumer. Rather than the high estate which the Hebrews assigned to man as the representative of God on Earth, for the inhabitants of Mesopotamia man was nothing more than the slave of the Gods and subject to their whims. Perhaps we still are.

The Old Testament then describes how God told Noah's descendent, Jacob son of Isaac and grandson of Abraham, directly that he was selected as patriarch of a tribe of unremarkable nomads to become the "Chosen People" and obtain special favors if they obeyed the rules laid down for them. He had twelve sons with two wives and two concubines and was renamed Israel by God. (Genesis 35:16-26) Their descendents kept disobeying the rules and worshipping other Gods, so they were disbanded, although a remnant of some 40 souls was preserved through enslavement in Egypt during a period of famine. After they were released from captivity 400 years later reluctantly by the Pharaoh with prompting of Moses and his miracle plagues, they were given a land by God that was already occupied by six tribes whose descendents have been trying to evict them ever since. "The LORD said, I have indeed seen the misery of my people in Egypt. I have heard them crying out because of their slave drivers, and I am concerned about their suffering. So I have come down to rescue them from the hand of the Egyptians and to bring them up out of that land into a good and spacious land, a land flowing with milk and honey, the home of the Canaanites, Hittites, Amorites, Perizzites, Hivites and Jebusites." (Exodus 3:7-8, Acts 13:19) [Canaan was the son of Esau, son of Jacob/Israel son of Isaac son of Abraham, while the others are assumed to be descendants of Ishmael, the son of Abraham and Hagar, the maid of his wife, Sarah who also was promised twelve tribes by God. (Genesis 16:15, 17:20)] The resident Arab tribes refused to surrender their lands to Moses without a fight and the war was on. Now it is being fought again as the resident Palestinians are trying to prevent being pushed off the land by modern Jews. [See their biblical history at Exodus 3:7-18, Exodus 6:4.]

Despite its ubiquitous disobedience, God persisted in giving this tribe of Jews his preferential treatment. (Ezekiel 20:39-44) They were given ten commandments by their leader, Moses, who claimed he received them directly from God on a set of stone tablets that he broke in a fit of anger at their worship of a golden calf. Later restored, the sacred tablets of God's law were preserved in an ark that got lost in history. Then Moses added 613 more dos and don'ts to the list for the total integration of religion and society, which Muslims claim is the only authorized relationship between God and mankind.

The remnant of the chosen sheeple broke the covenant by worshipping other Gods and lost favor with God for which he scattered them among the nations until they were nearly exterminated by Nazi Germany during WWII. "In his anger against Israel the Lord handed them over to raiders who plundered them. He sold them to their enemies all around, whom they were no longer able to resist." (Judges 2:14) "All this took place because the Israelites had sinned against the Lord their God, who had brought them up out of Egypt from under the power of Pharaoh king of Egypt. They worshiped other Gods and followed the practices of the nations the Lord had driven out before them, as well as the practices that the kings of Israel had introduced." (2 Kings 17: 7-8) [One may only wonder why God did not choose some tribe in India or China to be his chosen ones who may have been more obedient.]

After a period of punishment and exile, God promised the repentant, penitent Jews they would be again reconstructed in that land promised to Israel. "This is what the Sovereign Lord says: Although I sent them far away among the nations and scattered them among the countries, yet for a little while I have been a sanctuary for them in the countries where they have gone . . . . I will gather you from the nations and bring you back from the countries where you have been scattered, and I will give you back the land of Israel again. They will return to it and remove all its vile images and detestable idols. I will give them an undivided heart and put a new spirit in them; I will remove from them their heart of stone and give them a heart of flesh. Then they will follow my decrees and be careful to keep my laws. They will be my people, and I will be their God." (Ezekiel 11:17-20)

Under prodding by President Harry Truman, the United Nations granted ethnic Jews the special favor in 1947 of reoccupying the land they claimed that God staked out for them in the present land of Palestine, and renamed it Israel. The U.S. was the first country to recognize it as a sovereign nation. Naturally, the current Arabic inhabitants of Palestine, thought to be descended from the bastard son of Abraham named Ishmael and his wife's handmaid, are resisting this Jewish invasion just as they did the first time. About half the world's population of 13 million Jews migrated to establish reconstructed Israel, but the rest remain in the U.S. and many other nations of exile. Modern Israel has no friends among NATO and the Arab nations of the world so the U.S. must be its advocate alone. The Jewish lobby (The American-Israel Political Action Committee) is one of the strongest in Washington, D.C. AIGWOC . . . all in God's will of course.

You have two diametrically opposed cultures—Arabs and Jews—claiming God-given right to the same piece of barren land, so the result is perpetual war. [Is this insanity, or what? God started it and only God can end it.] After winning preemptive wars against its menacing Arab neighbors in 1967 and 1973, Israel began constructing settlements inside the boundaries of the West Bank and the Gaza strip to accommodate the burgeoning Jewish population. Both Palestinians and Jews continue making babies, needing food, education, jobs, etc. all of which require more land. Israel is surrounded and grossly outnumbered by who may be descendents of Ishmael promised by God to be the father of nations. (Genesis 17:20) But the U.S. still prefers officially to support Israel anyway. But the U.S. still prefers to support it anyway. Washington Post Jewish writer, Charles Krauthammer opined, "Since the Oslo accords in 1993 turned the West Bank and Gaza over to the Palestinians, their leaders built no roads, no courthouses, no hospitals, none of the fundamental state institutions that would relieve their people's suffering. Instead they poured everything into an infrastructure of war and terror, all the while depositing billions from gullible western donors into their Swiss bank accounts" [while imprisoning the sheeple in a restricted lifestyle of radical Islam.] So, both sides are poised for inevitable conflict. All in God's will of course . . . AIGWOC.

The U.S. support of Israel, spurred by Jewish lobbying and conservative Christians, is a primary cause of the ongoing worldwide Arabic-Muslim terrorism. Leaders on both sides have been assassinated for trying to make peace. [At this time, President Barack Obama has proposed a withdrawal of Jewish settlements and establishment of the Palestinian nation on territory defined before the war of 1967. Naturally, Israel opposes this idea and so the strife goes on.] Perhaps it all is necessary to prepare for the final battle in the Middle East at Armageddon as predicted in Revelation 16:16. Until God intervenes and changes hearts and minds there will be NO peace in the Middle East and the U.S. will continue to hemorrhage trying to make it so. But, one may appropriately wonder what he has in mind by all this bloodshed.

It is said that God, who could not prevent Homo sapiens from self destruction through disobedience after two attempts himself to recreate them, finally sent his only son as himself into the world through the womb of a virgin to save them. "Consequently, just as the result of one trespass was condemnation for all men, so also the result of one act of righteousness was justification that brings life for all men. For just as through the disobedience of the one man the many were made sinners, so also through the obedience of the one man the many will be made righteous." (Romans 5:18-19) Whoever permitted this declaration in the Bible goofed big time. This scripture obviously is false doctrine because the first sin of disobedience was committed not by the man, Adam, but rather by the woman, Eve. (Genesis

3·6-7) As for passing the condemnation of their trespass for all men, the story in Genesis contains no such thing, although the lives of Homo sapiens was forever changed. So, perhaps the whole need for sacrificial redemption should be assigned to mother Mary rather than to Jesus for it was by woman that many first were made sinners, and not the man, if at all. The veneration of Mary by Catholics thus may have considerable merit, but for the wrong reason. Perhaps she is the second Eve who got it right instead of wrong by her stoic obedience to the will of God and sacrificing her only son and thereby redeemed all women. Wouldn't that be a hoot?

Two of the New Testament gospels plus Apostle Paul are explicit in tracing the lineage of Jesus through his mother's fiance, Joseph, back to Abraham through the infamous king, David, who was an adulterer and a murderer in order to fulfill Old Testament prophecy. (Matthew 1:1-17, Luke 3:23-38, 2 Timothy 2:8) [By the way, Moses called by God to lead the Israelites out of Egypt, was a murderer and fugitive from justice after killing a guard if you recall.] But, if it was true that Jesus had human ancestors, he must have been conceived in the usual manner of Homo sapiens, not by the Holy Spirit, as claimed by the faithful. Apostle Paul emphasizes his personal selection as an apostle in addition to the twelve by claiming both the supernatural and the natural genealogy of Jesus, "Paul, a servant of Christ Jesus, called to be an apostle and set apart for the gospel of God, the gospel he promised beforehand through his prophets in the Holy Scriptures regarding his Son, who as to his human nature was a descendant of David, [does this imply a natural conception with a human father?] and who through the Spirit of holiness was declared with power to be the Son of God by his resurrection from the dead: Jesus Christ our Lord." (Romans 1: 1-5)

Apostle Paul actually does not proclaim the virgin birth. Could it be that Jesus was born as a man but was transformed into God as Christ through his resurrection? Or, maybe the story of crucifixion and resurrection of Jesus is a metaphor for crucifying the ego to purge the illusion of free will. "Nevertheless, not my will but thine." (Luke 22:42) [This prayer vigil in the life of Jesus occurred in complete privacy, so the faithful must believe that God told the reporter what to write since there could have been no witnesses. Apostle Paul had to argue intently to assure belief in the bodily resurrection of Jesus, which he never witnessed, without which there would be no salvation. (1 Corinthians 15: 12-19) Hey, whatever works. All in the will of God the Almighty One, of course.]

However, the four gospels present materially different accounts of his life, arrest, crucifixion, and resurrection. Neither the Gospels of Mark nor John makes any claims to his miraculous conception or birth by a virgin. Mark does not mention any temptations of Jesus during his initiating fast for forty days in the wilderness, which would kill a normal man. Besides, if God created all things would he also not have created Satan and caused him to tempt his own Creator, i.e., himself? Only Luke records a conversation between Jesus and two thieves who were crucified with him. Only in the Gospel of John does Jesus teach about the necessity of a second birth in order to enter the kingdom of Heaven. (John 3:3) John also is the only gospel that employs gnostic metaphysics to explain salvation through acceptance of Christ, which was a stumbling block to many. "I tell you the truth, unless you eat the flesh of the Son of Man and drink his blood, you have no life in you. Whoever eats my flesh and drinks my blood has eternal life, and I will raise him up at the last day. For my flesh is real food and my blood is real drink. Whoever eats my flesh and drinks my blood remains in me, and I in him." (John 6:53-56) "I am the resurrection and the life. He who believes in me will live, even though he dies; and whoever lives and believes in me will never die." (John 11:25-26) "If anyone comes to me and does not hate his father and mother, his wife and children, his brothers and sisters, even his own life, he cannot be my disciple." (Luke 14:26) Pretty fantastic stuff.

Many of his disciples left after hearing these words, and so do many today. D.M. Murdock [aka Acharya S] has chronicled all the many ways the four gospels are flawed and concluded in Who Was Jesus? (2007) "The Bible is not the inerrant Word of God. The reality is that the gospels are so riddled with such inconsistencies, inaccuracies, fallacies, questions, impossibilities, errors, repulsive doctrines, and contradictions as to bring into question the alleged history of the entire story . . . Contrary to popular belief, Easter does not represent the historical crucifixion and resurrection of Jesus Christ. In reality, the gospel tale reflects the annual crossification (sic) of the sun through the vernal equinox (Spring), at which time the sun is resurrected, as the day begins to become longer than the night. Easter celebrations date back into remotest antiquity and are found around the world, as the blossoming of spring did not escape the notice of the ancients, who revered this life-renewing time of the year, when winter had passed and the sun was born again."

This author emphasizes that there are no corroborating historical references supporting the life of Jesus. Some scholars now think the letters of Apostle Paul were written before the four gospels, which may have been issued after the church was organized to support its verbal contentions about the life of Jesus. Luke claims that "many have taken in hand to set forth in order a declaration of those things which are most surely believed among us . . . ," but not a single scrap of any such manuscripts have survived except his own. (Luke 1:1) The oldest extant text of New Testament writings is the Muratorian Fragment dating from the last half of the second century which contains reference to the Gospel of Luke and the Acts of the Apostles. None of the original manuscripts have ever been found.

The newest version is <u>The Five Gospels</u>, (1996) and <u>The Acts of Jesus</u> (1999) published by the Jesus Seminar, a group of some 150 self-selected hard thinking theologians organized by the Westar Institute of Salem, Oregon in 1985 which was founded by theologian, Robert W. Funk (1926-2005). Its goal was to take the controversies about Christ from academic cover into the world of public discourse. "This is an honest, no-holds-barred exchange involving thousands of scholars, clergy and other individuals who have critical questions about the past, present and future of religion."

They voted using a system of colored beads to reach a weighted-average consensus on their contemporary version of what Jesus taught and did. Fellows of the Jesus Seminar estimated that only about 18 percent of the Jesus quotes in the New Testament likely were spoken by Jesus himself with the rest being doubtful to uncertain. They also concluded the empty tomb is a fiction and Jesus did not rise from the dead, but was made to by writers after the fact. Why, they do not explain. How these honorable theologians came to do this project is curious, to say the least. Take your choice; it seems you must either consider the Bible as factual history even though it is riddled with inaccuracies and contradictions, or as spiritual truths hidden under allegorical stories for only a select few to interpret correctly, or as pagan fiction that carries no more worth than the story of Batman and Robin. It could be like worshipping Superman for all of his miraculous, but fictitious, powers. Whichever you choose is up to God the Almighty One of course.

We could go on, and we will. Obviously, if God created Jesus with no earthly biological father, he could not have any blood connection to King David and so would not fulfill the prophecy, but that little detail is just overlooked except for Jews who claim he was an imposter claiming to be the Messiah. Jesus himself seemed to refute this inheritance at one point, which confounded his disciples. (Matthew 22:41-44, Mark 12:35-37, Luke 20:41-44) You could look it up. Without a human father, he also would be lacking the 23 pairs of chromosomes that normally come from the male parent to pass along that hereditary information, which includes the Y-chromosome that establishes sexual determination. Whether such a person actually could exist is a medical mystery.

Virgin birth has been discovered in some bony fish, amphibians, reptiles and birds, and has been suspected among sharks in the wild. Two instances of apparent virgin births by sharks in captivity have been reported. Scientists who studied the sharks in Virginia and Nebraska said the newly formed pups acquired one set of chromosomes when the mother's chromosomes split during egg development, then united anew. Absent the chromosomes present in the male sperm, the offspring of an asexual conception had reduced genetic diversity and, the scientists said, may be at a disadvantage for surviving in the wild. The scientists said their findings offer intriguing questions about how frequently "automictic parthenogenesis" occurs in the wild.

Every plot needs a protagonist and an antagonist, so if God created Jesus, he also created Satan who was the fallen angel, Lucifer, and so they are brothers. (Isaiah 14:12 KJV) Unless, of course, that God did not create everything. Actually, the Bible makes no claim that he created Hell or Heaven. But, then he would not be God the Almighty One, would he? D. M. Murdock [aka Acharya S] asks, "Why would God need to take birth on Earth as his own son in order to give his life gruesomely as a ransom to himself so that he could remove the sins of his creation which he formed so badly, in his own image and likeness, that he needed to save them from eternal destruction that he decreed for the pitiful miscreants?" We could just as easily assume that God felt such remorse after creating a world of necessary suffering that he assumed the life of a human being and suffered death by crucifixion as the supreme act of atonement and reconciliation to earn the forgiveness of his creation. Of course, he had to return from death after crucifixion or God would be dead. But, if he really wanted to shake things up afterward, why didn't Jesus appear to the Jewish and Roman leaders or do a little lecturing to Pharisees in the Temple after his resurrection? If he had returned to Pontius Pilate or confronted the Sanhedran and Jewish high priest, returned to the Temple for some post-resurrection teaching and such, then maybe the Jews would have accepted him as their Messiah, Rome would have treated the Jews differently and history would record his presence and everything would be different.

Unfortunately, absent any of these events, it remains that the only claims for the resurrection are in the Bible itself which vary among the gospels, plus a few obscure hearsay comments by the first century Jewish historian, Josephus Flavius. (37-101 CE) and none at all from the philosopher and theologian, Philo of Alexandria (25 BCE-47 CE) who lived in Jerusalem and left several volumes of local history of the Jews. For those who claim the Holy Spirit empowered the Christians on the day of Pentecost to spread the word, whatever happened there still is a mystery. (Acts 2) When there was no reconstruction of the Kingdom of Israel afterward, the Jews revolted against the Romans, the message was abandoned and the gentiles/Greeks became the chosen sheeple.

Outside of the Bible there is little to no historical documentation that would prove Jesus ever really existed much less rose from the dead. And being God and all, why did he not just with the wave of his hand and the command of his voice create a manual of actions for all his creatures to follow for all time and place so there would be not doubt about his will? None of the gospel writers claimed to be eye witness of the resurrection because they wrote many years later, although some scholars assume the writers of Matthew, Mark, and John were the actual apostles. And of the 500 or more witnesses claimed by Apostle Paul, not one of them left a certified testimony of their experience. (1 Corinthians 15:7) The transforming experience of Paul occurred at some later time. Peter, the chosen apostle, merely mentions the resurrection in passing. (1 Peter 1:3) Neither does Apostle James provide any biography of Jesus' life or mention a virgin birth and resurrection in his short epistle, although scholars believe that he was the brother of Jesus mentioned in Matthew 13:55. One would expect his brother to let the world know all about him.

This gross omission is most unseemly. Besides, God being God and all, one would think he could come up with a better solution to redeem mankind than sacrificing his own son/self on the cross of crucifixion to save sheeple of his own creation from the consequences of sin that he also created by planting the tree of knowledge of good and evil way back there in the Garden of Eden. What we actually have is a form of midrash or chain letter as one writer after another built upon the previous one in ways to make it all hang together as a composite story. Moreover, the books of the New Testament are not collated in the order they were written. Lastly, none of the original manuscripts have ever been found; the oldest scraps found in Egypt date to about 200 CE. The earliest extant papyrus fragments are dated several centuries later, and no one knows how accurately they copy the originals. The first full compilations of the original Greek text rely upon copies from the fourth century which were compiled by scribes of the Roman Catholic Church into the Latin Vulgate. None of it would hold up in a court of law to determine the actual facts. We do not have the real Jesus, only shadowy reflections of him shown through a dark glass of misinformation and misunderstandings, according to Apostle Paul. (1 Corinthians 13:12)

Nevertheless, faith in this son of a carpenter named Jesus (called Christ) made Son of God on Earth, and maybe God himself, was so powerful his followers readily accepted death by sword and lion in order to preserve their belief after his death. The clincher for them was his promise to return again to destroy all evil and collect the disciples among the faithful, living and dead, and commune with them forever in the Kingdom of Heaven, which is left as a vague concept for the habitat of the "elect" who are chosen by God before they were born through Jesus to occupy it. (Matthew 24:31, Mark 13:27, Luke 10:22) Never mind that an abrupt removal of all born-again Christians would leave those left behind totally unable to conduct any form of functioning economy. Reason would conclude the ones remaining could not survive more than a few weeks with every process of normal life terminated by the absence of all those born-again Christians. Only the Asian countries might survive because they have so few Christians among their populations as the gospel was prohibited from them.

Obviously, the expected "rapture" of the church is full of imagination and myth without much reason to support it. Indeed, the Book of Revelation would be considered science fiction among today's literature, and Apostle Paul would be diagnosed a schizophrenic. So, maybe, would be Jesus. But, what about the historical landmark conversions reported by the likes of St. Augustine in 386 CE and Martin Luther in 1515 CE and John Wesley in 1738 CE, plus John Calvin. Whatever happened to Augustine, Luther, Wesley and Calvin, they left a faith-based mark in the world which had powerful long term consequences. How could this all be unless God willed it so?

Still, there is more. [Sorry about that]. There was that fellow named Joseph Smith, Jr. who claimed that he got a message from an angel named Moroni in the form of some golden tablets he found hidden someplace up in New York that he translated into the Book of Mormon, which was published in 1830. He claimed to have eight eye witnesses who saw the tablets, but they conveniently vaporized after he completed the translation. The tablets, not the witnesses. He migrated from New York to Pennsylvania to Ohio to Missouri to Nauvoo, Illinois, adding more followers and proclaiming each location as the new Eden. With his growing band of followers he created a new type of theocratic community with him as the cult leader and ran for President in 1844. But he was killed while imprisoned after being accused of setting up a theocracy, including plural marriage, as the revealed will of God the Almighty One. He may have married as many as thirty women, ten of them already married. His life story is full of twists and turns that reads like an adventure novel. Although he was assassinated, his leadership was accepted by a group of followers that has grown into the international Church of Jesus Christ of Latter-Day Saints after they migrated further to Salt Lake City, UT in 1847 led by his chief apostle, Brigham Young. Young also was a polygamist who sired 56 children and married some 50 women, which bordered upon white slavery.

Brigham Young, designated leader of the Mormon church wrote, "No man or woman in this dispensation will ever enter into the celestial kingdom of God without the consent of Joseph Smith . . . every man and woman must have the certificate of Joseph Smith, Junior, as a passport to their entrance into the mansion where God and Christ are . . . Joseph Smith reigns there as supreme a being in his sphere, capacity, and calling, as God does in heaven. Many will exclaim—Oh, that is very disagreeable! It is preposterous! We cannot bear the thought! But it is true." And they believed him, too. How could this be unless God willed it so? So long as

Utah was governed as a polygamous theocracy, it was denied statehood by the Federal government.

Although the Mormon church officially disavowed polygamy to gain statehood in 1896, it is still on the church books as a revelation from God to Joseph Smith, Jr. and some Mormons still practice it in remote villages. Mormons emphasize traditional family roles and perform ritual celestial marriages that are sealed for all eternity, which leaves no room for any alternative living arrangements under penalty of excommunication. [Jesus claimed that in heaven there will be neither marriage nor giving in marriage because souls will be like the angels, presumably asexual.] The Mormon Church also excluded blacks as agents of the devil until 1978 when its leaders received a new revelation and changed its position after blacks in Africa spontaneously accepted the faith. A unique Mormon temple ritual is baptism for the dead, including Jews, when they are recommended by members. Things change, and the Mormon Church continues to grow, cult though it may be.

Many sheeple believe in "mind over matter" in healing physical sickness and achieving life goals. Jesus taught that faith was the source of his healing miracles and he promised his disciples that they would do even greater things than he did. (John 14:12) Neurology now sees that worry, boredom, and resentment are big causes of fatigue which impacts the immune system making it more susceptible to disease. This is not new. The ancients in India developed the practices of Yoga to relax and stretch the muscles throughout the body in order to sustain physical as well as mental health. Sheeple in Latin countries who take the afternoon off for a siesta before going back to work may be onto something. When the body relaxes the mind is repaired and vice versa. The Bible teaches in many places that belief/faith is more powerful than anything. (Matthew 17:20, Luke 17:6) And if the Bible says so, it must be true . . . right?

More than a century after her death, followers of Mary Baker Eddy, (1821-1910) still are performing her instructions in churches of Christian Science. Founder of the Church of Christ, Scientist with the self publication of her book, <u>Science and Health with Key to the Scriptures</u> in 1875, Eddy was moved to see matter as a construct of mortal mind and therefore not real. It follows that what is not real cannot suffer sin, sickness, or death. Her theory of mutually exclusive duality in mortal and immortal/spiritual realms was mentioned, but not explained, by Jesus, "The spirit gives life, the flesh counts for nothing." (John 6:63-64) Although Jesus admitted that flesh exists and could be cured, she split the concept and taught that flesh does not exist, but it can be cured. True reality only exists in the world of Spirit/God/Mind that knows nothing of this realm. Her followers see nothing wrong in this illogical concept.

Her reasoning goes: God created all that exists that was good; God did not create sin, sickness and death; Therefore, sin, sickness and death do not exist. [Of course one could easily reason the opposite . . . God created everything; sin, sickness, and death exist, therefore God created sin, sickness and death.] Her reasoning is a plausible way out of human suffering, of which she had plenty, when the pain becomes more than bearable. It seems like she tapped into a lot of kindred sheeple with problems looking for solutions. Mrs. Eddy believed and taught that everyone had the power of healing demonstrated by Jesus . . . because he said so. "Whoever believes in me will do the works I have been doing and they will do even greater things than these . . ." (John 14:12)

Mrs. Eddy extended her ideas about mind/faith healing from self-proclaimed healer and agnostic Phineas P. Quimby, who got them from Charles Poyner who got them from Scottish hypnotherapist and surgeon James Braid, who got them from German physician Franz Mesmer, who got them from Helena Blavatsky who got them from God, believe it or not. Mesmer was discredited in Paris and disappeared from history but his notion of "animal magnetism" took root as a meme, i.e., contagious idea, and spread to America. Eddy saw all things material as illusions and all things immaterial as good. So instead of accepting thought as a phenomenon of matter, she saw matter as a phenomenon of thought, much like ancient Hindus. There is some basis for that idea in modern quantum mechanics that says atomic particles appear where ever one looks which includes being in more than one place at once. In the extreme withdrawal from sensory reality, one may be labeled psychotic, as some of her critics tried to label Mother Eddy, among them Mark Twain and Joseph Pulitzer. Pulitzer even tried unsuccessfully to have her committed to a mental hospital.

[Of Mrs. Eddy, Mark Twain (1835-1910) concluded after a liberal critique of her literary faults in his book, Christian Science (1907) "She has restored to the world neglected and abandoned features of the Christian religion which her thousands of followers find gracious and blessed and contenting, I recognize and confess; but I am convinced that every single detail of [the book] was conceived and performed by another." He could not go so far as calling that source God, and he apparently did not know she hired an editor.]

Mary Baker Eddy found enough willing followers to expand her metaphysical organization throughout New England and far beyond during her lifetime. Now it is found in some 68-70 countries. One historian named William Johnson wrote in 1885, "The public was ready for Mrs. Eddy. The time was opportune for a doctrine of this kind." How could that be unless God willed it so? Is this not a good example of memetics, i.e. contagious ideas, running amuck? Prior to her "divine discovery," the mental state of a sick patient was just one of the factors in the case. After her discovery of Christian Science in 1866, the year that Quimby died leaving 8,000 followers with no leader, she saw that mind itself is the patient. Thought is the arena where change must take place in order for healing to occur. Heal the mind, heal the body. To change matter, change thought.

Critics claim her ideas were not original and came from other such ideas long before her, including the Gnostics of first century Christianity. At her time the concept of placebo had not yet been fully developed, although her healing experiences now may be labeled as such. One might say that all thoughts emerge in good time as a chain of thoughts with one link building upon another crossing continents and centuries. All in God's will of course . . . AIGWOC. Doubtless Mrs. Eddy was driven by some higher power to challenge her critics and devote her later years to the organizing of churches and followers, and they responded in kind to her dictatorial cult leadership. She attributed all opposition and the work of her enemies and competitors obsessively to "malicious animal magnetism," (MAM) completing the necessary dichotomy for Mesmer.

Mrs. Edy denounced mesmerism, but it does seem that her followers were and still are mesmerized by the power in her energy a century after her mortal body appeared to die. It appears from various biographies that she may have had some undiagnosed mental disorder, mistaken as some kind of supernatural power . . . or vice versa . . . as could the founders of most religious movements. But she was not infallible. Consider one of her declaratives; "Nothing that lives ever dies . . . and vice versa." Here is the fallacy in Christian Science: Mother Eddy taught that the mortal body was good for nothing but "sin, sickness, and death," and that not in reality. She declares, "There is no disease." How can something that does not exist be healed? Why even attempt it? If the mortal body is so delusional and worthless then why bother treating it for illness which does not exist . . . why not just let it appear to die, the sooner the better? And more than that, how can something that does not exist reproduce and multiply? But wait, there is no money in that reasoning; no revenue without performing healing mind treatments. This just illustrates that God creates fallacy to balance truth in the principle of necessary opposites, and Mrs. Eddy knew a good revenue source when it was handed to her . . . but if her theory has such a big hole in it how come she still has many followers? . . . all in Gods' will of course . . . AIGWOC.

In any event, there are some physicians today who may agree with her. One among them being Deepak Chopra, from India by birth, who is a board certified endocrinologist with quite a following in mind-over-matter medicine documented in his numerous books. Chopra claims that "by consciously using our awareness, we can influence the way we age biologically. You can tell your body not to age." He has reportedly made millions of dollars marketing such messages along with books, lectures, tapes, and consumables based on a modern version of an ancient Indian healing system called ayurvedic medicine. Chopra promises perfect health to those who can harness their consciousness as a healing force.

Chopra claims that "remaining healthy is actually a conscious choice." He states: "If you have happy thoughts, then you make happy molecules. On the other hand, if you have sad thoughts, and angry thoughts, and hostile thoughts, then you make those molecules which may depress the immune system and make you more susceptible to disease." (It may be difficult to remain so happy if you are living in a FEMA trailer in New Orleans five years after Hurricane Katrina destroyed your house and all your possessions or in a tent in Haiti.) In 1994, Forbes magazine dubbed Chopra "the latest in a line of gurus who have prospered by blending pop science, pop psychology, and pop Hinduism." Harvard Medical School offers a course titled, "Spirituality and Healing in Medicine." There now are virtual Christian Scientists in about 1,000 congregations, 900 of them in the U.S. They claim documented evidence of some 75,000 case histories in faith healings to prove their hypothesis is true, but such anecdotes do not convince everyone.

[Pentecostal faith healers, like Benny Hinn, Todd Bentley and the late Oral Roberts, plus the late Katherine Kuhlmann, Aimee Semple McPherson, Maria Woodworth-Etter, and John Alexander Dowie among others, can pack stadiums with sheeple who are searching desperately for some solutions to their unbearable burdens. They were followed by Norman Vincent Peale, Robert Schuller and more recently, Joel Osteen in preaching that mind over matter is there for the asking. All you have to do is believe. Jesus said so. (Matthew 21:22, Mark 11:24) As these things usually go in the propagation of memes (contagious ideas), sheeple clustered around other teachers with similar views and there followed the development of the so-called "New Age" in religion organized in the churches called Unity, Science of Mind, and the more controversial and secretive Church of Scientology. The Unity School of Christianity was organized in Kansas City by Charles and Myrtle Filmore after she claimed a faith healing from tuberculosis and now is largely a family business run by their grandchildren. The Science of Mind, [aka Religious Science] was founded in 1927 by Ernest Holmes (1887-1960) in Los Angeles. He described his movement as "correlation of the laws of science, opinions of philosophy, and revelation of religions applied to human needs and aspirations."]

Each of these belief systems publishes a continuing stream of books and literature to attract and to convince followers of the benefits in their investments. Whatever possesses their followers to be infected with their memes (contagious ideas) is an ever more challenging question in psychology of religion and the incipient neurology of faith. Is the desire to affiliate with some religion based on a psychology that is no different from weekly attendance at football games, NASCAR races, or even following the careers of favorite movie celebrities? What is it about sheeple that needs to worship something in a group, even a virtual group on the Internet? Psychologists may call it the "herd instinct" that seems to be hard-wired into all humans, left over from the need of animals to cluster among large numbers for safety from predators. In modern applications, the herd instinct may explain stock market bubbles as sheeple follow the herd a little too long, such as the real estate bubble of 2008.

Of course, there is an opposite instinct, that of contrariness, which helps to explain the lone eagles among us who avoid the pack mentality in order to do their own thing, i.e,, be their own person, etc. However, it is odd how the lone eagles often attract the herds as followers and how the followers seek out the lone eagles to adore and to worship. Witness the flocks who follow Oprah Winfrey, for example. She needs only to mention a book and it becomes a best seller. Survivors of the infamous mass suicide of 909 members on November 18, 1978 at "Jonestown" in Guyana ordered by notorious communist cult leader, Jim Jones, all expressed remorse at following the herd, but they seem unable to explain why they did it. The ability of humankind to discern good leaders from bad leaders seems to be definitely limited. All in God's will of course . . . AIGWOC. But, besides the leaders and their followers, there is one more category . . . that of the "watchers," i.e., those who just observe what is happening without valuing or judging perhaps because fear keeps them frozen in place. They are growing in number as culture becomes more complex and threatening. Think you can handle that?

Another case in point is a fellow named L. Ron Hubbard (1911-1986) who wrote science fiction articles for magazines after he served briefly in the Navy during WWII. While he was living in Los Angeles he wrote a book titled, <u>Dianetics</u> (1950, 2002) based on some popular psychology of the time. It said that we all have a lot of scars and cobwebs called "engrams" in our brains that limit our adult achievement from bad experiences maybe from childhood needs unmet or some previous lives and by removing the engrams we can reach our full potential . . . getting clear . . . and if everybody in the world did it there would be peace and prosperity for all. The process of removing mental scars from painful events by recounting them in psychotherapy was called "abreaction" by Sigmund Freud and enjoyed a period of acceptance as normal treatment for post trauma stress, but now it is taken more skeptically. However, post trauma shock is a recognized disorder experienced by soldiers returning from combat. It really has nothing to do with God or religious transformation, but the book was a best seller and made Hubbard pay some big income taxes. To avoid the taxes he consulted with a law firm in LA and they said, "If you want to avoid taxes, call it a religion because that is where the money is," and they organized a new church. They started the Church of Scientology in 1954 when it really was a school in Freudian psychology restated by Hubbard. But he understood more about religious psychology than did Freud.

Hubbard taught that sheeple are at their core spiritual beings called "thetans" whose existence spans many human lifetimes which we have all forgotten. Sheeple are supposed to move closer to their true spiritual nature through extensive "audits" that seek to put them in a state of "clear." As they move higher up in the church echelons (and make regular payments) further revelations about the extraterrestrial origins of the Universe and other mysteries are disclosed to adherents who must keep their secrets from the public. Many of these have not been disclosed because that would eliminate their power, though the disclosure of the belief that an alien ruler named Xenu brought sheeple to Earth 75 million years ago in jet planes and planted them around volcanoes is one of the more unusual tenets that have come to light. Hubbard wrote a lot more stuff and the lawyers took control and still run the tax-exempt business that is now administered by his dogmatic heir, David Miscavige, who was indoctrinated (some might say brain washed) as a youth by Hubbard himself.

Scientology has spread all over the world and captured some movie stars, including Tom Cruise and John Travolta among others. It was sued several times and regularly sues others with a full time law firm, but the Supreme Court said it was a religion and therefore it is exempt from taxes. Hubbard was a playboy and lived mostly on his yacht off Florida with young women where he did most of his writing, and that was a lot. His genius for communicating his ideas cannot be disputed. The Church sells its materials to gullible sheeple and sucks them into buying more and more to get promoted to higher and higher levels of spiritual development. Reaching the highest level of "Operating Thetan" may cost several hundred thousand dollars. Whatever else Scientology is, it is a very successful tax-exempt education business. But then, so are most organized religions. Many sheeple think that if they just buy another book or take another course they will become healthy, wealthy, and happy . . . human nature at work. It is all legal by laws of the U.S. that make churches exempt from paying taxes under the First Amendment of the

Constitution . . . and all in the will of God the Almighty One of course . . . as there can be no other.

The latest in this line of "new age" religion attempts to merge Buddhism and Hinduism with their opposite, Catholicism, in a faith that will be attractive to Jews with a large dose of popular psychology. A Course in Miracles, (1975) was scribed by research psychologist Dr. Helen Schucman, (1909-1981) who claimed it was channeled from a voice named "Jesus." It states separation from God is impossible and guilt is unnecessary because sin never happened in the realm of spirit. Schucman hypothesized that fear which drives violence emanates from a sense of guilt, not from a sense of sinful disobedience, but guilt for separating from God which never happened and creating the ego for self control. By acknowledging that "mistake," one can recover the original status and be "resurrected" into the original state of at-one-ment in love and peace with all sentient beings. Schucman extrapolated from the accepted psychological understanding of the behavior of the child separated from its care giver to claim that human beings all have separation anxiety. In her view, they separated from God and the utopian garden of Eden and feel anxiety, fear, and respond with defense and attack as a result.

It seems that Dr. Schucman adapted this faith in New Age thought without attribution to its many predecessors in her supposed channeling of Jesus as follows: "The acceptance of sickness as a delusion of the mind is the basis of healing. A patient decides that this is so, and he recovers. If he decides against recovery, he will not be healed. Who is the physician? Only the mind of the patient himself. The outcome is what he decides that it is. Special chemical agents may seem to be ministering to him, but they only give form to his own choice. They are not actually needed at all. The patient could merely rise up without their aid and say I have no use for this. There is no form of sickness that would not be cured at once." Perhaps it was this power that Jesus tapped into for his miracle healings as he said to more than one, "Your faith has healed you." (Matthew 9:22, Matthew 15:28, Mark 5:34, Mark 10:52, Luke 8:48, Luke 18:42) Today, such faith healing sometimes runs into conflict with the law as when parents withhold medical procedures for children while they engage "practitioners" for such "mind treatments." Still, they report enough testimonials of success to make this form of faith healing worth more serious investigation if only to prove the efficacy of placebo effects. But, if the mind is this powerful, who or what controls the mind? Jesus may have given us a clue when he stated, "The spirit gives life, the flesh counts for nothing." (John 6:63) Nevertheless, both Mary Baker Eddy and Helen Schucman died when their times came. But their faith lives on. How could this be so unless God will it to be.

Schucman takes from Hinduism, which she apparently had studied but did not acknowledge, and writes that sheeple denied their true self and identified with their false, separated selves. Hinduism sees human beings, egos, as separated selves, called Ahankara, and as such must necessarily feel incomplete. Only return to the whole, called Brahman, Hinduism says, makes sheeple feel complete and not feel inferior. That is to say that separation from spirit is rooted in separation from God and his Son, our supposed real self. To the Hindu, God is not separate from creation residing in heaven, but rather is embodied within it, i.e., immanent. She applied Hinduism, Buddhism and Gnosticism to the psychology of her time before psychology turned to biological causal explanation of human behavior. In line with most religions, Helen Schucman writes that the Real Self is the son of God, a spiritual being. Recall that Jesus taught, "The spirit gives life, the flesh counts for nothing," (John 6:63) He healed, not to cure sheeple, but to show the power of God . . . as in the healing of a man blind since birth. (John 9:3) So, maybe she was onto something important . . . or not.

As Schucman saw it, we are unified spirit but desire to see separated selves housed in temporary bodies; we are one spirit but desire to be different egos in imaginary bodies. When this image of separation ends, peace comes. We dissociate from our true self, unified spirit, and place what we dissociated from, heaven, into our unconscious mind and choose to live instead in the realm of conscious matter, with all its sin, sickness, and death. Why, she does not explain. She did not demonstrate the reality of her supposition in her personal life but, rather, refuted it claiming at the end, "I know it's true, I don't believe it." Her genius, or marketing skill, was in wrapping her work in the voice of "Jesus," and thus giving psychology the power of infallible spiritualism to attract gullible believers. Whether this happened consciously or unconsciously, only she can tell. She, apparently, did not study neuroscience, that is, biological psychology and did not proffer opinions on it. Instead of claiming that this observation is hers, she projected it onto Jesus and so attempted to envelope it with religious infallability.

Schucman took no interest in publishing the work in her own name, possibly knowing the risk attached to her professional career, so she "kindly" let others take the copyright and publish it. Therein lies the story, because it was another Jewish psychologist, Dr. Kenneth Wapnick, who was wandering what to do with the rest of his life at the time who took the baton and made it his life work. It worked out well for him and the publisher, Judith Skutch-Whitson, who made a lifetime career of it through the Foundation for Inner Peace. [www.acim.org] At last count, the "Course" had been translated into nineteen different languages . . . all in God's will of course . . . AIGWOC.

It is not surprising that such a highly educated Jewish psychologist, who as a child was baptized as a conservative Southern Baptist, would create a Jesus that Jews could worship without him being the rejected Messiah come to set up a new kingdom on Earth. Or perhaps the "Course" is a call for reconsideration by Christians of the principles in Hinduism that proclaim only Oneness of all with no dualities. In any case, several million sheeple around the world consider it to be some form of new gospel, correcting the errors that make up the foundations of Christianity. But, not everyone.

Fr. Benedict J. Groeschel, C.F.R. who knew Helen intimately and gave a eulogy at her funeral, wrote, "This woman who had written so eloquently that suffering really did not exist spent the last two years of her life in the blackest psychotic depression I have ever witnessed [as she died slowly of pancreatic cancer]." During an October 1994 lecture on "Discernment" given at Holy Cross Church, Rumson, N.J., Fr. Groeschel, a psychologist and exorcist, stated that he believed that Schucman's experience with the channeled Jesus was possibly a true diabolic manifestation. Her disciple, Dr. Kenneth Wapnick was to observe; "It was almost as if Helen were determined to prove the "Course" was ineffective at best, deleterious at worst, enabling her to feel even more justifiably bitter about her life." But he seemed to like it very much.

Reading the original unpublished urtext carefully shows the dialog between Helen and "Jesus" appears to be a struggle between egos, hers and his, and he sounds suspiciously like a cult leader striving for control, which she continually resists but obeys. It could be diagnosed as schizophrenia. Their relationship seems to be like that of a child with an imaginary "friend," who discusses her shopping habits and what to wear. The "Course" states, "Anyone who elects a totally insane guide must be totally insane himself." What does this say about all those who purchase and study it . . . and the separation of ego that it proclaims? They must all overlook or be intentionally blinded to its glaring fallacy. The "Course" claims that God's will cannot be disobeyed . . . "In truth it is impossible." If true, the presumed separation that is the cause of all our troubles must be the will of God, so we have nothing to fear. Although Kenneth Wapnick claimed her religious experience with Jesus does not fall into any category of mental disorder in the psychiatric diagnostic manual, DSM-IV, (1994) her reactions to the inner "voice" of Jesus reflected a duality in conflict between two parts of her split personality.

[Actually, there is the psychiatric diagnosis of "Religious or Spiritual Problem," defined in DSM code: V62.89. Helen Schucman certainly fits the definition, but it was not available until 1994, long after she died in 1981. Its treatment is not funded by health insurance so it is rarely used.]

She described herself in a letter thus; "It seems that I have spent many years vacillating between being an evil priestess with a sincerely religious streak and a new or a real priestess of some kind with a persistent streak of evil." As with so many religious creators, Dr. Schucman did not live to see Dr. Kenneth Wapnick, her principle disciple, and many other teachers and commentators profit from her creative imagination. Had it not been for them, the original urtext, manuscripts of her personal journals, may have gathered dust in the closets of her offices with no impact whatsoever, except for her personal struggle. Their work in editing and formatting the original is as much a miracle as was the original inspiration. Perhaps there will be a rush to meme duplications among its teachers like the Koran and the Book of Mormon in religious inspirations . . . or not. As Jesus proclaimed, "Thus the saying one sows and another reaps is true. I sent you to reap what you have not worked for. Others have done the hard work, and you have reaped the benefits of their labor." (John 4:37-38)

It goes on. Nigerian psychologist, Dr. Ozodi Osuji explains in <u>Living From the Real Self</u> (2009): "We are on Earth to seem a separated self housed in a body. We want to enjoy bodily things: food, sex, etc. The enjoyment of these bodily things is the perpetuation of the ego. Any people who enjoy flesh tend to be egotistical and tend to be adjusted to this world. They tend to work hard to attain the things of this world. Americans are an example; they enjoy their food, sex and bodies; their whole civilization is geared towards making the ego and body live well, hence they study science and technology to make their chosen home, body, as comfortable as is possible. Those who see through the ego and body and do not seek enjoyment of sensate things seldom do well in the world of capital materialism."

Osuji claims one should never mix the four categories of being, Ego, Ego Ideal, Holy Spirit directed ego, and Spirit. 1) The ego adapts to this world and is comfortable in it. 2) The ego ideal sees this world as wanting and uses imagination to come up with ideational ideals; this is the abode of fantasy, neurosis and psychosis. 3) The Holy Spirit accepts this ego's world as it is but makes it lovely by urging folks to love and forgive one another. 4) Spirit is non-material and has no place in this world nor does it even see its existence. We merely dream separation but are not really separated. We merely dream and in our dreams seem to harm and kill other sheeple. What we do in dreams has not been done in reality. When we overlook the dream, the ego and its world, we return to the world of formless spirit, the world of God and his sons/children. Life in separated state, in ego, is transitory, ephemeral and does not satisfy the children/sons of God. What satisfies them is return to union with God and with all spirits in the oneness of creation. As in ancient Gnosticism, Schucman/Jesus considers our world evil and wants us to leave it and return to the world of God/Spirit. She does not want us to do what we have to do to adapt to this world, for why waste time in a dream when you could wake up in heaven? Her theology tries to teach sheeple how to negate this dream world and return to the real world; how to overcome the separated self, the ego, and return to the unified self, the Christ.

Beyond these beliefs, billions of sheeple believe in the many Gods of Hinduism and the noGods of Buddhism with its belief in reincarnation until souls reach perfection in the state of Nirvana. The body decays, the atoms return to the Earth as dust to dust, but the mind at its subtlest level continues into the next life, and the next, until all learning is complete and Nirvana is achieved. Dr. Michael Newton is one of a few psychologists who use hypnotism to access unconscious past "memories" of sheeple who have claimed they experienced consciousness between lives. His subjects described detailed encounters with authority figures in working out their plans for return to the Earth in new lives. His books are very popular among sheeple who want proof of reincarnation. Skeptics claim it is impossible, without other corroborative evidence, to distinguish a true memory from a false one. But, recent research indicates that hypnosis may have some validity in pain reduction according to the emerging theory of neurolinguistic programming. A professional hypnotist was able to endure surgery on his hand with no pain under self-hypnosis, and a few "superhumans" have demonstrated ability to turn off the pain reaction to intentional puncture wounds in lab experiments. Irish hypnotist, Keith Barry has demonstrated that normal sheeple can be induced to do some very strange things under his instructions to the subconscious mind. [You can see him on www.youtube.com.] Some religious rituals involve body piercing that normally could not be tolerated. For some sheeple it does appear that mind controls matter . . . sometimes.

Prof. James W. Fowler III described a six-stage theory of faith development in Homo sapiens that still is without peer in Stages of Faith (1981, 1995, 1999). They could be compared with growing through several grades in school, beginning with the trust of a child, confidence in teachers, wonder at the world, challenge of authority, and finally reaching a level of altruism and all-inclusive sense of being One with the Universe, which few ever achieve in this life. Most sheeple settle at some lower stage and never reach their full potential in spiritual evolution because each stage brings with it more than enough burdens to challenge the benefits of growth, and each stage is feared by those in stages below it. As such, stage six is rare and dangerous because Fowler says; "Stage six is very rare because it is the ultimate awareness of unity in all things. Universalizers are often experienced as subversive of the social structures (including religious structures) by which we sustain our individual and corporate survival, security and significance. Many persons in this stage die at the hands of those whom they hope to change.

Universalizers are often more honored and revered after death than during their lives. [Think of Martin Luther King, Jr. and Mohandas Gandhi.] The rare persons who may be described by this stage have a special grace that makes them seem more lucid, more simple, and yet somehow more fully human than the rest of us. Their community is universal in extent. Particularities are cherished because they are vessels of the universal, and thereby valuable apart from any utilitarian considerations. [Think of the individual pieces in a jig saw puzzle; which one is the most important?] Life is both loved and held to very loosely. Such persons are ready for fellowship with persons at any of the other stages and from any other faith tradition . . . or none."

Most organized religions cannot aid sheeple past stage three because stage four is one of questioning what no longer works and discarding dogma that needs replacing in order to move on to stage five, which is accommodation to reality by accepting Gods' will in all things, and giving thanks for it . . . why would any tax-exempt church intentionally do that and put itself out of business? However, (there is always a however) Jesus admonished, "I tell you the truth, unless you change and become like little children, you will never enter the kingdom of heaven. Therefore, whoever humbles himself like a child is the greatest in the kingdom of heaven." (Matthew 18:2-4) You may recall the children's hymn taught in Sunday school; "Jesus loves me, this I know, for the Bible tells me so. Little ones to him belong, they are weak, but he is strong." It seems like too much self confidence bodes ill in heaven. "Consider it pure joy, my brothers, whenever you face trials of many kinds, because you know that the testing of your faith develops perseverance. (James 1: 2-3) "Grieve, mourn and wail. Change your laughter to mourning and your joy to gloom. Humble yourselves before the Lord, and he will lift you up." (James 4:9-10) This is a little like swimming; if you struggle you drown but, relax and you float. "Blessed are the meek for they shall inherit the Earth." (Matthew 5:5) Humility seems to be the primary asset, but it is in short supply as the "Word of God" tells us that "every way of a man is right in his own eyes." (Proverbs 21:2).

Second among assets of the faithful is unwavering loyalty as demonstrated by Job throughout his undeserved suffering. "Though he slay me yet will I trust in him." (Job 2:8-10) And third is simultaneous fear and love of God, the Almight One. Consider this instruction by St. John of the Cross. (1542-1591) "When you most seek, and most anxiously desire, you will never find if you seek for yourself; not even in the most profound contemplation but only in deep humility and submission of heart." Again: "seek in reading and you will find in meditation. Knock in prayer and it shall be opened in contemplation." Catholics prefer to contemplate a suffering

Messiah on the cross, dying for their sins with a remorseful contrite heart that remains in perpetual sorrow for sins committed and contemplated. Protestants prefer to contemplate an empty cross with a risen absentee savior residing in heaven who completed the act of redemption for all sinners who believe in him.

The ancient Chinese wisdom of <u>Tao te Ching</u> states, "Each being in the Universe returns to its common source. When you realize where you come from, you naturally become disinterested, amused, and kindhearted. Immersed in the wonder of the Way, you can deal with whatever life brings to you. And when death comes, you are ready." One may say that Jesus walked up to the mount of Golgotha carrying his cross, knowing where he came from and where he was going. That sounds a lot like walking the labyrinth used as the model for this work. Take another look at the cover graphic.

Such childish trust is displayed in words of the hymn by Civila D. Martin, (1904)

> "Be not dismayed whate'er betide, God will take care of you;
> beneath his wings of love abide, God will take care of you.
> God will take care of you, through every day, o'er all the way;
> he will take care of you, God will take care of you.
> Through days of toil when heart doth fail, God will take care
>   of you;
> when dangers fierce your path assail, God will take care of you.
> All you may need he will provide, God will take care of you;
> nothing you ask will be denied, God will take care of you.
> No matter what may be the test, God will take care of you;
> lean, weary one, upon his breast, God will take care of you."

The Bible says, "God keeps his promise, and he will not allow you to be tested beyond your power to remain firm; at the time you are put to the test, he will give you the strength to endure it, and so provide you with a way out." (1 Corinthians 10:13). For a person totally disabled that is difficult to accept. [For example, consider all the soldiers returning from combat wounded for life, both physically and mentally.] And it does not explain those driven to suicide when their suffering becomes intolerable. One can only wonder how this Apostle Paul faced up to his own execution in Rome.

Every time you pass a test, ". . . Allah notices and makes plans to reward you in eternity," so says the Koran. The Bible also says, "Blessed are those who endure when they are tested. When they pass the test, they will receive the crown of life that God has promised to those who love him." (James 1:12). Since most sheeple obviously suffer some lack in this life, there must be something more that is beyond knowing. Of course, if you are the brain damaged woman who was blinded and had her face and hands ripped off by the pet chimpanzee of her friend, these words may not be much comfort. Same goes for all the Christian refugees of Darfur driven from their homes and abused by the Muslim government of Sudan that is being enriched by selling oil to China or those millions made homeless and killed by the monsoon floods in Pakistan. Also, the innocent fishermen who lost their business because BP polluted the Gulf of Mexico with its oil spill could have some difficulty with this line of thought.

[Almost finished now.] Mystical writer Abd-ru-shin [who was big on free will, intuition, and personal volition] declared, "All teachings/thoughts/ideas were at one time willed by God, precisely adapted to the individual peoples and countries, and formed in complete accord with their actual spiritual maturity and receptivity." If true, this declaration would have to include all the sacred writings of all the religions on Earth, The Bible, The Koran, including the latest "new age" spiritual tomes including, In the Light of Truth—The Grail Message, Science and Health with Key to the Scriptures, A Course in Miracles, The Urantia Book, The Book of Mormon, The Aquarian Gospel of Jesus the Christ, and Dianetics. Some sheeple think they are worth translating into foreign languages and studied throughout the world, excellent examples of memes, i.e.,contagious ideas. Although they appear to be works of fiction by authors with great imaginations, many sheeple take these documents as revealed truth from God. Are they all mentally ill or what?

Religions seem to have two things in common. They all are based upon imaginary unprovable claims by some guru, and they spawn a never-ending stream of books and speeches to clarify and expand their dogma. Consider how the teachings of Jesus given in the four gospels of the New Testament were immediately interpreted and reissued in various forms by the apostles, rejected by the Jews but accepted by the Greeks/Gentiles. Within the first group of Christians disputes over dogma arose and one Stephen was stoned to death, becoming the first martyr for this cause. Although the twelve apostles spoke and taught various interpretations, the most authoritative of all became Apostle Paul, the self-proclaimed "least of the Apostles" and not one of the original twelve. (1 Corinthians 15:9) Of course there is no explanation for why all this belief in the unbelievable varies so widely except . . . All in God's will of course . . . AIGWOC.

How can a reasonable person with neurons intact reconcile all these divergent and imaginary beliefs that are causes of ongoing suffering and struggles among Homo sapiens? Sigmund Freud and Joseph Campbell considered religion to be a myth, but one that is necessary. Campbell argued that without some form of moralistic social rudder, humans would be in a death struggle for resources. Therefore, in order for civilization to be possible, a code of behavior must exist which generates the necessary order and cooperation among rivals for scarce resources. This requisite behavior is codified in formal religions, where sheeple are taught to suppress their animal desires for goods, sex and sustenance, so that all will get a share and terminal conflict is avoided. Faith claims that the payback takes place after you die, where good deeds are rewarded with a place in heaven and evil deeds are punished in a place of firey eternal torment called hell. Freud noted that delaying the reward until after death then guarantees that the social behavior will last throughout ones life. In his book, The Selfish Gene, (2006) Richard Dawkins argues that much of our altruistic behavior can be explained by simple formulas whereby the behavior leads to more copies of our genes. The process of natural selection favors development of the behaviors elicited by religion. If his theory is combined with the valid points made by Freud and Campbell, then it is possible that the need for some religious belief is coded in our genes, and individuals have no control of their faith belief. They believe what they are given. All in God's will of course . . . AIGWOC. Think you can handle that?

A curious alternative version of belief is the development of secular humanism that grew up outside of church dogma. Every thought has its necessary opposite. Humanism was expressed in the manifesto of Karl Marx (1818-1883); "Man makes religion, religion does not make man. Religion is the self-consciousness and self-esteem of man who has either not yet found himself or has already lost himself again. Religious distress is at the same time the expression of real distress and also the protest against real distress. Religion is the sigh of the oppressed creature, the heart of a heartless world, just as it is the spirit of spiritless conditions. It is the opium of the people." The belief in secular humanism is a way of thinking and living that aims to bring out the best in sheeple so that everyone can have the best in life, sans a belief in any Gods or the need for a savior. It proposes the "golden rule" by German philosopher Johann Goethe (1749-1832); "Treat people as if they were what they ought to be, and you help them become what they are capable of being." All in God's will of course . . . AIGWOC.

Secular humanists reject as irrational the idea of God and the supernatural and believe that these are not useful concepts for addressing human problems. They affirm that we must take responsibility for our own lives and the communities and world in which we live. Secular humanism emphasizes reason and scientific inquiry, individual freedom and responsibility, human values and compassion, and the need for tolerance and cooperation. It presents the case for understanding the world without reference to a God, and works to separate Church and State and defends the rights of sheeple who do not accept religious beliefs. The issue of whether and in what sense secular humanism might be considered a religion, and what the implications of this would be has become the subject of legal maneuvering and political debate, but it is authorized nevertheless for tax exemptions same as religious organizations in the U.S. As such, faith in secular humanism is no different than faith in a dogmatic religion. It is, after all, a belief system based upon dependence in other than God, so it qualifies as a form of faith, and the definition of Aquinas above applies. So, perhaps Prof. Fowler was correct in assuming that everyone is in some stage on the same pathway to enlightenment whether it is based in organized religion or not.

It seems fairly likely that all faith is driven by desire of ego that things should be different when reality is intolerable. Faith may be the manifestation of dissociation, denial, and avoidance of reality, a necessary defense mechanism to help sheeple get through the day. As such, is faith-based behavior necessary for mental health, or is it a form of mental illness, or both? Psychologist, Dr. David Lukoff, founder of the Spiritual Competency Resource Center, [www.spiritualcompetency.com] claims surveys conducted in the United States consistently show a "religiosity gap" between mental patients who report themselves to be more highly religious and to attend church more frequently than mental health professionals. Lukoff was instrumental in amending the psychiatric diagnostic manual, DSM-IV (1994) to include the diagnosis of "Religious or Spiritual Problem," defined as follows: V62.89: "This category can be used when the focus of clinical attention is a religious or spiritual problem. Examples include distressing experiences that involve loss or questioning of faith, problems associated with conversion to a new faith, or questioning of other spiritual values which may not necessarily be related to an organized church or religious institution." His treatment methods are not covered by medical insurance so the diagnosis rarely is used . . . maybe it should be.

Is this the best that the omnipotent all knowing all being God the Almighty One could really do with this creation? How much education does it take to obtain liberation from religious beliefs that conflict with reality? There are many highly educated sheeple with Ph.D. degrees in science attending churches, temples, synagogues, and mosques every week. So, must true believers forever believe, and nonbelievers be forever scornful, with no possible middle ground? It seems that everyone must believe in something, even if it is atheism. Will a day ever come when all religions are merged into the One Source from which they all seem to come? Should that be a reasonable goal for Homo sapiens? Perhaps that day has come. You can get the full story of Theofatalism™ in <u>Lessons From Sedona.</u> The original book that describes five awesome principles of reality, <u>Voices of Sedona,</u> may be ordered from www.IUniverse.com, as well as the Amazon and local Barnes & Nobles book stores.

13. God always wins

Bottom line is that all we have for sure is the here and now . . . the past is gone and the future is indefinitely uncertain. And if things could be different they would be. One life story illustrates that idea implicitly. Only three miles from Mount Vernon, the home of George and Martha Washington, there is a little known and seldom visited historic preservation site that was the home of Eleanor (Nelly) Parke Custis (1779-1852) and her husband, Lawrence Lewis. It is called Woodlawn Plantation. Nelly was the adopted granddaughter of Martha. She was raised, along with her brother, as a member of the presidential household after premature death of her father. Her youth was full of the gayety and social acclaim fitting a President's ward. Perhaps she came as close as any to being the first American princess. At age 20 she married the president's widowed nephew, Lawrence Lewis, twelve years her senior who was engaged as Washington's private secretary. Washington gave the couple 2500 acres and plans for a mansion plus his distillery as a wedding gift in 1799 a few months before he died. [Many sheeple don't know that George Washington was the largest exporting distiller of corn whiskey in America for many years.]

After a youthful life of ease with the best education available in Philadelphia and suitors galore at party after party in New York, Washington, D.C. and Alexandria, Nelly became the mistress of a struggling farm and soon learned that life often takes a turn for the worse and then gets even moreso. By age thirty four, Nelly had birthed eight children, seven of whom she was to bury along with her husband before she died. The "vile Virginia clay soil" at the farm was not very productive for fruits and vegetables needed to feed her family and the two score slaves needed to run the operation, so her life was full of struggle and suffering. Not to mention that of the slaves.

Nelly retained a close friendship with Elizabeth Bordley Gibson of Philadelphia whom she met at school, and the two corresponded regularly throughout their lives. Elizabeth violated her promise to destroy the letters from Nelly and so a complete one-sided history of their correspondence exists in <u>Beautiful Nelly</u>, (1991) compiled by historian Patricia Brady. In her letters, Nelly, who wished to be called Eleanor after she married, chronicled her interests in the social connections initiated by her status in the first-first family that were eroded and eventually lost to the cares of her new life. Throughout her life she expressed her preference for the bright society of Philadelphia, and between the lines one can sense her disappointments and grief for the social life and children that she lost. Several times she lamented her situation to Elizabeth, who married late and well, and remained childless in contrast. "My friend, in never having been a Mother, you cannot conceive a Mother's trials . . . I have often told you, my dearest friend, that you were happier in being without those precious objects of devoted affection which bind our hearts to Earth, & although sources of happiness, are also sources of most heartrending anxiety & overwhelming affliction." [This could be true of dedicated fathers too.]

After her husband died, Woodlawn was sold and Eleanor fell onto even worse times. She lived with her widowed daughter-in-law at Audley Farm near Berryville, VA far from Parke in Louisiana, her surviving beloved daughter whose husband hated her and refused to let them visit for fifteen years. Her remaining son, Lorenzo died suddenly at age 43 leaving the women to run the farm. Audley now is privately owned, and only a roadside sign marks its history.

Of a young love that never flowered, in her last year at age 73 in 1852 Eleanor recalled in a letter to Elizabeth a youthful suitor in Philadelphia as follows: "I recall him to my mind now when only 18, how handsome, how healthy, how witty & how agreeable he was. He gave me a beautiful ode on my 15th birthday and altho I committed it to the flames just before I married & never copied it, it has never been forgotten. I can repeat it now perfectly. I certainly should have loved him had I not been too happy and gay to be susceptible." Eleanor approached death "very deaf." She was partially paralyzed by a stroke and felt "useless and helpless with no hope of being better . . . my knees are very weak and I totter when I attempt to stand or move without my cane." Her "rolling chair" was a blessing.

Through all her suffering and struggle, Eleanor maintained her belief in a higher power and felt "most grateful to the Almighty for all his mercies." She died on July 15, 1852 and lies buried with her beloved Grandmama and Grandpapa at Mt. Vernon. In 1846 the Woodlawn plantation was finally offered at public sale and the land was purchased by a group of Quakers who divided it into separate farms. The land passed through a succession of private owners until 1949 when a locally formed group, the Woodlawn Public Foundation, purchased the house and remaining land to begin restoration.

In 1957 the estate became the property of the National Trust for Historic Preservation. Today it is surrounded by encroaching development and there is scarcely any remnants left of the life that Eleanor once experienced there. Her home at Woodlawn awaits the tourists who seldom come, which may be a good thing.

Perhaps you also might wish that some things could have been different in your life. Maybe there was some lover in your youth that got away. Gravity does not care whether you acknowledge it or not and neither apparently does the will of God the Almighty One. You can disapprove of gravity but you cannot change it, and so with God. God always wins, and tells you what to think about it. We must take what he gives and give what he takes. Feel good inside no matter what happens outside.

14. RESOLVING DICHOTOMIES

FOR INNER PEACE

There is possibly no better example of dichotomies than the opposites in religion. Should Christians go to war to defend their nation or accept death as defenseless martyrs? Which scriptures prevail; the ones prohibiting violent vengeance (Matthew 5:13, Luke 6:21, Romans 12: 19) or the ones ordering obedience to government authorities? (Matthew 22:21, Romans 13: 1-7) Many such religious issues have no clear solutions. Many controversial social issues end in a tie. Elections in the United States usually are settled with very small majorities. If everyone eligible actually voted there likely would be more ties because opinions are so evenly divided on most issues. Polls on public opinions about such as gun controls, abortion rights, and other social issues usually end up close to even on both sides. Bigger government—smaller government; more spending—less spending; more borrowing—less borrowing; more taxes—less taxes; tighter controls—less controls . . . the debates are endless. Trying to make sense of it all drives the political pundits insane. But that is not all, y'all. Albert Einstein (1879-1955) concluded, "There are only two ways to live your life. One is as though nothing is a miracle. The other is as if everything is."

The former is the way of humanists who don't believe in a God who intervenes in affairs of life, and the latter is the way of Theists who believe nothing happens outside the will of God the Almighty One. In physics there is the dichotomy of light as both waves and particles. Search for either and you are likely to find what you search for, but one precludes the other. With eyes to see, dichotomies also occur in belief systems as in nature and physics. The Bible says, "And now, O Israel, what does the Lord your God ask of you but to fear the lord your God, to walk in all his ways, to love him, to serve the lord your God with all your heart and with all your soul." (Deuteronomy 10:11-13) This command to both love and fear God is given nine times by Moses and becomes the first great commandment. Note, there is an apparent owner of the soul as in "your soul," expressed 46 times in the Bible. This verse contains both obedience driven by fear, and service driven by love. How can anyone love someone and fear them at the same time? However, instructions to love and to fear God are almost equally divided in the Bible. Read on.

You don't hear much discussion of this idea in churches because they prefer to teach only that, "God is love." (1 John 4:8) But, the Bible also says, "Fear of God is the beginning of wisdom." (Psalm 111:10, Proverbs 1:7, 9:10) and Jesus warned, "Fear him who after killing the body has the power to throw you into hell . . . fear him." (Luke 12:5) He implied there is something left after you die. Many sheeple believe in reincarnation in which they get to come back again and again until they get it right. But, others believe sheeple are destined to have but one life and one death and, "after that the judgment." (Hebrews 9:27) Although assumed as self evident ever since philosophers took quill to parchment, the idea that we live in a world of diametric opposites such as love and fear has persisted, but there is more. The Buddhist tradition unites either/or into both/and synthesis and is balanced by antithesis as described by Hegel. Now, the Principles of Theofatalism™ extend this idea to a powerful, logical conclusion, that of immaculate immanence in which the opposites are fused as one. Opposites must be necessary to create the diametric center where there lies ultimate inner peace. Shrodinger's dilemma of coexisting mutually exclusive conditions prevails because they cannot be separated even though we may observe only one or the other at a time. It seems that God did not make any one-sided coins, although doubtless he could if he wanted to, but it would have to be shaped like a sphere.

From the commonly used antonyms in every language (up—down, hot—cold, sweet—sour, love—hate, piety—hedonism, compassion—brutality, charity—greed, failure—success, determinism—free will), there are plenty of examples of diametric opposites in daily living. In religion we even have Christ and anti-Christ, and in physics there is matter and anti-matter. Listed in the same order used by both Pope Gregory the Great in the sixth century, and later by Dante Alighieri (1265-1321) in his epic poem "The Divine Comedy," the seven deadly sins are as follows: lust, gluttony, greed, sloth, wrath, envy, and pride. Each of the seven deadly sins has an opposite among the corresponding seven holy virtues (sometimes also referred to as the contrary virtues). In parallel order to the sins they oppose, the seven holy virtues are chastity, temperance, charity, diligence, patience, kindness, and humility. What drives sheeple crazy is when something happens that seems to make no sense, when something that should be mutually exclusive coexists.

Take for example two opposing facts about American foreign policy. We have a trade embargo with Cuba, possibly the smallest and poorest communist country on Earth and we fought the Cold War to defeat Russian Communism, but our largest trading adversary is communist China. Any American can be fined up to $250,000 and imprisoned for ten years just for buying a Cuban cigar anywhere in the world. But we run a gigantic trade deficit with China for purchase of its cheap goods, inarguably the largest communist nation on the planet, while we ignore its many civil rights and environmental violations. With its central planning ability, China can and does target certain markets for world domination, i.e., its expansion in the export of apple juice has almost killed off the U.S. producers and reduction of exporting its rare-earth minerals. Its accumulated U.S. trade balance increased from $200 billion in 2001 to $1.4 trillion in 2007. It uses that money to build up its industrial base, modernize its new cities, to invest in Africa, and to buy even more U.S. treasury bills. Onto this mess we have overlaid a system of capitalism that requires corporations to maximize profits for stockholders at the expense of workers and consumers, while dumping their risks onto taxpayers. Heads they win, tails they win. All in God's will of course . . . AIGWOC.

Now we must depend on that debtor relationship with China to help control the international nuclear threat posed by North Korea and even support our treasury in its deficit spending that seems to have no limit. Plus, China buys oil from the Muslim government of Sudan so it blocks any U.N. resolutions that could help the Christian refugees in Darfur region of Sudan. As yet, China has not taken a position opposing our protection of Israel, but when they do we will be powerless to resist. We need China to help control North Korea and we also contend with the rivalry it has with India. Nevertheless, China is our largest creditor . . . how could that be unless God willed it so? Hmmm.

American consumers reward countries that exploit workers in abusive ways in order to buy cheap products and line the pockets of the importers and investors. Most of Nike sports shoes are made in communist Vietnam, where we lost 58,000 soldiers without winning. How come they did not set up some factories in Haiti where sheeple must live on mud pies because they are so poor? We spend billions for the war on illegal drugs at home while we send billions to Afghanistan, a country that depends upon growing poppies for opium exports, which accounts for 90 percent of illegal heroin and hooks sixteen million sheeple into hopeless addiction. Trying to destroy the $50 billion annual crop merely drives the poppy farmers to support the terrorist Taliban regime. Ironically, before the U.S. deposed the Taliban regime in 2003 it had almost totally eradicated poppy farming, which is prohibited by Islam.

And while our leaders say the fight in Iraq is for freedom, they debate how much torture is appropriate when depriving Muslim devotees of their freedom to live as they wish. America spends billions on border security with Mexico while the leaders of North America have been scheming to trade national sovereignty for a security and prosperity partnership without borders like the European Community. A defining move is allowing truckers from Mexico to deliver their freight anywhere in the U.S. taking the jobs of American truck drivers. How could this all happen outside the will of God the Almighty One? What kind of world is it that is composed only of friends and enemies . . . opposites for sure. Even Jesus observed that . . . "He that is not with me is against me." (Matthew 12:30) But such distinctions all are relative for friends of one may be enemies of another, and vice versa. In fact, politicians claim, "the enemy of my enemy is my friend and the friend of my enemy is my enemy," etc.

Perhaps the eternal dichotomy is that between the flesh and the spirit expressed by Jesus and felt by Apostle Paul. Jesus declared, "The spirit gives life, the flesh counts for nothing. (John 6:63) Science has no explanation among theories of physics, chemistry, biology and such for what is called life and neither do the religious. We can only say life is energy in the flesh. Its origin and purpose are unknown. Jesus commented, "No one can serve two masters. Either he will hate the one and love the other, or he will be devoted to the one and despise the other. You cannot serve both God and Money." (Matthew 6:24) The Apostle Paul also struggled with the dichotomy of flesh and spirit pulling him in opposite directions as a "wretched man." (Romans 7:24)

St. Teresa of Avila (1515-1582) also expressed this same duality; "On the one hand, God was calling me. On the other, I was following the world. All the things of God gave me great pleasure, yet I was tied and bound to those of the world. It seemed as if I wanted to reconcile these two contradictory things, so completely opposed to one another—the life of the spirit and the pleasures and joys and pastimes of the senses. I suffered great trials in prayer, for the spirit was not master in me, but slave. I could not, therefore, shut myself up within myself (the procedure in which consisted my whole method of prayer) without at the same time shutting in a thousand vanities. I spent many years in this way, and now I am amazed that a person could have gone on for so long without giving up either the one or the other . . . I can testify that this is one of the most grievous kinds of life which I think can be imagined, for I had neither any joy in God nor any pleasure in the world. When I was in the midst of worldly pleasures, I was distressed by the remembrance of what I owed to God; when I was with God, I grew restless because of worldly affections. This is so grievous a conflict that I do not know how I managed to endure it for a month, much less for so many years."

This struggle was expressed by the great Christian mystic, Meister Eckhart (1260-1327) also, "The two eyes of the soul of man cannot both perform their work at once: if the soul shall see with the right eye into eternity, then the left eye must close itself and refrain from working, and be as though it were dead. But if the left eye be fulfilling its office toward outward things, that is holding converse with time and the creatures; then must the right eye be hindered in its working; that is, in its contemplation of heaven. Therefore, whosoever will have the one must let the other go; for no man can serve two masters . . . Whoever possesses God in their being, has him in a divine manner, and he shines out to them in all things; for them all things taste of God and in all things it is God's image that they see." This idea is carried into the Constitution of the United States with its doctrine on separation of church and state. Realistically, it is impossible as sheeple must eat to live in order to contemplate Heaven and no one leaves his religion at home when he goes to work in the Federal government.

Another dichotomy exists between the torturing God and the loving God. Noted British theologian, C.S. Lewis composed this theodocy while suffering grief from untimely loss of his wife . . . "Take your choice, tortures occur. If they are unnecessary then there is no God or a bad one. If there is a good God then tortures are necessary (A Grief Observed, 1963) He concluded, "Not that I am in much danger of ceasing to believe in God. The real danger is of coming to believe such dreadful things about him. The conclusion I dread is, So this is what God's really like. Deceive yourself no longer." With belief in such a God, the reasonable response is fear and rage rather than love and worship. Yet, to be whole one must hold them all as both/and rather than either/or. Rabbi Joshua Liebman (1907-1948) instructed, "Maturity is achieved whenever a person accepts life as full of tension (between opposites such as fear and love.)" [C.G. Jung pursued the notion that suffering is kin to alchemy in which dross is converted into gold. Perhaps torture is necessary to crucify the human ego and to purify the soul for its ascension.]

The energy in good is the same as the energy in evil and the Bible says it all comes from the same source. (Isaiah 45:5-7, Deuteronomy 32:39, Collossians 1:16, I Samuel 18:10) Go ahead, look it up. Both seem to be necessary or it would be different. If there were no evil, how could good be defined or discerned? Where would beautiful and rich be without ugly and poor for comparison? [The richest man in India, Mukesh Ambani, who split his father's fortune with his brother, has built a personal billion dollar mansion twenty seven floors high (570 feet) with inside parking for 160 cars in the midst of the poorest slums of the city Mumbai where workers below labor for merely two dollars per day. His personal family maintenance requires 600 full time staff. All in God's will of course . . . AIGWOC.]

C. G. Jung's greatest contention with Christianity was just this failure to recognize that which is labeled the dark and evil sides of nature are as much a manifestation of God as that which we label good. Jung himself did not see the challenge of life as being the victory of light over dark but rather accommodation of their coexistence. St. Teresa of Avila (1515-1582) described her exquisite suffering, "The pain was so great, that it made me moan; and yet so surpassing was the sweetness of this excessive pain that I could not wish to be rid of it." The predator and the prey, perpetrator and victim, must coexist for each is the complement of the other in God's creation. As in Chinese Yin and Yang of Taoism, the whole must contain the moral and ethical opposites as much as the alternating light and darkness of physical existence. The greatest and yet unsolved moral dilemma for mankind is reconciliation of the two faces of God, Jesus and Satan if you prefer. The mere awareness of this problem creates panic and fear so intense that keeping a safe distance from it is the only port of safety. So we say that God only is love and mankind creates their own distress, and we ignore the issue until some crisis strikes. Socrates concluded during his trial for heresy in 399 BCE at Athens that "the unexamined life is not worth living." As then, today this is the road less traveled.

The latest confusion over dichotomies may be injected by publication of A Course in Miracles (1975) by Helen Schucman that proclaims this thought system that assumes necessary dualities is insane and anyone believing in dualities has lost sight of the original inseparable Oneness between God and the real Universe, as proclaimed in higher forms of Hinduism. She dispenses with the sensory Universe; "Nothing real can be threatened. Nothing unreal exists."

[Hinduism says that it is God (Brahman) himself who cast Maya, spell, on himself and went to sleep and dreamt this world and that the goal of religion is to enable us to remember that each of us is a part of God (Atman) who is one with God. In meditation one is supposed to break through the illusion of separation (mocksha) and attain Samadhi (union with God) after which experience one is said to be enlightened and illuminated to ones true self. Buddhism says much the same in claiming that sensory phenomena in this life are not real but only imagined for the same reason, that of avoiding suffering. Perhaps Helen Schucman, in her efforts to make Hinduism amenable to Christians, altered the sequences of events and said that it was the son of God who separated from God, hence the illusion and not God himself who is dreaming this world. Who knows?]

The "Course" claims the physical world of duality is nothing more than an unreal projection of human ego as in a dream, that brings the illusion of separation, suffering, and guilt for sins never committed. It proclaims,

"Nothing real can be threatened, and nothing unreal exists." Individuals often experience the emotion called "guilt" when our judgmental attitude assigns part of the blame we create for sin to ourselves. When blame is created, it has to be assigned either to ourselves or others. When we assign it to ourselves, we feel guilty and when we assign it others we feel anger. But, if sin does not exist, there is no reason for blame and guilt and anger disappear. This concept is very difficult to implement considering that three million sheeple are confined to prisons in the U.S. for their guilt and continuous wars are driven by anger.

The Course in Miracles (1975) claims that this world actually is a dream we created in order to prove the false separation from God, [why is not explained, but the perceived benefits must have exceeded the burdens] and that in the real world we all are one with God and his creation, so there is no superior-inferior relationship between the Creator and the created, no separation, and nothing that can be threatened, so there is no need for self defense or attack, hence no guilt and remorse either. It claims we have freedom to choose this ego-world or the true nature of Holy Spirit. But, it contradicts itself by proclaiming, "Disobeying God's will is meaningful only to the insane. In truth, it is impossible." If this is true, then whatever condition mankind, collectively and individually, is in must be the will of God and all the rest is moot and that includes accepting or rejecting the "Course."

This self-contradictory belief system would disassociate completely from the ego driven world of senses, emotions, and sin, guilt, remorse, and suffering to replace it with an imaginary and utopian world of spirit in which there is only perfection, oneness, inner peace, and tranquility all bathed in universal forgiveness, (which always is better than revenge) salvation, and love. Such a utopia lies buried under the reality of most everyone, waiting to be discovered. But, hey, forgiveness implies that someone did something wrong, which is impossible in the Course's imagined utopian world of Spirit. Its scribe, Dr. Helen Schucman expressed her delight in a poem titled, "Song to Myself," ". . . I never left my father's house. What need have I to journey back to him again?" C.G. Jung also alluded to such a place as he commented, "Whoever looks outward dreams, but whoever looks inward awakes." [Utopia is the name for an ideal community or society, taken from the title of a book written in 1516 by Sir Thomas Moore describing a fictional island in the Atlantic Ocean, possessing a seemingly perfect socio-politico-legal system. The wondering hero could only enjoy it a short time and then was driven back into the world with its suffering as well as pleasure.]

During her last weeks on Earth, Helen Schucman commented that she must die in order to "get out of its the way" so that others might teach and propagate the "Course," which is available in 19 different languages. It seems that she was working on the "Course" all her life subconsciously, but it took the convergence of several other sheeple to make it a published reality. But, for herself, she commented to publisher Judith Skutch-Whitson, "I know it's true, I just don't believe it . . . I don't believe in Utopia." Of her poems, she disclaimed, "They are beautiful . . . I hate them." Indeed, many of the personal ones read like a love letter to Jesus, not unlike the poetry of female saints throughout Catholic history. She claims in "Love Song," "My Lord, my Love, my life, I live in you. There is no life apart from what you are. I breathe your words, I rest upon your arms. My sight is hallowed by your single star . . . My arms are open, come my Lord to me and rest upon my heart. It beats for you and sings in joyous welcome. What am I except your resting place and your repose." No comment from her husband. It seems that Helen was driven to create a private Jesus fit for Jews, but she never fully crossed the bridge herself. She wrote that God's will cannot be disobeyed, so her disbelief must be God's will as there can be no other.

Kenneth Wapnick, organizer of the Foundation for Inner Peace and heir to the "Course" wrote in her biography, "In Helen's life there can be found an underlying tension that runs throughout, almost from birth, a conflict of two mutually exclusive identities [similar to the dichotomy of flesh and spirit described by apostle Paul?] and a conflict which appeared never to be resolved. Heaven or Helen, God or ego . . . witch or angel." In the end it appears that Helen Schucman died under resistance of the ego, which the "Course" claims created illusion to sustain the world of separation, rather than accepting the unity in Holy Spirit she was called to proclaim. Wapnick concluded, "That it aroused tremendous anxiety in her goes without saying, that she fought it tooth and nail and determinedly chose in the end not to practice its teachings was also, for her, painfully true." So, a course that teaches non-duality was written by a woman who was a living duality. How ironic is that? Helen Schucman perhaps was manifesting dissociative disorder or multiple personality disorder, and Jesus was one of her alter egos that she projected her personal theology onto. All that aside, what is interesting is why so many sheeple buy the "Course" and choose to study it. This can only be called a meme, a contagious idea, for which there is no earthly explanation. All in the will of God the Almighty One, of course.

The "Course" seems to be a modern restatement of the ancient Taoist idea dating back to 3000 BCE of "Wei Wu Wei," the oneness in all things, but laced with terminology that would seem familiar to Christians, with a Jesus that Jews could love. Taoism's central principle is that all life, all manifestation, is part of an inseparable whole, an interconnected organic unity which arises from a deep, mysterious, and essentially unexplainable source which is the Tao, the Way, itself. Various western translators have compared this concept to the idea of God, Universal Mind, or Absolute Reality. Gaining an awareness of universal unity and learning to cooperate with its natural flow and order, like floating down a river, enables sheeple to attain a state of being that is both fully free and independent and at the same time fully connected to the life flow of the Universe—being at one with the Tao. Such was the lifestyle of native American Indians before they were so rudely interrupted by the invaders from Europe. This is not the same as psychological dissociation as a defense mechanism to preserve the ego, but rather a manifestation of what Apostle Paul meant, "Do not conform any longer to the pattern of this world, but be transformed by the renewal of your mind . . ." (Romans 12:2)

From the Taoist viewpoint this represents the ultimate stage of human consciousness or Oneness among the opposites. It may also reflect the fourth and highest level of spiritual ecstasy described by St. Teresa of Avila (1515-1582) wherein the rain falls on the just and the unjust and the floods and droughts all are integrated into the whole, of which sheeple are an inseparable element. "Two things becoming one." Of course, the Tao te Ching and the Course in Miracles are examples of necessary dualities as they present a necessary opposite of duality, i.e., the absence of duality. Several million sheeple are attracted to the "Course" and its teachers, who make a living conducting seminars and selling books and videos to explain it all. Naturally, the Church opposes it as heresy and even worse, possibly demonic false teaching. Both the Church and the Foundation for Inner Peace are tax-exempt corporations that make a tidy living for their leaders and staffs. So, the struggle between duality and non-duality is itself a dichotomy. And it must be necessary or it would be otherwise.

C. G. Jung observed that struggles among his mental health patients over the clash among opposites was relentless and could never be eliminated because it was life suffering to continually rebirth itself, i.e., the eternal clash of spirit and flesh that Apostle Paul expressed as the "wretched man that I am." (Romans 7:14-25) St. Teresa of Avila (1515-1582) also expressed the struggle between spirit and flesh throughout her autobiography with obvious erotic inference. "O my Creator, pour not such precious liquor into so broken a vessel, for again and again Thou hast seen how I have allowed it to run away. Put not such a treasure in a place where the yearning for the comforts of this life has not yet disappeared as it should, or it will be completely wasted. How canst Thou entrust this fortified city and the keys of its citadel to so cowardly a defender, who at the enemy's first onslaught allows him to enter? Let not Thy love, eternal King, be so great as to imperil such precious jewels. For it seems, my Lord, that men have an excuse for despising them if Thou bestowest them upon a creature so wretched, so base, so weak, so miserable and so worthless, who, though she may strive not to lose them, by Thy help (of which I have no small need, being what I am), cannot make use of them to bring profit to any. I am, in short, a woman, and not even a good one, but wicked."

Perhaps Jesus is a necessary and sufficient male object for the expression of female libido among the celibate nuns who become his "brides." Jung laid out the resolution of flesh and spirit as the greatest of human struggles. "Instead of the propitiating praise to an unpredictable king or the child's prayer to a loving father, the responsible living and fulfilling of the divine will in us will be our form of worship of and commerce with God. His goodness means grace and light and His dark side the terrible temptation of power. Man has already received so much knowledge that he can destroy his own planet. Let us hope that God's good spirit will guide him in his decisions, because it will depend upon man's decision whether God's creation will continue. Nothing shows more drastically than this possibility how much of divine power has come within the reach of man . . . Somehow there seems to be a great kindness in the abysmal darkness of the deity."

The dichotomy prevails in life, but apparently not in spirit, psyche, or in the "collective unconscious," a term related to C.G. Jung. This could be another term for the Akashic records that date back to ancient Hindu Sanskrit and now are implied by modern physics that claims information never disappears once it is created even though it may be dispersed among energy throughout the Universe. During his journey through Africa in 1915-16, C.G. Jung become aware of the deep rooted primitive aspects in the DNA of modern mankind, since it appears that all modern humans emerged from central Africa originally around 50,000 years ago. In that plane, Jung observed his patients worked through their problems by outgrowing them in the mode of Taoist Chinese "wu-wei," doing by not doing, or letting things happen instead of struggling to make them happen. They were able to let the conscious mind and intellect get out of the way and let the subconscious engage. Then, instead of being in the storm, they could observe it from a distance without being demolished. Wu-wei also implies action that is spontaneous, natural, and effortless. This behavior simply flows through us because it is the right action, appropriate to its time and place, and serving the purpose of greater harmony and inner peace.

The transforming benefit of this unity gospel was expressed by a patient of C. G. Jung who wrote him this note; "Out of evil, much good has come to me. By keeping quiet, repressing nothing, remaining attentive, and by accepting reality unusual knowledge has come to me, and unusual powers as well, such that I could never imagine before. What a fool I was. How I tried to force everything to go according to my will. Now I intend to play the game of life, being receptive to whatever comes to me, good and bad, sun and shadow forever alternating, also accepting my own nature with its positive and negative sides. Thus everything becomes more alive to me."

In the context of modern day western living, to have no purpose is unthinkable and even frightening, certainly anti-social and perhaps pathological. Perhaps this is why the Rev. Rick Warren struck gold with publication of his simple-minded book, The Purpose Driven Life. (2006) It provided a welcome alternative for meaninglessness in modern society, i.e., God's will by proclaiming, "It is not about you." And yet obviously our current values have not promoted harmony and balance, either environmentally, internationally, or on an individual level. To allow oneself to wander without apparent purpose can be frightening to the western ego because it challenges some of our most basic assumptions about life, about who we are as humans, and about our role in the world. From the eastern Taoist point of view it is our cherished western beliefs—that we exist as separate beings, that we can exercise willful control over all situations, and that our role is to conquer our environment—that lead to a state of disharmony and imbalance, sin and sickness, and even wars.

If we can learn to follow the wu-wei, doing by not doing, then only what needs doing is done. This means trusting our own humanness, our thoughts and emotions, and also believing that the Earth will provide support and guidance. By allowing the Tao of God to work through us, our actions are truly spontaneous, natural, and effortless. We thus flow with all experiences and feelings as they come and go. [Presumably that includes encountering some natural disaster or human criminality, no matter how much blood is shed or how suffering is incurred, with neutrality and nonjudgmental observance.] We know intuitively, although maybe not consciously, that actions which are not ego-motivated, but respond to the needs of the environment and our fellow-man, lead toward harmonious balance and give ultimate meaning and purpose to our lives. Perhaps, this is what Jesus meant by teaching, "Give, and it will be given to you. A good measure, pressed down, shaken together and running over, will be poured into your lap. For with the measure you use, it will be measured to you." (Luke 6:38) Apostle Paul expanded this instruction thus: ". . . whatsoever a man sows, that shall he also reap. He which sows sparingly shall reap also sparingly; and he which sows bountifully shall reap also bountifully . . . The one who sows to please his sinful nature, from that nature will reap destruction; the one who sows to please the Spirit, from the Spirit will reap eternal life. (2 Corinthians 9:5-7, Galatians 6:8)

This principle of wu-wei has been proven in experiments where sheeple will return a favor to produce reciprocity, even by returning a Christmas card for one received from a stranger. It is the law of social reciprocity that glues soldiers and the mafia and street gangs together into self-sustaining groups as well as members of churches, country clubs, and political parties. By listening carefully within, as well as to our surroundings, by realizing that we are part of an interconnected whole, by realizing what we do to others we do to ourselves, by remaining still until action is called for, we can perform valuable, necessary, and long-lasting service in the world while cultivating our ability to be at one with the Tao, the Way. Such is the promise of wu-wei. This is similar to the Buddhist detachment that permits one to live with eternal suffering and struggle without being disabled or becoming psychotic or even suicidal. This outcome is the goal of all psychotherapy, and it is nothing less than accommodation of the subconscious with the conscious mind, the major duality in man.

The merger of opposites into Oneness is not a rational act nor a matter of will; it is a psychic process of unconscious development that expresses fantasies in thoughts and intuitive formulations in dimly lit abstract structures of principles, and sometimes it is discovered in a flash of light along the "Road to Damascus." Now, Theofatalism™ takes the world of dualities a giant leap forward using the Chartres Labyrinth as its Mandala or symbol of the necessary journey through life. At the center of all opposites there is serenity and contentment because all opposites cancel each other out according to the law of physics—for every action there is an equal and opposite reaction. Thus, love, compassion and charity necessarily are balanced with hatred, abuse, and criminality. The Catholic Church recognizes this both/ and dichotomy by teaching the seven deadly sins that are balanced by seven heavenly virtues. You can't have one without the other. Have you noticed that most conservative Christian leaders ardently support the right to bear arms and are some of the most bigoted, militant sheeple on Earth? They seem to ignore the absolute pacifism taught by Jesus. (Luke 6:20-49) Facing them now are militant leaders of Islam who use the Holy Koran as direction for jihad holy war against the infidel. The predator and prey, the perpetrator and victim, Creator and destroyer, both have their necessary place.

So whenever you hear someone say, "God is love," recall that, "The fear of the Lord is the beginning of wisdom." Where dichotomies are not perceived as either/or but rather both/and, there inner peace dwells. Think you can handle that?

15. Mysteries of the Universe

"In the beginning was the Word, and the Word was with God and the Word was God." (John 1:1) Orthodox Bible readers who claim it is the Word of God may believe that creation of Earth began at nightfall the evening before Sunday, October 23, 4,004 BCE according to some conservative Bible scholars based upon assumptions published in 1654 by Anglican Archbishop James Ussher (1581-1656) of Armagh, now in Ireland. Science sees it much differently. One who has attempted to reconcile the two in a way that could satisfy both is Dr. Gerald L. Schroeder, a Jewish professor of physics, who has written four books since 1990 which his followers and students may accept as a plausible reconciliation of physics and theology, i.e., a both/and approach to cosmology. However, a universal unification of theology and cosmology is yet to be seen. Aside from the rhetorical question, why does anything exist, we live in a very big place, and there is a lot of shaking going on, to paraphrase a standard of "rock n roll" music made popular by Jerry Lee Lewis.

Astronomers think we live on a planet formed from a swirling mass of gas and material elements clustered by the force named gravity about 4.7 billion years ago in a solar system energized by a star that is one of maybe 150 billion stars that are clustered into the "Milky Way" galaxy that is one of hundreds of billions of such galaxies. Our galaxy is one of thirty in a cluster of galaxies that in turn are strung into a band of galaxies with too many to count. Astronomers have discovered more than 300 planets orbiting stars outside our solar system, but they have done so indirectly, by measuring changes in gravity around stars that seem to wobble due to the pull of the planets in orbit around them. If there is life on other planets perhaps it could be far advanced from ours if it had billions of years longer to develop. The search for extra-terrestrial life is a serious project of NASA its search for extra-terrestrial intelligence. Cosmic distances in the Universe are beyond imagination and are measured in how far light travels in one Earth-year, or about 5,865,696 million miles, i.e., about 6 million million miles, based upon 186,000 miles per second. So the time it took light to arrive from the farthest visible stars is about 13.8 billion years ago. This is in marked contrast to the distances in sub-atomic particles that are measured in nanometers and nanoseconds. Light from the Sun reaches Earth in about eight minutes, but it takes more than four years to come from the nearest star neighbor in the Andromeda cluster. No one knows what is in the blackness of space, but it does not appear to be empty.

The farthest galaxy yet disclosed by the orbiting Hubble telescope [aided by a natural zoom effect in space and use of several large surface-mounted telescopes] is estimated to be somewhat more than too many miles to count, but very close to the assumed origin of the Universe 13.23 billion years ago looking backward in time because that is how long it takes light to reach Earth from the farthest galaxy. [Here is a homework assignment: If light travels at 186,000 miles per second, calculate the distance in miles of the farthest detected objects in space. To save you the trouble, one person calculated the distance to be 76,254,048,000,000,000,000,000 miles from Earth. That's 76 sextillion miles (and some change)! Astronomers also estimate there are some 300 sextillion stars in the various billion galaxies of the Universe, 500 of them have been identified with potential solar systems similar to ours.] The oldest galaxy, discovered in 2008 and called A1689-zD1, is so far away what we see now is a snapshot of how this galaxy looked 13.3 billion years ago, close to its formation about 700 million years after the "Big Bang," so named by astronomer Fred Hoyle, that scientists think originated the Universe.

The further out it looks the more Hubble seems to find, a Universe without boundaries, so the true age of the Universe may be indefinitely uncertain. Beyond the limits of vision there may be unknown galaxies receding so fast that light from them can never reach Earth. We don't actually know if there is anything out there now or not, since the light we see could be from objects that no longer exist, sort of like watching an old movie with actors who are long since dead. Maybe the only thing really left of the origin is the background radiation that seems to permeate radio reception. Theories about time and space as commonly known are being revised to the point of incredulity, baffling to the human mind. From assumptions of a definite beginning at the "Big Bang" to the idea of a mobius, that has no beginning or ending where space/time is always here/now, the Universe is a mystical puzzle. The biggest mystery is what the hell is it doing out there? And what part in all of it is the role of Homo sapiens on this planet? Few sheeple ever take a few minutes out of their busyness to contemplate the really big questions.

[One such was a fiction writer named Daniel Quinn who started a popular folk-lore series of books with "Ishmael" in 1992 that employs a gorilla who can communicate with humans to explain it all. His fear is that humankind are quickly destroying the planet with their unbridled population growth and consumption of natural resources in clustered cultures. His work inspired at least one disciple, James J. Lee, to take up arms against humans by attacking the headquarters of Discovery channel to effect change of its programming and got himself killed by police.]

Cosmologists, sheeple who study the origin, operations, and future of the Universe, claim they are getting closer to understanding it all. With modern computers to process complex mathematical models and ever more sensitive instruments mounted in space satellites, they are probing further out into space, which also means looking further back in time. Thanks to thousands of pictures in deep space taken by the Hubble orbiting telescope, astronomers estimate age of the space/time Universe to be at least 13.8 billion years since its eruption in the "Big Bang." This conclusion obtains by reversing the expansion of space as it is being observed. A big mystery seems to be why it seems to be expanding faster the further out one looks. International scientists celebrated the successful startup of a huge particle-smashing machine near Berne, Switzerland on Wednesday Sept. 10, 2008 aiming to recreate the conditions of the "Big Bang" that created the Universe.

[Experiments by the European Union of Nuclear Research using the Large Hadron Collider (LHC), the biggest and most complex machine ever made and located 500 feet underground in Switzerland, could revamp modern physics and unlock secrets about the Universe and its origins. It is funded by and built in collaboration with over 10,000 scientists and engineers from more than 100 countries as well as hundreds of universities and laboratories. Scientists hope to find a theoretical particle known as the "Higgs Boson," named after Scottish scientist Peter Higgs who first proposed it in 1964, as the answer to the mystery of how matter gains mass from pure energy like Albert Einstein calculated. Without mass, the stars and planets in the Universe could never have taken shape in the eons after the "Big Bang," and life could never have begun on Earth or if it exists, as many cosmologists believe, on other worlds either.]

As one cosmologist said, the Universe appears to be the only free lunch since it literally seems to be something from nothing. But maybe not. Some theories include the possibility that there was something before the "Big Bang," so that may not be the beginning after all. The latest theory proposes that maybe the Universe originated from a "Big Collision" between pre-existing matter and anti-matter, which liberated enormous energy and left a residue of residual matter composing the Universe as we see it. Still another theory claims time had no definite beginning. Perhaps it was just one event in a continuum with no beginning or ending, depicted by a mobius. The idea of a first cause or God has been challenged with theories of quantum physics. The lesson of quantum physics in that "something that just happens" need not actually violate the laws of physics. The abrupt and uncaused appearance of something can occur within the scope of scientific law, once quantum laws have been taken into account. Nature apparently has the capacity for genuine spontaneity. It is, of course, a big step from the spontaneous and uncaused appearance of a subatomic particle-something that is routinely observed in particle accelerators-to the spontaneous and uncaused appearance of the Universe. But the loophole is there to play with.

None of this astronomical study would be possible without the giant telescopes. Astronomer, George Ellery Hale (1868-1938) learned in 1904 that the Carnegie Institution was prepared to fund his new space observatory in the sum of $150,000 by the Carnegie Foundation and the Rockefeller Foundation. It wasn't until 1917 that the giant mirror needed finally arrived from France. Mount Wilson at 6,000 feet, in the San Gabriel Mountains outside Los Angeles, would become home to the largest telescopes in the world for the next four decades. The man who best exploited the power of the Mount Wilson telescope was Edwin P. Hubble, (1889-1953) whose first great discovery was to show in 1923 that the faint smudges that populated the heavens were in fact remote galaxies, each one consisting of billions of stars. In 1929, Hubble made an even greater discovery while working with his assistant Milton Humason, who had been promoted from mule driver to the most accomplished astronomical photographer in the world. They used the 100-inch telescope to show that the other galaxies were moving away from our own Milky Way galaxy, and the further away they were the faster they were going.

Moreover, matter is not just spreading out in space, but space in the Universe itself is expanding. Furthermore, the speed of recession was consistent with what would be expected if the Universe had started with a "Big Bang." Hubble's observation supported the then maverick theory that the Universe was created a finite time ago, as opposed to being an eternal cosmos. The spirits of Edwin Hubble, George Ellery Hale and Mount Wilson live on in the discoveries of their successors. The orbiting Hubble Space Telescope, in name and ambition, proves that astronomers continue to push the limits of astronomy. A telescope launched into orbit by a space shuttle might seem far removed from one hauled to a mountaintop by mules when the sky above Los Angeles was still clear of smog, but both are the result of an insatiable curiosity and a never-ending obsession about the mysteries of the Universe.

From the smallest spec of galactic dust to the largest imploding burnt out star called a supernova, the Universe seems to be on the way to somewhere far beyond the imaginations of sheeple who study it. While they ponder what might have happened in some instant of time nearly fourteen billion Earth years ago, they also are probing the skies to see what is happening now that could affect life on Earth as we assume to know it. With the aid of the orbiting Hubble telescope, astronomers have detected images of galaxies out to 13.8 billion years from Earth with no end in sight. An object seen 13 billion light years away is assumed to be that old because its light is just now reaching Earth. The Universe seems to have no circumference edge and no center, at least none that can be found. Imagine that. And the further out they are the faster the objects seem to be moving away from each other, leading to the assumption that space itself is expanding.

Whatever the cause, it appears that the expansion of time/space has been accelerating for five billion years after it appeared to be slowing previously and is carrying the galaxies along with it. In fact, at the outer observable boundaries of the Universe it appears that space is expanding faster than the speed of light so that whatever is out there cannot be seen because it is receding faster than its light can flow back to Earth. Something seems to be counteracting gravity and making it so that in billions of years, the Universe will be an even vaster, emptier realm, filled with stars and galaxies flickering out one by one until there is only darkness. How this could be so still is being debated by astrophysicists. In that regard, they have focused on four fundamental forces that seem to be driving everything . . . or maybe five.

The four fundamental forces seem to be gravity, electromagnetism, and the weak and the strong nuclear forces. Albert Einstein (1879-1955) began a world wide effort to discover a theory that would integrate and explain all four of these forces. British physicist Stephen Hawking has spent his life clumped into a wheel chair trying to make sense of it all. His helpers all over the world are looking for a single theory that will put it all together. It appears that integration of three of them is nearly possible, but putting them all together into a single theory of everything still seems to be a bit beyond reach of current knowledge. The latest is called "string theory" which has everything made up of vibrations . . . and maybe ten or more different dimensions. Instruments that could prove the mathematical assumptions are not yet available. From the discoveries of Sir Isaac Newton (1642-1727) that seem to govern the laws of physics on Earth to the interplanetary and now the galactic discoveries made from space, the wonders of it all appear to be beyond the comprehension of average humans. The connections between matter and energy, time, space, and gravity all seem to be far removed from the day to day living of Homo sapiens. And yet, they are dependent upon all of it for their existence without realizing it.

New discoveries seem to add mystery to what already is a concept beyond the imagination of average sheeple. Stars are being formed from seemingly random clusters of matter and older ones are dying out with a gigantic nuclear implosion, called a super-nova, leaving a "black hole" with gravity so dense not even light can escape. Stephen Hawking developed some equations that seem to indicate the gravity in a black hole goes to infinity as matter is compressed to a tiny spot leaving only a "singularity," which is a word that means "we have no clue." Black holes appear at the center of many galaxies and some wonder if they are not birthing other Universes we cannot yet detect. Scientists now are trying to explain the existence of many black holes that are discovered by watching stars that appear to be in an accelerating orbit around something undetectable at the center. The blips of light detected in the starry sky may only be visible remnants of stars that no longer exist in the vast arena of space and time. However, an opposing theory is being developed by Jacob Barnett, age 12, who is the latest mathematical genius to tackle mysteries of the Universe. He claims that he can prove Einstein was wrong.

What is unobservable in space includes something assumed to be "dark matter," proposed by astronomer Vera Rubin in the early 1970s, which is necessary to account for the amount of gravity measurable but unaccounted for by the amount of matter that is observable. Fully eighty-five percent of gravity is unaccounted for by detectable matter. Scientists estimate that 90 to 99 percent of the total mass of the Universe is missing matter. Only 4.6 percent of the mass in the Universe appears to be atomic particles so the invisible matter must be composed of something different. Actually, "dark matter" may be misleading; it's really the ability to detect it that is missing with current technology. Scientists can tell that the "dark matter" must be there, but they cannot see it. Bruce H. Margon, chairman of the astronomy department at the University of Washington, told the New York Times, "It's a fairly embarrassing situation to admit that we can't find 94 percent of the Universe." "What it is, is anybody's guess," adds Dr. Margon. "Mother Nature is having a double laugh. She's hidden most of the matter in the Universe, and hidden it in a form that can't be seen." If this be so, then black space is not empty as it seems to the available methods of detection.

Dark matter is thought to be ten times the weight of known matter, so a whole new theory of the cosmos may be necessary as more becomes known about it. This problem has scientists scrambling to try and find where and what this dark matter is, but it demands reworking the laws of gravity and that is taboo because science still does not know where gravity comes from or why it behaves as it does. For one thing, dark matter it seems to fly right through the densest forms of matter known without impacting any molecules or atoms. For this reason it is being called weakly interacting massive particles (WIMPs) or anti-matter. In one experiment, housed a half mile into the Earth to capture dark matter in an abandoned iron mine in Minnesota, it was discovered in 2009 that perhaps they had isolated two samples of something like that. [Since it was reported that Jesus appeared to pass through walls and locked doors after his resurrection, perhaps his new body was composed of dark matter. (John 20:19) Was Jesus really a visitor from outside our solar system?]

Would you believe there also is postulated the existence of anti-matter which is equal to but with opposite charges to matter? When the two collide they destroy each other leaving only energy, which cannot be created nor destroyed. Are you following this? For years, astronomers have been baffled by the source of anti-matter. Physicists at the CERN laboratory near Geneva, Switzerland have succeeded for the first time in trapping atoms of anti-matter hydrogen, or anti-hydrogen. That feat takes researchers one step closer to seeing how anti-hydrogen might differ from normal hydrogen. That, in turn, could reveal all sorts of things about gravity and perhaps shed light on what happened to all the anti-matter that theoretically should be, but isn't, present in the Universe. Anti-matter is the same as regular matter except that each particle has an opposite charge. Recall that Jesus was reported to enter rooms after his resurrection by going through the walls, so perhaps his new body was anti-matter? Are you keeping up?

If anti-matter equals matter then the Universe must add up to zero, but it apparently doesn't so that leaves a mystery yet to be solved. Researchers say the matter-annihilating material is generated when stars get ripped apart by black holes or neutron stars, leaving only gamma rays as evidence. The undetectable force behind this development is being called "dark energy." Dark energy may be a force opposite to gravity. Whatever it is, science thinks it is expanding space faster and faster, blowing up like a balloon at increasing speed. All in God's will of course . . . AIGWOC.

Albert Einstein said his biggest mistake was refusing to believe in dark energy. He may be forgiven by a group of scientists in Hawaii who organized the Resonance Project Foundation to explore a unified theory of matter that would integrate the work of Einstein with other physicists to explain everything from subatomic particles to galaxies in outer space. Their stated goal says; "Instead of seeing ourselves as separate from everything around us, this view allows us to recognize that we are embedded in a fractal feedback dynamic that intrinsically connects all things via the medium of a vacuum structure of infinite potential. [Did you understand that?] A fundamental understanding of the dynamics of this inter-connectivity redefines the lens through which we see the Universe and our place in it, and leads to theoretical and technological advancements that move us towards a sustainable future." If this leaves you feeling very small, helpless, and insignificant, welcome to the human race.

There is a fairly well established explanation for the formation, existence, and termination of stars from condensing swirls of gas and matter by the force of gravity. But, a theory connecting them with the affairs of life forms on Earth has been elusive. The ancient astrologers developed a complex theory for control of mankind by stellar forces, but it still awaits some acceptable proof to convince the skeptics. Throughout the cosmos it appears that all beginnings come with endings and endings are followed with new beginnings, as modeled by a "mobius." [A mobius is a mathematical curiosity made by making a single twist in a narrow strip of paper and attaching the ends. It makes into a continuous edge and side with infinite traverse.] This notion was penned by T.S. Eliot (1888-1965), "In my beginning is my end and my end is my beginning." Perhaps that rule includes the lives of all species Homo sapiens . . . or not. Some cosmologists are trying to figure out how the Universe itself will end. Our own Sun appears to be about half way through its expected life cycle of some ten billion Earth years. How the downside of its inner nuclear fusion reaction will affect Earth can only be modeled by mathematical equations. But cosmologists think it will end in a fiery ball of molten helium gas, a red giant, that will engulf the Earth and incinerate the adjacent planets with it about four billion years from now. Whether or not there are any duplicates of Earth in the cosmos is a continuing question of intense speculation. Hundreds of stars have been detected with a suspicious wobble that may indicate some form of planets orbiting them as with Earth and its Sun.

The planets in our solar system are assumed to be kept in their orbits around the Sun precisely by the force of gravity which warps space to keep them in motion. A little more and they would crash into each other and a little less and they would spin out to space. They follow a pathway determined mysteriously by the space-time distortion caused by gravity which creates an energy vortex that keeps them spinning like an object tossed into a toilet. Energy radiated from the nuclear fusion occurring in the Sun is just enough to maintain all the seasons on Earth. The sun is 400 times larger than the moon of Earth and just about 400 times the distance away so that the moon causes a full solar eclipse for a few minutes whenever it aligns properly for viewing about once every 36 months. This is the only time that science can see and study the corona, the exploding band of gases that surrounds the Sun, which seems to be in constant uproar.

One mystery is why the outer corona is so much hotter than the surface of the Sun. Science believes that stars like our Sun were made when clusters of gaseous materials cooled into solids and then compacted from gravity to the point where they spontaneously ignited into a nuclear reaction, like the combustion inside a diesel engine. The originator of it all is a big mystery. The biggest mystery of all may be the source and purpose of a fifth fundamental force, the force that initiates and sustains what is called life and its nearest ally called consciousness among sentient beings. The Psalmist observed, "When I consider your heavens, the work of your fingers, the moon and the stars which you have set in place, what is man that you are mindful of him, the son of man that you care for him? You made him a little lower than the heavenly beings and crowned him with glory and honor." (Psalms 8: 35)

Possibly the most famous, if not the most honored, physicist is a man totally paralyzed by Amyotrophic Lateral Sclerosis, Lou Gehrigs Disease. Stephen Hawking, British professor of astrophysics, is himself a great paradox of the most wonderful mind locked in a physically wasted body. From his wheel chair he has formulated and replaced theories about the Universe that will take years to unravel. One of them is that there might well be an infinite number of parallel Universes. Another is that black holes actually are absorbing matter, information, and energy and eventually turn into "nothing." But he changed his mind about that recently and now claims that positive and negative particles are separated at black holes, with half of them being re-injected into space . . . what is called Hawking radiation. It may be from just such a "nothing" that the whole Universe originally emerged, i.e., a singularity. Perhaps each black hole observed in the center of each galaxy is birthing a new Universe. But, how and why is unknown.

With the modern invention of chaos and string theories, physics has moved beyond the practical ability of mortal minds to envision and has entered a world that only exists in mathematical equations. This leads to the enormous question of whether what is called "mind" exists apart from the neurons in the brain that we can envision. Modern physics might say that it does and it does not. Neurologists think there is a hidden layer of mind in which the electro-chemical blips between neurons in the brain are converted into conscious thoughts. There seems to be a universal need to accommodate opposites that appear to be mutually exclusive, even in the apparent impossible truth of both general relativity and quantum mechanics in physics. The latest evolution in physics is string theory, which says everything merely is energy vibrations, and there may be as many as eleven different dimensions of space, not just the three that we can sense. The giant Hadron particle collider located near Berne, Switzerland may soon validate this theory . . . or not . . . well, that is repeating ourselves.

Stanford Prof. Leonard Susskind, speaking of string theory has observed, "The beginning of the 21st century is a watershed in modern science, a time that will forever change our understanding of the Universe. Something is happening which is far more than the discovery of new facts or new equations. This is one of those rare moments when our entire outlook, our framework for thinking, and the whole epistemology of physics and cosmology are suddenly undergoing real upheaval. The narrow 20th-century view of a unique Universe, about thirteen billion years old and ten billion light years across with a unique set of physical laws, is giving way to something far bigger and pregnant with new possibilities. Gradually physicists and cosmologists are coming to see ten billion light years as an infinitesimal pocket of a stupendous megaverse. If there exists a mind-bogglingly huge enough number of Universes (10 to the 500th power and growing), then inevitably ours, however unique or special it may seem to those of us who contemplate its apparently fine-tuned laws, is just a run-of-the-mill inevitability."

At the same time theoretical physicists are proposing theories which demote our ordinary laws of nature to a tiny corner of a gigantic landscape of mathematical possibilities. Susskind says that all matter may actually all be inside a giant Black Hole. When you think about it, life is full of black holes that suck you into an abyss after you cross a threshold from which there is no return possible, what is called the "event horizon" in cosmology. This may be true of your career choices, your finances, your relationships, and your beliefs. The final threshold is death, sort of like going over Niagara Falls in a barrel where there is a definite point of no return once you enter the Niagara River, i.e., the river of life and death.

You may be floating down the river on a houseboat having a party, but the waterfall awaits just around the bend. Fortunately, humans are spared from this realization until the middle of life by avoidance of death. C.G. Jung declared the second half of life should be preparation for death, but very few have learned this lesson. Comparing a human life, no matter how powerful or influential, to the barely imaginable space/time of the Universe, makes one feel quite small and insignificant, doesn't it. And, yet, in 2004 both Russia and the U.S. launched a new competition to put human explorers onto the surface of Mars by 2030. This immense task presents challenges far beyond that of the human exploration of the moon. While conditions for life on planet Earth are being threatened by global warming and nuclear catastrophe, it remains to be seen how and whether mankind will evolve in the future.

There are some physicists who wonder if the Universe really exists or is it just a function of human imagination or some nonmaterial presentation, like a hologram. [A hologram is a projection of some object in space by intersecting beams of laser light.] The new theories of quantum mechanics suggest it may only exist for those who look for it because at that level all that exists are the probabilities that anything exists. It seems that the Universe appears to those who look for it but does not exist if you are not looking. Imagine that. Most traditional theists, including Jews, Christians and Muslims, assume that this is the only possible Universe, created by God, although writers of the Bible could not dream that big. Modern day science, which physicists fully admit is incomplete, shows that our particular Universe has a number of constants, a slight change of which would likely make life as we know it impossible. This has been seized upon by theists as proof of God's existence and His creation of the Universe. Others believe there could be an infinite number of Universes, one for each logical possibility, separated only by an invisible membrane. Unfortunately, this is both incomplete science and bad theology. Both fail to satisfy just as much as did God's answer to Job, "where were you when I created all these things?" The fundamental question as posed by philosophers from Aristotle to Leibniz is, "Why is there something rather than nothing?"

The debate among philosophers goes on trying to prove one way or other if the Universe is real or only imaginary and whether it had a creator or not. Proof of its existence depends upon an assumed imbalance between matter and anti-matter with matter winning the race, but only barely. Moreover, one knows life when it is present or absent but no one can define it or describe its source nor account for its absence, even though Jesus declared, "The spirit gives life, the flesh counts for nothing." (John 6:63) If energy can neither be created nor destroyed, does birth and death on Earth merely recycle the constant amount of energy around into different sentient beings? After all, there is no doubt that a man and a tree both are alive. So are bees, elephants, and whales. What about all those binary bits that exist in all those personal computers? Will they always exist no matter how many times we erase the hard drives?

A few scientists are suggesting that we all are just some manifestation of a computer program, a virtual simulation as it were. Were such ideas always there just waiting for the machine that would make them manifest or did they just come from nothing? Are ideas created or discovered? Are there any other sentient beings living in other places in the Universe? Are they friend or foe? When you consider a human life in the scope of universal time and space, it is such a small slice as to be inconsequential, and yet apparently it is absolutely necessary for each one to exist for its time. What came before the big bang? What makes gravity? What is dark matter and dark energy? Why are there black holes? Is this the only Universe or could there by infinite Universes? Is the species Homo sapiens the only form of life that contemplates the mysteries of the Universe and its greatest mystery of all . . . why does it exist? Of what purpose is the species Homo sapiens in the big plan of it all? Of what value is the pitiful life of a single person? Is every insignificant individual absolutely essential to completion of the whole?

The ultimate cosmic mystery is whether or not there is life as we know it elsewhere in the Universe. The Search for Extra-terrestrial Intelligence (SETI) is attempting to find out, but don't hold your breath. The odds are so limited that only the will of God could ever make such a discovery possible. If it turns out that we are here alone that will make our planet all the more precious and mysterious, and if it turns out we are not alone our connection with other forms of life will be just the beginning of something totally unimaginable. Physicist, Stephen Hawking warns us to be wary of such a discovery because he says it might turn out like the impact on resident natives after Columbus discovered the new world. They and their lifestyles are mostly all gone now.

We must wait for some future time to sort out these mysteries. Only the questions remain. Meantime, each individual human life seems insignificant among the vastness in space/time of the Universe . . . but still an absolute necessity and indispensable . . . or it would be different. Why we are here is the ultimate existential question. And what is there about some human brains that wants to know while others just go off and play? So, we must live with the existential anxiety of indefinite uncertainty. That is part of being human. Get it? Feel good inside no matter what happens outside . . . if you can.

16. The day Earth dies, if not before

The ancient Egyptians worshipped the Sun as a God, and well they might because it is our source of all energy to sustain life on Earth. It is so big that it could contain a million planets the size of Earth. Its location 93 million miles away requires its light 8 minutes to reach Earth, just right to avoid death by freezing or combustion. Whenever the Sun hiccups, the Earth trembles, reminding us that all beginnings come with endings. Its regular corona magnetic storms impact the magnetic field of Earth with little damage, but a gigantic one could fry all the computers and disable the electrical grid for a whole continent, leaving us all to slowly starve to death. More immanent than that, some rogue enemy could detonate a nuclear weapon over the continent that would destroy all the web-based computers containing all the business records from personal bank accounts to corporate records. From time to time prophets of doom have predicted the end of the world that never happened, but it will.

The prophet Joel predicted in the last days of Earth, "the Lord will show wonders in the heaven above and signs on the Earth below, blood and fire and billows of smoke. The sun will be turned to darkness and the moon to blood before the coming of the great and glorious day of the Lord." (Joel 2:28-32) Scientists estimate the sun bombards the Earth every second with enough energy to power the entire North American continent for a year, so only a slight variation up or down could be disastrous. The ancient Maya calendar seems to end on December 21, 2012 and no one knows that comes next. On that date the Sun is expected to enter the center of the Milky Way, thus ending a 5,000 year period of this age. What is interesting about this is that numerous prophesies from ancient traditions around the world also have pointed to this time as a period of great upheaval and change, perhaps the most important in human history. The alchemists of Europe built the

231

Cross of Hendaye to describe it. The Qero Indians of Peru call it the "Pacha Kuti" and the ancient Egyptians referred to it as the "Zep Tepi" or The First Time. In the Indo-Tibetan tradition it is equated with the final throes of the Kali Yuga, the Age of Iron. This date also figures in the prophecies of sear, Nostradamus and psychic, Edgar Cayce.

Each of these traditions tells us that a great transformative moment could be at hand. One fearful event could be a gigantic solar storm on the Sun that would damage the magnetic field of Earth so badly it would cause a gigantic blackout among the highly integrated electrical power grid that could take years for recovery. Imagine a life without refrigeration, or lighting and electrically powered communications and data processing. Other scientists fear that the gigantic 60-mile wide super volcanic caldera called Yellowstone Park may erupt with such devastation that sunlight could be blocked from the Earth for several years, causing massive famine and extinction of life. Someone must be taking all this seriously as there is a super secret storage vault in Norway that is being stocked with all the food seed specimens in case repopulating the planet will be necessary, if there is anyone left alive to do the work. Those who believe in Bible symbolism may see a prophecy coming true in the story of the fig tree attributed to Jesus. Fig trees are symbols of sustenance provided by God for his faithful ones of Israel, along with grape vines and pomegranates, in the Old Testament. So when he cursed a fig tree because it was not bearing fruit and later warned his disciples to watch for the time when the fig tree should produce new leaves, he may have referred symbolically to the destruction of Israel by the Romans and its later renewal by the United Nations in 1948 . . . or something far bigger than that. Those who see meaning in such things assume this means the end times are nearing. (Matthew 21:19, Matthew 24:31-33) No one knows for sure, but there are many ideas and theories about it because all beginnings seem to come with endings.

Andromeda and our Milky Way galaxies are the two big dogs of our galactic neighborhood. Andromeda is the closest major galaxy to us, about 2.5 million light years away. The distance of a light year is about 5.9 trillion miles, hence looking out into space also is looking backwards in time. Are you getting this? The Milky Way and Andromeda are heading toward each other at about 75 miles per second. They are so far away from each other that the big crash is about four billion years away. And even that might be nothing more than a reshuffling of the night sky or the creation of one super-sized galaxy. Astronomers have known for decades that galaxies consume each other, sometimes violently, sometimes just creating new mega-galaxies. Many times cataclysmic events have seemed like the end of the world to those annihilated by them, but the Earth is still here. Many prophecies, including invasions from outer space, collision with an asteroid, shift of the magnetic pole, and return of Christ attempt to explain this phenomenon.

If you believe the Bible is the Word of God, heaven and Earth are predicted to end through a very mystical chain of events that cannot be deterred followed by the creation of a new Earth and a new heaven. Jesus predicted, "But in those days, following that distress, the sun will be darkened, and the moon will not give its light; the stars will fall from the sky, and the heavenly bodies will be shaken." (Mark 13:24-25) Apostle Peter restated it, "The heavens will disappear with a roar; the elements will be destroyed by fire, and the Earth and everything in it will be laid bare . . . But in keeping with his promise we are looking forward to a new heaven and a new Earth, the home of righteousness." (2 Peter 3:13) Scholars and prophets have been attempting to figure what that means and how and when it will occur ever since. But Jesus said only God knew when it would all happen, and not even the son of God was given to know the details. King Solomon lamented for all men, "Since no man knows the future, who can tell him what is to come." (Ecclesiastes 8:8) Jesus, himself, disclaimed knowledge of the end times, "Heaven and Earth will pass away but my words will never pass away. No one knows about that day or hour, not even the angels in heaven, nor the Son, but only the Father." (Matthew 24:35-36) Are you worried yet?

St. John, the assumed writer of Revelation, said the present age must culminate with a gigantic battle between good and evil at Armageddon that will destroy the unrighteous and set Christ upon the throne in Jerusalem for a thousand years before the final necessary demolition and recreation of heaven and hell that presages creation of a new heaven and a new Earth. This prophecy seems passingly odd for a God that could create the Earth and all its life by the sound of his voice in only six days. Why resort to a very human battlefield and wait for a thousand years when he could just say the word and get whatever he pleases in an instant. Moreover, it seems that Jesus was confused because several times he prophesied his second coming would occur within the lifetimes of his disciples . . . or not. "There are some standing here, which shall not taste of death, till they see the Son of Man coming in his kingdom." (Matthew 16:28) "No one knows about that day or hour, not even the angels in heaven, nor the Son, but only the Father. Be on guard! Be alert! You do not know when that time will come." (Mark 13:31-33) But, who is man that he should challenge the Word of God . . . Hmmm.

Skeptics say that Bible prophecies of doom are not inevitable predictions, and humanists say if sheeple are just good enough they can avoid the ultimate annihilation. But, C. G. Jung concluded that wholeness requires humans to embrace their "shadow," i.e, the negative, repulsive, and socially rejected aspects of our natures. The argument about which prevails, faith or works, compassion or brutality, is as old as first century Christianity. Jesus said that sheeple must be reborn as little children in faith, but he also illustrated in a parable that faith without works will get you eternal punishment. (Matthew 25: 34-46) Compare any child under age two with any adult to see this contrast in human nature. It was an ongoing struggle in the writings of Paul and James in the New Testament, and it persists through Arminianism and Calvinism to this day.

Nevertheless, there is no end to the prophets of doom who think they have it figured out as each generation produces one or more preachers who claim that current events prove the Bible predictions are literal and imminent. Several prophets have selected a specific date in the past for the end of the world that never happened. They are so numerous there is a body of end-time literature called eschatology, study of the end. A lot of it is based on the images in the book of Revelation which have various interpretations. Some of it is plain fiction, but it earns a good living for the authors. Among the current genre, possibly the most popular books are <u>Left Behind</u> (1996) by Tim LaHaye and <u>The Late Great Planet Earth</u> (1998) by Hal Lindsey. The latest Catholic interpretation is <u>Eschatology, Death and Eternal Life</u>, (1988) by Pope Benedict XVI [aka Joseph Cardinal Ratzinger.] He concluded, "The new world cannot be imagined. Nothing concrete or imaginable can be said about the relation of man to matter in the new world. Yet we have the certainty that cosmos leads to a goal, a situation in which matter and spirit will belong to each other in a new and definitive fashion." Apostle Paul observed, "The prophecy awaits its time. If it seems to be slow, wait for it. It will surely come." (Hebrews 10:37)

However, since the Bible was written, knowledge about our planet and its solar system has increased far more than was predictable back then. Science now predicts that our planet will not last forever. The details are debated by scholars, but we know now that life on Earth is totally dependent upon energy from the Sun and, that too, will not last forever. One of its mysteries is why the Sun is much hotter at its outer corona than in its surface. During full eclipses studies of the corona have created fears of what could happen to Earth if one of its super eruptions were to disrupt the magnetic field that regulates life on the planet. Perhaps the ancients who worshipped the Sun God were not so wrong after all. They just needed to go one step further and worship the Creator of the Sun. Astronomers believe that the Sun is a gigantic ball of helium with a hydrogen nuclear fusion reaction ongoing at its core. Scientists imagine they have figured out that the hydrogen fuel of the Sun will be consumed by its nuclear fusion reaction in about five billion more

Earth-years. They think this was proven from knowledge gained in the first hydrogen nuclear fusion bomb test on November 1, 1952.

The fusion reaction in the Sun got started when its matter became so condensed its hydrogen exploded spontaneously about ten billion years ago—sort of like continuous combustion in a diesel engine. The Sun is not large enough to condense into a supernova when its fuel is gone as much denser stars do when they die, so as it shuts down it will implode inward creating immense heat that instantly will begin burning up its helium. As the helium burns more rapidly, it will explode into a giant fireball called a red giant that will engulf the orbits of the nearby planets, including Mars and Earth. The Sun will expand three hundred times bigger and its radiance will be 2,000 times brighter. This may begin to happen about one billion years from now but it could be even sooner, perhaps 50 million years. As the Sun expands, first the oceans will all boil away and then Earth will be consumed like a twig in a fireplace almost instantly, and the very small nugget of ash remaining of the Sun will float into space cooled to a small burned out cinder. Believe it, or not. There are some astronomers seriously searching for other planets similar to Earth that might provide a new home for Homo sapiens. They have discovered more than 100 so far. All we have to figure out is how to get there and set up housekeeping. That is, unless they annihilate themselves even more quickly. With billions of years to go, the life of mankind is put into a very small niche in the overall scheme of things. To put Homo sapiens in perspective, if you scale the ten-billion year lifecycle of the Sun to 24 hours, mankind has occupied only little more than one second of its existence.

More easily imagined during the lifespan of Homo sapiens is the phenomenon of a total solar eclipse. A solar eclipse occurs when the moon passes between the Sun and the Earth so that the Sun is wholly or partially obscured. This can only happen during a new moon, when the Sun and Moon are in conjunction as seen from the Earth. At least two and up to five solar eclipses occur each year on Earth. Total solar eclipses are nevertheless rare at any location because during each eclipse totality exists only along a narrow corridor in a relatively tiny visible area of Earth. In ancient times, and in some cultures today, solar eclipses have been attributed to supernatural causes. Total solar eclipses can be frightening for sheeple who are unaware of their astronomical explanation, as the Sun seems to disappear in the middle of the day and the sky darkens in a matter of minutes. It turns out that the ratio of the size of the moon to the Sun is 400:1, the same as the ratio of its distance to Earth and the Sun. That is why the small moon can seem to blot out the much larger Sun completely. Is that a coincidence, or what?

There is another celestial coincidence that seems to be planned very specifically. The core of the Earth is thought to be a molten mass of hot iron, hotter than the surface of the Sun. It is exposed through a volcanic rift that circles the planet under the oceans and landmass like the seam around a baseball and explodes periodically onto the surface with much destruction through vents called volcanoes. The rotating mantel of the Earth spins around the core, inducing an electric current that creates a natural magnetic field that surrounds the Earth, protecting it from cosmic radiation from outer space. All this makes the surface a conductor of electricity that is vibrating at a resonant frequency of eight cycles per second. Perhaps one day the role of this magnetic field surrounding Earth in sustaining life on the planet will be understood better. Astronauts circling the Earth have reported seeing flashing lights, even with their eyes shut, now believed to be caused by cosmic particles that were able to enter their space crafts through its molecules of matter and directly impact their optic nerves. Where they come from no one knows. Some astronauts have developed cataracts as a result.

In any event, the core of Earth is cooling albeit very slowly and may eventually freeze into a solid mass that terminates the magnetic field, sending Earth into a silent death, much as may have happened to Mars, our closet planetary neighbor. Scientists also think the magnetic field surrounding Earth may have shifted abruptly in the past, some 171 times over 70 million years, and that it could shift again. Because a wide range of commercial and military navigation and attitude/heading systems are dependent on models of the magnetic field, these models need to be updated periodically. The magnetic field's strength and direction and their rates of change are predicted every 5 years for a 5-year period. The North magnetic pole has been moving towards Siberia ever since it was first located a century ago which could mean the shift has begun. During the past century its speed of relocation has accelerated from 10km per year to 40km per year. What that would do to life on the planet is unknown. Whether this will happen before the Earth is consumed by the imploding Sun is not presently understood. The bottom line is that Earth will not exist in its present form forever. Each day is one more and one less, just like your life which is a small zit on the scale of space/time marking life on this planet.

Planetary events are not mere curiosities because they are impacting Earth as you read this. Tides are caused by the gravitational pull of the moon, and solar winds, flairs, and corona storms affect life on Earth more than you know. Coronal mass ejections from the Sun bring intense radiation storms that can disable solar powered satellites or cause cancer in unprotected astronauts inside their spacecraft. Scientists predict that solar storms likely will peak during the current cycle which began about 1859, around 2012, bathing the Earth in enormous clouds of radiant energy and impacting the magnetic field of Earth in unpredictable ways. It is curious that the calendar dating by the Maya of Central America from five thousand years ago or more ends exactly on December 21, 2012, and the French soothsayer, Nostradamus also apparently predicted the end of the world on that date. The ancient Chinese oracle, the I-Ching also seems to converge on that date. The ancient astronomers obviously imagined that date marked the end of something. What comes then will be interesting to observe by Homo sapiens living at that time.

Observable galaxies seem to have a "black hole" in the center of such immense concentration of matter, a million times more than our Sun reduced to a few miles in diameter, that its gravity sucks in everything with such force that not even light can escape. Streaming out of the black hole is immense "Hawking radiation" that can destroy adjacent galaxies, but also blow particles together with such force as to create new stars and even new galaxies. Thus, the Universe seems to be creating and destroying matter simultaneously. What goes on inside a black hole and why is still a mystery of the cosmos. In about three billion years, experts predict that the Milk Way and Andromeda, the nearest galaxy, will collide with unimaginable consequences. At the center could be formed a super black hole, and as its core gravity approaches infinity, time approaches zero and may come to a stop. Thus may end the Milky Way, which houses our Sun and its solar system. What happens to the Sun and its solar system is unpredictable if that happens.

In addition to these conditions known to exist between the Sun and the Earth, what possible unknown conditions might exist between all the unimaginable bodies in the Universe that could impact Earth and destroy it? About 5,000 asteroids have been detected and are being tracked. They are thought to be debris remnants of the formation of our moon that did not get captured by its gravity and are wondering off into space by themselves, sometime knocking into each other and sending them into random trajectories. Some 400 of them could be directed towards Earth by the slingshot force of gravity produced by the giant gas planet Saturn, 1,000 times bigger than Earth, sort of like a lethal game of dodge ball with bullets the size of houses speeding up to 40,000 milers per hour. Of all the undetected asteroids spiraling around our solar system as space debris left from formation of the planets, how many might impact Earth with total devastation such as the one that impacted the Yucatan and thought to have destroyed all the dinosaurs and many other species about 65 million years ago, no one knows.

One such impact may have occurred in Siberia during 1905 when it appears that some explosion in the atmosphere much larger than the atomic bomb destroyed a large area of timber. If it had been a city, the whole place would have been demolished. Scientists believe one such asteroid is on a collision course with our planet and could impact as soon as April 13, 2036 when it gets so close it could be pulled in by the gravity of Earth. Who knows if the ancient astrologers were not correct In their assumptions about the impact of planetary forces upon the lives of human beings? It appears to archeologists that ninety-nine percent of species that have occupied the Earth have come and gone, so perhaps shall the end come for the current species Homo sapiens. So as you prepare for sleep tonight, think about the fact that you have completed one more day in your finite life and one less day remains in the uncertain life of the solar system and planet Earth. One more is one less. That is the law of necessary opposites. Both/and.

Beyond the end of Earth, there are wild speculations about the end of the Universe. While it seems to be expanding at an increasing rate, one theory says it may eventually reverse direction and return to its original big bang in a "big crunch." Another notion has it expanding forever, and still another has it slowing down and eventually coming to a deep freeze as time stops altogether, while still other experts say it may continue expanding and contracting forever. Pope Benedict XVI, [aka Joseph Cardinal Ratzinger] dispensed with time in his "Eschatology" (1988) thus, "The contradiction between faith and the present world order is not resolved by reference to some privileged moment nor to the world of eternity. The all important time for Christianity is the future." His imagination knows no bounds because no one knows the future. Considering the shortness of average life spans of Homo sapiens compared with the imagined remaining lifespan of the Sun, you might be more interested in how you will spend the former rather than the latter. Thoughtful sheeple will experience anxiety of the unknown future as they ponder the possibilities of their own endings and what comes next, if anything. Considering the brevity of their existence, some thinking Homo sapiens may wonder why they are here at all and fear for lack of an answer. They call that existential anxiety, angst for short. We would not be normal without it. All according to the will of God the Almighty One, of course.

17. Whose Will Is It?

Some things really are amazing. The role of the History Channel in cable television is a case in point. Just a little watching of its well documented stories will open the eyes of even the most ardent atheist to the will of God the Almighty One. Three programs recently observed will help to illustrate and maybe challenge your belief in free will among Homo sapiens.

The life of Werner von Braun (1912-1977) is rapidly fading into history. Doubtless many sheeple reading this never heard of him and could care even less. But, his impact on their lives is more than just coincidence. Born in 1912, he had a burning desire for space travel from an early age. To him, exploring the planets would be the highest achievement of mankind. Unfortunately, there was no way to escape the gravity of Earth so he set out to learn how to do it. From his days as a student at the Technical University of Berlin in 1930 he began a lifelong struggle to visit other planets. He obtained some grants for his research and was close to achieving his Ph.D. degree when the Nazi regime took control of Germany under Adolf Hitler. Rocketry research was diverted to weapons development and von Braun quickly became identified with the V-2 rocket that bombarded London during the last year of WWII. Although his infamous rockets killed 5,000 sheeple and wounded thousands more, their production in a secret cave factory took even more lives. Estimates are that 25,000 laborers who were conscripted from concentration camps died during their production.

When it became obvious that the allies were closing in on Berlin, von Braun used his commission in the SS Corps to enable his crew of nearly 500 engineers to sequester all the tons of engineering records in an abandoned iron mine until he could surrender to the American forces. Had he been captured by the Russian army, the outcome of the Cold War might have been quite different. In America, von Braun became head of the Army's rocket program and later head of the project to put men on the moon. The latter took some convincing of President Kennedy to pursue manned space rocket development. Nevertheless, von Braun led the program to its successful completion only to once again see his dream of space travel submerged in the Cold War with Russia and budgets shifted towards military uses for rocket science. Although he finished his career as technical director for NASA, he retired in 1972 with his dream of a space station still just a paper recommendation. He died in 1977 at age 65 from colon cancer. No one doubts that Werner von Braun was the father of modern space rockets that make the international space station possible. How close he came to being responsible for the destruction of London during WWII we will never know.

Another story on the History Channel was that of constructing the Empire State building in New York City. It was during the depths of the Great Depression shortly after Gov. Al Smith had returned to obscurity after leading the state as its dynamic governor who lost his campaign for President against Herbert Hoover. Smith was a "wet" politician who opposed the "dry" policy of alcohol prohibition. A group of financiers were casting about for a project to uplift the unemployed and bring hope to the suffering masses, and they somehow hit upon constructing the tallest building yet in the middle of Manhattan Island. Al Smith was hired as the project manager by the Empire State Corporation. He led a team of architects, engineers, and constructors to complete a project that could scarcely be done today at all, much less within the budget and schedule that he sustained.

The Empire State Building was designed by Gregory Johnson of the architectural firm Shreve, Lamb and Harmon, which produced the building drawings in just two weeks, [without any computer aided drafting] possibly using its earlier design for the R.J. Reynolds Tower in Winston-Salem, North Carolina as a model. The availability of steel fabricated in Pittsburg made it possible to reinforce concrete and provide the frame needed for such a structure, and the available labor, highly motivated, got the job done. A tribe of Mohawk Indians from Canada was employed for the high level steel erection. Since there was no ground space for storing materials, the arrival and installation of products was timed carefully for maximum efficiency. An indispensable feature was the electric elevators that replaced the necessity of trudging up stairs and so limited the number of floors tenants were willing to rent.

Beginning in 1930, the building was completed in only 410 days at half the budget due to the declining dollar, hardly possible with the technology of today. In its first year of operation, the observation deck took in more than a million dollars, as much money as its owners made in rent that year. But, the building would not become profitable until 1950. It stood as the world's tallest building for more than forty years until completion of the World Trade

Center North Tower on December 23, 1970. The Empire State Building was designated as a National Historic Landmark in 1986. In 2007, it was ranked number one on the List of America's Favorite Architecture according to the American Institute of Architects. The building houses 1,000 businesses, and has its own zip code. As of 2007, approximately 20,000 employees work in the building each day, making the Empire State Building the second largest single office complex in America, after the Pentagon, before loss of the World Trade Center. During WWII, a B-25 bomber off course during fog flew into the structure at the 79th floor, doing only minimal damage with loss of fourteen sheeple plus the plane's crew. Strange, when you think of the loss of the World Trade Center on 9/11/01 as planes flew right through the towers.

The History Channel also documented another miracle of engineering and construction hardly replaceable today. As the population of southwestern states zoomed during the early 20th century the need for water to irrigate the arid farm land and support the need for electricity led to the wild scheme to dam up the Colorado river. Several locations were scouted and the final decision to make it happen about 30 miles from Las Vegas on the Nevada-Arizona border was spurred through Congress by Herbert Hoover as both Secretary of Commerce and as President. Early plans called for the dam to be built in Boulder Canyon, so the project was known as the Boulder Canyon Project. The dam site was eventually changed to Black Canyon, but the project name remained the same. Construction began in 1931 and was completed in 1935, more than two years ahead of schedule. The dam and the power plant are operated by the Bureau of Reclamation of the U.S. Department of the Interior. Listed on the National Register of Historic Places in 1981, the renamed Hoover Dam was designated a National Historic Landmark in 1985. Lake Mead is the reservoir created behind the dam, named after Elwood Mead, who oversaw the construction of the dam.

The contract to build the Boulder dam was awarded to Six Companies, Inc. on March 11, 1931, a joint venture of Morrison-Knudsen Company of Boise, Idaho; Utah Construction Company of Ogden, Utah; Pacific Bridge Company of Portland, Oregon; Henry J. Kaiser & W. A. Bechtel Company of Oakland, California; MacDonald & Kahn Ltd. of Los Angeles; and the J.F. Shea Company of Portland, Oregon. The chief executive of Six Companies, Frank Crowe, invented many of the techniques used to build the dam. One in particular is very interesting. Because of the desert climate, it was necessary to circulate refrigerated water through tubes in the concrete to remove the heat generated by the chemical reactions that solidify the concrete, since the setting and curing of the concrete was calculated to take about 125 years. Six Companies, Inc. was contracted to build a new town called Boulder City for workers, and the construction schedule for the dam was accelerated in order to create more jobs in response to the onset of the Great Depression. During the first summer of construction, workers and their families were housed in temporary camps while work on the town progressed. To maintain family security and safety, gambling, drinking and prostitution were not permitted in Boulder City during construction.

Overseeing the operation of this model town was a 69-year-old former newspaper editor and Justice Department employee named Sims Ely. Ely possessed all legal, moral, and judicial power in Boulder City. To this day Boulder City is the only location in Nevada that prohibits gambling, and the sale of alcohol was illegal until 1969. There is enough concrete in the dam to pave a two-lane highway from San Francisco to New York. There were 104 deaths associated with the construction of the dam. The first person to die was J. G. Tierney, a surveyor who drowned in the Colorado while looking for an ideal spot for the dam. Coincidentally (?), his son, Patrick W. Tierney, was the last man to die working on the dam 13 years to the day later. The seventeen hydroelectric turbine—generators at Hoover dam generate a maximum of 2,074 megawatts of hydroelectric power. There is little doubt that without Hoover, Crowe, Ely, and Mead, the Hoover Dam would not exist today and sheeple of the southwest would need other ways to power and irrigate their lifestyles.

Many sheeple know the story of Amelia Earhart, probably the most famous female aviator in history. She was a true pioneer in aviation, and won many awards. On June 1, 1937, Earhart began an around-the-world flight from Miami, Florida in a twin-engine Lockheed Electra with Fred Noonan as her navigator. They reached Lae in New Guinea on June 29, having flown 22,000 miles with 7,000 more to go. Earhart and Noonan never found Howland Island, their next refueling stop after leaving Lae, and they were declared lost at sea on July 18, 1937 following a massive sea and air search ordered personally by President Roosevelt. Although Earhart's disappearance has spawned innumerable theories, her true legacy as a courageous and dedicated aviator and an inspiration to remains strong today.

In comparison, very few sheeple probably have ever heard of Elizabeth "Bessie" Coleman (1892-1926). On June 15 1921, Bessie Coleman received the first pilot's license issued to an African American, male or female, from the Federation Aeronautique Internationale of France. Coleman was a bravely independent and determined woman, who decided that learning to fly provided an exciting challenge. However, in the early years of the 20th century she had two strikes against her: her race and her gender. Unable to secure flight training in the United States, she went to France and earned her license. She returned to the United States in September of 1921, and began to perform in the Chicago area, doing aerobatic loops and figure eights.

Her ultimate goal was to establish a flying school for African Americans. In 1925 she moved to Houston and performed throughout the South, drawing multi-cultural crowds. She had nearly reached her goal of opening a school, when on April 30, 1926, she went up for a practice flight for a May Day celebration in Orlando, Florida. About ten minutes into the flight, the Curtis Jenny biplane, piloted by her mechanic and publicity agent, William Will, went into a nose dive and flipped over. Coleman, who had not fastened her seatbelt, was thrown from the plane and plunged to her death. However, her brief flying career inspired many young African Americans to enter the field of aviation and her legacy continues in the form of aviation clubs and tributes, including the 1995 U.S. postal stamp issued in her honor. Each year on the anniversary of her death, African American pilots fly over "Brave Bessie's" grave in Chicago to drop flowers in her honor.

History is full of stories about a few special men . . . and women . . . called to perform a special service during their lifetimes. Take, for example, the 56 signers of the Declaration of Independence. They were lawyers, merchants, preachers, farmers, and doctors, all leaders from the thirteen British colonies who despised what they perceived as oppression by the Crown. There is a theory among some intellectuals that a few super-wealthy families actually control all the nations on Earth. The presidents and prime ministers and dictators merely are doing their will, which is to control the wealth of nations and thereby to control the world. Those who believe this notion say their goal is nothing less than a one-world government without any national sovereignty that would make it even easier for them to control everything. They point to growth of international free trade agreements as evidence this is happening. They claim that organizations, such as the Council on Foreign Relations in the U.S., the World Bank, and the Trilateral Commission are agents of their will. Some see the symbol of these super-controllers in the pyramid and all-seeing eye shown on the reverse of the U.S. one dollar bill. In comparison with the rest of us, such sheeple seem to have a special calling. But, when you look a little deeper into history, you may realize they could have done nothing without the aid of many unnamed men and women who supplied the flesh and blood necessary to get the job done. Millions gave their lives. But, what if everyone refused to fight in future wars, no matter the cause?

Every day, events are occurring that may never be shown on the History Channel. But they are no less significant to the sheeple experiencing them. Psychologist, Martin E. Seligman and his cohorts have attempted to show how sheeple learn through experience that some things, but not all things, are beyond human control so it is futile to worry about them. They claim it is an error of thinking to assume that because we cannot control some things we cannot control anything. They call this "learned helplessness" and say it is the root cause of pessimism and depression. They say it comes from the baby's memory within us that did not get fed or changed when needed and was ignored by adults who had ultimate control over its survival. They say that adults can take control of their own lives and must assume responsibility for their own behavior by avoiding over generalizing. Seligman says: "The optimists and the pessimists: I have been studying them for the past twenty-five years. The defining characteristic of pessimists is that they tend to believe bad events will last a long time, will undermine everything they do, and are their own fault. The optimists, who are confronted with the same hard knocks of this world, think about misfortune in the opposite way. They tend to believe defeat is just a temporary setback, that its causes are confined to this one case. The optimists believe defeat is not their fault: Circumstances, bad lack, or other sheeple brought it about. Such sheeple are unfazed by defeat. Confronted by a bad situation, they perceive it as a challenge and try harder."

The reasoning of Seligman and his cohorts is no less flawed than that of their subjects. They avoid discussion of what makes pessimists and optimists because they don't know. There is always an opposite view. If you are not scared and confused you just don't know what is happening. Residents of Hollywood, CA live with the dichotomy between haves and have-nots in plain view. The highly successful movie types live in mansions, drive expensive cars and shop on Rodeo Drive. But the wannabes drive taxis and serve in restaurants and bars hoping for their great discovery often for a lifetime. Los Angeles writer Julie Gray concluded, "In a city, a country and a time full of people convinced that money and material trappings are equal to success and happiness, can you still know that this is not true and be happy just to be living and breathing?" In reply, Abraham Lincoln said he believed that "everyone is just about as happy as they choose to be." But he also said that that he did not control events but rather events controlled him. A wise sage concluded, "If at first you don't succeed, try and try again but then quit because there is no sense in making a damn fool of yourself."

A God who controls some things but not all things would leave sheeple with only a gamblers chance of success in achieving any task. In fact, any achievement requires unlimited connections between forces that are unseen and uncontrollable by the achievers, but all are necessary links in the chain to the goal. The impotence of Seligman's theory against the power of God the Almighty One might be seen in the lament written by Viennese classical music composer Franz Schubert (1797-1828) to a friend after he contracted untreatable syphilis which claimed his life at age 31; "I feel myself to be the most unfortunate, the most miserable being in the world. Think about a man whose health will never be right again and who from despair over the fact makes it worse instead of better. Think of a man, I say, whose splendid hopes have come to naught, to whom love and friendship offer nothing but, at best, pain; whose passion for beauty (at the least the kind that inspires) threatens to disappear, and ask yourself whether he isn't a miserable fellow. My peace is gone, my heart is sore; I shall find it never, nevermore. So might I sing every day since each night when I go to sleep I hope never to wake, and each morning merely reminds me of the misery of yesterday." His work was not recognized until decades after his death.

Georges Bizet (1838-1875) was another tragic classical composer. At the premier performance in Paris of his opera, "Carmen," the audience walked out in silence with no applause after the close. He was so devastated that he had two heart attacks on consecutive days and died at age 37 without knowing his work would become famous and would appeal to audiences world wide, with popular and critical acclaim. To this day, "Carmen" is among the top five most produced operas. All in the will of God the Almighty One, of course.

Where this life of Homo sapiens is all going is uncertain, but a few sheeple seem to think they know. Apostle Paul wrote to young Timothy, who was going to be the pastor to the church in Ephesus, "I charge you therefore before God and the Lord Jesus Christ, who will judge the living and the dead at His appearing and His kingdom: Preach the word! Be ready in season and out of season. Convince, rebuke, exhort, with all longsuffering and teaching. For the time will come when they will not endure sound doctrine, but according to their own desires, because they have itching ears, they will heap up for themselves [false] teachers; and they will turn their ears away from the truth, and be turned aside to fables." (2 Tim 4:1-4). If this prophecy was to be fulfilled, whose will was it? Jesus said, "If your hand causes you to sin, cut it off. It is better for you to enter life maimed than with two hands to go into hell, where the fire never goes out." (Mark 9:43) This instruction is repeated for eyes and feet several times by the writers of Mark, Matthew, and Luke. It seems that he thought there was some force beyond consciousness controlling human behavior.

Clearly, the New Testament writers thought that there was some force in play that was not part of the conscious human will. Ever since Apostle Paul lamented his personal struggle between the will of the spirit and the will of the flesh that made him a "wretched man," sheeple have been living with awareness of this conflict. A Course in Miracles (1975) makes it a universal conflict between ego and spirit, and it must be necessary or it would not exist. The "Course" states, "No one can die unless he chooses death . . . and no one dies without his own consent." But, then it also says, "There is no death, but there is a belief in death." Those who believe in reincarnation may also state that no one is born without his own consent either. So, who controls life, God or man? Actually, the only way we can see God is to look around at his creation . . . all of it. But, it takes special eyes to see God everywhere in everything or the shock would be too great.

The writer of James, assumed to be the brother of Jesus, invoked the Lord's will. "Now listen up you who say, Today or tomorrow we will go to this or that city, spend a year there, carry on business and make money. Why, you do not even know what will happen tomorrow. What is your life? You are a mist that appears for a little while and then vanishes. Instead, you ought to say, If it is the Lord's will, we will live and do this or that." (James 4:13-15) The Koran says much the same thing to Muslims. So, why do sheeple insist on believing that they are in control of their own lives? Proverbs 1:7 states, "The fear of the Lord is the beginning of knowledge, but fools despise wisdom and instruction." But, you better not call anyone a fool because Jesus said that could send you to hell. (Matthew 5:22) Apparently he only could render such judgment. Remember that. Feel good inside no matter what happens outside.

18. UNCONSCIOUS CONSCIENCE

At first glance these two words may seem to be perfectly incompatible; an oxymoron. The word "consciousness" begs a definition that goes beyond the obvious dichotomies of either/or materialism or spirit realms. There is no theory connecting brain, mind and consciousness so what drives human behavior still is unknown. The Church teaches children they are born in sin and desperately need a savior to avoid eternal suffering in Hell. No wonder so many sheeple grow up fearing God more than loving Him. Nevertheless, there seems to be something more buried in the genes of Homo sapiens that produces guilt and needs to be assuaged by a savior. Semanticist, Alfred Korzybski (1879-1950) observed, "God may forgive your sins, but your nervous system won't." C.G. Jung concluded the cure of most mental distress was getting right with God. This problem is so ubiquitous that one expert counted up more than 140 different modes of treatment in psychology to address it. Nowhere is this problem more significant than among army veterans returning from combat duty after killing fellow human beings on orders from superior officers who label them "enemy."

During combat in wars, the struggle between morals and orders must always be won by orders. So long as the enemy is remote and faceless as in attacks by pilots flying unmanned aircraft or dropping bombs from high elevations that obscure the lives below, the psychic damage is not so severe. But those killing the enemy with hand weapons drawn face to face return with post trauma stress disorder (PTSD) that is not easily assuaged. The dichotomy between professional soldier and moral civilian just is too wide for many of them to navigate as they recycle to combat and return to families numerous times. It is so wide that more soldiers committed suicide in 2010 than died in combat. We need to realize that if mankind was made in the image and likeness of God that includes all the behaviors resulting from desires derived from God and from God only. All this struggle over guilt and remorse could be eliminated by believing 1) we are powerless over God and 2) nothing happens outside the will of God. But, unfortunately, sheeple are burdened by belief in free will that brings with it much suffering of guilt and remorse for consequences of choices that did not turn out so well. Thus, we need to learn how to forgive God for the sins of mankind because there is only one Source of all and nothing happens outside of its will. If we assume humankind has free will, then problems pile up in the unconscious conscience until something breaks.

Sigmund Freud and the various schools of psychology have shown that repression or sublimation of sinful desires by religion does not eliminate them, but rather drives them into the subconscious where they create chaos in the psyche. Peace of mind requires that they be exposed and acknowledged for what it means to be human . . . made in the image and likeness of God. But, in addition to the learned social rules of moral behavior that keep us safe among others, there seems to be some universal code of behavior that demands its own form of obedience to sustain peace of mind. The Australian parliament reversed itself by an act of collective conscience when it repealed a law it passed in 1996 legalizing assisted suicide after nine months to think about. Similar laws in Oregon and Washington have been upheld by the U.S. Supreme Court. But the subject of end of life planning had to be abandoned by the U.S. Congress during debate on medical reforms because the emotional backlash was too hot to handle. Why should a woman have the right to terminate a pregnancy but the aged suffering souls be prohibited from getting help from a physician to end their lives at the time of their own choosing? Why is the one taboo overcome but the other one seemingly insurmountable?

A primitive tribe in central Africa assumes that any evil deed will be disclosed even if the perpetrator tries to keep the secret . . . even the grass under his feet will scream the accusation of guilt. When Cain killed his brother Abel, the Bible says God knew it because ". . . your brother's blood cries out to me from the ground." (Genesis 4:10) Perhaps the feeling of guilt and remorse for doing "wrong" can be attributed to a function of the "holy spirit" as defined in fundamental Christianity. Convicting sheeple of their sin is supposed to be one of its primary functions. "When the Holy Spirit comes, he will convict the world and show where right and wrong and judgment lie." (John 16:8) This opinion was described by one theologian; "Some in the modern church have made an industry of solving the guilt symptom to the spiritual demise of many. We pay money to have someone in church pulpits make us feel good without repentance; to give us the temporary illusion of God's approval of our sin; to assuage our guilt with smooth words. But unless the sin which caused the guilt is dealt with, any relief is only temporary and may make the problem worse. After all, conviction is the first work of the Holy Spirit!"

[This lesson was learned by those who experimented with open marriage and free sex in the communes that sprang up mostly on the west coast during the late 1960s. After some years of emotional suffering they just naturally disbanded leaving a trail of broken hearts and guilty consciences in their wake. But they have been replaced with serial cohabitation now instead of marriage. There does not seem to be much conscious prohibition of abortions among the supporters of this form of birth control. But they must hide it under claims for health of the mother in order to avoid the emotional restraint.]

One definition of psychiatry is, significantly, treatment of sick souls, i.e., those not right with God. C.G. Jung thought this was the primary goal of the second half of life . . . getting behavior and conscience in order. Proponents of this view say that the central problem of mental health is subconscious guilt. If mankind contains both a Jesus and a Devil, what determines which one wins? And if the brain controls the body, who/what controls the brain? Some might call that "Mind." Some mental health patients appear to be cured, not by drugs, talk therapy, or even electro-shock treatments, but rather by a new relationship with their subconscious conscience that occurs more or less spontaneously. Could that be the will of God the Almighty One?

Depression, anxiety, hostility, fear, tension and, in more serious cases, psychosis such as PTSD may really be ailments of the conscience—symptoms that result from violating the conscience's promptings and refusing to live honestly and responsibly according to some unconscious moral standards. On this basis, the only way to have the good life is to live a life that is being good, however that is defined differently in the many cultures and individuals of humankind. Guilt seems to be built into the emotions of Homo sapiens, like anger and fear so it must have a purpose or it would be eliminated by natural selection. From guilt there arises remorse and from remorse comes a call for amends. Without guilt and remorse there likely would be no compassion or charity, and such a one-sided world cannot apparently exist. Are such things instincts in the collective unconscious or learned behaviors or really derived from the Holy Spirit?

Children are taught very early that there are rulers who make rules, and consequences for breaking them. Religions almost all extol virtues and condemn vices; all have sinned, cleanliness is next to Godliness, etc. The Prophet Muhammad taught, ". . . when a person's intellect overcomes his sensuality he is better than the angels, but when his sensuality overcomes his intellect he is worse than the beasts." Apostle Paul wrote, "Do you not know your body is the temple of the Holy Spirit within you which you have from God and you are not your own?" (1Corinthians 6:19-20) He also lamented the struggle between spirit and flesh, and expressed lack of control for doing what he would and avoiding what he would not, and he labeled himself a "wretched man." (Romans 7:15-25)

In university research, both girl and boy babies usually choose to affiliate with dolls and puppets that exhibit cooperation and compassion while avoiding those representing competition or threats. As they grow older children affiliate with others of similar gender likes and dislikes; boys become competitive and girls become cooperative and later they must be taught the opposites again. Eventually, they form into nations that either support or threaten other nations. In the extreme, they make war to support the prodding of their conscience. The matter of conscience is not moot during wartime because there is a fine line between bravery and atrocity. Conscience must be redirected in Homo sapiens by military training that disables the ego in order to get them to kill each other in battle on the orders of their commanders. Napoleon observed and made use of this human psychology; "A soldier [with ego disabled] will fight long and hard for a piece of colored ribbon." Afterwards, it is quite common for soldiers to experience post trauma shock or cognitive dissonance, which could be manifestation of remorse built into human ego for wrongs and pain inflicted upon fellow human beings.

In the early 19th century, there was a growing number of Christian writers who advocated pacifism and total non-resistance to violence, using the teachings of Jesus for authority. (Luke 6:27-35) By the U.S. Civil War, a host of nationalist orators and writers arose to oppose this attitude, and tried to prove the sinfulness of non-resistance, both from scripture and on common-sense grounds. They might have invoked the teaching of St. Paul from Romans chapter 13 to advocate obedience to the establishment. When the war ended, President Lincoln declared, "With malice toward none, with charity for all, let us strive on to finish the work that we are in . . . to do all which may achieve and cherish a just and lasting peace among ourselves and with all nations." Too bad that John Wilkes Booth did not agree and shot and killed the President. None of the losses incurred during the war on both sides could ever be resurrected. Since then life in America has been marked by wars and preparations for wars. Now we seem to have embarked upon a war of conscience between opposing religions . . . Christianity vs. Islam . . . and that could be the worst kind.

The debate over slavery during the Civil War was an example of the necessary opposites in human thinking, and in many cases the nationalists were right, i.e., in regard to persons who did not renounce the benefits they received from the government and yet tried to avoid the hardships of military service to protect them. However, Christian authors invoked the binding nature of the rule of non-resistance for a Christian given in Luke 6: 20-40, pointing out that this command is perfectly clear, and is enjoined upon every Christian by Christ and his disciples without possibility of misinterpretation. "We ought to obey God rather than men." (Acts 5:29) Others proclaimed the "divine right of kings" in the words of Christ, "Give to Caesar what is Caesar's and give to God what is God's." (Matthew 22:21) "Submit yourselves for the Lord's sake to every authority instituted among men: whether to the king, as the supreme authority, or to governors, who are sent by him to punish those who do wrong and to commend those who do right." (1 Peter 2:13-14) St. Paul also declared the authorities were established by God and should be obeyed. (Romans 13: 1-7)

Military conscription was used to man the U.S. Civil War, WWI and WWII, as well as wars in Korea and Vietnam. Heavyweight boxing champion, Muhammed Ali [aka Casius Clay] refused involuntary military conscription and paid dearly in professional and personal retribution. In contrast, singer-actor Elvis Presley was drafted and served obediently in the army for three years. President Nixon reverted to an all-volunteer force although registration of young men still is required. Jesus said there will always be wars and rumors of wars, but the end is not yet. (Matthew 24:6, Mark 13:7) The dichotomy of conscience goes on, and military psychology says those who fight best are those who fight willingly. However, that willingness is bought at a very high price to the taxpayers, and possibly to the nervous system of each soldier too.

Being good is a relative matter. The nation's highest medal of honor is given for killing the enemy in battle. Normally, sheeple are repulsed and feel disgust when their peers behave like animals, up to a point, otherwise pornography would not be so popular and no one would pay to see professional wrestling. Most everyone would agree that a serial killer who dismembers and eats the bodies is more animal than human, but the same ones may think nothing of their attraction to Internet pornography, committing adultery, violence in the movies and video games, or cheating on their income tax, even if just a little bit. It seems that some laws are made to be broken. If all the traffic laws were to be enforced without exception there would not be enough policemen to do the job. Actually, law enforcement is an oxymoron because we don't punish sheeple for crimes they don't commit. But, sheeple also feel uplifted or inflated by little acts of charity and compassion. Even watching such on television makes one want to do likewise, whether it is reality or fiction.

Thomas Jefferson (1743-1826) a slave owner who had a slave mistress observed, "When any act of charity or gratitude is presented either to our sight or imagination, we are deeply impressed with its beauty and feel a strong desire of doing charitable and grateful acts also," so he recommended reading literature about benevolence to improve the level of society. The emotion of disgust obviously is balanced by the necessary opposite of compassion. What is more baffling is how much acceptable and prohibited behaviors vary from culture to culture from time to time. For example, you can select a live cat or dog for your dinner in some lands while that would be totally abhorrent to pet lovers in the U.S. who think nothing of dunking a live screaming lobster into a boiling pot of water. A social transition occurred last century that converted "single mother" from a social taboo and a family disgrace into a badge of honor among some U.S., but not Muslim, culture. By 2009, about 41 percent of births were to single mothers and among some ethnics, the figure was up to 70 percent. Obviously, there is a lot of relativity when it comes to right and wrong, and it changes whenever God wants it to.

Criminology is a case in point. Criminals are said to lack self criticism, to be short of empathy, and to see themselves as victims; they tend to see themselves as good persons while seeing other persons as bad persons, to not want to make efforts to get what they want out of life, to not take responsibility for their negative and antisocial behaviors, to not learn from their past mistakes, to be intensely afraid unconsciously but instead to pretend to be tough persons, to have a need to control other persons, to perceive themselves as unique and better than other persons, and to believe themselves the rightful owners of all things, including what they did not work for and what other persons worked for. These traits can be seen in some very young children by trained observers. Criminals feel no empathy for others. If they pass an accident victim who is in pain and or dying they do not feel an urge to help him; instead, if no one is looking they would steal from the suffering and or dying person and not feel bad about themselves for doing such a dastardly thing! Perhaps it is because their "mirror neurons" are turned off, all in God's will of course . . . AIGWOC.

[In Philadelphia, the "City of Brotherly Love," a couple homeless drug addicts were seen on security video to steal the watch off a man who died on the floor in an emergency room awaiting treatment for a heart attack. Normal sheeple are said to have "mirror neurons" in their brains that tend to make them feel the suffering of others, a trait called empathy. The mirror neurons in doctors, nurses, morticians, socio-paths and soldiers must be turned off to enable them to do what they must do.]

Generally, criminals do not feel guilty for their wrong doing; they do not feel guilty at all. Instead, they feel happy at the suffering of other persons who somehow seem to deserve what they get. Those who have progressed to a sadistic state actually derive pleasure from other persons' pain and suffering and consciously inflict pain on their victims to satisfy their perverted pleasure. Whether they are born that way or made so by their social and family environments is continuously debated. Our laws do not ban criminal thoughts or speech, but only criminal behaviors, so society must wait for illegal action to impose a reaction. By that time serious pain may be inflicted upon their victims. One child molester was released from prison after serving 21 years only to rape and murder a young woman barely six months after his release. He was subsequently executed for that crime. But Jesus claimed that thinking lustful thoughts was the same as an act of commission, at least in the case of adultery. "I tell you that anyone who looks at a (married) woman lustfully has already committed adultery with her." (Matthew 5:28) [Does this mean that thinking about diet and exercise is the same as doing it? It is a good thing that jurisprudence disagrees because we punish sheeple for their actions and not their thoughts.]

Some thinkers propose there are no victims, just complementary partners. Thus, enemies align on battle fields with precise tactics from God. It is uncanny how the predator and prey seem to be at the right time in the same place for crimes to occur. And, once acts that damage unconscious conscience are committed, none of the parties can redo anything differently. Occasionally, though, a criminal does express remorse and a few make serious attempts to change their behaviors, but most do not. Although some prisons are equipped and staffed to encourage such rehabilitation, it seems that criminals are hard wired for the lives that they lead. Insanity can be used, but rarely, as a defense in criminal trials.

Most of the time courts assume that criminals can control their behavior to disobey the law if they choose to do otherwise. As such, free will of the defendant is assumed in most all criminal cases. However, new research may be indicating mental illness is more prevalent among criminals than most courts will admit. Mental patients cannot be restrained against their will until they demonstrate they are an imminent threat to themselves or others. Of course, by then it may be too late. It may be possible to attribute all illegal behavior to some malfunction in the human brain someday. But again, if the brain controls behavior, what controls the brain? Psychiatry may claim that a schizophrenic is not in control of his own thoughts . . . but who or what is it that is not in control? And what are thoughts, anyway? What is the difference between one killing under the command of God and one killing under the command of superior officers . . . established by God? . . . Hmmm.

Neurology postulates that behavior is all a function of the human brain and that thoughts occur as chemical blips among neurons before they become conscious by about 100-300 milliseconds. Research at the Bernstein Institute of Mathematical Neurology in Germany has telegraphed brain waves of human actions by up to six seconds before conscious awareness in MRI scans of the brain. A baseball batter must start his swing before the pitcher releases the ball and a football passer must release the ball before the receiver is in position. How the mind makes such decisions and signals the body to take action is unknown. This finding suggests that belief in free will is an illusion. [A scientific research project ongoing at the University of Southern Florida managed by Prof. Alfred R. Mele may produce some new conclusions about the debate surrounding human free will. It is funded by the John Templeton Foundation and hopes to apply multi-disciplines to the investigation of assumed free will. Visit: www.freewillandscience.com]

But, a person with normal ego seems to decide unconsciously if an act is appropriate or not before committing it . . . unless the ego is disabled and overrun by some higher authority. A sociopath is defined as someone without conscience who has neither empathy nor sympathy for his victims. A schizophrenic is one who hears voices commanding bad things, but what of voices commanding good things, like that of Mother Teresa? A good soldier is one who obeys legal orders unquestioningly. Conscience is that function that tells the difference. But, since a dead brain and a sleeping brain obviously are quite different, we are left with many anxious unknowns. We are aware of being aware when awake and unaware when sleeping, but how that works is uncertain. Who or what is aware of being aware? Those researching near death experiences have documented cases of sheeple feeling sublime happiness and contentment while seemingly unconscious and still aware, but not all. Some of them report unease and even fright and terror facing some peril beyond human explanation. Could these be effects of unconscious conscience?

Inside this cloud there must lie some way to separate right from wrong, or is there. Dr. Robert Lawrence Kuhn proclaims that "passionate uncertainty is closer to truth." Much of what is claimed to be the Christian ethic seems to have been copied from the "Teaching of Amenemope," a sage of Egypt who wrote a 30-chapter instruction on ethics some 1300 BCE. His rules for happiness, i.e., "Better is bread with a happy heart than wealth with vexation . . . better is a bushel given to you by God than five thousand gotten through wrongdoing," sound a lot like the Proverbs, "Better is a little with the fear of the Lord than great treasure and trouble with it." (Proverbs 15:16) Similarly, the ancient wisdom of Confucius and Buddha can be read today with altogether familiar concepts. The Buddha provided the eight-fold path to enlightenment through right speech, action, livelihood, effort, mindfulness and right concentration which, of course, implies there must be a necessary opposite of eight wrongs too. Perhaps they all are part of the collective unconscious that C.G. Jung claimed was the common denominator among Homo sapiens passed from generation to generation.

The law requires that sheeple must be in conscious control of their acts to be held responsible, and volition is a necessary prerequisite to punishment. But, not always. Accidents do happen. And insanity is a legal defense. There is a very fine line between bravery and atrocities in wartime on the battlefield. President George W. Bush authorized water boarding [faux drowning] as a way of exacting information from suspected Muslim terrorists even though it is generally condemned as a form of torture. The fear is what we do to them they may do to unto us. Was his action an order from the Higher Power? Now, science is debating whether free will is an illusion or not, albeit maybe a necessary one. Nobel writer, Ernest Hemingway (1899-1961) observed, "What is moral is what you feel good after." So, what is immoral must be what you feel bad after. If this were true in all cases, professional soldiers would not have to contend with cognitive dissonance after a battle from killing their human fellows in cold blood.

Sheeple who are lying secrete increasing sweat involuntarily that changes the conductivity of skin in measurable ways, making the "lie detector" admissible in a court of law . . . or not. No one can measure a feeling or a thought but we all know they exist. So one may ask where does that judgmental feeling or thought come from? To be sure, the bounds of conscience vary quite widely, some would say due to socially intruded norms or learned religious dogma or even the threat of legal consequences. In Christianity, one must feel convicted of sin in order to accept Jesus as savior. Where does such conviction of conscience come from? Jesus claimed it was a function of the Holy Spirit. Sinful behavior is neutralized by confession, forgiveness and amends in the Catholic Church. This does not mean it should become a habit. Jesus told the woman taken in adultery to "go and sin no more" after he saved her from certain stoning to death. (John 8:11)

A Course in Miracles (1975) would reverse all that and replace normal ego-driven behavior that includes rational fear, anger, and guilt for self preservation, with a perfect world of spirit that makes room for only forgiveness and love. It presents folks with an either/or dichotomy in which fear and love cannot coexist because one drives out the other. The writer who claimed she was an involuntary scribe of Jesus, Dr. Helen Schucman, (1909-1981) was a self-proclaimed Jewish atheist, although she was baptized as a child. She expressed this belief in a poem, "Song to Myself;" ". . . Holy am I; in sinlessness complete . . . beyond all thought of sin and wholly pure. Who could conceive of suffering for me? Surely the mind that thought it is insane. I never left my Father's house. What need have I to journey back to him again?" This seems to be the ultimate in dissociation from the body, but since the "Course" claims the body does not really exist, dissociation is moot and nothing that it appears to do really happens. Mary Bake Eddy taught a similar concept in separating material bodies from immaterial Spirit in two different worlds for her followers in the Church of Christ Scientist. Such a concept appears to be found in the first century Gnostics faith.

Obviously, this notion is quite different from Christian dogma that claims, "All have sinned . . ." (Romans 5:12) and therefore we need a savior. In contrast, the "Course" and religious science teaches that ego has created the illusion of guilt and fear so all we need to do is forgive ourselves for believing in the illusion that we are separated from God which we created. Instead of becoming as little children as Jesus instructed, (Matthew 18:3) we are to assume that we are as God created us originally, innocent and sinless. Since God is assumed to be omnipotent and the source of all, what the "Course" declares to be illusory belief in an unreal world of ego and senses must also be the manifestation of the will of God the Almighty One, as there can be no other. The "Course" claims that disobeying God's will is impossible. If this is true, all else is moot. If fear and guilt are needless illusions based upon original sin and punishment that never happened, as the "Course" proclaims, why should they exist at all? Indeed, it says that they don't; only Love exists. All else is illusion . . . but if so, from where? Perhaps these thoughts are but examples of necessary opposites. For every thought there must be an equal and opposite thought. Reality and illusions. The duality exists so it must be necessary.

Philosophers have debated for centuries the implications of concepts such as "good" and "well-being" as opposed to "legal" and "illegal" to describe desirable and undesirable behavior. We have the two schools of ethics; one is absolute and the other is relative. "Thou shalt not kill," except in self defense whether real or assumed and in wars legally conducted by nations. Some claim the highest good is maximizing well-being, while others say maximum well-being occurs at the point of balance between what is good for self and what is good for others. Now, we must also include what is good for the planet. Self-sacrifice to the point of martyrdom is extolled by Islam and has been enthroned by the Church and the state throughout history. Putting one's self before others is often criticized as hedonism, while self-sacrifice merits sainthood. The Golden Rule says to do unto others as you would have them do unto you. And some say that giving and receiving are the same. Jesus claimed, "There is no greater love than a man who gives up his life for his friends." (John 15:13) Shakespeare had Hamlet wrestle with this concern in the famous soliloquy, "To be, or not to be: that is the question: Whether 'tis nobler in the mind to suffer the slings and arrows of outrageous fortune, Or to take arms against a sea of troubles, And by opposing end them? . . . Thus conscience does make cowards of us all . . ."

Nevertheless, sheeple totally isolated from conscious boundaries, as infants and aging dementia patients, still seem to make choices that vary from person to person which appear to be guided by some definite motives and constraints they were born with. For example, a ten year old boy who stole his grandmother's car and wrecked it exclaimed, "It is fun to do bad things." Thus, one auto driver may adhere strictly to legal traffic laws [admittedly a rare example] even though criticized by more aggressive drivers, and one who feels hungry may seek a job, even a demeaning one, in order to earn money for food. Other drivers may intentionally and consciously ignore traffic laws, including maintaining a driving license, and some sheeple may forcefully take the food they desire by stealing and robbing others of their possession. In extreme cases, some sheeple would rather die homeless than harm anyone, while the sociopathic serial killer apparently has no restraint of conscience to deter his grizzly behavior.

Leo Tolstoy (1828-1910) captured the issue in describing Levin in "Anna Karenina,"(1877) "Yet, when he did not think but lived, he constantly felt in his soul the presence of an infallible judge who decided which of two possible actions was better and which was worse; and whenever he did not act as he should, he felt it at once." There seems to be something in every normal person that produces the feeling of guilt when their behavior violates it. Sigmund Freud called this moderator of Id (just do it) and the super-ego (just say no) the Ego. Apostle Paul was no stranger to this dilemma as he lamented the war between spirit and flesh that made him do things which resulted in his woe; ". . . what a wretched man I am." (Romans 7:15-25) This is why it is so easy to convince sheeple that they need a savior to avoid punishment for their sins.

There is an inherent paradox between choice and its realization: making a choice inevitably leads to renouncing a choice—for every yes there must be a no, each decision eliminating other options. To do "this" we must renounce "that." We simply can never know with certainty if we are making a right decision. There are only predetermined decisions and unknown consequences, and there is no understanding how the mind makes connections between cause and effect. However, some mystics claim existential anxiety from uncertainty can be transcended and replaced with a sense of existential joy. This requires the synthesis of opposites (such as predictability and uncertainty, being and nothingness, life and death, separation and belonging, etc.). This is not to say that this frame of mind makes life a bed of roses. Anyone with such an attitude will still experience unpleasant feelings or be unhappy, some from threats and some from conscience, but if they are not thrown back into the world of opposites, the underlying feeling of joy can be maintained, which would enable one to face whatever comes with less anxiety. Sheeple who study such things find roots in fields including sociology, law, religion, philosophy, psychology, psychiatry, and more recently in neurology and genetics. Unless one assumes that sheeple all act from unconscious valuing of benefits and burdens in making any behavioral decision, any attempt to understand the wide variations in unconscious conscience runs into barriers at every turn. Let's take a few cases in point.

In a highly celebrated case, the family of the late Terri Schiavo (1963-2005) fought out in courts all the way to the U.S. Supreme Court whether or not to remove her from life support after sustaining her for more than a decade in a "persistent vegetative state," with no hope of improvement, against her previously stated will to avoid such suffering. Medically, only her brain stem survived, enabling nothing more than autonomic functions such as breathing and digestion. She had to be sustained by a feeding tube and needed constant personal care. Schiavo's higher brain functions, and with them her personhood, had been irretrievably lost by a bulimic diet. The Florida courts that allowed her removal from artificial life support recognized this, as petitioned by her husband. But, her family could not accept that decision. What made the legal decision so difficult for her mother, father, and brother to accept was anticipation of loss of the remembered whole person, an actual social and personal existence that had been but was no more. The permanent loss of this person was something with which they were unable to cope because they held onto the hope that it could be recovered, while her husband was ready to let her go and move on to his new family.

Most everyone finds insurmountable the assumption that physical vulnerability extends to the core of our selves. Nevertheless, many sheeple often want every means possible to be used in preserving their pitiful lives at all costs, long after any hope of return to normalcy is passed. As the generation of baby boomers ages, decisions such as this concerning their life support will be made routinely, if not painlessly. In those cases, life extension measures may cause families excruciating dilemmas before the best solution becomes clear. But, the fact is that society cannot afford to keep all the aged alive as long as medical science can, and the resulting conflicts must be settled by some Higher Power. [The fact is that the economic boom driven by the 76 million baby boomers is over and the sooner we accept its consequences, the better. Without their incomes, taxes, and consumer demands the overall national standard of living must decline. One survey indicated that 60 percent of them are helping to support their failing adult children and about one third are caring for their aging parents as well in a so-called "sandwich generation." For a discussion of issues in aging faced by the generation born from 1945-1965 refer to Baby Boomer Lamentations by this author.]

The Catholic Church is arguably the most powerful arbiter of moral behavior among Homo sapiens. Among its dogma are the central commandments of God, including "thou shalt not kill" and "thou shalt not commit adultery" among eight others. These two rules of behavior are connected together in the Church's stand on reproduction. You may have seen the bumper sticker: "You can't be Catholic and pro-choice." Its most conservative interpretations require that coitus be engaged only for the purpose of procreation with no impediments among Church sanctioned married couples, and that once fertilized, the human egg becomes a human fetus with all the rights of survival and protection of any adult. However, members of the Church bend these rules according to their own consciences, and that results in a wide range of sexual behaviors. Repressing normal sexual desires leads to pornography and abuse. The results include priests accused of sexually molesting young sheeple in their charge, sexually mature sheeple wallowing in fornication, and a national law that grants pregnant women the right to an abortion as the ultimate form of contraception without consent of the father. The Bishop of Rhode Island refused the communion of Eucharist to Rep. Robert Kennedy (D-RI) for his support of abortion. He commented, "If one's faith conflicts with one's occupation, the occupation should be changed." Conservative preachers seem to agree with them. Women who have abortions often complain that they suffer pangs of conscience the rest of their lives.

The Rev. Mark H. Creech, Executive Director of the Christian Action League commented, "Are we so foolish as to believe that we know better than God—that we can break His commandments and not be broken by them? Do we believe we can divest our laws from His laws and not destroy ourselves in the process?" There is no doubt that mediating the rights of the unborn and their parents requires conscious conscience, but what accounts for the wide range of unconscious variations in such behaviors? And, why does the Catholic Church demand obedience to the Ten Commandments but ignores all the other laws of Moses, while Islam demands obedience to all of them? The basic conflict between Christianity and Islam seems to be deciding what are God's laws. The Church as well as the Jews abandoned the archaic rules of Mosaic law centuries ago, while Islam declares they are still valid and should be integrated in all forms of government through its law of shari'ah. It is claimed that Muhammad declared, "I am commanded to fight until everyone believes there is no God but Allah and Muhammad is his messenger." The Koran instructs, [4.74] "Therefore let those fight in the way of Allah, who sell this world's life for the hereafter; and whoever fights in the way of Allah, then be he slain or be he victorious, We shall grant him a mighty reward."

We are a nation "under the rule of law," so we are told. But the law is not a black and white matter. For example, there are gradations of illegal killing that range from accidental to manslaughter to second degree to first degree murder . . . and there are established defenses of insanity and self defense. The highest military honor is bestowed upon warriors for killing their fellow man in the name of national defense. Celebrated attorney, Clarence Darrow

(1857-1938) quipped, "The law does not punish everything that is dishonest. That would interfere too much with business." Most criminal cases are settled by decisions of a jury with rules of evidence that vary from state to state and by elected or appointed judges responsible for their implementation. Thus a trial in one jurisdiction may have an outcome that could be different in another jurisdiction or with a different set of jurist participants.

In many cases, punishment is left to the discretion of the presiding judge so that variations in sentencing on the same facts can exist from court to court. We tolerate drunk drivers who kill thousands each year to assure personal freedom to consume alcohol legally to the point of delirium. Again, the matter of unconscious conscience comes into play that seems to be beyond the control of the court process, because a different set of actors can produce a different result. No case could illustrate this better than that of former football star, O.J. Simpson, accused of killing his estranged wife and her boyfriend. He was found innocent in a criminal court but guilty in a civil court on grounds of the same evidence but under different rules of jurisprudence. He escaped restitution in both cases, but later was jailed for committing a different felony. Also, it is not unusual for some convicts to be released upon discovery of new evidence that confirms their innocence. Justice may be blind but it also can be dumb.

These examples are but a small fragment of the larger issues surrounding what is considered to be moral, ethical, and legal among the wide ranging societies of Homo sapiens upon the Earth. Will we someday come to the conclusion that free will is an illusion and, therefore, no one can be held responsible for their criminal behavior? How about the changes in social issues that raise issues of conscience? Up until the "no-fault" divorce laws adopted in the 1960s marriage was a sacred contract between God and man that was not easily revoked, except for abuse, adultery, or abandonment. Jesus reinforced it by quoting, "For this reason a man will leave his father and mother and be united to his wife, and the two will become one flesh. So they are no longer two, but one. Therefore what God has joined together, let man not separate." (Matthew 19:4-6) But alas, that attitude no longer prevails in many marriages. The late Senator Ted Kennedy was able to buy a divorce from his first wife although they obviously had children and were joined together in the Catholic Church, presumably by God. Facing death from a brain tumor, it is said that he sent a contrite letter to the Pope asking him for special prayers to forgive his many sins. And, why do so many sheeple, even very young ones, feel so much guilt for their behavior and fear of eternal punishment that they easily accept the ultimate sacrifice of Jesus as Christ on the cross to save them from their sins? It must be their unconscious conscience. All in God's will of course . . . AIGWOC.

Apostle Paul claimed to be controlled by forces beyond his will; "We know that the law is spiritual; but I am unspiritual, sold as a slave to sin. I do not understand what I do. For what I want to do I do not do, but what I hate I do. And if I do what I do not want to do, I agree that the law is good. As it is, it is no longer I myself who do it, but it is sin living in me. I know that nothing good lives in me, that is, in my sinful nature. For I have the desire to do what is good, but I cannot carry it out. For what I do is not the good I want to do; no, the evil I do not want to do, this I keep on doing. Now if I do what I do not want to do, it is no longer I who do it, but it is sin living in me that does it. So I find this law at work: When I want to do good, evil is right there with me. For in my inner being I delight in God's law; but I see another law at work in the members of my body, waging war against the law of my mind and making me a prisoner of the law of sin at work within my members. What a wretched man I am! Who will rescue me from this body of death? Thanks be to God—through Jesus Christ our Lord! So then, I myself in my mind am a slave to God's law, but in the sinful nature a slave to the law of sin." (Romans: 7:14-25) This scarcely sounds like the same man who seems to transcend this dichotomy when he elsewhere writes, "I have been crucified with Christ and I no longer live, but Christ lives in me." (Galatians 2:20) Which came first, his guilt or his reclamation? Perhaps they each are ongoing elements of what it takes to be human . . . balancing issues of both/ and instead of either/or.

The dogmatic claim that everyone is born a sinner and needs a savior can be refuted easily by scriptures in the Bible. [See the essay titled "The Fraud of Christianity," Chapter 5.] The only reasonable explanation worthy of belief for what drives many sheeple to seek a savior to save them from their sins and avoid everlasting punishment in hell is that something must be happening at some unconscious level that is beyond the control of the individual consciousness. It is as though God, who created the illusion of free will and the consequences of it, also embedded in his creation the feeling of a guilty conscience in addition to the perception of disobedience. Since this is natural state of humankind there may be no need to go home because we never left. C. G. Jung discovered that, "Whoever reflects upon himself is bound to strike upon the frontiers of the unconscious which contains what above all else he needs to know." Elsewhere he claimed, "I do not need to believe . . . I know, because I have been touched by something that sheeple call God . . . this is the name by which I designate all things which cross my willful path violently and recklessly, all things which upset my subjective views and plans and intentions and change the course of my life for better or worse. In accordance with tradition I call the power of fate in this positive as well as negative aspect as much as it is beyond my control, God . . . Although my experience can be good or evil, I know the superior will is based upon a foundation that transcends human imagination."

Jung expressed that "something" in his psychology of religion, which is nothing less than the universal struggle between right and wrong. In every human being there is a sense of right and wrong, but why does that vary so much? Conservative Muslims think nothing of beheading the infidels to gain control of those who resist shari'ah law in the name of Allah. It is the voice of their conscience, dictating to us a law we did not make, for this voice protests whether other men know our conduct or not. This voice often is quite against what we wish to do, warning us beforehand, condemning us after its violation. The law dictated by this voice of conscience supposes a lawgiver who has written his laws in our hearts. And as God the Almighty One alone could do this, sheeple assume that He exists.

The tree of knowledge of good and evil was planted in the Garden of Eden by God, himself. Sheeple who are given to believe this myth may blame God for all their troubles, if it were not for their own false assumption of free will. Guilt arising from that first disobedience must have some benefit to humanity, or natural selection would have eliminated it by now. Hence, some sheeple appear to be born with the need for a savior to remove the consequences of their sins in previous lives. Without some mythically based rules to follow, Homo sapiens may be vulnerable to demonic forces beyond their control to balance their compassion and charity with brutality and torture. And even with civilized rules, religious zealots committed some atrocious acts in the name of their religions, like the infamous Catholic Inquisition and the infamous Crusades during the Middle Ages and the acts of slavery among the U.S. plantation owners who assumed that God made some humans inferior to others, not to mention the current generation of Islamic suicide bombers. [One may smile at what slave owners would think of the black athletes now who are millionaires.] When you take that idea up to the President of the United States and the members of Congress and the Supreme Court and include terrorism by radical Muslims under the rule of Jihad, the subject of conscience gets rather sticky.

Soldiers deployed in combat are expected to suspend they own egos and to obey the chain of command to kill the enemy. They are taught, "Your enemy is always your enemy until he is dead." The highest honor bestowed by the U.S. on its citizens is the Congressional Medal of Honor, awarded for killing fellow human beings who are labeled "enemy" in the name of national defense. When surviving battle heroes return they often are confused about what is right and wrong and without some retraining, they may become disoriented with cognitive dissonance. The line between willful criminality and mental illness is difficult to discern even by experts in courts of law.

Since the actions of nations derive from the actions of their leaders, the role of unconscious conscience, or the lack of it, at the top cannot be overlooked, although it may never be controlled. When President Clinton was asked why he had that affair in the oval office with Monica Lewinski he replied, "Because I could." Perhaps he could have said, "Because I had to."

Martin Luther King, Jr. declared that sometimes a man must do something, not because it is popular or politic or safe, but because his conscience tells him it is right. His conscience got him killed. Think you can handle that? May God help us all to feel good inside no matter what happens outside . . . or not. Welcome to the School of Theofatalism™ where everyone is a member and no one can be expelled or resign. Read the full text in <u>Lessons From Sedona</u> available at Barnes & Noble book stores and online at www.iUniverse.com and www.amazon.com.

19. THE GREATEST MIRACLE

If you ask sheeple what they think is the greatest miracle, you might be surprised by their answers. Of course many will say the Christ child, and if it were true that might suffice. After all, sending his only son through a virgin woman and sacrificing his only son by crucifixion to make amends for all the troubles God has caused his creation would be a miracle. The resurrection, if true, would be even more fantastic. The idea of God, itself, is quite a miracle come to think of it. [Ancient Hindus thought of G.O.D. as generator, operator and destroyer.] Beyond that, perhaps some might say the greatest miracle is the gift of memory because it connects the past with the present and makes learning possible.

A few very rare sheeple, called savants, can recall from memory anything they ever observed, and scientists have no idea how that works. Others might suggest the greatest miracle is the ability to communicate in order to transfer knowledge from one to another. Language seems to be what separates humans from animals, as the experience of Helen Keller (1880-1968) illustrates, deaf and blind running on pure instinct until she was taught to communicate with signs tapped into her palm by her teacher. Muslims might recommend the Koran and Mormons might suggest the Book of Mormon as the greatest miracle. Some would select the Bible and its many derivatives, including A Course in Miracles (1975) imagined to be dictated by the voice of Jesus to its scribe, Dr. Helen Schucman. Others might select the imagination of Helena Blavatsky who published her version of the Hindu versions of the Akashic records and organized the Theosophical Society or the revelations of Mary Baker Eddy who proclaimed the discovery of Christian Science. Still others could invoke the modern theories of physics that describe a strange existence of parallel Universes and up to ten or more different dimensions of matter plus time which only can be described with exotic mathematics.

Human imagination has to be right up there at the top because it was the source of all these results. Imagination also may be what dreams are made of, and without them where would we be? C.G. Jung developed his theory of active imagination in 1913-16 to help enable clients with troubled souls to access the contents of their subconscious through dreams in order to heal their wounded psyche. When he discovered his own subconscious Jung said, "… it was as though the ground literally gave way beneath my feet and I plunged into the dark depths." He concluded it is the content of the subconscious that drives all conscious behavior like the unseen base of an iceberg. Of course, acting out whatever is in the subconscious without the modulating control of ego can get one into trouble. Napoleon Bonaparte (1769-1821) concluded, "Imagination rules the world." Albert Einstein (1879-1955) concluded that "imagination/intuition is more important than knowledge." Retired Episcopal Bishop, John Spong has observed, "Even sin must be imagined before you can do it." Did not God create sin so that he could have something to forgive? Aye there's the rub, for imagination itself has no moral compass. Minds that can create computers also can create the viruses to destroy them. The problem with human imagination (all benefits come with burdens) is that it goes off in all directions … sometimes straggling and sometimes exploding. You can see imagination at work among little girls playing with their dolls as well as little boys and their video war games. Without such diversions, reality for some children would be unpleasant to intolerable. One scientist at the Jet Propulsion Lab in Pasadena, CA has imagined that all life on the planet merely is a computer simulation conducted by the great programmer in the sky, called God.

C.G. Jung separated fantasy from creative imagination, claiming, "… active imagination means that the images have a life of their own and develop according to their own logic; if your conscious reason does not get in the way … all the works of man have their origin in creative imagination." Such may include the popular online fantasy, "Second Life," in which players assume a fictitious identity and conduct business in a virtual world of interacting computers on the Internet. By converting virtual money into dollars the line between reality and fiction in the computer simulation, "Second Life" almost disappears. Imagination also would have to include all the weapons of mass destruction now possible in wars. Business schools teach the secret to success is, "Find a need and fill it." But, no one realizes a need until they see or invent a product to fill it and that is the result of imagination. Without imagination there would be little human progress. All in God's will of course. AIGWOC. Think you can handle that?

Imagination, intuition, and faith all seem to be related in many ways. Intuition has a long tradition of use in philosophy, mathematics, business, psychology, engineering, linguistics, art, music, literature, religion, and science, particularly with reference to the creative process. Plato called it "divine madness," in contrast to reason, the senses, and the madness of mental infirmity. Many thinkers and inventors have attributed their discoveries to intuition, whatever that is. The basic definition is "direct perception of truth, fact, etc., independent of any reasoning process; immediate apprehension." Another definition from the same dictionary refers to intuition as "a keen and quick insight." Other definitions stress that the intuitive process is itself unconscious. Intuition, then, is "knowing without knowing how you know." The matter of religious faith rests upon the existence of this human function called imagination or intuition. In fact, some thinkers have suggested that imagination is a necessary and sufficient condition for the formation of all religions. Imagination could be another word for the "holy spirit" or third person of the Godhead expressed in Christianity. It may be the manifestation of God's will among mankind. Without imagination, or holy spirit, children could not be enticed to good behavior with the promise of heaven and the threat of hell. There is no greater imagination than that of relationships between Catholics and their favorite saints.

Consider, for example, how St. Teresa of Avila (1515-1582) described her gratitude to St. Joseph. "I have never known anyone to be truly devoted to him and render him particular services who did not notably advance in virtue, for he gives very real help to souls who commend themselves to him. For some years now, I think, I have made some request of him every year on his festival and I have always had it granted. If my petition is in any way ill directed, he directs it aright for my greater good. If I were a person writing with authority, I would gladly describe, at greater length and in the minutest detail, the favors which this glorious saint has granted to me and to others. I only beg, for the love of God, that anyone who does not believe me will put what I say to the test, and he will see by experience what great advantages come from his commending himself to this glorious patriarch and having devotion to him." Now, how could one be so truly devoted to both the Jesus of God and his earthly father at the same time unless the Holy Spirit intervened with a generous dose of imagination? Could there be more than a little subconscious family incest going on here? After he set a new world record in swimming by winning eight gold medals with a little help from his teammates at the 2008 summer Olympics, Michael Phelps said, "Nothing is impossible. With so many people saying it couldn't be done, all it takes is an imagination, and that's something I learned and something that helped me." He never mentioned St. Joseph.

Perhaps science provides an explanation. Experiments in neurology seem to show that the mind acts before a thought becomes conscious by some 100 to 300 milliseconds, i.e., mind over matter is true. Thoughts are initiated by pre-cognitive detectable actions in the brain, but what drives the brain is unknown. Perhaps that is why sheeple buy lottery tickets with literally no chance of winning, except for the one that does. But, what controls the mind? Neurologist, Robert Burton thinks it could all be in our genes plus the biochemistry of the brain, which helps him explain why two sheeple draw different conclusions from the same facts, or even see the facts differently from the same observations.

Burton concluded, "One day the know-it-all and the perennial skeptic might be seen as the two extreme on-and-off positions of the genes for the feeling of knowing . . . To expect that we can get others to think as we do is to believe that we can overcome innate differences that make each of our thought processes as unique as our fingerprints." They are like parallel lines that never converge, even to infinity. If so, what controls the genes? Unfortunately, there literally is no way of telling the difference between a mind that creates great works of fiction and another that creates great works of art or music or even great acts of criminal infamy. All the great industrialists were driven by confidence in the visions of success that they perceived. So were the political despots. For example, compare Henry Ford with Adolf Hitler. Both men had great imaginations. Moreover, science fiction writers, Jules Verne and H.G. Wells, described journeys to the moon and nuclear bombs a hundred years before science made it possible. But, where that comes from and who controls it is a mystery. All in the will of God the Almighty One, of course.

Imagination is defined as: "the act or power of forming mental images of what is not present, the act or power of creating new ideas, and the ability to understand the imaginative ideas of others." As such, perhaps nothing happens that has not been imagined beforehand, and memory merely is imagination of what happened in the past. Scientists all pursue experiments to prove hypotheses that are first imagined. The modern development of controllable prostheses for amputees was foreseen by surgeons in the sixteenth century, long before they became possible. What could be more miraculous than documented examples of creative visualization that helps slow down and even reverse growth of cancer cells. The boundary between neurology and psychiatry is as hazy in medical science as it is in real life.

There is a man in Turkey, Esref Armagan, who is challenging theories about the way the brain perceives sight. He was born without eyes but paints incredible landscapes complete with the right colors and the right perspective angles using only his fingers. An MRI scan shows that the visual section of his brain is active when he paints, just like a normally sighted person. He correctly sketched a three dimensional outline of the hexagonal "Baptistery" in Florence, Italy. No one knows how he does it. Linear perspective in art employs an imaginary spot to which all horizontal lines converge to create the illusion of depth perception on a flat surface. The first linear perspective of that building was painted by Filippo Brunelleschi in 1415. However, experiments in "remote viewing" conducted by the U.S. Government in "Project Stargate" by Dr. Russell Targ with normal sighted sheeple to assess its validity proved to be inconclusive, although the results did appear better than random chance would allow. Irish hypnotist, Keith Barry has demonstrated his ability to drive a car while totally blindfolded through the eyes of his passenger. You can see him on www.youtube.com. The research into this practice is formalized by the International Remote Viewing Association. Strangely, a Google search turns up thousands of sites for remote viewing but there is very little that is known about this function called imagination in the human brain. But if it did not exist the world of Homo sapiens likely would be very much different. Let us count some ways.

Let's begin right at the top with religion, which is the supreme creation of imagination and takes many forms among Homo sapiens. Voltaire [aka Francois-Marie Arouet (1694-1778)] said, "If God did not exist, it would be necessary to invent him." Indeed. What could be more imaginative than the notion of God choosing a sinless virgin mother to bear his only son to save the world through his sacrifice by crucifixion and resurrection. Children sit in awesome wonder as their Catholic nuns and Sunday school teachers proclaim the "communion of saints" who minister to the poor mortals from the threshold of heaven, and the punishment of eternal hell for those who don't comply. They are reminded of their sin and guilt with the symbol of Jesus hanging upon the cross . . . all for them. Nothing is more universal among Homo sapiens than praying to some imagined deity as an act of worship or penitence or thanksgiving or petition. The varieties of practice in prayer are limitless and seem to have roots among prehistoric tribes. There is a remote tribe in Indonesia that depends upon fishing for its survival. After they make a new dugout canoe from a tree, they imagine they must make up a shrine and pray to the tree God for forgiveness to prevent the canoe from sinking. None of them has ever thought to test their belief by refusing to ask forgiveness of the tree God.

A perfect example of inspired native imagination is the legend of Pele, (pronounced PAY-lay in English) the Goddess of fire, lightning, dance, volcanoes and violence. She is a daughter of Haumea and Kane Milohai, and her home is believed to be the fire pit, Halema'uma'u crater, at the summit caldera of Kilauea, one of the Earth's most and continuously active volcanoes; but her domain encompasses all volcanic activity on the Big Island of Hawaii. There are several traditional legends associated with Pele in Hawaiian mythology. To this day, tales of Pele's power and peculiarities continue. Whispered encounters with Pele include those of drivers who pick up an old woman dressed all in white accompanied by a little dog on roads in Kilauea National Park, only to look in the mirror to find the back seat empty. Pele's face has mysteriously appeared in photographs of fiery eruptions, and most sheeple who live in the islands—whether Christian, Buddhist, Shinto, or other—speak respectfully of the ancient Goddess. After all, she has destroyed more than 100 structures on the Big Island since 1983, and perhaps even more awesome than that, she has added more than 70 acres of land to the island's southeastern coastline.

Pentecost Island is part of the Republic of Vanuatu (formerly the New Hebrides), a chain of 183 tropical islands in the southwestern Pacific, between Australia and Fiji. A tribe of its native sheeple practice what they call "land diving." It is the original form of bungee jumping to invoke plentiful crops. Young men jump off a 100 foot tower tethered by an unforgiving vine rope that is measured to graze the ground with their bodies as they land. A tribe in Africa that worships its ancestors invokes their blessing by drinking fresh blood from the necks of sacrificed goats and chickens while dancing themselves into a trance state. Practitioners of the faith called Voodoo in Haiti think that some sheeple can live without a soul, sort or like walking cadavers. That, of course, assumes there is something called a soul which seems to be a rather common notion among both philosophers and religions. In the city of San Francisco, Mexico, devout Catholics make an annual pilgrimage to the church to invoke the blessings of their patron saint, St. Francis, who lies on a bier in the form of a plaster statue, which many of them take for real. Among the tribe of Taos Pueblos in New Mexico there is this belief expressed by their high priest; "We are a people who live on the roof of the world, we are sons of our Father the Sun, and with our religion we daily help our father to go across the sky. We do this not only for ourselves but for the whole world. If we would cease practicing our religion the Sun would no longer rise, and then it would be night forever." And he really believes it. All in God's will of course . . . AIGWOC.

The "Ghost Dance," was the central ritual of the messianic religion instituted by a Paiute Indian medicine man named Wovoka about 1870. The religion prophesied the peaceful end of the westward expansion of whites and a return of the land to the Native Americans. The ritual lasted five successive days, being danced each night and on the last night continued until morning. Hypnotic trances and shaking accompanied this ceremony, which was supposed to be repeated every six weeks. Other Native Americans sent delegates to Wovoka to learn his teachings and ritual. In a remarkably short time the religion spread to most of the western Native Americans. The ghost dance is chiefly significant because it was a central feature among the Sioux just prior to the massacre of hundreds of Sioux at Wounded Knee, S.D., in 1890. The Sioux, wearing shirts called ghost shirts, imagined they would be protected from the soldiers' bullets. They got revenge with the massacre of U.S. soldiers under General George Custer at the Battle of the Little Bighorn.

It gets better . . . or worse. Conservative Christians imagine that Jesus is who St. John of the Bible claims he is, that the gospel writers all reported exactly what he said, and the churches they attend are ordained by God so they are exempt from rule by governments. Among very conservative modern Christians there is the belief that everyone will burn in eternal Hell unless they acknowledge Jesus of Nazareth is the Lord and Savior who was sacrificed by his father God as recompense for all the sins of mankind . . . who were created by that God like the potter uses clay in his image and likeness. Some sheeple even imagine they have a personal relationship with the living resurrected Christ who they imagine died for their sins which they imagine they were all born in. Catholic nuns imagine they are the brides of Christ. And Catholics imagine that the bread and wine served during the Mass magically turn into the body and blood of Christ. Pre-Christian Jews were not the only sheeple to practice blood sacrifice to appease their Gods, but in the Last Supper event it is carried to the macabre extreme of ritual cannibalism as Jesus says of the bread, "Take and eat; this is my body." (Matthew 26:26) In John 6:53-55 he says, ". . . unless you eat the flesh of the Son of Man and drink his blood, you have no life in you." Imagine that. Further, they imagine this edict comes from scraps of parchment that were scribbled by unidentified writers during the first century CE who were Jewish tribesmen under the rule of the Roman Empire in the area now designated as Israel around the city of Jerusalem.

The Tarsus-born Roman citizen Saul renamed Paul, a Jew from the tribe of Benjamin, imagined that Jesus called him after the crucifixion to organize a spiritual kingdom among the Gentiles after he was rejected by the Jews. And today, the Jewish sheeple of Israel imagine that the only God selected their patriarch, Abraham to sire a chosen people to occupy the land occupied by the Canaanites, now Palestine, and to engage the rest of the world in that endeavor or risk destruction for its disobedience. Today twelve million Jews scattered worldwide still look for their deliverer to come as Messiah because Jesus did not set up the conquering Jewish kingdom that they imagined is decreed by God in the Old Testament. (Ezekiel 20: 39-44). Conservative Christians imagine that he will return any time now to do it, although reformed Jews imagine that world peace will only be made by social actions of enlightened sheeple.

Meantime, conservative Muslims imagine there is no God but Allah and Muhammad is his messenger, to be obeyed at all costs, while Christians and

Jews should be annihilated. Throughout the world there still are primitive tribes that believe they must shed blood to assure good crops and healthy heirs from their Gods. Of course, some sheeple imagine there is no God at all and go play golf or tennis on Sunday morning. In fact, the rabid support of professional athletic teams on weekends may not be so far removed from the tribal warfare of previous generations. Sheeple seem to be hard-wired for engaging in conflict to prove their tribe is better than another tribe. Isn't that what the international Olympic games is all about? Imagine what the world would be like if warfare could be replaced with athletic contests, maybe like cage fighting. First they used sticks and stones and now they use aircraft carriers and nuclear submarines, but the underlying instinct is the same. How long will it be before Homo sapiens outgrow this absolute nonsense?

George Beverly Shea, the baritone singer for the Rev. Billy Graham's evangelistic crusades made his signature hymn this ode to Jesus, which anyone can see is based more on imagination than reality: "I'd rather have Jesus than silver or gold; I'd rather be His than have riches untold; I'd rather have Jesus than houses or lands, I'd rather be led by His nail pierced hand. Than to be a king of a vast domain or be held in sin's dread sway, I'd rather have Jesus than anything this world affords today." It seems that Homo sapiens are made to believe in one religious myth or another and if it is not Christ it will be Muhammad or Joseph Smith, Jr. or L. Ron Hubbard or Mary Baker Eddy. Take your pick.

Jesus made specific promises in the Bible about how prayer is supposed to work, but sheeple don't seem to have enough imagination to make it happen. What would happen if we all got down on our knees and prayed to God in this way: Dear God, almighty, all-powerful, all-loving Creator of the Universe, we pray to you to cure every case of cancer on this planet tonight. We pray in faith, believing you will bless us as you promised in Matthew 7:7, Matthew 17:20, Matthew 21:21, Mark 11:24, John 14:12-14, Matthew 18:19 and James 5:15-16. In Jesus' name we pray, Amen. What if we pray sincerely, knowing that when God answers this completely heartfelt, unselfish, non-materialistic prayer, it will glorify God and help millions of sheeple in remarkable ways. Jesus says in several different places that he and God will answer your prayers if you just ask in faith, believing, you will receive whatever you ask. (Matthew 21:22, Mark 9: 23, Mark 11:24) [Son of a Baptist preacher, Dr. O. Carl Simonton, founded a cancer treatment center in Malibu, CA to test that hypothesis and found some reason to conclude that patients who applied happy thoughts to their treatment got better results in many cases.]

Others are showing it is possible to reprogram the brain with neurofeedback techniques like using brain waves to control a video game run by software that implements theories about mind control initiated by Franz Mesmer. The program senses brain wave frequencies like an electroencephalogram (EEG) and feeds back results the patient can consciously use to actually move the mouse courser. Mary Baker Eddy (1821-1919) said if we could clear the material mind from its illusion of sin, sickness, and death, the immortal Mind of God would demonstrate its universal health. Imagine that. And Christians believe Jesus because he is God incarnate and God cannot lie. But, that makes no sense because to be God he must be able to do anything he wishes, including ignoring your prayers. Even lying, too. So, you get the picture. Nevertheless, religious imagination has produced some of the world's greatest architecture, music, art, and literature. If we assume all this religious creativity is imaginery, the question remains; why does it still exist? And where does it come from?

Meantime, another religious group called Muslims imagines that the Christians and Jews got it all wrong and that Moses had it right from God in the first place. [Actually, any religion that imagines it only has "the Truth" is a cult.] They imagine the Koran is the voice of God and that Muhammad is his latest and last ordained prophet, and that government should be based upon strict shari'ah law. Some scholars imagine Muslims are descendents of Ishmael, the illegitimate son of Abraham and his wife's Egyptian servant, Hagar. (Genesis 16-17) Further, they imagine that one named Muhammad was given the message from the angel Gabriel to set things straight by conquering nations to live by the laws of Moses for all time.

Since Muhammad was unable to write, others who heard him speak took notes and wrote down all the messages they imagined came directly from God and compiled them after his death in 632 CE in their holy book, the Koran. The most extreme among them imagine that anyone who disputes that message must be executed in order to create a pure society where sheeple can live in peace and prosperity, so long as they obey the rules they imagine were given by God. Muhammad said, "I have been commanded [by whom?] to fight people until they confess that there is no God but Allah and that Muhammad is Allah's Messenger." The extreme Christians and Jews and Muslims imagine that the others are creatures of the Devil called Satan and several other names found in their religious books made holy by their imagination. The Devil is imagined as the perfectly evil antithesis of God which is imagined as perfectly good. But, if God created Satan then he and Jesus must be brothers. If Satan was not created by God, we have a problem.

We haven't even begun to look at the religions of Asia where some Hindu sheeple imagine they will be purified by bathing in the polluted Ganges River, and imagine that cows are sacred animals while dogs and cats and insects may be eaten freely. Running through the faiths of Asia is the idea of reincarnation of souls through many lifetimes and the keeping of a library of universal thought called the "Akashic records." C.G. Jung may have integrated them into his theory of the "collective unconscious" in which all the previous lives of all humanity are somehow included in the psyche of each individual. There is a recurring genre of books assuming to prove that sheeple have had previous lives, often based on the fantasies disclosed by subjects under deep hypnosis. Sorting out fact from fiction in such cases is impossible of course, but imagination seems to thrive on their continuance. The ego apparently wants to be immortal, and will support any form of evidence no matter how imaginary. This could explain the insane success of such inspired tomes of creative writing as the Holy Bible, the Holy Koran, The Grail Message, the Urantia Book, A Course in Miracles, the Book of Mormon, and Dianetics, all self-proclaimed works from God.

But this could be said of all thoughts, ideas, and discoveries if there is only one common Source of All. Abd-ru-shin [aka Oskar E. Bernhardt (1875-1941)] wrote, "All teachings/thoughts/ideas were at one time willed by God precisely adapted to the individual peoples and countries, and formed in complete accord with their actual spiritual maturity and receptivity." Thus, no information is created by mankind, but only discovered when the time is right. That also could help to explain the support in the West of a form of New Thought or New Age religion that seeks to combine elements of Asian philosophy with Christianity.

The anchor church of this movement may be the Agape International Spiritual Center in Culver City, CA organized by Dr. Michael Beckwith in 1986. Preachers in this faith rarely quote the Bible but rather prefer the creative writings of intuitive authors among their population. In contrast are those, like pastor Dr. John Hagee, seemingly called to concentrate on Old Testament pro-Israel eschatology who imagine that prophesies of inevitable immanent end of times are being fulfilled right before our eyes in the news every day. One might call what they do on television "religious theater," because it looks much like a rock concert. Beckwith even calls his Sunday performance a "show." All in God's will of course…AIGWOC.

There are many more imagined versions of religions among Homo sapiens, but you get the picture. All of them are imagined to be true by their devotees and that belief causes much of the trouble between Homo sapiens. So, we might insert the advice of St. Thomas a Kempis, (1380-1471) "It is more profitable to leave everyone to his own way of thinking than to give way to contentious discourses . . ." about their differences. Although they all seek imagined universal health, wealth, and happiness, none of them are given to tolerate extremes in the others. From such imaginations there come wars and continuous struggles for power and control, which leads to some of the most horrendous crimes and tortures imaginable. But, there are benefits from wars because all burdens come with benefits.

Wars have prompted some of the most amazing developments among Homo sapiens and brought out some of their most noble qualities as well as their brutality. Gunpowder was apparently discovered in China before the fourth century but was not applied to portable weapons until it appeared simultaneously in several areas around the early 14th century. Consider developments in medicine, manufacturing, communications, and civil engineering to name just a few benefits that have been stimulated by wars. The U.S. Civil War stimulated such battlefield developments as canned food, reconstructive surgery, and telegraph systems. Unfortunately, they came at the cost of more than 250,000 combat deaths and did not prevent loss of as many more from various battlefield diseases. Airplanes and submarines, germ warfare, and gas weapons plus the automatic machine gun enabled mass destruction during WWI. Several amazing inventions were developed during WWII, including radar and the atomic bomb that killed more than 55 million sheeple in Europe and nearly 20 million in the Pacific front.

By imagining and creating ever more efficient killing machines, productivity in all battle fields has been increased beyond imagination. Early on it took one soldier to kill another one on the battlefield. Now, thanks to imagination, one soldier can kill millions if he/she is the pilot of a plane that delivers a nuclear bomb. He/she does not even have to be in the plane to fly it anymore because radio controlled drones now can be flown directly to the target with GPS guidance from an air conditioned office while sipping coffee anywhere in the world, thanks to the imagination that produced satellite navigation and the global positioning system. Of course, it also can be used to direct a cab driver to find your house but that is not nearly so much fun.

War making helped create the most expensive weapons imaginable, including nuclear powered aircraft carriers [they cost $2.5 million per day to operate] and submarines, plus intercontinental missiles and space stations. No place on Earth now is remote enough to hide from spy satellites that can read auto license plate numbers from space. Do you think the bicycle merchants, the Wright brothers, could have imagined those developments while they struggled to make their first flight at Kitty Hawk, NC in December 1904? Richard Jordan Gatling (1818-1903) received the first of his 50 patents for agriculture implements at age 18, but he is mostly known for inventing the repeating machine gun that dramatically raised the killing productivity of field soldiers during the Civil War. The latest machine gun that uses his technology can spray 3,000 bullets per minute at the enemy.

Imagination in Asia preceded that of the West by centuries. Marco Polo opened trade between Europe and China, but when he returned to Venice from his initial discoveries in 1295 CE his tales of their advanced culture were disbelieved. How about the discovery of gun powder by the Chinese that can be used both for celebration fireworks and also as propellants for bullets? A Chinese inventor who thought of lashing gun powder to arrows for the first rocket launched missiles around 1150 CE is lost in history. The Chinese also invented paper made from bamboo and the mechanical clock escapement. They also invented printing from movable type seven hundred years before Johann Gutenberg. They created the first iron and steel and the weapons to be made from it. They make ten times as much steel now as does the U.S. The Chinese also perfected the lodestone compass and ocean sailing centuries before Europeans. After being dormant for centuries, nowadays China imagines becoming a world power in business and the Olympics. They also have the largest land-based army in the world. All in the will of God the Almighty One.

Don't forget that Russia and the U.S. both still possess enough nuclear bombs and warheads to destroy everyone on the planet, probably about 70,000 each. There is no counting the ones possessed by the other nuclear powers. But, the doomsday weapon currently feared most is a gigantic electro-magnetic pulse generated by a nuclear bomb detonated high in the atmosphere that could "fry" all the computer microchips on the continent and destroy our entire information infrastructure in one instant. Consider the imagination that it took to create those kinds of things. But none of these massive weapons can prevent a suicide bomber from killing scores of sheeple plus himself because he imagines that he will enjoy 72 virgins for eternity in a garden of delight with rivers running through it for his personal sacrifice. One wonders what female suicide bombers imagine their reward will be.

Science fiction sometimes is imagined to be reality. How else can one explain the faith sheeple place in the Book of Mormon, the Koran, A Course in Miracles, and even the Bible? Or the recently discovered encoded messages found hidden in the Bible that convince some mathematicians they are accurate predictions of world events, even to destruction of the Earth in 2012 by impact of an asteroid? And, what about those folks who imagine they have encountered aliens from outer space and were kidnapped to be examined aboard Unidentified Flying Objects?

To see the results of modern human imagination one need only look at the spurious architecture of Dubai in the United Emerites. Using oil money, they are creating the most futuristic city imaginable including manmade island communities and the tallest buildings ever designed. A new 2.3-square kilometer pyramid-shaped "Ziggurat" building concept proposed for Dubai would be able to house over 1 million sheeple and be almost totally self-sufficient energy-wise. By tapping into the planet's renewable resources, designers assert that it could practically be carbon-neutral, and given that transport within the structure would be connected by an integrated 360-degree network, fuel-burning cars would be pointless. It seems to be true that whatever man can imagine man can create if only he has enough money.

Well, as you can see the world likely would be a much different place without human imagination. Would there be no symphony orchestras, marching bands, museums, art galleries or public parks or skyscrapers? Would there be no treatments for cancer, diabetes, heart attacks, etc? Come to think of it, there needs to be a lot more imagination for medicine to cure all the diseases, especially, for the little innocent children of the world. But, then what do you imagine we would die from when all the diseases are prevented? Would anesthesia, concrete, and steel exist without imagination? How about Christmas? Would there be no Wi-Fi, video cell phones, personal computers, television or automobiles? Maybe there would be no Internet either or space exploration. Would the National Football League exist without imagination? How about NASCAR or baseball and soccer and basketball and all the other professional sports that enrich their owners and the players at the expense of the fans? Perhaps all the oil and coal and natural gas would still be in the ground without human imagination. Perhaps there would be no marriages or divorces either, because both are driven by imagination, are they not? And what about all the other life forms on Earth? Is imagination a programmed function that drives their migrations across the planet or must we look elsewhere for explanations of such phenomena?

Can anyone wake up and decide to imagine discovery of the next great human development? Did Steve Jobs willfully decide to imagine the computer empire known as "Apple?" Did Bill Gates willfully decide that all personal computers would come with his Windows operating system installed? Jesus reportedly taught that you can perform miracles if you have faith the size of a mustard seed and believe it is possible. But, alas, although it does not seem to work that way for us mortals, the video game world does seem to work that way. The Japanese inventor of the first video game, PacMan, claimed that he got the idea from looking at a round Italian pizza with a slice cut out. It's first English translation came out PuckMan, but it was changed for obvious reasons. Trip Hawkins conceived of video games almost a decade before the computers needed were being sold so he could organize his firm, Electronic Arts, that pioneered the modern stream of violent and pornographic home entertainment medium. Now, they are used to help train combat soldiers for the U.S. Army and to help in recruiting. A video game developed by a patient is helping young cancer victims to defeat the "bad guys" of rampaging cancer cells by stimulating their immune systems.

The ingenious virtual video world simulation called "Second Life," created by Linden Research, Inc. uses fictitious humanoids called "avatars" to socialize and transact business with others world wide through buying and selling virtual products and services that would not be possible in the real world. There currently are more than thirteen million players and several hundred thousand of them operate their own virtual businesses apart from their real lives. Second Life is not alone as there now are several competitors providing similar virtual escapes. There seems to be no limit to the virtual uses of personal computers that are being offered daily for the playing publics. It takes a great deal of imagination to enjoy these new virtual video environments.

Alexander Fleming discovered the effects of penicillin inadvertantly in 1928 at St. Mary's hospital in London, but his paper on it in the "British Journal of Experimental Pathology" drew no attention. A cancer researcher at Oxford named Ernst Chain who worked for Howard Florey rediscovered Fleming's paper in 1938 and researched penicillin as an antibiotic. As WWII began, research funded by the Rockefeller Foundation leaped across the ocean to find a way of manufacturing it for treatment of battlefield wounds. Someone discovered that corn and rotting cantelope from Illinois made excellent cultures. By the end of WWII, 21 companies were producing 650 billion units of penicillin per month, and countless lives had been saved. Fleming shared the Nobel Prize for Physiology in 1945 with Florey and Chain. Florey commented later, "People sometimes think that I and the others worked on penicillin because we were interested in suffering humanity. I don't think it ever crossed our minds about suffering humanity. This was an interesting scientific exercise, and because it was of some use in medicine is very gratifying, but this was not the reason that we started working on it."

The limits to imagination are unknown. Jesus said if you have a little faith you can move a mountain and that believers will do even greater things than he. (John 14:12) A pastor in Ohio once gave his members each fifty dollars and, according to the parable of the talents, (Matthew 25:14-30) ordered each one to go out and multiply it for charity. The number of ways many members increased the money was miraculous. Many discovered idle talents they could put to use and doubled the money. Here is another story of imagination. At the age of 12 and 13, the Bergquist family children heard that soldiers in Iraq were charging cell phone calls back home so they started a non-profit business recycling used cell phones and using the proceeds to buy prepaid calling cards for the troops.

Researchers studying epilepsy at Washington University in St. Louis reported that an afflicted teenager was able to move a video icon just by thinking of it. In other experiments at Duke University, subjects are able to move robots remotely located merely by thought waves. Such a capability may enable amputees to control prostheses by thinking the movements. It might be possible even to transfer the thought patterns he uses for that perfect golf swing from Tiger Woods to any old duffer. So, perhaps Jesus was right after all. But, if he really was the son of God, why don't Christians live by his teaching? "Everyone who hears these words of mine and does not act on them will be like a foolish man who built his house on sand." (Matthew 7:26) Perhaps his teachings as in Matthew chapters 5-7 or Luke chapters 15-19 would be just as much a stumbling block today to the healthy, wealthy, and happy among us as they were then.

Albert Einstein (1879-1955) observed, "The intuitive mind is a sacred gift and the rational mind is a faithful servant. We have created a society that honors the servant and has forgotten the gift . . . The intellect has little to do on the road to discovery. There comes a leap of consciousness, call it intuition or what you will, and the solution comes to you and you don't know how or why." He also said imagination is more powerful than knowledge. A moment of thought will produce a long list of discoveries and inventions proving this is true. Navigation, gunpowder, calculus, anesthesiology, cement, steel, the cotton gin, the assembly line, rubber tires, silk, banking, the disc operating system, electric lights, hypnotism, placebos, telephones, radio, television, lasers, radar, GPS, Christian Science, . . . or heaven and hell . . . inventions and discoveries; the list is endless.

The mystery about such things is why they emerge from the mind of one person and not another. Who makes that assignment? One may only wonder what Einstein would say about the emergence of New Age channelers who claim that they transmit voices from the beyond and the followers of cult leaders who imagine they are miracle workers or the insane use of credit cards as though they were cash. Space scientists are seriously considering attempting to fly a paper shuttle back from space even though they have no way of instrumenting or tracking it. "Just imagine, children around the world would be anxiously waiting for the return of our origami shuttle, perhaps looking up into the sky from time to time," the designer said. "That would be great fun." Sir Richard Branson has almost done it with his commercial orbiting space shuttle. Others are seriously imagining colonizing the planet Mars after they build a base camp on the moon. They really are.

Young children are known to have very creative imaginations but they often get stifled with warnings by adults who have outgrown theirs who are aware of danger ahead in life from hard lessons of experience. Children also learn to imagine that bad things will happen if they misbehave, and so as adults they may continue to be restrained by the threat of punishment. The ultimate may be imagining eternal heaven and hell. That is what makes us self-conscious human beings and law abiding citizens. Imagine what the world might be like if that did not happen and we saw no danger, only possibility. Of course, there always are the opposites. The imagination that created nuclear power also created nuclear bombs. And the imagination that creates marriages also creates adultery. The imagination that stimulates a child into creative arts can also stimulate a troubled adult into accusing parents, relatives and others of childhood abuse that arises from repressed memories, whether or not it actually happened. The mind that imagines healing drugs also imagines harmful addictive illegal drugs, as in harvesting poppies for heroin. To imagine the future includes the good with the bad, the pain with the pleasure, and the fear of the unknown as in what comes after death. There are always necessary opposites. Thomas Edison, (1847-1931) who patented invention of the light bulb, tried unsuccessfully to make houses out of preformed concrete panels because he said, "Nobody had any imagination so I gave up and quit." When you extend imagination into the extended future of time, the possibilities challenge the understanding of reality.

But as with everything, there is a negative side to imagination. As Bishop John Spong observed above, even sin must be imagined before you can do it. Humans are gifted with ability to imagine time as past, present, and future. Those who can imagine trouble in the future may avoid it by adequate preparation, except for death and taxes. Trouble is, some sheeple cannot imagine bad consequences so they do things that get them and others into trouble without thinking. If you cannot imagine trouble, you cannot avoid it. The sociopaths in prison may have some form of distorted imagination, "do this, don't get that, escape punishment." All change contains both threat and opportunity and the one you choose is the one you imagine subconsciously comes with most benefits. Those who choose opportunity in change have different brain neurons from those who see only threats. Most sheeple choose the threat first, but if you cannot imagine any punishment or harm, sheeple can do very dangerous things, and evil could win out.

Perhaps there is no boundary between imagination and insanity, only a continuum as in the Chinese concept of Yin and Yang or the symbol of the mobius. When you think about it, perhaps the greatest imagination of all is that one about God and some immortal life in a new Earth for believers and suffering in hell eternally for sinners. Of this coming world, Pope Benedict XVI, [aka Joseph Cardinal Ratzinger] wrote in his "Eschatology," (1988) "The new world cannot be imagined. Nothing concrete or imaginable can be said about the relation of man to matter in the new world. Yet we have the certainty that cosmos leads to a goal, a situation in which matter and spirit will belong to each other in a new and definitive fashion." We won't bother here with what Muslims imagine will happen in their eschatology. But, we can imagine the trouble it will cause on Earth as the two mutually exclusive religious systems clash in the struggle for power and control.

There are some benefits to negative imaginations. Dale Carnegie (1888-1955) instructed in How to Stop Worrying and Start Living, (1948) "Imagine the worst thing that can happen and plan to accept it." [If God did not intend for us to worry then why even make it possible in the first place? Worry must have its necessary place in life or it would not exist. Get it?] Carnegie probably did not imagine a world war between religions that could be the last nuclear holocaust. But, it could happen if the Muslims do not reject instructions from their leaders to interpret the Holy Koran as a call to war against the infidels. They have plenty of evidence for such in the various commands to fight in the cause of Allah until everyone admits "there is no God but Allah and Muhammad is his messenger." So long as the western nations cannot imagine this happening they cannot prepare for it. But if you look at the strife in Iraq, Afghanistan, and Pakistan, with suicide bombers of the Taliban striking almost weekly, the possibility can be seen just around the corner.

Unless they take words in the Koran as seriously as the Muslims do, Christians cannot hope to avoid the destruction of Christianity and the way of life that it supports. But, of course, if Christians take the teachings of Jesus as seriously as Muslims take the teachings of Muhammad, they lose. So far attacks by the Taliban are local and not coordinated internationally among Muslim nations. But if a strong leader emerges to mobilize all their power, beware the shadow of the Apocalypse. Perhaps such leadership is emerging from the Muslim Brotherhood of nations. Perhaps we are seeing the beginning now among rebels in Arab nations in revolt against their dictators who have made deals with the West. It appears that the Suny and Shiite branches of Islam are uniting against a common enemy, Israel, and its main sponsor, America. Of course, the Bible says that all this must be to prepare for the last great battle between the good guys and the bad guys at Armageddon. From time to time a "prophet" emerges who claims that he has been given special insight to interpret current events in light of Bible prophecies about those end times. Of course when their deadline for end of times passes without incident, they just move the date forward again. Imagine that.

Obviously, Christians don't act as the Gospels teach or we would not have the professional war making machines we do, all in the name of national defense. Jesus actually taught absolute passivism and non-defense in response to aggression, but who can imagine living in a world like that? (Luke 6:

20-49) Go ahead, read that scripture. The aggressor would always win and soon Christianity would disappear. Nevertheless, Jesus reserved his severest criticism for the hypocrites, those Pharisees who talked the talk but did not walk the walk. "You snakes, you brood of vipers. How will you escape being condemned to hell?" (Matthew 3:7, 12;34, 23:23, Luke 3:7, Romans 3:13). And the Apostle Paul imagined that all authorities are to be obeyed because they are installed by God. (Romans 13: 1-7) Is that crazy, or what? How can we decide which of his instructions were given by God and which came from his inner imagination? Think about it.

But, hey, you can feel good inside no matter what happens outside. All you have to do is imagine that nothing is outside the will of God the Almighty One, and everything that happens must be as it is or it would be different. Imagine that.

20. The Coming Energy Crisis is Here

We use 20 million barrels of oil per day, that is 10,000 gallons per second, but we produce only seven million barrels per day. We have to import the rest mostly from Arab nations who don't like us very much. The second largest consumer of oil is China, and it is catching up rapidly. That is why U.S. presidents are so concerned about what happens in the Middle East, where all the oil is located. So we support rebels throughout the unfriendly Arab oil countries without knowing what the outcome will be. If you thought the banking meltdown in 2008 was scary, just wait for the next oil embargo. Ever since mankind first discovered that coal would burn, followed by oil and natural gas, we have been on the inevitable pathway to self destruction, intoxicated on fossil fuels. You can thank Henry Ford and his assembly line for the present crisis since until him the manufacture of automobiles was too expensive for average workers to afford. Where he got that idea must be left up to God.

Worldwide demand for fossil fuels has exceeded population growth, and it cannot be sustained by increasing supplies forever because they are finite resources of planet Earth. The pending consequences of this situation are so politically dangerous they cannot even be discussed in public, so it is couched under the umbrella term of "energy." We prohibit oil companies from harvesting the mainland reserves for environmental reasons and create worse unintended consequences. The explosion and environmental disaster in the Gulf of Mexico during summer of 2010 merely illustrates that future oil exploration will be ever more dangerous and costly, and there is no reversing that trend.

The fact is we need oil to fuel transportation, cars, buses, trains, and ships and planes and the lack of optional alternatives is leading to catastrophe. Although several attempts to create a national energy policy have failed, the need is desperate. Those who wish for renewable sources like wind and solar to replace fossil fuels for cars, buses, trucks, airplanes, ships, and such must wait a long time. For comparison, a typical coal or gas power plant produces 1,000 megawatts of power while the largest solar array produces only 75 megawatts and a typical wind turbine produces only a meager 2.5 megawatts. Without a unified plan we stumble from one fuel crisis to another. Still, many confused politicians claim we can replace oil with wind mills and solar panels. They just don't get it. President George W. Bush said, "America is addicted to oil." He got it, but he could not fix it. We import 13 million barrels of oil per day and if we produced all that is estimated to be possible from domestic supplies currently off limits, perhaps 2-3 million barrels per day could be removed from imports. That is not good for a product that is diminishing in supply worldwide.

All the projections for future world oil production, divided into proven reserves, undeveloped reserves, and undiscovered reserves are based on assumption, hope, politics, and downright illusion with little to no chance of verification. More than two thirds of the lushest oil fields are in the Middle East, mostly under Saudi Arabia which is a Muslim theocracy run by the house of King Saud. It is all controlled by the oligarchy called the Organization of Petroleum Exporting Countries (OPEC) cartel of eleven nations, which is led by Saudi Arabia followed by Kuwait in terms of the largest reserves. We saw in 1973 what happens when they cut off our deliveries, but most sheeple have forgotten already. Experts estimate the U.S. has proven oil reserves that would last only seven years at current usage rates without any imports. But they also claim that we have undeveloped oil resources that exceed that of OPEC, if they only were removed from environmental restrictions that prohibit their development. Since sheeple will not change until it hurts too much not to, the price of oil and gasoline must rise further to create public demand for these resources to be developed.

The biggest oil discoveries were made in 1965 and each year foreign producers find less than the previous year at ever increasing costs. For every five barrels being consumed, only one new barrel is being discovered, world-wide. The future of oil appears to be bleak in the near term and bleaker in the long term unless restricted lands are released for exploration. The numbers are so huge an average person can scarcely envision them, and that is part of the problem. Can you imagine daily production of 87 million barrels at present? That is 3,650 million gallons . . . per day. Some experts say world oil production has peaked or soon will, and future discoveries will be more and more expensive to find and deliver. As world oil production declines, the competition for remaining supplies will heat up and markets could easily degenerate into violence when bidding becomes emotional.

It's not just a crisis in oil, but also in electricity and power in all forms. Whether generated by coal, nuclear, oil, water, or solar and wind renewables, the economy depends upon it and the homes of average sheeple could not function without it. With only five percent of its population, the fact is that America consumes far more than its fair share of the finite resources of Earth, and it cannot continue growing at this pace. A curtailment is long overdue. But, the average American does not want to hear about it and the vast majority of our political leaders are reluctant to support any policies that would require any sacrifice on the part of any of their constituents. Americans don't like to hear they cannot have whatever they want. So nature will have to take its course. All in God's will of course . . . AIGWOC. Get it?

Two-thirds of the world's oil reserves are in just five countries: Saudi Arabia, Iran, Iraq, Kuwait, and United Arab Emirates. Of the world's known gas reserves, 45% are located in Russia and Iran. If you include the other Middle Eastern countries, the total rises to 65 percent. All of them are driven by Muslim religious zealots who believe the Koran tells them how we should all live. And think about the transportation of the oil and gas coming from the Middle East where many countries are engaged in civil wars. The major collection point is in Kuwait on the Persian Gulf, then it goes by tankers through the Straits of Hormuz, a narrow outlet surrounded on the north and east by Iran. Eighty percent of the oil produced in the Persian Gulf, and 25 percent of the world's oil, or 13 million bbls/day, passes through the Straits of Hormuz. It would not take much effort to stop exports if Iran, or any terrorist organization, were to choose to do so.

These issues are scary enough, but there is another. Banking deregulation adjustments in the 1990s caused the credit crisis. And now, our financial markets have been propped up by sovereign oil wealth from none other than Saudi Arabia, China, South Korea and Singapore. We're not out of this mess yet, not by a long shot. And Americans just do not get it so there is not an informed public to guide our politicians.

The future world production of oil is unpredictable because estimates vary so widely, but the fact is that skyrocketing world fossil fuel prices are threatening our economy, and no one in the U.S government seems to have a comprehensive solution. The only way to get off of oil is to decouple it from our economy, especially transportation and no one has any alternative for that. Planes, trains, trucks, buses and autos cannot run on wind or solar, and there is not enough land to grow food plus enough biofuels to replace gasoline. We are getting dangerously close to violence as the government is impotent to engage the issue on a rational basis; emotions are getting raw. This could be the "Achilles heal" of capitalism as oil profits soar and consumers become more outraged. Secretary of Defense Robert M. Gates has said, "It only requires a relatively small amount of oil to be taken out of the system to have huge economic and security implications. If we wait until a crisis occurs to act, the nation will have access to few, if any, effective short-term remedies." But, it always seems to require a crisis for our government to get together on a solution to any problem. All in God's will of course. I hate to keep repeating that, but it seems to be necessary.

The fact is that easy access to cheap oil under American control is over and adjusting to that reality is going to be very painful. In spite of tripling investment in exploration, American oil companies are producing only half as much as they did at their peak in 1950, mostly because 85 percent of public areas that may contain oil are off limits by public policy. For example, the trans-Alaska pipe line is only bringing half as much oil daily from Prudhoe Bay as its peak output thirty years ago, and it is costing more than a million dollars a day to maintain. There is more oil in Alaska and some other states, but it is off limits. The United States is the only country in the world that denies its citizens access to its own natural fuel resources. Increasing U.S. oil production would require overturning decades-old moratoriums that limit offshore drilling and leasing of federal lands. It may come down to whether eagles and black bears mind oil exploration in the regions where they live.

If we could get all the known U.S. reserves on and off-shore they may provide about a ten-year supply all together. Opening the restricted lands may be the only way to save Americans from gas and oil prices so high that their spending for food and medicine is being threatened. But, when producing companies can make more money on rising prices than they can by increasing costly production, the latter will decline and consumers will suffer. And, since the U.S. government does not own oil and gas companies, yet, there is little that can be done to change that. Meantime, the Organization of Petroleum Exporting Countries (OPEC) operates freely as a cartel that controls oil production for their own interests. Even if we could increase U.S. production the OPEC countries easily could retaliate by reducing their output, keeping the world demand ahead of supply.

Many experts say oil production is close to peaking world-wide and the consequences are so horrific that most sheeple prefer to ignore them until they encounter the rising prices for gasoline at the pump. The level of oil consumption by the U.S. cannot be sustained or increased much longer without major economic penalties.

Natural gas is getting more usage in power plants and buses, so imports of liquefied natural gas (LNG) have quadrupled since 1985, but no one wants another liquid natural gas port anywhere close. Principle LNG suppliers are Trinidad, Egypt, Nigeria, Norway, and Qatar. Pipeline gas is imported from Mexico and Canada. Yet, some advocates with financial interests in gas recommend that all commercial trucks and buses should be converted to natural gas to avoid another oil shock. Energy companies have proposed 35 new LNG terminals in 10 states and five offshore areas near the coast. The majority of the projects are proposed for the Northeast, which has seen huge price increases for heating oil and public distrust of nuclear power; California, where natural gas is in high demand for power generation; and the Gulf Coast, where LNG processors can easily plug the finished gas product into interstate pipelines. Russia is the largest supplier of gas to Europe, and it has demonstrated its ability to hold its customers hostage for higher prices by outright curtailments.

Because nuclear power is expensive and too dangerous for many sheeple, electric utilities burn increasing amounts of natural gas. There is no long term solution for storing and safeguarding the radioactive waste products, as proven by the recent natural disaster in Japan. Attempts to store it underground at Yucca mountain in Nevada have been thwarted for more than twenty years so it languishes in pools of water at the generation sites, increasing by a couple thousand dangerous tons each year. Shifting energy supplies away from fossil fuels to more renewables like hydrogen, solar, wind, and biomass are years away from meeting more than a small fraction of demand and they do practically nothing for transportation needs. Meantime, supply and demand for oil and gas are making some very strange bedfellows, like the chummy relationship between Iran and Venezuela. Fossil fuels that took millions of years to form during evolution of mother Earth could be discovered and used up in only a couple centuries. There are currently 98 oil producing countries in the world, of which 64 are thought to have passed their geologically imposed production peak and, of those, 60 are in terminal production decline. We use one fourth of it and most needs to be transported in 4,000 ocean tankers, while the U.S. companies own only 57 of them.

Producers of oil want desperately to believe that there is no limit to its supply, if there were no environmental restrictions on exploration. Nevertheless, exploration produces less and less for the money invested and technological breakthroughs will be too slow and voluntary conservation will be too shallow to avert widespread disruption of economic activity, especially transportation and consequently food distribution. Lacking the political and social will to make conscious, rapid, drastic changes, Americans will be subjected to Mother Nature's adjustments. The fact that the United States must import two thirds of its oil, a tenth of its refined gasoline, and much of its natural gas from Muslim and socialist nations that hate our way of life can only bode more trouble ahead. Ever since President Roosevelt negotiated a defense-for-oil deal in WWII with Saudi Arabia, there has been only the shakiest of bonds between the buyers and sellers of oil and gas. Every U.S.

President since him has avoided insulting the Saud family kingdom for fear of oil embargoes such as the one staged in the 1970s that threatened the economic health of the world when we supported the Shah of Iran. Nearly 80 percent of world oil reserves are controlled by Arab nations that have no sympathy for the plight of consumers in the U.S. And oil prices are set by a new population of unregulated international commodities traders, just like corn and soybeans.

The present war on terrorism is the only one in which the United States has financed both sides, insane as that sounds. We buy oil from the Arab nations that vow to wipe Israel off the Earth. We give military aid to Israel for self defense, and we then finance the clean up and reconstruction of damages they inflict upon Gaza with it. The struggle between Jews and Arabs is a war to the death paid for by U.S. taxpayers. On the other hand, petro dollars are financing some of the most advanced architecture in the world among Muslim nations in the Middle East [Saudi Arabia, Iraq, Iran, Kuwait, Emerites] while western nations become ever more dependent upon them for economic survival. Canada claims to have a hundred years supply of oil locked up in tar shale in the province of Alberta that could help supply the U.S., but there is a pipeline planned to the ocean at British Columbia paid for by China for its own interest. China survives and grows from all its exports of cheap goods bought by U.S. consumers. China will need to double its oil imports to sustain its growth the next decade. And the gasoline engine still runs on and on and on with imported gasoline because oil refinery capacity in this country has not been increased to keep up with demand. The public silence of oil company executives is deafening. They have said that they intend to rely upon rising prices to increase their return on investment rather than invest in raising production.

Many experts predict unsettled times ahead as world oil production peaks and spiraling demand spreads to undeveloped countries. Pirates from Somalia have found that capturing oil tankers for ransom is a quick way to make some easy money. Towns that once were eroded by years of poverty and chaos now are bustling with restaurants, Land Cruisers and Internet cafes funded by the ransoms collected. Residents also use their gains to buy generators, allowing full days of electricity, once an unimaginable luxury in Somalia. One may ask how a handful of pirates can stop a super tanker that is bigger than an aircraft carrier on the ocean and take command of its crew. Surely the Arab oil suppliers will take note of it. But they will not allow the price of oil to rise high enough to reduce demand or to stimulate alternatives unless world oil supplies decline in spite of all efforts to maintain production. Exactly this is predicted to happen within the next decade as rising prices will no longer produce increasing supplies. The regulations for operations of all commodity futures markets were revised by Congress in 2000 so that now oil prices no longer are based upon costs, but rather future expectations. Even if all the known reserves available to the U.S. were released for drilling, not likely with all the environmental constraints, they could not keep up with increasing demand that this economy requires to fuel its growth. Oil prices now are based upon trading "paper barrels" rather than consumable crude. Closing all the loop holes among international oil trading markets would be impossible. We have entered a realm of economics where traditional theories no longer apply, where rising prices do not stimulate changes in either supply or demand for oil, what economists call inelasticity, and where it goes no one knows.

The U.S. economy is based on energy that comes from other problematic fuels too. Coal is our most abundant fossil fuel resource, but it burns dirty and it is dangerous to mine. The collapse of a mine in West Virginia killing 29 workers was caused by allowing endless appeals of citations for safety violations by the company to favor production more than safety. The amount of coal it takes to drive half of all steam electric generators is staggering to the imagination, 80 million tons per year. We consume about twenty railcar loads of coal per second . . . that's right . . . twenty carloads per second . . . to produce electricity. The real cost of coal includes its environmental impacts but that is not factored into the price of electricity. Mining it disrupts the Earth and takes human lives, burning it produces toxic ash and emits carbon dioxide and other noxious gases which many scientists claim adds to global warming, and transporting it by rail uses up precious petroleum reserves. Efforts to clean it up require separating CO_2 and storing it much like waste fuel from nuclear power plants, possibly in depleted oil caverns. This process is expensive and not yet commercially feasible. Coal can be converted to liquid fuel as they do in South Africa, but no one takes it seriously here because it costs too much. Meanwhile, China has become an importer of coal from American mines. We are shipping the pollution over to them so it can drift back across our land.

Nuclear power plant construction expense and eternal storage of spent plutonium make further construction of nuclear power plants difficult, if not impossible, since they cost up to ten times as much as an equivilant coal plant to build and operate. Natural gas is no savior because most of it lies under Russia, Iran, and Quatar. U.S. reserves are being consumed rapidly in power generation plants. Renewable resources including solar, wind, geo-thermal and bio-mass technologies still are not reliable or cheap enough to make much of a dent in demand for the next decade or more and they do nothing for transportation. You cannot make electricity from the sun in the dark. Exotic energy alternatives like hydrogen fuel cells still are mostly dreams in research and development labs, except for their use in space where cost is no object. And the hydrogen must come from natural gas. Shifting auto fuel to ethanol appears to be less attractive than it seemed at first because it takes petroleum to make it and its consumption of corn changes the market for animal feedstocks, raising the price of all foods. The cost of vegetables is climbing and the supply of meat is being threatened by the shift of farming resources to growing corn for ethanol, and we are forced to import wheat that is taken out of production. We cannot hope to duplicate the success of Brazil, which obtains its ethanol from sugar cane.

To complicate matters, reports indicate that man-made greenhouse gases from burning fossil fuels are depleting the ozone shield protecting the planet from harmful rays from the sun. Glaciers and the frozen ice at the north and south poles are melting faster and faster. Global climate changes seem to be upon us and the results could disrupt life as we know it for much of the species on this planet before a generation is passed. The sluggish actions of Homo sapiens in response cast some doubt on whether they are the highest of life forms after all. The conservators of clean air have successfully kept the fuel efficient diesel engine out of many American cars although they are most preferred throughout Europe, but commercial truckers rely upon diesel engines with clean air exemptions. Volkswagen and Daimler-Benz have shown it is possible to build an efficient diesel auto engine that meets U.S. clean air standards. In Europe, cars are required to get 50 mpg by 2015, so why is it not the standard in the U.S. where the goal is a modest 35 mpg by 2020? Oddly, our tax rules provide a dollar per gallon credit to oil companies for blending biodiesel fuels for export to other countries. Converting the auto fleet to electric vehicles is not the answer because of the massive strain on the power generation industry that also must burn coal or use dangerous nuclear fuels. Even so, Tesla Motors of California, funded by Toyota, is selling electric vehicles with highway performance that Detroit big three auto makers can only dream about. This is possibly due to the fact that big investors have too much money in both oil and auto company stocks to let electric vehicles make a serious attack upon oil consumption for gasoline engines. All in the will of God the Almighty One, of course.

Several U.S. Administrations have hopelessly confused the public by attempting to propose increased renewable sources as a solution for the addiction to oil. There is no way that solar, wind, and geothermal will replace oil for use in transportation. Moreover, the Obama administration and congressional Democrats have proposed a major cap-and-trade system aimed at reducing carbon dioxide emissions from coal fired power generation and burning gasoline in vehicles. Under the cap-and-trade system, the federal government would limit the total volume of CO_2 that U.S. companies can emit each year and would issue permits that companies would be required to have for each ton of CO2 emitted. Once Issued, these permits would be tradable and could be bought and sold like commercial paper, establishing a market price reflecting the targeted CO2 reduction, with a tougher CO2 standard and fewer available permits leading to higher prices. Companies would buy permits from each other as long as it is cheaper to do that than to make the technological changes needed to eliminate an equivalent amount of CO2 emissions. Companies would also pass along the cost of the permits in their prices, pushing up the relative price of CO2-intensive goods and services such as gasoline, electricity from coal, and a range of industrial products. In theory, consumers would respond by cutting back on consumption of CO2-intensive products in favor of other renewable forms of cleaner power. While increasing costs to U.S. consumers, this plan does not affect the rapidly growing use of fossil fuels in China and India and so would have little affect on global warming. Shifting the U.S. economy to more renewable energy sources like solar power and wind generation to save the planet by "going green" may sound very patriotic, but they will cost a lot and whatever slows down the economy is not good for sheeple whose jobs depend upon fossil fuels. There are lots of them. Environmentalists avoid the fact that in going green, the poor who depend upon fossil fuels will be hurt the most by increasing their costs. So, the fight is on.

Jesus said there would always be wars and rumors of wars, but he could not predict that they would be fought over energy issues. There always seems to be something that nations can find to fight about, and oil reserves may well be the next battlefront. Indeed, wars use up natural and human resources faster than any other activity of Homo sapiens, but they are very profitable for bankers and makers of weapons of mass destruction. If world oil production peaks soon as predicted, the present international struggles may be merely the foothills of a challenge to western civilization that can barely be imagined as buyers and sellers duel for dwindling supplies of lower quality petroleum. Although the bulk of those supplies are under Muslim nations, it seems that western consumers are blind to the real issues they face. A collision between secular and non-secular society seems to be emerging, and those who control the most oil could win. Not since the Crusades have the forces been so perfectly aligned by maligning religious dogma on both sides. If you are interested in prophesies about the end of times perhaps this is it. If the Muslim oil producing nations get together they could demolish the economies of the Christian nations easily in a few weeks. But then they would have to contend with the demands of Asia, and such nations as China and India could contend for the oil supplies, and possibly set off a new world war between East and West. When you have conservative Muslims who own the oil and conservative Christians who want it both declaring they are led by

God, you have the "war between the rights." That could be the last one. How could this be unless God willed it so?

Why should other countries accelerate depletion of their oil resources in order to fuel the insatiable usage of Americans? It is understandable that western countries either must placate the Muslim and other rogue nations that own most of the world's oil or engage in war to assure its delivery at economical prices. But, our political support of Israel propels the Arab nations further towards opposition. They cannot defeat our military, but they can squeeze us into economic destruction by controlling the prices of oil and natural gas. About 70 percent of retail gasoline prices is spent on buying crude oil and is rising rapidly. Free markets could be overruled by energy politics. Although he was politically incorrect, retired chair of the Federal Reserve, Alan Greenspan wrote that the war with Iraq "is largely about oil." Many experts warn that it is too late to avoid major economic woe and wars over the remaining supplies of oil. A geophysicist named Dr. M. King Hubbert (1903-1989) predicted in the 1950s that U.S. oil production would peak about 1970, and some think he was right. He also predicted world oil production would peak about now, and it seems to be on track. How much is left that can be recovered is uncertain but it certainly will cost more and more to get and to refine. The consequences are so dire that no one wants to contemplate them. Perhaps we should take a look at how the poorest 500 million sheeple in Africa are living without electricity and own no cars. If we don't learn to travel without oil, that could be our future.

At the bottom of it all are the international energy corporations and investors that must pursue the highest profits in the interest of stockholders at the expense of consumers in our current economic system. As energy prices soar and profits become obscene, forces for and against capitalism will engage in more and more combative attempts at resolution. Energy companies claim they need the high profits to invest in meeting ever increasing demand against competition from companies owned by foreign governments. Costs for a typical gallon of gasoline at $4.00 are claimed to be $2.80 for crude oil plus about .92 for refining and distribution, leaving about 28 cents in profit for exploration and development. While the profits are large in absolute terms, they do not exceed other corporate rates by capitalist standards, and all of it is badly needed to fund research on alternatives which is not being done. Moreover, prices do not include the environmental and social costs of oil production because the corporations have been able to pack the regulating government agencies with industry sympathizers. If the true cost of oil were priced accurately, there would be a consumer revolt and cars would need to get 50 miles per gallon. To see a true-cost pricing of oil, take a look at gasoline prices in Europe.

Exxon-Mobil claim it invests a billion dollars a day in developing new oil supplies, each new barrel of which costs more than the last to recover. How high the price of gasoline and natural gas must go to begin reducing demand by U.S. consumers is uncertain, but the more they pay for energy the less is available for other consumer durables. They will have to pay more to consume less, something that is downright un-American. If the energy producers insist on maximizing their profits at the expense of national interest, there may soon develop a demand for government takeover to secure American national interest. The ultimate political solution may be to nationalize the oil and gas and coal companies to eliminate the profit motive, ration fuel, and control prices with government rules . . . thereby assuring scarcity. But there may have to be social revolution and depression, and continuous wars, before that happens.

If God the Almighty One is so perfect, could he not have created a better arrangement than that? Doubtless he could but he didn't, so it must be necessary as it is. This conclusion is called Theofatalism™, and you may read all about it in <u>Voices of Sedona</u> available at www.IUniverse, www.amazon. com, and local area Barnes & Noble book stores.

21. WOLVES, LAMBS, AND HOMELAND SECURITY

Thinking sheeple are beginning to be concerned, and the rest should be, about the rise of militant Islam and the role of suicide bombings and other attacks by radical Muslims against nonbelievers in Allah and the prophet Muhammad. The assassination of 13 unarmed troops and wounding of some 30 others at Fort Hood, Texas by U.S. Army Maj. Nidal Hasan, a psychiatrist and Muslim, has raised some issues about religion in the military that sheeple have a hard time addressing if they are not well informed. Islam is not just a religion, but a total way of life that seeks nothing less than total integration of secular and religious life because God/Allah says so in the Holy Koran. Why this fact is so much avoided in the present political dialogue can only be the will of God the Almighty One. So, the purpose of this essay is to remove the blindfold from those blinded to the reality of religious dichotomy that is facing the western world.

This is nothing less than a resurgence of the religious wars of the Middle Ages that saw Islam expand to engulf the seat of Judaism and Christianity in Jerusalem and take over much of Europe. It bloomed through the Ottoman Empire until after WWI when the empire was disbanded and present nation-states were formed in the Middle East. However, the zeal of jihad holy war has only been dormant and was not extinguished. Now, it is rising again fueled by those conservative Muslim teachers and imams who see in the Holy Koran commandments to fight the infidel and unbelievers until they all are subdued and live under the shari'ah law of Allah as it was manifested by the prophet Muhammad. Christianity may be at risk for its survival because it teaches total passivism and nonviolence to enemies to the point of death. Muslims read the Holy Koran, and it is past time for U.S. politicians to read it also. If they did, perhaps their claim that the First Amendment covers the practice of Islam could be at least debatable.

[The brief 30 minute Christian sermons on Sunday are not enough to give sheeple enough fuel to go on the rest of the week and to make Sunday school lessons relevant to life. Indeed Jesus said that his kingdom was not of this world and his ministry said very little to help the Jews survive under Roman rule, so they revolted and we know the rest of the story. Christianity needs to find some way of bridging that gap between the spirit world and the real one in which sheeple must live and work every day and in that it is failing. If current demographic projections of immigration continue, birth rates among the EU nations will make Islam the dominant faith in one more generation. Its pace is growing rapidly in North America too. It integrates the secular and non-secular into one unit without the separation of church and state that dominates the first amendment to the U.S. Constitution. Maybe that is why Islam is the fastest growing religion. Islam is not just one hour on Sunday, but rather a 24/7 lifestyle, like it was in the day of Moses and the Torah. Unless religion can help sheeple get through this life on a daily basis what good is it? Perhaps that is why so many sheeple leave the church; it just has become irrelevant to real human life . . . maybe always was . . . except for the times it was invoked by force. Hence we are given Theofatalism™ as the solution . . . and why it is illustrated with contemporary as well as historical events in these essays to make it relevant to the real world.]

There are few voices crying in the wilderness for nations to wake up to the parasitic threat of Islam. In Slavery, Terrorism and Islam (2009) Dr. Peter Hammond explains that Islam has religious, legal, political, economic, social, and military components. The religious component is a beard and shroud for all of the other components. Islamization begins when there are sufficient Muslims in a country to agitate for their religious privileges. Typical is the plan to build a new mosque within two blocks of ground zero in New York where Muslim terrorists fire bombed the World Trade Center into rubble on 9/11/01. When politically correct, tolerant, and culturally diverse societies agree to Muslim demands for their freedom to practice their religion, some of the other components tend to creep in as well, like a parasite taking over a host. Only after the proportion of Muslims in society reaches a critical mass does it become apparent that their goal is nothing less than total cultural and political domination, all according to the will of Allah of course. The progression can be seen by comparing nations with few Muslims to those that have become Islamic theocracies, as for example France and Turkey. Once they reach the point of domination there's supposed to be peace, because everybody is a Muslim, the madrasses are the only schools, shari'ah is the only law, and the Holy Koran is the only word of God, and Muhammad is his prophet.

The official U.S. response is stifled by the First Amendment to the constitution that stipulates "Congress shall make no law respecting an establishment of religion, or prohibiting the free exercise thereof..." Christians cannot display their symbols on public property, but Muslims who claim they come in peace are given the right of way for political correctness. Remember the Trojan Horse? This restriction on addressing religious dogma that would threaten the safety and continued freedom of Americans is not a trifle, and it must soon be faced up to if the threat of Islamic terrorism is to be defused. Several decisions by the Supreme Court over the years have addressed the issue of freedom of speech and religious action that would threaten to overthrow the government, but now it seems that political correctness has paralyzed the nation from seeing the great threat of Islam and taking defensive action. No small element of the issue rises from tenants of Christianity that many would like to hold as the basic principles of the founding fathers, freedom of speech and such. But, a careful look at the Bible complicates the matter more than many political and religious leaders want to discuss. Consider the dichotomy in opposed teaching of Islam and Christianity. It seems that very few sheeple actually know the principles of their own faith and are blindfolded to the situation that faces them. Here are a few eye-openers for starters in the Holy Koran. [Of course, conservative Muslims will claim any translation of the Koran from its native Arabic renders it false and heretical.]

Fighting orders for Muslims . . .

[2.190] And **fight** in the way of Allah with those who fight with you, and do not exceed the limits, surely Allah does not love those who exceed the limits.

[2.191] And kill them wherever you find them, and drive them out from whence they drove you out, and persecution is severer than slaughter, and do not fight with them at the Sacred Mosque until they **fight** with you in it, but if they do **fight** you, then slay them; such is the recompense of the unbelievers.

[2.193] And **fight** with them until there is no persecution, and religion should be only for Allah, but if they desist, then there should be no hostility except against the oppressors.

[2.217] They ask you concerning the sacred month about fighting in it. Say: **Fighting** in it is a grave matter, and hindering (men) from Allah's way and denying Him, and (hindering men from) the Sacred Mosque and turning its people out of it, are still graver with Allah, and persecution is graver than slaughter; and they will not cease **fighting** with you until they turn you back from your religion, if they can; and whoever of you turns back from his religion, then he dies while an unbeliever—these it is whose works shall go for nothing in this world and the hereafter, and they are the inmates of the fire; therein they shall abide.

[2.244] And **fight** in the way of Allah, and know that Allah is Hearing, Knowing.

[3.13] Indeed there was a sign for you in the two hosts (which) met together in encounter; one party **fight**ing in the way of Allah and the other unbelieving, whom they saw twice as many as themselves with the sight of the eye and Allah strengthens with His aid whom He pleases; most surely there is a lesson in this for those who have sight.

[4.74] Therefore let those **fight** in the way of Allah, who sell this world's life for the hereafter; and whoever **fights** in the way of Allah, then be he slain or be he victorious, We shall grant him a mighty reward.

[4.76] Those who believe **fight** in the way of Allah, and those who disbelieve **fight** in the way of the Shaitan [Satan/Devil]. **Fight** therefore against the friends of the Shaitan; surely the strategy of the Shaitan is weak.

[4.84] **Fight** then in Allah's way; this is not imposed on you except In relation to yourself, and rouse the believers to ardor maybe Allah will restrain the **fight**ing of those who disbelieve and Allah is strongest in prowess and strongest to give an exemplary punishment.

[8.39] And **fight** with them until there is no more persecution and religion should be only for Allah; but if they desist, then surely Allah sees what they do.

[8.57] Therefore if you overtake them in **fight**ing, then scatter by (making an example of) them those who are in their rear, that they may be mindful.

[9.12] And if they break their oaths after their agreement and (openly) revile your religion, then **fight** the leaders of unbelief—surely their oaths are nothing—so that they may desist.

[9.13] What! will you not **fight** a people who broke their oaths and aimed at the expulsion of the Apostle, and they attacked you first; do you fear them? But Allah is most deserving that you should fear Him, if you are believers.

[9.14] **Fight** them, Allah will punish them by your hands and bring them to disgrace, and assist you against them and heal the hearts of a believing sheeple.

[9.29] **Fight** those who do not believe in Allah, nor in the latter day, nor do they prohibit what Allah and His Apostle have prohibited, nor follow the religion of truth, out of those who have been given the Book, until they pay the tax in acknowledgment of superiority and they are in a state of subjection.

[9.36] Surely the number of months with Allah is twelve months in Allah's ordinance since the day when He created the heavens and the Earth, of these four being sacred; that is the right reckoning; therefore be not unjust to yourselves regarding them, and **fight** the polytheists (the Trinity) all together as they **fight** you all together; and know that Allah is with those who guard (against evil).

[9.111] Surely Allah has bought of the believers their persons and their property for this, that they shall have the garden; they **fight** in Allah's way, so they slay and are slain; a promise which is binding on Him in the Taurat and the Injeel and the Quran; and who is more faithful to his covenant than Allah? Rejoice therefore in the pledge which you have made; and that is the mighty achievement.

[9.123] O you who believe! **fight** those of the unbelievers who are near to you and let them find in you hardness; and know that Allah is with those who guard (against evil).

[16.81] And Allah has made for you of what He has created shelters, and He has given you in the mountains places of retreat, and He has given you garments to preserve you from the heat and coats of mail to preserve you in your **fight**ing; even thus does He complete His favor upon you, that haply you may submit.

[22.39] Permission (to **fight**) is given to those upon whom war is made because they are oppressed, and most surely Allah is well able to assist them;

[33.25] And Allah turned back the unbelievers in their rage; they did not obtain any advantage, and Allah sufficed the believers in **fight**ing; and Allah is Strong, Mighty.

[48.16] Say to those of the dwellers of the desert who were left behind: You shall soon be invited to **fight** against a people possessing mighty prowess; you will **fight** against them until they submit; then if you obey, Allah will grant you a good reward; and if you turn back as you turned back before, He will punish you with a painful punishment.

[49.9] And if two parties of the believers quarrel, make peace between them; but if one of them acts wrongfully towards the other, **fight** that which acts wrongfully until it returns to Allah's command; then if it returns, make peace between them with justice and act equitably; surely Allah loves those who act equitably.

[61.4] Surely Allah loves those who **fight** in His way in ranks as if they were a firm and compact wall.

Many more discussions can be found in Islam and among the teachings of Muhammad that guide Muslims into the modern form of jihad. For a complete display, visit www.prophetofdoom.net. For an opposing view, visit www.submission.org.

[Presently, the young sheeple in several Arab countries appear to be initiating a period of revolution to remove dictators who have allied with the West and oppressed their civil rights. It remains to be seen what form of government will replace them. It could range from mostly secular to mostly theocratic Islam because they think of themselves more in terms of religion than nationality. If Islam, as in Saudi Arabia, Iran, Iraq, Egypt, Turkey, Pakistan, etc., how conservative and reliant upon shari'ah law they will be is indefinitely uncertain. An American CIA operator working in Pakistan was pardoned for killing two natives he claimed was self defense after the U.S. paid "blood money" to the bereaved families in accord with shari'ah. We use it when it works for our purpose.]

Prof. Akbar Ahmad, chair of Islamic studies at American University claims those Muslims who would interpret these scriptures above in the Holy Koran literally are stuck in the middle ages. He would invoke another view expressed in Surah 2:256, . . . "let there be no compulsion in religion," to support his claim that modern Muslims do not take the Koran calls to fight seriously, but rather see them as archaic history that does not apply to modern times. However, as the eldest son of one of the founding leaders of Hamas, Mosab Hassan Yousef has written a new book, Son of Hamas, (2010) detailing his youth growing up with the propaganda of Muslim imams and his stint as a spy for Israeli intelligence, plus his surprising conversion from Islam to Christianity. Now, he characterizes the prophet of Islam as a killer and claims that neither Israel nor Hamas are honest with their sheeple. While Yousef admits the death threats he faces now have left him with some regrets about writing the book, he says his story needs to be told. It includes his conversion to Christianity and the conviction that peace in the Middle East will come only when both the Palestinians and the Jews become Christians and love each other instead of killing each other. That will take an act of God because conservative Muslims call Yousef a heretic worthy of execution. Peaceful Muslims claim that jihad actually is a struggle for control between the inner and outer, flesh and spirit, that Apostle Paul described which made him a "wretched man." However, they don't seem to be in control of Islam at the present time. All in God's will of course. AIGWOC.

Christian Non-Fighting Words . . .

Some scholars point to the Old Testament and its commands to the Israelites to attack and subdue the occupants of the Promised Land as well as all their surrounding enemies as authority for violence of the worst kind. The error here is in applying those commands to modern times. No modern branch of Judaism follows the Old Testament rules for battle anymore with its commands to rape and pillage, although the historical battle for occupied land still is being waged by Israel. One must compare the teachings of Jesus in the New Testament with the Koran in order to get a comparison for modern times. Muslim schools for male youth all require memorizing the Koran. There are no such academic institutions in Christianity, even in the seminaries that educate ministers. A basic unresolved issue among Christians is the presence of evil throughout the world. That there are many evil doers in the world is self evident to anyone who gets the daily news. Evil takes many forms and seems to be ubiquitous. In fact, evil seems to be more powerful than good. One of the most heinous of crimes is the abduction, rape, and murder of little children by pedophiles. One of the most bizarre cases involved a husband and wife who abducted an eleven year old girl and kept her imprisoned in a shack in their back yard, undetected for 18 years. When they finally were exposed the young woman had birthed two daughters by her rapist, had never attended school, and had seemingly adapted to her condition.

Loss of a child is one of the most painful of all grievances, but there are many others, and they all appear to be part of God's will as the Creator of all evil, as there can be no other. "I make peace and create evil. I the Lord do all these things." (Isaiah 45:7) "When a disaster comes to a city, has not the Lord caused it?" (Amos 3:6) The Holy Koran says the same thing; "No calamity comes, no affliction occurs, except by the decision and preordainment of Allah." (64.11) How shall we respond to painful suffering in life that is caused by God? What guidance does the Bible provide for those who consider themselves Christians facing such woes in life? Here are some of its responses from Jesus to these matters. He ordered his disciples to follow his commandments. See what you think of them.

"You have heard that it was said, Love your neighbor and hate your enemy. But I tell you: Love your enemies and pray for those who curse you and persecute and mistreat you . . ." (Matthew 5:43-44, Luke 6:26-28)

"But love your enemies, do good to them, and lend to them without expecting to get anything back. Then your reward will be great, and you will be sons of the Most High, because he is kind to the ungrateful and wicked." (Luke 6:35)

"But I say to you not to resist evil . . . bless those who curse you, pray for those who mistreat you. If someone strikes you on one cheek, turn to him the other also. If someone takes your cloak, do not stop him from taking your tunic . . . Give to everyone who asks you, and if anyone takes what belongs to you, do not demand it back." (Matthew 5:39-41, Luke 6:28-30)

"Do not judge, or you too will be judged. For in the same way you judge others, you will be judged, and with the measure you use, it will be measured to you . . ." (Matthew 7:1-3)

"Do not judge, and you will not be judged. Do not condemn, and you will not be condemned. Forgive, and you will be forgiven." (Luke 6:37)

"And when you stand praying, if you hold anything against anyone, forgive him, so that your Father in heaven may forgive you your sins." (Mark 11:25)

"If your brother sins, rebuke him, and if he repents, forgive him. If he sins against you seven times in a day, and seven times comes back to you and says, I repent, forgive him." (Luke 17:3-4)

"For this very reason, Christ died and returned to life so that he might be the Lord of both the dead and the living. You, then, why do you judge your brother? Or why do you look down on your brother? For we will all stand before God's judgment seat." (Romans 14:9-10)

"Do not take revenge, my friends, but leave room for God's wrath, for it is written: It is mine to avenge; I will repay, says the Lord." (Romans 12:19, Deuteronomy 32:35)

Given these scriptures, how can any Christian take up arms to defend himself or his country and still call himself a Christian . . . huh? It would appear from the above scriptures that a pacifist Muslim and a militant Christian both are hypocrites, and it was those for whom Jesus lost his temper, "You snakes, you brood of vipers. How will you escape being condemned to hell?" (Matthew 3:7, 12;34, 23:23, Luke 3:7, Romans 3:13). In spite of their professions of faith, most Christians and their religious leaders do not actually follow the teachings of Jesus as taken literally. If they really believe he was the divine son of God and the New Testament contains his word, then why do they not obey it? "If you love me keep my commandments." (John 14:15)

The loyal Christian and the loyal Muslim seem to be caught in a mutually exclusive dichotomy. To be truly Christian is to invite martyrdom by the sword of Islam. How could this be unless God willed it so? Those Christians and philosophers who claim some accommodation of violence with "just war" stretch the teachings of Jesus beyond endurance. One may fairly ask who is being truer to the faith; Muslims who want to conquer Christians or Christians who want to conquer Muslims? Consequently, if Christians be Christian and Muslims be Muslim, then the latter take over the former, surely as the wolf kills the lamb. Peace comes only when everyone declares "there is no God but Allah and Muhammad is his messenger."

There is an incipient but growing population of young sheeple born in this country of Arab extraction who are learning the power and rewards of Islamic jihad in mosques on weekends while attending our public schools. Countless Muslim children are being taught the power and rewards of Islamic jihad in Muslim owned madrasses (schools) funded by Middle East oil money that escapes scrutiny by homeland security officials because the U.S. Constitution prohibits "any law respecting the establishment of religion . . ." So, the killing of 13 soldiers and wounding of dozens more at Ft. Hood, Texas by Maj. Nidal Hasan, psychiatrist and Muslim, would seem to be a role model for things to come. All in the will of God the Almighty One, of course.

Unfortunately, a large measure of ambiguity was injected into Christian dogma by Apostle Paul in his letter to the church at Rome. He recognized the sovereign power of the state, presumably to the point of obedience to war and slaughter of fellow human beings upon command of the authorities. Recall he may have been a prisoner in Rome when he wrote this: "Everyone must submit himself to the governing authorities, for there is no authority except that which God has established. The authorities that exist have been established by God. Consequently, he who rebels against the authority is rebelling against what God has instituted, and those who do so will bring judgment on themselves. For rulers hold no terror for those who do right, but for those who do wrong. Do you want to be free from fear of the one in authority? Then do what is right and he will commend you. For he is God's servant to do you good. But if you do wrong, be afraid, for he does not bear the sword for nothing. He is God's servant, an agent of wrath to bring punishment on the wrongdoer. Therefore, it is necessary to submit to the authorities, not only because of possible punishment but also because of conscience. This is also why you pay taxes, for the authorities are God's servants, who give their full time to governing. Give everyone what you owe him: If you owe taxes, pay taxes; if revenue, then revenue; if respect, then respect; if honor, then honor." (Romans 13:1-7)

Many scholars have tried to reconcile the teaching of Jesus regarding pacifism with this scripture by dividing the secular from non-secular, saying that obedience to God and to man are both condoned by the will of God. In addition Jesus split the issue by instructing, "Render unto Caesar what is his and render unto God what is his." (Matthew 22:21, Mark 12: 17, Luke 20:25) But in order to make this work they must also divide human existence into the physical and the spiritual realms. In order to placate Rome, Catholic leaders concocted the "just war" concept that tries to have it both ways. Thus, we have religious chaplains serving in the military, and chapels of worship are constructed on defense bases. Analysts of this situation ultimately run into a logical dead end and leave the matter up to individual conscience. So we end up with those who volunteer to conduct military warfare, whose who serve involuntarily under state conscription, and those who are excused from military duty as conscientious objectors. All in the will of God the Almighty One, of course.

Obviously, the role of religion in the military needs to be debated and changes need to be made to protect the national security . . . or not. In 2007, the U.S. House of Representatives passed a bill to establish the National Commission on the Prevention of Violent Radicalization and Homegrown Terrorism (H.R. 1955-110). The Senate referred it to the Committee on Homeland Security but no further action was taken. Rallies by opponents were held from Maine to California, and numerous civil liberties, religious freedom and American Muslim and Arab organizations issued action alerts encouraging voters to contact their congressional representatives in an effort to stop the Senate companion bill, S. 1959. It worked. Caroline Fredrickson, director of the Washington Legislative Office of the American Civil Liberties Union declared, "Law enforcement should focus on action, not thought. We need to worry about the people who are committing crimes rather than those who harbor beliefs that the government may consider to be extreme." If you see no flaw in her logic, welcome to Fort Hood and Maj. Nidal Hasan.

Since sheeple will not change until it hurts too much not to, perhaps it will have to wait upon many more families to lose loved ones to the sword of Islam before the political correctness for religious tolerance and diversity can be debated. How many Americans must die by suicide bombers before the threat is recognized? How many? Well, consider that we tolerate more than 16,000 murders each year without blinking an eye and as many more are killed on the highways by drunk drivers (13,846 in 2008). Switzerland, which prides itself on neutrality and tolerance for diversity, is the first nation to amend its constitution prohibiting construction of minarets, the missile like towers for call to prayer, within Muslim mosques. Other restrictions on freedom of religion to protect national security from radical Islam are yet to be debated.

"The wolf will live with the lamb, the leopard will lie down with the goat, the calf and the lion and the yearling together, and a little child will lead them." (Isaiah 11:6) Obviously, this prophecy has not come true yet and may never unless this dichotomy in religion is addressed. Jesus warned his disciples, "I am sending you out like sheep among wolves, therefore be as shrewd as snakes and as innocent as doves." (Matthew 10:16, Luke 10:3) Christianity and Islam seem to be mutually exclusive. And both claim that sheeple will not change unless God/Allah makes them do so. (John 6:64-66, Surah 14:15) How could this be unless God willed it so?

If this brief discussion has troubled your complacency, perhaps it is time to begin developing a belief system that can accommodate the reality of life in a world of mutually exclusive opposing dichotomies, in this case freedom of religion and shari'ah law of radical Islam. The necessity of dichotomies is one of the powerful five principles developed in Voices of Sedona, and in these Sedona essays, comprising the course in Theofatalism™. If you are ready, the teacher has come and her name is Sedona. Buy Voices of Sedona and Lessons From Sedona at www.IUniverse.com, www.amazon.com and Barnes & Noble book stores. Feel good inside no matter what happens outside.

22. THIS THING CALLED LOVE

Researchers have learned that mating among the animal kingdom is very complex and ritualized. Males must compete and impress females for the opportunity to pass on their genes to reproduce the species through uniting of chromosomes donated by both mother and father. [Before discovery of human female eggs, which required invention of the microscope, common sense said that males deposited their "seed" inside the female where it gestated into an infant.] Among Homo sapiens the mating process is distorted by the inclusion of an emotion called "love." Apostle Paul described love as an action verb and not a feeling, and stated that without it, "I am nothing . . ." even though he might have received . . . "all knowledge, the gift of prophecy, poverty, and faith sufficient to move mountains."

He went on to describe these traits of love. "Love is patient, love is kind, love is not jealous, love is not arrogant, love does not brag, does not act unbecomingly, does not seek its own, is not provoked, does not take into account a wrong suffered, does not rejoice at unrighteousness, bears all things, endures all things, and never fails." Further, in the same passage he noted that ". . . when I became a man I did away with childish things . . ." and as between faith, hope, and love, ". . . the greatest of these is love." (I Corinthians 13:1-10) It seems that Apostle Paul had reached a stage of maturity that distinguished love from its childish counterfeit, what often is called "romance." Love is an action verb that describes unconditional giving, not getting. In the King James translation of that scripture, love is recast as unconditional charity from the Greek "agape^." In this context, one does not "make love." That is a common phrase for sex that really defines "making babies." Of that, the first Earl of Chesterfield [aka Phillip Stranhope (1584-1656)] said, "The pleasure is momentary, the position is ridiculous, and the expense is damnable." The only thing more pathetic than a man in love is a woman in love because she can get pregnant. Both are out of control and neither can look out for their personal interest. So, let's get these things straight.

It is quite normal for sheeple who feel incomplete to use other sheeple to fill up the holes in their character. One cannot have healthy relationships until they can live alone happily and contented. Sex is used by such sheeple to fill up their holes . . . literally. Sex is not love and love is not sex. One gets sex but gives love, i.e., unconditional charity. We have confused the latter with demands of the female body to reproduce, reproduce, reproduce and for men to help them do it. Of this female instinct, libertarian diarist and novelist Anais Nin (1903-1977) wrote, "Man can never know the kind of loneliness a woman knows. Man lies in a woman's womb only to gather strength, he nourishes himself from this fusion, and then he rises and goes into the world, into his work, into battle, into art. He is not lonely. He is busy. The memory of the swim in amniotic fluid gives him energy, completion. The woman may be busy too, but she feels empty. Sensuality for her is not only a wave of pleasure in which she has bathed, and a charge of electric joy at contact with another. When man lies in her womb, she is fulfilled; each act of love is a taking of man within her, an act of birth and rebirth, of child-bearing and man-bearing. Man lies in her womb and is reborn each time anew with a desire to act, to BE. But for woman, the climax is not in the birth, but in the moment the man rests inside of her." So it appears that filling the womb is a goal separate from orgasms for women.

This is but a poetic way to describe the basic purpose of human females, reproduce, reproduce, reproduce, and it drives them to couple up with all manner of undesirable males. The growing number of single mothers shows just how strong is the urge for a full womb among normal women. [Within the female ovary, a follicle consists of one potential egg cell surrounded by special cells to nourish and protect it. But these are not true eggs yet, and will never complete meiosis (a special type of cell division) and become true eggs unless they are first fertilized by a male sperm which is, of course, the primary goal of life. A human female typically has about 400,000 follicles/potential eggs, all formed before birth. Only several hundred (about 480) of these "eggs" will actually ever be released during her reproductive years. One month the left ovary will release a potential egg and the next month the right ovary will release a potential egg. All in the will of God the Almighty One of course.]

This ancient yearning to merge is practiced in Tantra Yoga, where a form of energy is assumed, called kundalini, that is stored like a coiled serpent at the base of the spine. In Tantra Yoga, kundalini is an aspect of Shakti, the divine female energy and consort of male God Shiva. In a fully functioning person, this energy rises through the seven portals called chakras to emerge from the skull upward, activating the main physical activities of Homo sapiens. If the energy is blocked the person exhibits behavior related to the area of blockage. If the third chakra prevails, sheeple may be obsessed with food and overeating. For many it seems the kundalini energy gets blocked at the lowest chakra of sexual arousal. Unless it rises to the mind and produces clear thinking, sheeple often think with their lower portions. This drive is so strong that some young unmarried women intentionally get pregnant repeatedly with no money and no prospects of raising the children normally. Think of the single mother with six kids who had eight more by artificial insemination . . . all at one time. Or imagine the woman, a nursing assistant, who killed five of her babies and stuffed them in a closet over several years without her husband or boyfriend being aware of her nasty habit.

There obviously are forms of love between family members that are not sexually driven, but arise from the heart chakra. But kundalini must pass through the lower chakras first. The emergence of kundalini is most often associated with long term practice of meditation and some forms of yoga, but most everyone has such an experience even if they don't want to talk about it. Liberation of the energy contents in the subconscious may be a troubling experience. Some of the known problems associated with a "kundalini rising" experience include: death, pseudo death, psychosis, pseudo psychosis, confusion, anxiety, itching and headaches, panic attacks, depression, sadness, suicidal thoughts, urges to self-mutilate, homicidal urges, irregular heart beat, exacerbation of prior or current mental illness, insomnia, inability to hold a job, inability to talk, inability to drive, sexual pains, temporary blindness, and headaches. Since the kundalini experience is not often included in psychiatric training, these side effects may be misdiagnosed and poorly treated in western medicine. [Until 1952, when the diagnosis was changed, psychiatry considered a woman under the influence of kundalini to be suffering from "hysteria." Primitive doctors actually thought the womb became disconnected and migrated throughout the body, causing the symptoms.]

The originator of psychoanalysis, Sigmund Freud (1856-1939) thought that all forms of love hide an unconscious desire for prohibited sexual union with the opposite sex parent. Imagine that. Exposing this taboo and letting go of the unconscious desire for the opposite sex parent was the basis of his therapy. Each child must let go of the opposite sex parent at puberty if they are to develop their own healthy adult relationships. Evidence does seem to indicate that many adult dysfunctions may possess a component of mismanaged relationships with opposite sex parents, either too much or too little. The most common issues relate to absent or detached fathers in the lives of their sons and daughters. Absent the role of parents, children will attach to other role models, some of them not so healthy and even criminal. This has been shown in experiments with infant monkeys who will attach to an inanimate mother/father substitute when the real one is missing. But always there is the "primal scream" when children recognize they will never be the paramour of the opposite sex parent because they have each other. Parents must disillusion the opposite sex child during puberty by affirming the marital bond, and if this does not happen the child may not develop a mature relationship with the opposite sex in adulthood. Adolescents who do not make this transition often are unable to develop and maintain healthy adult relationships. Obviously, in single parent households the potential for dysfunction is increased.

It could be that romance is all in your head, or maybe your nose, just like animals. [Don't laugh.] Neuroscience using MRI brain scans is discovering areas of the brain that indicate activation of emotions such as love, lust, and attachment. Kissing releases the same neurotransmitters in our brains as sky diving, bungee jumping, roller coasters and running. Brain scans show that during sexual orgasm the entire neo-cortex of the brain goes idle. Little wonder it is called, "the little death." A Google search for "love hormones" discloses research linking feelings of romance with chemicals produced in the hypothalamus. Science is discovering a whole cocktail of brain chemicals to account for everything from lust to love between a couple that sometimes lasts a lifetime but often does not. Research shows that they decline with familiarity and are re-stimulated by new partners. [Surprise, surprise.] Under their spell, the "love hormones," (including phenylethylamine, adrenaline, noradrenaline, dopamine, testosterone and a dash of oxytocin) apparently disable reasoning neurons in the brain. This combination of hormones releases endorphins in the brain that produce morphine, and we all know how addictive that substance really is. This explains why "love is blind" and dumb too. This is obvious from the all too common affairs by men and women in public positions who ruin their careers and families by illicit romance outside the box of social approval.

Before the unconscious love hormones were understood, C.G. Jung (1875-1961) observed, "When a highly esteemed professor in his seventies abandons his family and runs off with a young red-headed actress we know that the Gods have claimed another victim. This is how demonic power reveals itself to us." Perhaps he was speaking from experience because his wife and children had to share the house with Toni Wolff, his mistress for many years. However, his wife Emma expressed appreciation for what Toni brought to his life that she could not. Perhaps this also explains the reverse, when an esteemed female teacher has an illegal and taboo affair with a juvenile male student, or several. Among animal primates, males must compete for their ability to pass along their genes, but human females will mate with any available male when the hormones are driving their choices. [In contrast, when he was asked what he looked for in a woman, a clear-headed bachelor replied, "flaws."] Many of them are miserable wretches who cannot avoid their plight. Pity their poor suffering children and the taxpayers who must pay for raising them. All in the will of God the Almighty One, of course.

Sigmund Freud used the term "cathexis" early as 1895 to explain the fixation of libido, or sexual energy, upon a specific person, as in having a "crush" on someone. A person under control of the flood of sex hormones is said to be in cathexis, or is cathected to the love object. They are like deer frozen in the headlights; their pitiful brains are frozen into fixation upon the love object at the exclusion of all else. A person in this state is no more under control than a schizophrenic hearing the voices telling him to kill his mother. Sheeple in this condition act out a pathological behavior that often ends very badly. And breaking up in this condition can be as painful as withdrawal from alcohol, tobacco, or illegal drugs. It seems that kissing, petting and such kinesthetic and tactile foreplay releases this cocktail so if you don't want the full meal, avoid the appetizers. Freud thought of cathexis as sort of an electrical charge which some can feel through orgasm. It is not unlike an addiction on release of endorphins in the brain, so that may be why breakups are so painful. Sex addicts will put their lives in danger to get their next fix, and wars have been fought for a love object. Where is the free will in that?

The power of this hormone cocktail apparently captured the great King Solomon who wrote the "Song of Solomon" in praise of a young woman whom he took captive in a battle who could never return his affections. A person driven by this love cocktail may find someone very attractive who normally would not merit a second glance. Getting married while in this state of euphoria is a sure recipe for divorce. Watch any of the cases on "Divorce Court," and you can see how insane sheeple can be under the influence of this love cocktail. In that condition, married or not, they often produce babies that they cannot care for, causing much of the real misery in the world. Sheeple in cathexis also exhibit lower levels of serotonin, the same indicator for obsessive-compulsive disorder, and show reduced action among neurons that help distinguish desirable social characteristics. Under the influence of love hormones, sheeple often confuse love with wanting to get laid to bring sperm and egg together, damn the consequences. After all, it is the strongest human urge after needs for food and shelter. The hormones make you feel temporarily all nice and gooey towards the object of your desire. Their effect on the body is pretty fast, but their effect on the brain and your emotions is instantaneous.

Sheeple who research such things estimate that, on average, women potentially have up to ten times the capacity for sexual pleasure as men, maybe to compensate for the pain of childbirth. Some women have had ecstatic orgasms with a partner who negatively reacted to the overwhelming intensity of such heightened sexual energy and was driven off by fear of it. At this level there is a spiritual ecstatic component to sex that transcends the mere orgasm, perhaps the kundalini energy awakening described in ancient culture of India. Some women can reach orgasm just from tickling their nipples, which aids bonding with nursing babies and stimulates ovulation during foreplay. This stimulation also may have been intended for bonding with a lover to assure creation of a family as a stable platform for raising children. Some women who have moved into whole body spiritual ecstasy found that their partner was unable to tolerate their sexual response because it seemed too intense . . . the ultimate pleasure.

Although the hormones may come from your head, they seem to be triggered in your nose. [Stop laughing.] Scientific research has speculated that dating and mating are highly influenced by pheromones, powerful air-borne chemicals produced by the body. You can't see them or smell them, yet they can be powerful enough to instantly draw another person like a magnet. Dr. Virgil Amend explains, "Scientists have known for decades about an organ just inside the nasal cavity called the vomeronasal organ (VNO). It appears that the sole function of the VNO is to detect trace amounts of pheromones, and in turn, stimulates the limbic region of the brain, also known as the Seat of Emotions. Specialized nerve pathways run directly from the VNO to the limbic region in the brain. These specialized nerves were thought to remain dormant most of the time, but they have now been confirmed to become quite active when subjected to specific human pheromones. A precise concentration of pheromones can kick off a rush of chemicals in the brain within a matter of seconds, and can make people feel a strong emotional and physical response. The best part is this response can be triggered intentionally."

Dr. Amend's proprietary formulation of pheromones for men allegedly taps into the power of nature's chemistry by triggering the signals women are programmed to sense and respond to. It is called "Pheromone Adventure" if you have a mind to try it. "Humans naturally produce their own pheromones." Dr. Amend continues, "However, our cultural habits can wash away, distort or hide our natural pheromones with frequent bathing, detergents, antiperspirants, perfumes, etc. By supplementing with a few drops of the Pheromone Advantage formula, men can not only replace natural levels of these pheromones, but boost levels to the extent that the attraction is unavoidable in their presence." The good doctor does not explain how sheeple seem to make the particular selections that they do or why desire seems to rise and fall in cycles. Women who are ovulating give off unsensible levels of odors called "copulants" that trigger a surge of testosterone in men urging them to mate with the women. Not much different than animals, huh.

Among females, "hysteria," [think horny] was classified as a treatable medical condition up until 1952 when it finally was removed from the psychiatric diagnostic manual. One medical author estimated that three-quarters of American women presented symptoms of this malady in the late 19th century. [No similar data was found for men.] If no outlets are found, the repression can manifest in physical symptoms, panic attacks, sleeplessness, heat flashes and fainting spells. Doctors and midwives were given the cumbersome task of massaging women to orgasm to alleviate it. [Men seemed to need no outside interventions.] It was a lucrative business because there was no cure and required repeated treatments. Doctors reluctantly deferred their lucrative services to personal electrical vibrators which many women welcomed soon as these appliances became available in the Sears, Roebuck catalog. Concurrently the diagnosis of hysteria disappeared from medical journals along with the symptoms. Perhaps the vibrator is the main threat to marriage and the family because Gloria Steinem, voice of modern feminism, observed that "a woman [with a vibrator] needs a man like a fish needs a bicycle." She eventually got married at age 66. [Maybe the batteries quit.]

Cathexis is a temporary malady that fades in time with familiarity. If it is not replaced with love, the relationship sours and turns bad. In contrast, French Philosopher and bachelor Blaise Pascal wrote, "The heart has its reasons, of which reason knows nothing." English philosopher of inductive reasoning Sir Francis Bacon (1561-1626) observed, "It is impossible to love and to be wise." Could release of this hormone cocktail be the unconscious process by which sheeple "fall in love," an appropriate phrase for losing logical control to the reproductive instinct? Dr. Helen Fisher, anthropologist at the American Museum of Natural History, investigated love at first sight . . . the copulatory gaze . . . dinner dates . . . jealousy . . . intimacy . . . homosexuality . . . infidelity . . . in her history of the human species, The Anatomy of Love, A Natural History (1992). You cannot read her and still believe in free will, unless it is the will of God the Almighty One to so believe in free will.

Great addictive romances have driven human history, e.g. Anthony and Cleopatra, Sampson and Delilah, David and Bathsheba, Ronnie and Nancy, Bill and Monica. Alabama Senator and vice presidential candidate, John Edwards, was having an affair that produced a child while he renewed his marriage vows with his wife who had cancer on their thirtieth wedding anniversary. Under the spell of cathexis, sheeple sometimes cross legal and social boundaries and incur international infamy. Was it the love cocktail that required King Edward VIII to abdicate his British throne in 1936 to marry the twice divorced American commoner, Wallace Simpson? But the feelings of cathexis often wear off with familiarity, the intellect resumes control, and love becomes a matter of reason. Jesus reasoned love apart from cathexis as follows: "Greater love has no man than this, that a man shall lay down his life for his friends." (John 15:13.) Someone interpreted this to mean that a bird falls into the mouth of the cat as an act of love by the bird. In this view, prey are willing gifts to the predator. Of course, Jesus knew nothing about love hormones or suicide bombers, or did he?

No correlations have been found yet between sexual desire and fertility, or orgasm and conception. Some women who find it unusual to climax find no difficulty getting pregnant. But, sheeple seem to have a certain quota for release of orgasmic energy, and they strive for that goal until the energy runs out. For some, it is the ultimate addictive pleasure. No matter that up to 70 percent of babies are born to single mothers among some ethnic groups, the urge to merge seems to overcome common sense. So where does the power of reproductive choice lie—in the female, in the male, or in the creator of the brain chemicals and receptors among cells in the reproductive organs that drive such mindless behavior involuntarily? Do we see someone who seems attractive and then get hit by the chemicals, or do the chemicals make someone within sight seem attractive? How do blind sheeple fall in love?

Could it be that the impact of cathexis is transmitted from one to another like a contagious disease with the outcome just as unpredictable? A company in Japan sued a man for calling the free 800 number repeatedly. His defense was that he fell in love with the sound of the recorded female voice answering the phone call. And why do we confuse love with cathexis so hopelessly? Why do we tend to love sheeple who are good to us and even some who are abusive? Perhaps the distinct difference between love and sex can be explained only as the will of God the Almighty One. In that regard, A Course in Miracles (1975), thought by some to be a new revelation from Jesus states, "Disobeying God's will is meaningful only to the insane. In truth, it is impossible." If that were true, then everything that happens must be necessary or it would be different. And that includes creation of vibrators and suicide bombers.

How does marriage fit into all this? Not very well. Marriages that endure for a lifetime seem to cycle through three phases of romantic love, mutual respect, and compassionate charity during troubles and crises. But, they are the exceptions now. Often this is too much commitment when they realize that one will have to watch the other one die. Marriage was created as a social obligation among humans to protect the taxpayers from profligate spending and the cost of rearing children by combining two parents into a single legal entity. The Bible and the law see married couples as "one flesh." "For this cause a man shall leave his father and mother and cling unto his wife and they two shall become one flesh." (Genesis 2:24) True legal commitment requires that a couple must share everything with each other, 24/7. Many sheeple don't like that idea even though marital infidelity still is a social and religious taboo, attested by the criticism heaped upon golfer Tiger Woods for his many confessed marital infidelities and the impeachment of President Bill Clinton for lying about his affair with Monica Lewinski in the oval office. The traditional marriage vows still include forsaking all others, in sickness and in health, for richer or poorer, til death do us part, monogamy, etc. But alas, for all those things to exist, there also must be opposites including infidelity, distrust, polygamy, etc. according to the Principles of Theofatalism™.

[A minor tweak of the gene that maps out a receptor for the feel-good neurotransmitter, dopamine, may be all it takes to explain the promiscuous beats of the cheating heart. Researchers have found that people born with this genetic variation are twice as likely to cheat or engage in risky sexual behaviors, such as one-night stands, according to a study published by researchers at Binghamton University of the State University of New York. It would seem that science has provided the cheaters among us with the ultimate excuse; their genes make them do it. But unknown is why some sheeple with the cheating gene do not carry out the wish. Perhaps their unconscious conscience gets in the way. More study is needed to determine how religious education or moral teachings come into play.]

Moreover, Sigmund Freud observed that kids seem to fall in love with their opposite sex parents and often marry a replica to continue with all the family dynamics. Sheeple may feel attracted to their opposites, but are most comfortable with their mirror images. Spouses and couples seem to come in several combinations: independent-independent, independent-dependent, dependent-dependent, and enmeshed. There is a lot of psychological literature describing these combinations. Each of them has an equal chance of success if both partners are content with their respective benefits and burdens in the relationship. Intimate relationships all tend to survive so long as both partners want them to, i.e., so long as the benefits exceed the burdens, but only until then. Anthropologist, Helen Fisher has studied mating behaviors all over the world and, by combining personality traits with brain scans, she has concluded that sheeple of both sexes are programmed both to hook up in pair bonds that suit their respective personalities and to practice polygamy with multiple partners. She does not attempt to explain why one or the other wins out.

Many Homo sapiens are not unlike bonobo monkeys who would rather screw than just about anything except eat during their reproductive years.

[Bet you did not know that. Forewarned is forearmed.] It seems that many if not most sheeple would practice polyamory and polygamy if it were legal to do so. Many sheeple want the impossible, close family intimacy with personal autonomy, separate bank accounts, investments, careers, plus sexual freedom, etc. These seem to be opposing opposites that are mutually exclusive; a zero-sum game in which one set drives out the other soon after the honeymoon. Someone said that marital fidelity depends upon the available options, and some have more than others. For this reason, society has not completely expelled either polygamy or polyamory. The only problem is that most sheeple in prisons come from broken single parent homes, so the future of our society is indefinitely uncertain. All in God's will of course. AIGWOC . . . think you can handle that?

The range of desire for independence and dependence is wide and few couples intentionally seek a perfect match. The most miserable are those who stay together, because both are mutually codependent, through physical abuse and infidelity. Plus, differences in values and personalities develop with aging that cause ruptures between couples unless they are understood and successfully navigated. The religious claim that God ordained marriage between a man and a woman and ". . . what God has joined together let not man separate." (Matthew 19:6, Mark 10:9) The Romans attempted to sustain legal marriage by making adultery illegal in 40 BCE while making prostitution as a substitute legal. Sex for sale became illegal after the Catholic Church abolished the sexual excesses of the Roman emperors. Conservative Muslims still advocate punishment of adultery by public stoning to death. But, major social changes occurred during the 1960s that all but abolished religious marriage dogma in the West. The birth control pill for women was approved in 1960, no-fault divorce laws were passed in all the states but Louisiana, and abortion was legalized by many states and finally by the U.S. Supreme Court in Roe vs. Wade in 1973. Since then more than 45 million legal abortions have been reported and more than half of marriages end in divorce. Whether by divorce or death, the end of a marriage always is costly and painful.

Women's liberation also removed the stigma from living together with an ad-hoc partner after the 1960s. Cohabitation as an alternative to marriage has increased so rapidly that the data about it haven't kept pace with the growing numbers, researchers say. The latest U.S. Census for 2008 reported 13.6 million unmarried heterosexual couples living together, and that does not include the gay couples. Researchers say 50% to 60% of couples who marry today lived together first; some predict that 70% of young adults will cohabit. Most couples who live together either marry or break up within two years. Homo sapiens seem to be hard-wired for infidelity. Just like animals, they desire as many sexual partners as possible to assure propagation of the species. Contraceptives and abortions have made it possible for sheeple to enjoy as much coition as desired without the responsibility of children. The Church attempted to stifle lust, labeling it one of the seven deadly sins, to no avail, and governments have made adultery punishable with divorce, but this was not always so. Polygamy was practiced among the kings of Israel and polyamory is acceptable in some cultures. "Loving More" is a non-profit organization attempting to legitimize the very human ability to love more than one at a time.

Marriage was created as a social institution to provide a stable platform for raising children after the rush of hormones subsides, although that role seems to be fading rapidly in modern society as up to 70 percent of babies are born to single mothers among some ethnic groups. Research shows beyond argument that children need to bond with an available and dependable "mom and dad" for several years, and that requires a stable home with a working father to make it possible. But, that role has been overlooked by too many couples. No one gets married "til death do us part," anymore but rather for so long as it works or some new sex object takes over. And the no-fault divorce laws make it too easy to dissolve a marriage that it is threatened as a social institution merely for "irreconcilable differences." It is no wonder that so many kids do drugs or join gangs to compensate for lack of a normal family, the threat to society be damned. Self medicating to mask temporarily the pain of family dysfunctions cannot remove the dysfunctions or enhance the acceptance of their consequences.

Marriage counselor, Willard F. Hartley, Jr. has been able to classify most of the responses of couples in troubled marriages into ten unmet needs: admiration, affection, conversation, domestic support, family commitment, financial support, honesty and openness, physical attractiveness, recreational companionship, and sexual fulfillment. Obviously the way to keep a husband and wife happily married is for each of them to meet the needs that are most important to the other. Couples need to identify the combinations of needs that are unique to their marriage if it is to survive and grow with age. In other words, do unto your mate as they would have you do unto them. Many couples cannot do that without professional help, so they are either unhappily together or unhappily divorced. To accommodate them, a growing number of Internet dating services for married sheeple are making money matching up folks who feel the need to cheat. [Isn't capitalism wonderful?] The welfare of children scarcely matters to adults who want only ad-hoc relationships and the option to swing whichever way their hormones take them. This new culture bears very little resemblance to the concept of total marital commitment enjoined by Jesus, "But I tell you that anyone who divorces his wife, except for marital unfaithfulness, causes her to become an adulteress, and anyone who marries the divorced woman commits adultery." (Matthew 5:32) The penalty for adultery was execution by stoning in public back then, and still is among conservative Muslims.

Historically, marriage has so many variations in cultures and times that it hardly bears on the topic at all, except as an attempt by states to assure taxpayers do not have to pay for the children that result. In that, society is losing. Retired Episcopal Bishop, John Spong disagrees with the Catholic dogma that says sexuality is a gift from God to assure procreation in a family that should not be abridged in any way. Spong says, "Sexual intercourse, not God, produces babies. Does one imagine that God wills a dozen children for some, i.e., Catholics, while demanding sexual abstinence for others, i.e., Catholic priests and nuns? Would not effective family planning that requires responsible decision making be a better alternative for everyone?" Of course, the Church tried to make marriage a prerequisite for children, but that did not work even for Adam and Eve because they never got married. The high divorce rate shows that love and marriage often do not go together. Infidelity is quite common among couples as sheeple seem to have a natural tendency to be promiscuous. Perhaps that is necessary to learn how to handle their passions, as C. G. Jung observed, "A man who has not passed through the inferno of his passions has never overcome them." He should know. Falling into temptation seems to be a good thing. Even that great one had two known mistresses while being married to one of the richest women in Switzerland and siring five children.

That the ancients had perfected sex and love is shown in the erotic works of literature and art from Egypt, India, and the Roman Empire. Nothing comes close to the tale of unrequited love in the Song of Solomon, that obscure and often overlooked book of romance in the Old Testament. The great King seems to have fallen in love at first sight with a maiden in love with another. Although he woos her with all manner of erotic poetry, she never relents and eventually he lets her go back to her first love, which makes her very happy. One interpretation has this story being an allegory illustrating the love between Christ, the bridegroom, and the church, his bride. Of course, everything has its opposite, and the opposite of love is fear which breeds hate and that leads to war and crimes against our fellow man and away from compassion and cooperation. Love manifests as compassion while fear manifests as attack. They are two sides of the same coin and their power always adds up to one. The two are mutually exclusive and cannot coexist at once. Love drives out fear and vice versa. "There is no fear in love and perfect love casts out fear." (1 John 4:18) How much you choose of either could be a matter of free will or the will of God the Almighty One, whichever you must believe . . . for now.

There is much discussion of "unconditional love" in religious literature, like when Jesus died on the cross for all sinners no matter how undeserving they are. He instructed, "Greater love has no one that this; to lay down one's life for his friends." (John 15:13) He left unspoken the criteria for establishing friends. A Course in Miracles, (1975) claims that when we accuse or judge others, we are projecting our own fears and guilt that are buried in the subconscious onto others, which blocks the natural flow of love. We see in others whom we fear what we reject in ourselves. We can choose either to project our fears and guilt onto others through defense and attack, which promotes conflict and wars; or we can extend pure love through compassion and charity, which promotes inner peace and cooperation. In real life, sheeple juggle such love with fear of its consequences. They always are balancing love with imagined gain or loss, such that the balance sheet is continually tilting towards one side or other.

Buddhism teaches that unconditional love does not know fear and guilt or use it in the equation, so there is no need for defense or attack. The "Course" says that conflicts are our own doing by rejecting love and choosing ego; so conflicts can be undone by choosing again to abandon ego and let the power of love work. But the Bible presents fear of God and love of God as necessary opposites side by side throughout scriptures as in a child's love/ fear relationship to his father. "Fear God and keep his commandments, for this is the whole duty of man." (Ecclesiastes 12: 13) "Love the Lord your God with all your heart and with all your soul and with all your strength." (Deuteronomy 6:5) Comedian Bill Cosby captured this dichotomy with his famous threat to his beloved son, "I brought you into this world and I can take you out." Sheeple who are driven by their love hormones often marry sheeple whom they quickly come to fear and hate. Divorce courts are full of them. One might even speak of loving to hate, but that is a topic for another essay.

Note that this discussion has not mentioned affection, which should be used only to reward desirable behavior and then only very sparingly for maximum effect. Never use affection to solicit desired behavior. That goes for humans as well as pets. Sheeple, like dogs, develop behavior in response to rewards. Napoleon Bonaparte (1769-1821) observed that, "a soldier will fight long and hard for a piece of colored ribbon." Affection that is inappropriate or unearned can be detrimental to both dogs and humans. Although it is counter-intuitive, withholding affection until it is earned may get you more of what you want. Affection reinforces the behavior that immediately preceded it in both dogs and sheeple, so be conscious of the behavior you are reinforcing.

Reward only the behavior you want and ignore the rest. The big secret is that affection must be given within seconds of the behavior you want to reinforce or it will do no good, and may actually be misinterpreted as an indicator of lust. Giving affection at the wrong time is worse than none at all.

As you can see, there is more to matchmaking than meets the eye of untrained sheeple. When it comes to love and sex, most sheeple don't know what the f . . . they are doing. Perhaps it is all in God's will of course as there can be no other . . . AIGWOC. Feel good inside no matter what happens outside.

23. Invisible links make visible chains

History is composed of events that are chained together linking one cause to another until we reach the present time and place for each living sentient being. Each individual member of humankind, as well as all species of life, has his or her indispensable role to play in the unfolding evolution of reality. Although it may seem that your contribution to life is insignificant, it is indispensable to the chain that came before and will follow your death through all the heirs to come. Few ever stop to think of their place in the Universe, and if they did they might be so amazed they could be blinded by exposure to the cosmic forces controlling each life. We are blindfolded to reality because seeing it as it is could be too much for mortal minds to absorb without going insane. Poet, T.S. Eliot (1888-1965) said, "mankind cannot stand much reality." Here is a glimpse at that challenge to see how much reality you can stand.

You may recall that more than 55 million sheeple were killed during WWII in Europe during 1940-1945. Or, maybe not. But what you may not know is how the Nazi leader who started it named Adolf Hitler got the notion of Germany as the superior race of Aryans who could take over the world during his youth. The Aryans were described by Russian mystic, Helena Blavatsky (1831-1891) in her wild and mystical writings as descendents of the lost continent of Atlantis which was described by Greek philosopher, Plato. Her work was later distributed throughout Germany and influenced the mind of Hitler during the period when interest in the occult and communication with the dead was in vogue. Neither Plato nor Blavatsky could have foreseen Adolf Hitler and his Nazi party, but God did and linked them up in his plan for Germany. Get it? The argument that they had free will to do something different falls apart when you realize no one can go back in time and do anything differently. What was done is done. Some scientists think there is evidence that the Earth is about four and a half billion years old. If that time were scaled to a year, scientists estimate the existence of Homo sapiens on

Earth would be less than two seconds. So they have not had much time to evolve much beyond the animals from which they came, according to Charles Darwin.

Obviously, the life of an individual such as Plato, Blavatsky, and Hitler, is a small nanosecond of the whole cosmos. In their brief time Homo sapiens have used up more than half of the natural resources and put the whole planet at risk of survival with weapons of mass destruction while poisoning themselves with toxic wastes, not to mention all the mayhem they have brought onto each other. Makes you wonder what this species is all about doesn't it? In its short time, its various branches have developed into a wide range of variations. At one extreme are those who live by a personal computer, cell phone, and GPS receiver and could not survive if their modern machines were to disappear. The accelerated growth in high speed communications technology made possible by fiber optic cable and microprocessor chips and satellites orbiting the Earth leaves sheeple who cannot use them out of participation in modern life. The technology is neutral but its applications can be either very good or very bad. On the other extreme are those primitive tribes of Homo sapiens who still live on the land much like their ancestors did thousands of years ago and linked with ancestors in a chain of events impossible by mere chance with need for none of the modern inventions to sustain their survival. Although there are wild variations, among Homo sapiens there are some similarities in cultures and beliefs. They all came from somewhere through an amazing process of evolution connected together by indispensable connections between invisible links. Only by looking at the complete chain of events throughout evolution are the links disclosed.

British historian, James Burke (1936-) documented a series for public television titled "Connections" in which he circled the globe to show how events separated by decades and continents linked up to get us to the many variations in modern civilization. Sheeple often made a contribution to the chain without realizing they were creating a link that was absolutely necessary to human history. Take the cell phone for example. You may think it began with the telephone that was invented by Alexander Graham Bell in 1876. But his work depended upon a patent filed a few weeks before by Elisha Gray from developments by Philip Reir who built the first audio transmitter and receiver in the 1860s from theory proposed by Frenchman Charles Bourseul in 1854 who extended it from workings of the telegraph that was developed by Samuel F. Morse in 1838.

The personal computer has even a longer chain of events and unsung heroes leading up to its present state. Claude Shannon (1916-2001) is called the father of the information technology age because he discovered the system of digital information that makes it all possible while working for Bell

Labs. But, Intel could not produce those ubiquitous microchips and Apple could not make any of those handheld communicating devices unless British mathematician George Boole (1815-1864) developed the system of binary logic making possible digital arithmetic with no idea what it could be used for more than a century earlier. Indeed, binary arithmetic based on his system of ones and zeros has become the basis for digital computation and all manner of information exchange now throughout the world of humankind. And, it was there all the time just waiting for Boole to find it. Was Boole created just so he could be the one to discover it? . . . and was his mother and father specially chosen to birth him into this life for that purpose? . . . and were their parents indispensable in the chaining of computers leading up to NOW . . . . etc. etc. etc . . . . all in God's will of course . . . AIGWOC.

Sheeple consume a lot of potato chips and chocolate without ever wondering how they developed. Chocolate is the most complex food known. It contains 1500 different compounds. The nearest second is wine with 500 separate compounds. Chocolate was harvested 3,000 years ago in Mesoamerica for drinking in a bitter tea. No one knows how it was discovered or how sheeple first learned to process the bitter cocoa bean seeds into delicious food. The Nestle company was first to market it in Europe in the 16th century. Milton S. Hershey failed in three candy company attempts before he perfected his unique sweet chocolate recipe in 1899 by adding milk and plenty of sugar. However, his chocolate melted in summer temperatures without air conditioning and refrigeration and so was a seasonal product. It took the inspiration of Forest Mars, son of the founder of the Mars candy empire, to create the M&M coated candy that "melts in your mouth, not in your hand." Chocolate was blended with oats to create a concentrated food bar for soldiers in WWII. The rest is history.

Nothing would be possible at present had not a series of indispensable events occurred that led up to this time and place, whether for good or evil. Any slight variation or omission among the invisible links and the present time and place would be much different. Often, it takes a disaster to create some of the links. The unsinkable cruise ship, "Titanic" sank on its maiden voyage in 1912 after colliding with an iceberg with 1,250 doomed souls aboard because the engineers permitted its rivets to be made of substandard steel, and the British Admiralty permitted it to sail with only half the number of lifeboats normally required because they thought it was unsinkable. The closest ship that could have responded, the "Californian," was only 15 miles away, but its captain never got the distress call because his only radio telegraph operator had gone to bed after telegraphing a warning about the ice field that "Titanic" never acknowledged. And who put that iceberg there in its pathway? Where do icebergs come from anyway? But, just like icebergs, most of the events compiling human history are beneath the surface, much much bigger than the part above that is exposed above. And, the top must go where the bottom takes it.

In the Buddhist tradition everything is relational, and nothing exists in and of itself; nothing is immune to the forces of cause and effect. For anything to happen, everything preceding must be in place, and when everything is in place something happens necessarily. This awareness is like the calm waters that lie far beneath the surface of a raging sea or the calm air high above the turbulent weather. But there is always an opposing view. Physicist, Victor Stenger warns in "Quantum Gods" (2009) that no law of physics requires a given direction in time, so effects may actually precede causes, every process is reversible, motion does not require a mover, and flat tires might spontaneously re-inflate. Can you believe that? He explains that the necessity of a First Cause came from Aristotle in 350 BCE, and no longer applies in modern physics. He also claims that science has no need to postulate the existence of Spirit to explain laws of the Universe. Then he contradicts himself by writing, "But this does not rule out the possibility of a deist God who created the Universe and endowed upon it the ability to act creatively to carry out his own plans." Jesus plainly said that his kingdom was in a different dimension where laws of physics may not apply at all. (John 18:36) But don't expect to get younger with time.

When the time was ripe and everything had been put in place, Martin Luther (1483-1546) was able to rise up against the corrupt reign of Roman Catholic Popes and issue his famous proclamation in 1517 that changed the course of western religion. He left the abusive rigidity of private schools and entered a monastery to become a priest. What if he had become an accountant instead? Luther's theology challenged the authority of the papacy by holding that the Bible is the only infallible source of religious authority and that all baptized Christians are a universal priesthood. "Therefore, it is clear and certain that this faith alone justifies us . . . Nothing of this article can be yielded or surrendered, even though heaven and Earth and everything else falls." (Mark 13:31) With the aid of the newly invented printing press, Luther's writings circulated widely, reaching France, England, and Italy as early as 1519, and students thronged to Wittenberg to hear him speak. Luther was excommunicated by Pope Leo X in 1521. At his hearing he intoned, "Here I stand. I can do no other. God help me. Amen." Luther was declared a heretic, which made it a crime for anyone in Germany to give him shelter, food, or drink. That also made it legal for anyone to kill him without legal consequence.

Luther was protected by friends in Wartburg, where he translated the Bible from Greek into German and wrote many religious tracts explaining his new beliefs. Thus was begun the protestant movement. What may not be well known is that Martin Luther's vehement anti-semitic views against Jews, whose ancestors chose to free Barabbas and to crucify Jesus, were not repudiated by Lutheran churches until the 1980s. (Matthew 27:25) Toward the end of his life he became less and less tolerant of the human condition. After debilitating chronic illness including blindness in one eye, he died in 1546 at age 63. The rest is history. Speaking of that, had he not been assassinated, Dr. Martin Luther King, Jr. might have been just another civil rights leader. But, in death he has become larger than life with a legacy that equals that of his namesake.

Among the U.S. presidents, some are called to more challenges than others. Born in 1767 and orphaned by age 14, seventh President of the U.S., Andrew Jackson ("Old Hickory") grew up hating the British and the Indians, for good reasons. His father, mother, and brother died from hardships of the Revolution. Although orphaned at age 14, he became a self-taught lawyer and representative and senator from the frontier state of Tennessee where he owned a cotton plantation with up to 150 slaves, called the "Hermitage." He also was commissioned a Colonel and, with no formal military training, he gained a national reputation for killing 800 Creek Indians at the Battle of Horseshoe Bend in 1814, defeating the British at the Battle of New Orleans during the War of 1812, and for liberating Florida from Spain without authority from Congress. He was a paradox; a demanding leader of troops and slaves, but a polarizing politician with disdain for formal authority for those above him including Congress. He caused a scandal by marrying Rachel before her divorce was final, and revered her for life although she died unexpectedly just after he was first elected before he took office.

Jackson believed in "manifest destiny," the divine right of settlers to occupy Indian lands and to own slaves. During his administration (1828-1836) treaties with the Indians were ignored and the "trail of tears" was blazed as the Indian Removal Act, declared unconstitutional by the Supreme Court, required all Indians east of the Mississippi to vacate their homes and hike into the western wilderness at the point of military bayonets. Jackson refused to enforce the law against Georgia militia and permitted the Indians to be displaced. Thus began the westward expansion of the nation . . . and the genocide of Native Americans. The settling of the West was a lawless, dirty, and brutal historical episode. The "inalienable rights" of Americans were taken, not earned.

The settlers, who were aided by the U.S. Army, were relentless in taking possession of Indian lands and hunting grounds. They cleared the virgin lands and introduced cattle and agriculture that eventually took over the continent. They also formed new corporations and a banking system that began to shift power from elected representatives to the captains of industry, which Jackson rightly feared. Look where that has got us to now. He tried to deter the flood of capitalism by killing the central bank that was established by George Washington and Alexander Hamilton, but his victory was only temporary. [The central bank was reinstituted with creation of the Federal Reserve System in 1913. The age of capitalist industrialism had begun, leading to the present age of banking, insurance, and corporations "too large to fail." The Federal Reserve did not prevent the stock market crash of 1929 and it did not prevent the real estate market crash of 2008, so what good is it? And it cannot prevent the fiscal crisis that faces America now.] During Jackson's second term, the stage was set for the turmoil to come that divided corporations from workers and poor from rich as the political structure became organized around democrats and republicans, and divided slaveholders from abolitionists. The Civil War was then inevitable. Jackson left no heirs, but his heritage is an indispensable link in the chain of American history.

The original residents of North America can be traced back thousands of years before the British, Spanish, and French explorers in the 16th century. They appear like ants moving from one colony to another. All we can do is review the "what" without knowing the "why." Theories about man, matter, and the Universe continually evolve, and sometimes they defy common sense . . . like there is only ONE and each of us is an indispensable and equal part of it. The ancient Chinese Taoist philosophy says the river of life flows along and we all are like folks riding a raft to a water fall. The Tao te Ching proclaims, "The Way flows and ebbs, creating and destroying, implementing all the world, attending to the tiniest details, claiming nothing in return. It nurtures all things, though it does not control them; It has no intention, so it seems inconsequential. It is the substance of all things; though it does not control them; It has no exception, so it seems all-important. The sage would not control the world; he is in harmony with the world." [Think of the disaster caused by the raging tsunami wave that crushed the northern coast of Japan after the earthquake of 2011. That, too, is The Way.]

Greek philosopher Heralitus observed that life is a series of challenges and constant change so you cannot put your foot into the same river or meet the same person twice. There is nothing like returning home from a funeral to realize the truth in that. Others say your choices in response to challenges are fight, flight, avoid, or submit. Which you choose is up to God, of course. Life includes risks and unavoidable pain. But the more things change the more Homo sapiens seem to stay the same, and the more mistakes sheeple make the more mistakes they discover to make. Sheeple reproduce and strive to survive at the expense of others through mutual support and defense bounded by some form of isolation and separation. As of now, Homo sapiens are defined more by their insistence upon differences than their similarities. Elaborate social constructs have been created to maintain their separate identities, including various languages, religions, cultures, sports teams, nations, and governments. Although their branches spread out first to Europe and then in all directions about 135,000-150,000 years ago, their roots are traceable by DNA to some origin in central Africa and some evolutionary transition from a previous species, in spite of myths that would have them spring full blown in a single act of creation by a creator God that couldn't seem to get it right in a garden called Eden.

Why have Homo sapiens come this far and where do they seem to be going? Indeed, why do they exist at all? They are not the only species of life that continually seeks safety and control on planet Earth, and then social belonging, and then social superiority. Just like among other vertebrates, while the rank order in a pack of human animals is clear to everyone and accepted by most everyone, peace prevails. But, individual humans continually compete for power and invent more and more expensive and complex instruments of mass destruction, while at the same time they create greater monuments to their existence, even while depleting the resources of Earth that sustains them. [After a generation of peaceful dictatorships, now it appears that spontaneous revolts have erupted among several Arab Muslim nations. Their common denominator is OIL. So, the U.S. and the E.U. are cautiously watching what develops.]

What makes Homo sapiens believe that they are superior to all the other species on the planet? Why have they not yet learned that they all are part of the global chain of relationships that link them together through time and space? What is there about the brains of Homo sapiens that enabled them to go to the moon while they worship the Gods of their imaginations? How come they can soar to the cosmos of imagination but also fall into all manner of degradation and disease? Why do they see the links connected in the chain of history but stubbornly assume they have free will to make each link of life as they please?

How can the chain of events accommodate compassion and charity combined with brutality and slavery unless God wills it so? If we all are links of an invisible chain, does it have a beginning and an ending like the Bible claims . . . or is it just a circle like the Chinese symbol of Yin and Yang or the mysterious mobius that has no beginning or ending? Is everyone a necessary link in the chain? When you look back on your life, do the individual links in the chain become more apparent among your history? Is your present "here and now" the result of inevitable and indispensable links in the chain of your life? [Make a list of the most significant decisions you have made in your life and try to imagine what would be different now if you had chosen another option. Some physicists now are theorizing there may be as many Universes as there are options. There may be no mistakes, only inevitable choices and consequences. All in God's will of course . . . AIGWOC.] Who or what is behind this inevitable evolution of change? And, where is it going? Why is it even here? Is it all real or merely a fantastic illusion that exists only in our imagination?

Find the answers in Theofatalism™ described in <u>Voices of Sedona</u>, and <u>Lessons From Sedona</u>. Buy online at www.amazon.com, www.IUniverse.com and Barnes & Nobles bookstores . . . feel good inside no matter what happens outside.

24. THE LAST WORD

In the news recently were several accounts that make belief in Theofatalism™ not only plausible but highly desirable. Otherwise, we are left with events that pose such fear and confusion for thinking sheeple they may not survive the insanity that rages among mankind in the guise of common sense. In one situation a retired 69-year old retired Marine living in a Chicago suburb kept an award-winning lawn and placed signs to protect it proclaiming, "Keep Off." His 23-year old neighbor permitted his dog to pee on the lawn so the Marine shot and killed him. [The neighbor, not the dog.] In another case, a woman jumped onto the subway tracks in New York City to retrieve her fallen jacket. Her companion jumped in to help her and both of them were hit by an oncoming train. He died but she survived to think about it. We could assume that in both cases, the id that says just do it took control and disabled the role of ego in logical reasoning. Certainly if they had applied reason these sheeple would have acted differently. But, no one can go back and do anything over differently so we must live and die with consequences of our choices, no matter what. All in God's will of course . . . AIGWOC.

In other news, you may have read about the explosion of an oil rig in the Gulf of Mexico that spilled oil all over the area that provides grounds for a vast fishing industry as well as pristine beaches for public enjoyment along a thousand mile coastline. It seems that the oil company had punched a hole in a deep well a mile under water with no contingency plan for the worst-case scenario. Perhaps if they had realized the positive power in negative thinking they would have anticipated the worst-case scenario and prepared for it. Thousands of other deep water oil rigs operate in that area, supplying nearly one fourth of the oil needed by U.S. transportation, that also could potentially cause similar disasters. One may only wonder why such highly trained and experienced experts in oil drilling could incur such a tragic disaster unless, of course, it was the will of God. On the other side of the Earth, sheeple in Japan who could not escape it were swept away by a gigantic tsunami wave caused by a great earthquake under the ocean. Thousands were killed and thousands more made homeless. Manmade structures were instantly destroyed. The marvel is that such things are not unusual. Is that God's will or what?

There is more. The children of baby boomers are not making enough babies to pay for all their entitlements, so the southern U.S. border was opened to increase the population and increase tax revenues. But it has not worked out as planned because illegals send money home to families and avoid paying taxes rather than become citizens. You may have read about the new law passed in Arizona requiring that police officers question suspected lawbreakers about their immigration status. While more than a dozen other states are considering similar laws, there has been a massive reaction by opponents, crying about racial profiling, who are boycotting the state of Arizona because they favor an open southern border and unlimited immigration, which also opens doors for drug trafficking and related crimes. The border patrol forces are prohibited from disrupting Federal protected lands along the border, but not so the drug dealers and illegal immigrants. Consider the illegal immigrant charged with aggravated rape in Washington state after being deported nine times for previous crimes committed in a string of states. Is that crazy or what?

Meantime, the Federal government refuses to enforce immigration laws and to close the southern border while drug wars are being exported from Mexico to more than 230 U. S. cities. In Mexico the drug cartels now are so powerful they can force local police departments to hire their agents to assure there will be no prosecution of drug business . . . all because God has made drug addicts of 20 million sheeple in the USA. And the border control agents cannot stop the flow because most of the border is public land protected by U.S. Federal law from threats to the local fauna and flora and designated endangered species, which causes delays in access, pursuit and apprehension. Only 130 miles of the 2,000 mile southern border are classified as controlled. Is that God's will or what? Indeed, some claim the southern border is not the Rio Grande, but it is rather the northern boundary of states that were part of Mexico before the treaty of 1848 ceded all that land as the booty of war. Mexico apparently never ratified that treaty. Congress has been impotent to address the Hispanic immigration issue because the democrats want their new votes and the republicans want their cheap labor and both want their taxes. Meantime, the states affected directly by the surge of poor Hispanics must support the millions of immigrants who have swamped their service providers and driven them to near bankruptcy. All in God's will of course . . . AIGWOC.

Another crazy situation is the mountain of debt being piled up by the Federal government in order to prop up the sagging economy in a futile attempt to maintain our unsustainable standard of living. As the baby boomers retire, i.e., those born from 1945 to 1960, beginning now at the rate of 7,000-10,000 per day, their shift from producing and buying to taking entitlements will stress Social Security and Medicare commitments beyond sustainability. [For special essays in Theofatalism™ for baby boomers and their families, read <u>Baby Boomer Lamentations</u> by this author.] The southern border was opened to unlimited illegal immigrants to increase the population and create more economic growth, but the burdens have outstripped the benefits as they send their earnings home to help support indigent families. Meantime, corporations outsource manufacturing of consumer products to the countries with cheapest labor and we send vast amounts of dollars to countries like communist China to buy them. Then, they use the dollars to buy our debt which threatens our national security because, as the Bible says, the borrower is servant to the lender. (Proverbs 22: 7)

[It seems the world is dividing into sovereign official governments and the informal power of corporate elites. They have no allegiance to any nation and work only for their own benefits, including their donations to causes they support. They seek a world with no national barriers to international trade and banking. The formal governments are losing control to these moguls and seem to be irrelevant to their pursuit of goals that average sheeple cannot understand, while billions are spent in electing politicians who make no dent in the real world of international finance. All in God's will of course. AIGWOC.]

British nobleman, Alexander Tytler (1747-1813) reportedly predicted, "A democracy is always temporary in nature; it simply cannot exist as a permanent form of government. A democracy will continue to exist up until the time that voters discover that they can vote themselves generous gifts from the public treasury. From that moment on, the majority always votes for the candidates who promise the most benefits from the public treasury, with the result that every democracy will finally collapse due to loose fiscal policy, which is always followed by a dictatorship." The U.S. Federal government has been promising more than it can afford for decades, whether it is tax breaks for the rich or entitlements for the poor and borrowing more and more to finance the deficit. At this time, 40 percent of the Federal budget is financed with borrowed money . . . that is $188 million every hour . . . every hour. Before long, interest on the national debt will cost almost a trillion dollars . . . every year . . . if we can keep on finding lenders to give us the money. This is just like sheeple who max out their credit cards until they can only pay the required minimum monthly interest payments, and finally they go into default and bankruptcy. The Democrats want to keep all the public entitlements and pay for them by taxing the richest among us while the Republicans want to maintain tax breaks for the wealthy and pay for them by cutting benefits for the middle and lower classes, and neither is willing to compromise enough to balance the budget. Republicans claim the deficit is caused by too much spending and democrats say it comes from too little taxing . . . necessary dichotomies or what, God's will?

Ever since President Ronald Reagan declared, "Government is the problem," the government has grown like a cancer eating up the economy during both republican and democratic control. The acute dependency upon unregulated credit financing that caused the Great Depression of 1929 was repeated in the Great Recession of 2008 and what happens next definitely is indefinitely uncertain. But there is always an opposite view, and one economist claimed the U.S. government could spend as much as it wants without negative consequences because it can print more money without limits to offset lagging growth in the private sector. Ex-vice President Dick Cheney remarked, "Ronald Reagan taught us that deficits don't matter."

This attitude came from economic theory of British economist, John Maynard Keynes (1883-1946) that he promoted to overcome the Great Depression of the 1930s and smooth out the ups and downs in free market economies with deficit government planning. It took massive spending on WWII to break the Depression. Keynes was a very likeable and intelligent fellow, which made international acceptance of his theory even more devastating to free market capitalism. His chief opponent was American economist Milton Friedman (1912-2006) who promoted free markets and open unregulated international trade, but not so successfully because he had no solution for the poorest of the poor. Republicans claim you stimulate a lagging economy by reducing taxes and democrats claim you do it by increasing deficit spending . . . necessary opposites, for sure. Meantime, corporations lobby for what is best for stockholders at the expense of workers and consumers. All in God's will of course . . . AIGWOC.

[The U.S. economy needs 20 million new jobs to employ its idled workers, many of whom have college degrees and thousands in debt on college loans. In a few years the economy has gone from one driven by home ownership to one of investors and renters as the baby boomers enter retirement and shift from consuming to saving. Not good. During 2000-2009 about 50,000 American factories were closed and 2.5 million manufacturing jobs were moved overseas to countries with cheap labor while the share of Federal revenues from corporation taxes declined from 30 percent to only six percent, thanks to tax breaks enacted by President George W. Bush. So the argument by Republicans that reducing corporate taxes helps create jobs for Americans is nonsense.

There are hardly any consumer goods sold in department stores made in America anymore. China makes about 85% of all solar panels and 50% of all wind generators and will make all of the above within five years. GE closed its last plant in the U.S. making incandescent light bulbs and set up production of compact fluorescents in China. Apple computer designs its products in California but makes them in China. Nike makes most of its shoes in Vietnam although headquartered in Washington state. Corporations operate independently of national interest in the global markets and there is nothing anyone can do about it. The time may come soon when national governments are subordinate to international corporations and bankers who control the supply and cost of money. Thomas Jefferson warned that controlling banks were more dangerous to the country than an invading army, but no one listened. And with all the loopholes which they initiated, corporations pay little to no income taxes on the outrageous profits. Meantime the incomes of corporation executives have soared. Is all this national suicide, crazy, free will, or God's will? [This country is so diversified that the only thing which can unite it seems to be a war . . . so we have the wars on terrorism, drugs, poverty, etc. Perhaps we need a war on dying since that is such a common threat.]

In consequence, U.S. corporations and the rich have been relieved of taxes and manufacturing jobs have been shifted overseas, destroying the American middle class. If the tax code of 1951 had been sustained the U. S. national deficit would be only half as much as it is, and if the tax loopholes were closed the deficit would disappear. Things will only get worse as the 76 million baby boomers retire beginning now and reduce their consumption while demanding their entitlements. The only way to prevent fiscal disaster is to both curtail Federal spending and increase taxes to balance the budget, not to mention beginning to pay down the debt . . . something not possible under present politics. So the mounting debt is passed on to future generations and fiscal balance is put at risk. We are on a boat heading for a waterfall and no one can seem to prevent it from going over. [In early 2010 the U.S. Supreme Court gave corporations the right to contribute to political candidates anonymously just like any person can, and susceptible voters promptly elected republicans to win the House. Perhaps next comes the Senate and the White House too.] How could all this be unless God willed it so?

There are many similar items in the daily news if you have eyes to see . . . if you have the right internet connection. And if you look into it, history is full of events that make no sense unless you can believe that God willed it so to be. How can such seemingly insane events be happening among apparently intelligent and highly educated sheeple when it seems that their minds go out of commission to allow the most unbelievable events to occur, unless God willed them so to be? Surely, humankind has enough intelligence to avoid such events . . . or do they?

When you come to the end of logical reasoning trying to make sense of nonsense, there are only two alternative explanations . . . random chance or intelligent design by some Higher Power. If the latter, how much of it can we ever understand? Albert Einstein, (1879-1955) a rational humanist, tried to merge religion and science but he failed. He concluded, "The religion of the future will be a cosmic religion. It should transcend a personal God and avoid dogmas and theology. Covering both the natural and the spiritual, it should be based on a religious sense arising from the experience of all things, natural and spiritual as a meaningful unity." This unity of religion and science seems to be just as far from reality now as it was then because they still seem to be mutually exclusive. Whether they can ever merge into One still is indefinitely uncertain. But, if you can look up at the stars at night and not be overwhelmed at the true greatness of the Universe, you just have not looked.

If you think about it there probably are many events in each life that you wish you could go back and do over differently or might have been avoided. Unfortunately, since you cannot do that it is necessary to live or die with the consequences. Although many sheeple seem to enjoy fruits from trees they did not plant, it is more likely that everyone wishes for the best out of life that they think is possible from their own actions. But, it is not always logically true that you reap as you sow. When "do this—get that" no longer works it can be a revolting development, but its acceptance is a sign of personal growth.

[You might think that becoming President of the United States would assure fortune as well as fame, but eight of them endured poverty and suffering in their final years; Jefferson, Madison, Monroe, Harrison, Lincoln, Grant, McKinley, and Truman. It has only been since WWII that presidents have enjoyed legacy libraries and book publishing deals after serving in office.] Not having any kind of social or political platform upon which to build fame and public awareness, this present work may never be discovered unless God wills it so. Even Jesus expected most of his teaching to be lost on rocks and blown away in the wind. (Matthew 13:13-15) Unfortunately, life is not always fair and often the innocent suffer for the misdeeds of the guilty. There may be no mistakes, just choices and consequences. This must be so or it would be different. Nevertheless, the perceived benefits must always outweigh the burdens in the subconscious mind of the doer, and so it is.

For example, we accept more than 15,000 traffic deaths each year caused by drunk drivers in order to maintain freedom to drink alcohol legally to the point of delirium. Like Jesus said in the Bible, the rain falls on the just and the unjust, on the righteous and unrighteous. (Matthew 5:44-45) Often the suffering comes from natural disasters that one may call the acts of God. Consider the plight of the refugees living in tent villages in Haiti with no fresh water, absent sewage treatment, and sans medical aid, displaced by the earthquake that destroyed homes of more than 200,000 sheeple. Where do you turn when your world is shaken and you realize that God is doing the shaking? Is it possible to feel good inside no matter what happens outside? Enter belief in Theofatalism ™.

Theofatalism™ is expressed in these five principles: 1) Everything is happening as it must or it would be different, and that includes everything from the smallest sub-atomic particle to the largest galaxy in the Universe plus all of the life on planet Earth; 2) The Universe consists of diametric opposites; for each thought there must be an equal and opposite thought just like in the laws of physics; 3) decisions are made from motives that are subconscious but the values of the perceived benefits always exceed the burdens; 4) nothing about the future is certain so we must all live with the existential anxiety of indefinite uncertainty; 5) life is like a jigsaw puzzle without the picture on the box; it can only be completed one way and the outcome becomes more apparent only as we approach the end.

The symbol of Theofatalism™ is the Chartres Labyrinth; there is only one way in and one way out. Such is life. Now, if you can apply these principles of Theofatalism™ to all the situations described above in these essays perhaps you will see how one could feel good inside no matter what happens outside. The giant leap comes in applying them to all the situations in your own life, especially the ones you desperately wish were different or never happened. Perhaps they are ways in which God reminds us who really is in control. In such a circumstance, there are two responses; either calm submission or resistance. Which you apply will be the one you are given. With calm submission there will be inner peace and contentment and with resistance there will be suffering and discontent. Both options must exist or they both would not be possible. The thinkers among you will easily deduce that choice too must conform to the principles of Theofatalism™. So, whether you feel good inside or not is not for your conscious choice. AIGWOC . . . all in God's will of course. Get it?

Perhaps this paraphrase of a poem by Edwin Markham (1852-1940) expresses the idea of Theofatalism™. It contrasts the imaginary and the real state of humankind where everyone is included and nothing can be outside the will of God the Almighty One.

> They drew a circle that shut me out,
> Heretic, rebel, a thing they flout.
> But the will of God had a way to win;
> It drew a circle that took me in.

In this circle of life we all appear to be simultaneously insignificant but indispensable. If you have not got it by now, after all the anecdotes, scriptural references, and the expert opinions, we can only assume that you were not meant to . . . yet. It takes a certain spiritual maturity to let go of learned but unexamined myths and to step into the reality of indefinite uncertainty, while living in calm submission to God the Almighty One. Unless and until the human ego is crucified it may be impossible. So do not despair, but please pass this work along to another who may be ready to receive these lessons from Sedona. Or keep it in a safe place for some future time when you may become ready. On the other hand, if you do get it, welcome to the virtual School of Theofatalism™, where everyone is a member and no one can resign or be expelled. Now that the blindfold has been removed and you can see reality as it is, perhaps you also will be able to help others who are ready to achieve the same level of enlightenment . . . or not.

Here is a summary of the matter in four quotes that you might choose to memorize or to frame in order to help them remind you of these last words . . . feel good inside no matter what happens outside.

"Disobeying God's will is meaningful only to the insane.
In truth, it is impossible."
Helen Schucman, <u>A Course in Miracles</u>, 1975
"All teachings were at one time willed by God, precisely
adapted to the individual peoples and countries, and
formed in complete accord with their actual spiritual
maturity and receptivity." Abd-ru-Shin, <u>In the Light of
Truth – The Grail Message</u>, 1926
"It is more profitable to leave everyone to his way of
thinking than to give way to contentious discourses." St.
Thomas a Kempis, <u>The Imitation of Christ</u>, 1427
"My Father is always at his work to this very day, and I too
am working." Jesus Christ, <u>John 5:17 (NIV)</u>

Remember the Chartres Labyrinth and try to obtain one to walk through often [you can buy tabletop versions at www.labyrinthcompany.com] to help remind you there is only one way in, one way through, and one way out of this life for each one of us. It illustrates that God does whatever he wants with whoever he wants any time he wants however he wants. To read the derivation of the five principles of Theofatalism™, refer to <u>Voices of Sedona</u> available from www.IUniverse.com, www.amazon.com and local Barns & Noble book stores. Feel good inside no matter what happens outside. All in God's will of course . . . AIGWOC.

APPENDIX: START A DISCUSSION
AND SUPPORT GROUP

Perhaps this discussion has motivated you to start something big, like a new belief system to replace the antiquated one that does not work anymore. Anthropologist, Margaret Mead (1901-1978) observed, "Never doubt that a few thoughtful, committed people can change the world." The flight crews of the suicide flights that attacked America on 9/11/01 certainly proved that. You may be called to start something new with these principles of Theofatalism™ but it could take some help from others in your neighborhood. Finding them and organizing them may be your calling...or not. No one can fulfill their destiny alone. Even Jesus needed help. He proclaimed, "Whoever is not with me is against me and whoever does not gather with me scatters." (Matthew 12:30)

Discussion groups can be convened by average sheeple to deal with a wide variety of life issues that can be explained by the course in Theofatalism™. All you need to do is invite a group of sheeple who want to work together on common issues in managing stressful living amongst struggle and suffering. Merely having a mutual interest in helping each other can produce effective results. Perhaps you are called to get such a group started in your neighborhood among families dealing with spiritual issues not being met by the churches of America.

A few basic ground rules of operation can help make group discussion a very effective growth experience.

[Note: This is not professional therapy for clients seeking counseling for mental or emotional distress. Anyone seeking such treatment should be referred to competent professionals or local government agencies for appropriate services.]

1. Choose a quiet meeting place without distractions and make it a regularly scheduled event that is convenient in the weekly calendar of activities. Sometimes churches or other public facility managers will make such a place available for weekly meetings at a convenient time for the participants. Homes are suitable meeting places if a quiet room big enough is available. Avoid refreshments until after the meeting.

2. Open each meeting with a short restatement of its purpose, e.g., healing the stress of life with the Principles of Theofatalism™. Select the essay for discussion and print out a copy for the participants who may not have the book. Read the selected essay and ask for discussion that relates it to current experience and understanding of the members.

3. Start and end each meeting precisely at the agreed-upon times. Keep the sessions to two hours or less. Give each newcomer a few minutes to share his/her background and objective for joining the group. Then have those in the group who volunteer to do so give a short summary of their backgrounds to the newcomer.

4. Use first names only, following with the first letter of the last name, unless participants specifically decide to share their full names. Exchange telephone numbers or e-mails and encourage members to call each other between meetings to share further. Often close friendships are developed this way.

5. During the meeting, members may focus discussion on one of these essays. Other members may then comment on the way the same material has affected their lives and offer feedback to the originator if permission is asked and received. However avoid crosstalk between members and specific responses directed to one who has just spoken. Such crosstalk can be harmful to the healing process and creates a codependent environment, especially if it involves judging or advising by unqualified speakers. You want to create a safe place where sheeple can be free to express their thoughts and feelings without being judged, rejected, or ill-advised. Each member should share only his or her own experience, thoughts, feelings, strength, despair, or hope.

6. If it is part of the agreement, take a collection at each meeting to compensate the space provider for snacks and compile a central account for occasional group socials, publicity, and the like. Members might be chosen to keep the records, make plans, and safeguard any financial resources. However, no formal organization is needed or recommended.

7. Encourage expressions of negative and positive feelings alike, complete with profanity and tears or laughing and hugging if a person wants to make such a disclosure. Let all expressions of emotion be OK without judging them. Do not deny or prevent expression of any strong emotions or belittle tears and rages. Have some soft tissues handy.

8. Alternate leadership of the group regularly, so no one person becomes a teacher or takes on responsibility for fixing broken members of the class. Each person must be free to work out his or her own healing in relation to God. Leaders should not display fear, tension, nervousness, or insecurity around the group. They should be detached, but interested facilitators during their period of service.

9. Encourage everyone to leave the group when their work is well along, so they can transition to spiritual evolution on their own, and make room for others. Support groups should not become a lifetime crutch or substitute for self-reliance, but they often can provide the baseline for launching lifelong evolution of growth in consciousness.

10. If the group grows beyond ten to twelve members, consider starting a second group. Participation may be attenuated if too many sheeple prevent adequate time for sharing. Caution: If any member of the group seems uncontrollably disruptive or misbehaves to the point of alarming or threatening other members, that person should be carefully, but seriously, invited to leave and encouraged to get professional help. If there is evidence of actual mental disorder, insist that the person see competent medical professionals.

When the worst kinds of things happen, many cannot reconcile reality with their traditional assumptions alone. That may be more or less difficult for you to do, depending on how you are made. The secret to growth is in expecting that benefits of your new life will far exceed the burdens of giving up your old life. Some sheeple seem to accept the benefits of growth more easily, while others resist giving up the familiar burdens; in other words, they hang onto legacy behavior and beliefs because it hurts too much to give them up. Psychologists call this the "mormalcy bias," i.e., wanting things to remain the same. C. G. Jung observed that all growth is painful, so if you are not hurting you are not growing. Learning means change and that always is fearful, but it can be exciting too. Many are called to walk alone, but it helps to have partners in your walk through the suffering growth of life.

Personality plays a role in group participation. It may be that extraverts, who respond to events, sheeple, and things outside themselves, will be less able to give up their externally driven stimulants, while introverts, who respond more to ideas, concepts, and Information from inside themselves, are less prone to being controlled by events outside themselves. However, extraverts may feel more comfortable sharing their thoughts in groups than introverts. Extraverts must speak to know what they are thinking, and introverts must think to know what to say. It is said that if you don't know what an extravert is thinking, you haven't listened, and if you don't know what an introvert is thinking, you haven't asked.

All growth is painful and scary, as we must let go of familiar discomfort to move into uncertain futures. In comfort there is no growth. The psyche/soul must grow or decline, like an airplane that must fly faster than its stall speed or it will crash. A soul that is not growing is dying. The continuous process of discovery can always benefit from renewal through group therapy. One who learned this lesson said, "It is like spring cleaning. You get to dust off everything and sort through stuff. You get to throw a lot of junk away." Another said it is like weeding your garden: "once is never enough." The Dutch have a saying, "We grow too soon old and too late smart." Perhaps these essays will help to soften the shock of reality for those who can't handle the truth. Unfortunately the truth about wisdom is by the time we gain it there may be no time left to use it. Let the reformation begin. All in God's will of course . . . AIGWOC.